The Nebraska hardcover edition includes:

The Journals of the Lewis and Clark Expedition, Volume 1
Atlas of the Lewis and Clark Expedition

The Journals of the Lewis and Clark Expedition, Volume 2
August 30, 1803–August 24, 1804

The Journals of the Lewis and Clark Expedition, Volume 3
August 25, 1804–April 6, 1805

The Journals of the Lewis and Clark Expedition, Volume 4
April 7–July 27, 1805

The Journals of the Lewis and Clark Expedition, Volume 5
July 28–November 1, 1805

The Journals of the Lewis and Clark Expedition, Volume 6
November 2, 1805–March 22, 1806

The Journals of the Lewis and Clark Expedition, Volume 7
March 23–June 9, 1806

The Journals of the Lewis and Clark Expedition, Volume 8
June 10–September 26, 1806

The Journals of the Lewis and Clark Expedition, Volume 9
The Journals of John Ordway, May 14, 1804–September 23, 1806,
and Charles Floyd, May 14–August 18, 1804

The Journals of the Lewis and Clark Expedition, Volume 10
The Journal of Patrick Gass, May 14, 1804–September 23, 1806

The Journals of the Lewis and Clark Expedition, Volume 11
The Journals of Joseph Whitehouse, May 14, 1804–April 2, 1806

The Journals of the Lewis and Clark Expedition, Volume 12
Herbarium of the Lewis and Clark Expedition

The Journals of the Lewis and Clark Expedition, Volume 13
Comprehensive Index

Sponsored by the Center for

Great Plains Studies,

University of Nebraska–Lincoln

and the American

Philosophical Society, Philadelphia

A Project of the Center for Great Plains Studies, University of Nebraska–Lincoln

GARY E. MOULTON, EDITOR

The Definitive Journals of
Lewis & Clark

Joseph Whitehouse

VOLUME 11 of the Nebraska Edition

University of Nebraska Press

Lincoln and London

LIBRARY OF CONGRESS CATALOGING-IN-PUBLICATION DATA
Journals of the Lewis and Clark Expedition. Volume 2–8
The definitive journals of Lewis and Clark / Gary E. Moulton,
editor ; Thomas W. Dunlay, assistant editor.
p. cm.
Vols. 7–8: Gary E. Moulton, editor.
"A project of the Center for Great Plains Studies, University of
Nebraska–Lincoln."
Paperback edition of v. 2–8 of the Journals of the Lewis and
Clark Expedition, originally published in 13 v. by the University
of Nebraska Press, c1983–2001.
Includes bibliographical references and index.
Contents – v.2. From the Ohio to the Vermillion – v.3. Up the
Missouri to Fort Mandan – v.4. From Fort Mandan to Three
Forks – v.5. Through the Rockies to the Cascades – v.6. Down
the Columbia to Fort Clatsop – v.7. From the Pacific to the
Rockies – v.8. Over the Rockies to St. Louis.
ISBN 0-8032-8009-2 (v.2: alk. paper)– ISBN 0-8032-8010-6 (v.3:
alk. paper)– ISBN 0-8032-8011-4 (v.4: alk. paper)– ISBN 0-8032-
8012-2 (v.5: alk. paper) – ISBN 0-8032-8013-0 (v.6: alk. paper) –
ISBN 0-8032-8014-9 (v.7: alk. paper) – ISBN 0-8032-8015-7 (v.8:
alk. paper)
1. Lewis and Clark Expedition (1804–1806). 2. West (U.S.) –
Description and travel. 3. Lewis, Meriwether, 1774–1809 – Dia-
ries. 4. Clark, William, 1770–1838 – Diaries. 5. Explorers –
West (U.S.)–Diaries. I. Lewis, Meriwether, 1774–1809. II.
Clark, William, 1770–1838. III. Moulton, Gary E. IV. Dunlay,
Thomas W., 1944– . V. University of Nebraska–Lincoln. Center
for Great Plains Studies. VI. Title.
F 592.4 2002 917.804'2–dc21 2002018113

ISBN 0-8032-8023-8 (vol. 11: alk. paper)

Contents

Preface

This volume and the previous two rely largely on the editorial work of previous books in this edition. Therefore, the editorial notes and supporting material in these three books owe a debt to former consultants and friends of the project. Once again we extend our great appreciation to the unselfish work of these generous people.

Nevertheless, we have several persons to thank specifically for help with this volume. Both the original and fair copy versions of Private Joseph Whitehouse's journal are at Newberry Library, Chicago, where we were assisted by Robert W. Karrow, Jr., Administrative Curator of Special Collections. At our host institution, the University of Nebraska–Lincoln, help came from John R. Wunder, Linda J. Ratcliffe, and Gretchen Walker of the Center for Great Plains Studies, and from Thomas W. Dunlay, Doris VanSchooten, and Mary Higginbotham of the project.

The project received financial support from Samuel H. Douglas, III (Whittier, California), Nelson S. Weller (Piedmont, California), the Lewis and Clark Trail Heritage Foundation, and the National Endowment for the Humanities, an independent federal agency.

We extend our most sincere appreciation to these individuals. Any shortcomings in the present work, however, are entirely the fault of the editor.

Editorial Procedures

For volumes 9, 10, and 11, the final journal-volumes in this edition of the journals of the Lewis and Clark expedition, the principal editorial goal remains that stated in volume 2, that is, to present users with a reliable text largely uncluttered with editorial interference. Readers can find a fuller statement of editing principles in the Editorial Procedures in volume 2. The following paragraphs explain the purpose and extent of editorial annotation included in the present volumes, since the approach to annotation here differs from the method followed with the journals of Lewis and Clark.

Believing that the annotation to Lewis's and Clark's journals in the previous volumes furnished the essential information needed to understand the events, persons, and inquiries of the expedition, we deemed it unnecessary to reproduce those notes in their entirety in these enlisted men's volumes. We assume that most users turn to Lewis's and Clark's journals as their primary source of information on the expedition and use the enlisted men's journals as supplements. Where the enlisted men provide new or substantially different material in their journals, however, we have commented on that fact and explained the matter as extensively as we did in the captains' journals.

The annotation for the present three volumes falls under four large categories: people, places, animals, and plants. These have been the fields of greatest interest to users of the journals and were the areas most often noticed by the enlisted men. These were also the points on which these men were most likely to provide information not found in the captains' journals. Our aim was to establish a method that was not unnecessarily redundant to previous volumes but that provided readers with essential information so they did not need to refer constantly to other books.

In these volumes the notes have been abbreviated considerably. For example, authoritative sources are not listed in most notes since that information was provided in previous volumes. We do not provide geographic locations for every point mentioned in the enlisted men's journals, nor do we necessarily locate each day's campsite: these locales were discussed in detailed notes to the captains' journals. In the present volumes we try to give a sense of place from day to day by locating the major physical features passed each day. In this way readers should have no trouble determining the party's location at any given time. For natural history matters we provide both the popular and scientific names for flora and fauna. Occasionally we direct readers to notes for the captains' journals for extended discussions of difficult identifications. For the most part the enlisted men were observing and commenting on the same plants and animals as the captains. In fact, there appears to be only one instance in which a biological specimen was mentioned by an enlisted journalist but was not also identified in the captains' journals.

Wherever possible we recognize every Indian tribe noted by the journalists, no matter how indirectly, and name all Indian individuals whom we are able to identify. We also transliterate and translate native terms that have not previously been addressed or direct readers to fuller explication in earlier volumes. Sergeant John Ordway seems to have been the only enlisted man to mention Indian terms not noted by Lewis or Clark. It is in fact likely that the enlisted men copied the scant scientific information they have in their diaries from the journals of Lewis and Clark. Because of this we try not to add repetition in the notes to necessary redundancies in the text. Our hope is to give readers sufficient annotation to understand the text without reporting the obvious.

Introduction to Volume 11

The essential, definitive record of the Lewis and Clark expedition is contained in the journals and observations of the two captains, "the writingest explorers of their time," in the words of Donald Jackson.[1] If no one else associated with the enterprise had written a word we would still have a marvelous narrative replete with geographic, zoological, botanical, and ethnographic information. In fact, however, at least four other members of the party did set down their own daily accounts. This edition brings them together with those of their commanders for the first time.

President Thomas Jefferson did not order the actual keeping of separate journals by anyone other than the captains. In his final instructions to Lewis, however, he did suggest that "several copies of these as well as of your other notes should be made at leisure times, & put into the care of the most trust-worthy of your attendants, to guard, by multiplying them, against the accidental losses to which they will be exposed."[2] All this would seem to require is that some of the "attendants" copy the captains' journals verbatim. Apparently Lewis and Clark, at an early stage, decided to do something else. On May 26, 1804, less than two weeks out from River Dubois, the captains noted that "The sergts . . . are directed each to keep a separate journal from day to day of all passing accurences, and such other observations on the country &c. as shall appear to them worthy of notice.—"[3]

In his last communication to Jefferson from Fort Mandan in April 1805, Lewis wrote: "We have encouraged our men to keep journals, and seven of them do so, to whom in this respect we give every assistance in our power."[4] Lewis had a sense of history; in departing westward from the Mandan villages he compared his little fleet of pirogues and canoes to the vessels of Captain Cook.[5] The significance of his enterprise warranted as complete a record as possible. It might be too much to ask any enlisted men to copy their officers' voluminous journals, but those so inclined could be encouraged to add their bit to the record.

At least some of the men who went with Lewis and Clark seem to have shared that sense of history. They were volunteers, after all, and although some of them no doubt simply hoped to escape from irksome military discipline or to find good beaver streams, others evidently knew very well that this was the chance of a lifetime, that they were involved in something that would survive them, something greater than their individual contribution. The combination of that sense of history with a degree of literacy and considerable diligence made a few of them journal keepers.

To appreciate the work of these men, let us remember the conditions under which they wrote. Most days of the voyage involved hard physical labor, working canoes upstream, loading and unloading bulky equipment, hunting and butchering, tanning leather, making moccasins, cooking, chopping and shaping wood, caring for horses and searching for strays, mounting guard, portaging around falls and rapids, all while exposed to every kind of weather and to the attacks of insects and grizzly bears, with the constant danger of physical injury from accidents. At the end of such a day, perhaps while others were dancing to Pierre Cruzatte's fiddle, a journal keeper would have to write by the light of a campfire in notebooks somehow kept safe from the elements. According to Lewis, seven of the thirty-odd men had the perseverance and the sense of destiny to try.

They wrote under the same conditions as the captains, and like them wrote not only for themselves. It seems probable that they examined each other's journals, and perhaps Lewis and Clark read them, too. We know that on July 14, 1804, having lost his notes for the previous day, Clark had "to refur to the . . . Journals of Serjeants." The enlisted men's journals were intended as part of the record; they were public documents and we cannot expect any deep psychological revelations. No one recorded explicitly, for example, his opinion of Lewis or Clark or Sacagawea.

Literacy was the first requirement. It is probable that some of the men could not even write their own names. Historians have expressed considerable humor over Clark's awkward grammar and his versatility as a speller, but he was little worse than many contemporaries who like him were men of affairs, government officials, and army officers. Comparison of Clark's journal with those of the enlisted men should keep us from laughing too much at Clark. Nor should we be overly amused at the enlisted men, for none of their journals suggests stupidity or dullness. They tried to the best of their ability to record an extraordinary experience.

Sergeants in the army had to be literate, since they kept records for their companies, and it is not too surprising that three of the four enlisted men's journals that we now have are those of sergeants. John Ordway and Charles Floyd held that rank from the start of the trip, and Patrick Gass was promoted some three months out to fill the place of the deceased Floyd. Joseph Whitehouse is the only private whose journal we now have. Ordway's spelling and grammar are, if anything, better than Clark's. We cannot judge Gass's performance for we do not have his original writing. Floyd and Whitehouse apparently struggled with writing, but there is rarely doubt about what they meant.

We have four enlisted men's journals, in one form or another. Lewis indicated that seven men were keeping journals, and the discrepancy requires some notice,

although few hard conclusions can be made. Since the other sergeants were expected to keep journals, one would assume that Sergeant Nathaniel Pryor would
also do so, but no document demonstrating this has come to light. Pryor served later
on as an army officer and an Indian agent, but other men who could barely sign
their names filled those posts on the frontier. On August 12, 1806, Clark noted that
Pryor had left behind saddlebags containing his "papers," but Pryor had just returned from being separated from the main party, and the papers might have consisted only of letters he was supposed to deliver to a Canadian trader, and perhaps
a journal of his separate trip, which began barely three weeks before. In any case,
Pryor went back and recovered the saddlebags, so the papers, whatever they were,
were not then lost. There is simply no clear evidence to show that Pryor was one of
the seven journal keepers mentioned by Lewis.

It is fairly certain that one private besides Whitehouse kept some sort of journal,
because Robert Frazer announced his intention to publish by issuing a prospectus
soliciting subscribers barely a month after the party returned to St. Louis, promising
"An accurate description of the Missouri and its several branches; of the mountains
separating the Eastern from the Western waters; of the Columbia river and the Bay
it forms on the Pacific Ocean; of the face of the Country in general; of the several
Tribes of Indians on the Missouri and Columbia rivers . . . ," and with all this "a
variety of Curious and interesting occurrences during a voyage of two years four
months and nine days." The account, Frazer made clear, was "Published by Permis-
sion of Captn. Meriwether Lewis."[6] If the journal was anything like what Frazer
promised, that it was never published is a great pity. Given the importance of the
expedition this is surprising, especially since Patrick Gass was able to secure publication of his work the next year and since there were six further editions of his book
in six years. Clearly it was not lack of public interest in Lewis and Clark's discoveries
that held Frazer's work back. Whatever the problem was, Frazer passed from view
and so did his journal; we have no clue as to its fate.

In April 1805, when Lewis wrote that seven men were keeping journals, Floyd was
already dead. If we accept Pryor and Frazer as journal keepers, along with Gass,
Ordway, and Whitehouse, we still have two others to account for. It is possible that
Lewis counted Floyd, whose journal was sent back from Fort Mandan, even though
his record had ceased the previous August. There is a possibility that Private Alexander Willard kept a journal, and with Willard and Floyd we would have Lewis's
seven journal keepers.[7] One way or another a considerable part of the record appears to be lost, perhaps forever.

The journals that remain belong with those of Lewis and Clark, supporting them
to the best of their ability as they did during the voyage. After the return Lewis
evaluated his men, each according to his individual merits, and then wrote of them
all: "the Ample support which they gave me under every difficulty; the manly firm-

ness which they evinced on every necessary occasion; and the patience and fortitude with which they submitted to, and bore, the fatigues and painful sufferings incident to my late tour to the Pacific Ocean, entitles them to my warmest approbation and thanks."[8]

JOSEPH WHITEHOUSE

Of Joseph Whitehouse we know even less than about Ordway, Gass, and Floyd, less indeed than we know even about some expedition members who kept no journals. He said he was born in Fairfax County, Virginia, in about 1775; his family moved to Kentucky in 1784. He first enlisted in the regular army in 1798 and ended a standard five-year enlistment in 1803, having served in Daniel Bissell's company of the First Infantry.[9] He evidently reenlisted since, like Ordway and Gass, he was serving in Captain Russell Bissell's company of the First Infantry at Kaskaskia when he joined Lewis, probably in November 1803. In the introduction to the fair copy of his journal he said that "I was led at an early period of my life to enter into the Army of the United States, by views I had to acquire military knowledge, & to be acquainted with the Country in which I was born." We may take this to mean that, like many young men, he joined up for adventure and travel. He claims that during his service at Kaskaskia he conversed with traders doing business with the Missouri River tribes and began thinking "that there might be a practicability of penetrating across the Continent of North America, to the Pacific Ocean by way of the Missouri River." If this is an accurate account of his thoughts, then it may be that when Captain Bissell was ordered to furnish men for the Corps of Discovery he picked Whitehouse, knowing that he was interested in such an enterprise. Whitehouse did not say that he volunteered; he thought that he was "fortunate in being chosen" as one of the party, "which contributed much to quicken the execution of my favorite project, and of satisfying my own ambition." The words may be those of Whitehouse's scribe or editor, but there is no reason to assume that a humble private was incapable of dreams and ambitions like those nourished by Meriwether Lewis for years before the expedition.

On December 26, 1803, Clark refers to him as "Corpl. White house," perhaps an error since nowhere else during the expedition does he appear with this rank. Sometime in April 1804, Clark notes that "Wh[itehouse] wishes to return," which can be interpreted in at least two ways. Either Whitehouse was dissatisfied and wanted to return to his old company at Kaskaskia, or he was one of the expedition members expelled for misconduct at Camp Dubois, who were then allowed to return to the party after expressing repentance.[10] At any rate, Whitehouse did not choose to leave the expedition and was one of those chosen for the permanent party.

There was little else about Whitehouse's service with the Corps of Discovery that was remarkable. On May 17, 1804, he was one of the members of a court-martial trying William Werner and Hugh Hall for disobedience. He was almost bitten by a rattlesnake on July 11, 1805, and was nearly killed in a canoe accident a month later. He took his discharge soon after the return to St. Louis and received $166.66⅔ in pay and a land grant which he promptly sold to his comrade George Drouillard. Civilian life apparently presented difficulties not encountered in a trek to the Pacific; Whitehouse was arrested for debt in Missouri in 1807, and he reenlisted in the army in December of that year. He was stationed on the western frontier, serving at Fort Osage in 1808; he was there when he again reenlisted in 1812. In the War of 1812 he served on the Canadian border and was in combat in the Niagara Falls area in 1814. In August 1813 he was reduced in rank from corporal to private. He may have been one of those old soldiers who are at their best on active service but get into trouble on garrison duty. In 1816 he served for a time in the Corps of Artillery, reenlisted, and then deserted in February 1817. Clark could learn nothing of him in the 1820s. Descriptions in his service records indicate that he was five feet, ten inches tall, had light brown hair, a fair complexion and hazel eyes, and was a skin dresser by trade.[11]

Whitehouse's journal begins with the official start of the expedition on May 14, 1804; what we have of the original runs to November 6, 1805, but a paraphrased version continues to April 2, 1806.[12] Whitehouse tells us that "In this Voyage I furnished myself with books, and also got from captains Lewis and Clark, every information that lay in their power, in order to compleat and make my journal correct (p. 6)." This statement not only indicates some intellectual curiosity on Whitehouse's part but may suggest that his journal originally ran to the end of the expedition and was "compleat" in that sense. Whitehouse also notes that Clark kept his journal for him "when I was on a fatigue party." That statement provides one of the few insights into the relations between the captains and their men, and Whitehouse has more to say on that subject. These words, written when he was no longer under their command, praise "the manly, and soldier-like behavior; and enterprizing abilities; of both Captain Lewis, and Captain Clark . . . and the humanity shown at all times by them, to those under their command, on this perilous and important Voyage of discovery."

It has been suggested that Whitehouse gave up writing his journal because writing was too much of a burden for a man of his limited education. Yet if we examine his work we find that his entries become fuller and more informative with time, as he got into the rhythm of his task and understood better what he was about. At Fort

Mandan and Fort Clatsop, when less was happening and there were no new sights, his entries become briefer, and gaps appear, but when there were new and varied experiences to report and new country to describe, Whitehouse would give it a try, in spite of weather, fatigue, grammar, or spelling.

Whitehouse's original journal, as we now have it, consists of a single volume of three parts bound in animal skin, running from May 14, 1804, to November 6, 1805. It was once thought that he ceased writing on that last date, but we now know that this is certainly not the case. On his deathbed, Whitehouse gave the original journal to his Catholic confessor, Canon di Vivaldi; this may have been around 1860. Later, Gertrude Haley of San Francisco loaned the priest money, and he gave her the journal in return. It passed into various hands, including those of the New-York Historical Society. Haley regained possession and tried to sell it to the Library of Congress, which would not pay her asking price. Finally, Dodd, Mead and Company purchased it for the use of Reuben Gold Thwaites in his edition of the expedition journals.[13]

Seeing Whitehouse's difficulties with the language, Thwaites and others assumed that he had simply grown weary of writing in November 1805 and stopped. That notion was exploded by another of the fortuitous discoveries that mark the entire history of the Lewis and Clark journals. In February 1966, Professor George White, a geologist from the University of Illinois–Urbana, visited Philadelphia and in a bookstore was shown the manuscript of a journal by Joseph Whitehouse. Returning home, he told his university colleague Donald Jackson, editor of the *Letters of the Lewis and Clark Expedition,* who in turn informed the Newberry Library of Chicago, then and now holder of the original journal. The Newberry obtained the new find and Jackson was able to examine it. It was a single notebook, written by someone other than Whitehouse himself, running from May 14, 1804, to April 2, 1806. Just before the March 23, 1806, entry there is a heading, "Volume 2nd"; this would seem to indicate that there was a good deal more to come, and that Whitehouse may have completed his journal to September 23, 1806. This paraphrased version fills in some gaps in the original as we now have it.[14]

Jackson finally concluded that the new find, interesting as it was, did not provide enough new information to justify publication on its own.[15] It does, however, extend Whitehouse's record of the expedition by several months, and appears here so that this edition may be as complete as possible.

Notes

1. Donald Jackson, ed., *Letters of the Lewis and Clark Expedition with Related Documents, 1783– 1854* (2d ed., 2 vols. Urbana: University of Illinois Press, 1978), 1:vii.

2. Jefferson's Instructions to Lewis [June 20, 1803], ibid., 1:62.

3. See the Orderly Book entry for May 26, 1804.

4. Lewis to Jefferson, April 7, 1805, Jackson, ed., *Letters*, 1:232.

5. See Lewis's journal entry for April 7, 1805.

6. The Robert Frazer Prospectus [October 1806], Jackson, ed., *Letters*, 1:345–46.

7. On Willard's journal, see Olin D. Wheeler, *The Trail of Lewis and Clark, 1804–1806* (2 vols. New York: G. P. Putnam's Sons, 1904), 1:124; and Robert B. Betts, "'The writingest explorers of their time': New Estimates of the Number of Words in the Published Journals of the Lewis and Clark Expedition," *We Proceeded On* 7 (August 1981): 7–8, 8 n. 34.

8. Lewis to Henry Dearborn, January 15, 1807, Jackson, ed., *Letters*, 1:369.

9. Joan M. Corbett to Donald Jackson, July 2, 1970, in Donald Jackson's Whitehouse file, based on Corbett's research in RG 94 and RG 98 in the National Archives, Washington, D.C.

10. See vol. 2, p. 194, for the undated entry; Paul Russell Cutright, *A History of the Lewis and Clark Journals* (Norman: University of Oklahoma Press, 1976), 244–45.

11. Ibid., 242–64; Charles G. Clarke, *The Men of the Lewis and Clark Expedition: A Biographical Roster of the Fifty-one Members and a Composite Diary of Their Activities from All Known Sources* (Glendale, Calif.: Arthur H. Clark, 1970), 55–56; Clark's List of Expedition Members [ca. 1825–28], Jackson, ed., *Letters*, 2:639; Corbett to Jackson, July 2, 1970, Whitehouse file. Jackson notes that Whitehouse's being a skin-dresser would explain "the many notations in his journal to the effect that he was busy making and repairing the men's clothing." Jackson to Corbett, July 6, 1970, ibid.

12. An additional entry, predating the start of the expedition, is found in Whitehouse's fair copy. This entry, dated November 17, 1803 (see notes under Whitehouse's entry of May 14, 1804), is not found in any other enlisted man's journal. It provides a more detailed description of St. Louis than any previous journal keeper but is also notable for its misinformation. The main party did not leave St. Louis on the date given; they were still at the mouth of the Ohio and did not reach the town until December 11, 1803. Whitehouse himself was apparently not with the party on November 17, but with Captain Bissell's company and stationed at Kaskaskia, Illinois. His official date of entry into the Corps of Discovery was January 1, 1804, but he may have reached River Dubois earlier. Whitehouse's scribe must have added this entry based on information from Whitehouse, and it somehow became garbled.

13. Cutright, *History of the Lewis and Clark Journals*, 114–15. The story as Thwaites obtained it from Haley may be a bit confused.

14. Ibid., 247; see also Appendix B and Appendix C, vol. 2, for further description.

15. Cutright, *History of the Lewis and Clark Journals*, 248.

The Journals of the Lewis & Clark Expedition, Volume 11

The Journals of Joseph Whitehouse, May 14, 1804–April 2, 1806

Chapter Fifty-Five

Up the Missouri

May 14–September 24, 1804

Monday 14th May 1804.[1]   hard Showers of rain.   this being the day appointed by Capt. Clark to Set out, a number of the Sitizens of Gotian[2] Settlement came to See us Start.   we got in readiness.   Capt. Lewis is now at St. Louis but will join us at St. Charls.   about 3 Oclock P. M. Capt. Clark and the party consisting of three Sergeants and 38 men[3] who manned the Batteaux and perogues.[4]   we fired our Swivel[5] on the bow hoisted Sail and Set out in high Spirits for the western Expedition.   we entered the mouth of the Missourie haveing a fair wind Sailed abt. 6 miles and Camped on the North Side.—[6]

1804 Monday May 14th[7]   This day being appointed for our departure, from Wood River, a number of the Inhabitants (Americans) from Goshen settlement came to see us start for the Western Ocean; we got in readiness, at 3 o'Clock P. M. Captain William Clark, Three Sergeants and 38 Men, who mann'd the boat, and Two pettiaugers;[8] fired the Swivel from the Bow of the Boat; hoisted Sail, and set out in high spirits, for our intended Western expedition: we entered the mouth of the Mesouri River, having a fair Wind from So East, and Rain; we sailed up the said River about Six Miles, and encamped on the North side of it.—   The River Misouri is about one Mile wide, and on the South side of it near its mouth is an Island and its waters are always muddy occasion'd by its banks falling in, the current Runs at about five Miles & a half p hour; the banks are very steep, and the bottom very

Map of Expedition's
Route, May 14, 1804–
September 23, 1806

PACIFIC OCEAN

WASHINGTON

Columbia River

Clark Fork

Camp Disappo
(July 22-26,

Blackfeet Fig
(July 27,

See Inset B

Le
Cl
(July

Palouse R.

Fort Clatsop
(Dec. 7, 1805-
March 23, 1806)

Beacon Rock
(Nov. 2, 1805)

Oct. 21, 1805,
April 22, 1806

Columbia R.

Lolo Pass
(Sept. 13, 1805,
June 23, 1806)

Travelers' F
(Sept. 9-11
June 30-Ju

Nov. 4, 1805,
March 30, 1806

Willamette R.

The Dalles
(Oct 25-28, 1805,
April 15-18, 1806)

Oct. 19, 1805

Umatilla R.

Thr
(July 2
July

John

Deschutes R.

Day R.

Salmon R.

Celilo Falls
(Oct. 22-23, 1805,
April 21, 1806)

Snake River

Lemhi Pass
(Aug. 12 and 26, 1805)

OREGON

IDAHO

Camp F
(Aug. 17
July 8-10,

Snake River

▲ Lewis and Clark Site
▼ Lewis and Clark Locale
■ Lewis Party Site
◆ Lewis Party Locale
▣ Clark Party Site
◈ Clark Party Locale
● Modern Town

0   100
Miles

Columbia River

WASHINGTON

Clark Fork

Inset

MONT

Palouse River

N. Fork Clearwater R.

Oct. 13, 1805

Snake River

Lolo
(Sept.
June 2

Yakima R.

Kennewick
(Oct. 16-17, 1805)

Waitsburg
(May 1, 1806)

Canoe Camp
(Sept. 26-Oct. 7, 1805)

April 27-30, 1806
Columbia River

Walla

Lewiston-Clarkston
(Oct. 10, 1805,
May 4, 1806)

Camp Chopunnish
(May 14-June 10, 1806)

Oct. 19, 1805

Walla R.

Umatilla R.

Gib
(Ju

OREGON

Salmon River

Lost Trail Pass
(Sept. 3, 1805)

IDAHO

Snake

Salmon
(Aug. 21 and 31, 1805)

0   60
Miles

Lem
(Aug. 12 and 26

CANADA

Milk River

June 3-12, 1805,
July 28, 1806 (Lewis)
May 29, 1805,
July 30, 1806 (Lewis)

Missouri River

Judith R.

lls,
-July 13, 1805,
7, 1806)

May 8, 1805,
Aug. 4, 1806 (Lewis)

May 20, 1805,
Aug. 1, 1806 (Lewis)

Musselshell River

July 30, 1806

Yellowstone R.

April 26, 1805,
Aug. 3, 1806 (Clark),
Aug. 7, 1806 (Lewis)

Little Missouri River

Knife River

Heart River

Fort Mandan
(Nov. 13, 1804-
April 7, 1805,
Aug. 14, 1806)

Bismarck
(Oct. 21, 1804,
Aug.18, 1806)

NORTH DAKOTA

ONTANA

Yellowstone River

Pompeys Pillar,
(July 25, 1806)

Livingston
(July 16, 1806)

Bighorn River

Tongue River

Powder River

Grand River

Moreau River

Mobridge
(Oct. 8, 1804,
Aug.22, 1806)

SOUTH

Cheyenne River

Bad River

White River

Pierre
(Sept. 24, 1804,
Aug. 26, 1806)

DAKOTA

WYOMING

North Platte River

Niobrara River

NEBRASKA

See Inset A

rre
pt. 24, 1804,
j. 26, 1806)

SOUTH
DAKOTA

Inset A

Mississippi River

rara R.

Vermillion
(Aug. 24, 1804)

Sioux City
(Sept. 4, 1806)

IOWA

EBRASKA

Council Bluff
(July 30, 1804)

Omaha
(Sept. 8, 1806)

Camp White Catfish
(July 22, 1804)

te River

Republican R.

ILLINOIS

Camp Dubois
(Dec. 13, 1803-
May 14, 1804)

St. Joseph
(Sept. 12, 1806)

MISSOURI

Missouri River

Jefferson City
(June 3, 1804,
Sept. 19, 1806)

KANSAS

Kansas River

Kansas City
(June 26, 1804,
Sept. 15, 1806)

St. Louis
(Sept. 23,
1806)

y Hill River

Osage River

muddy. Wood River lies in Latitude 38° 54° North & the mouth of the River Mesouri 38° 54 39' North & Longitude 112° 15 West from Greenwich.

1. Whitehouse's first daily entry in the first part of his three-part original notebook journal covering the period May 14, 1804, to May 27, 1805. The pages of this portion of the notebook are approximately 7⅜" × 6"; the notebook as a whole is covered in animal skin. On the first page the words "Joseph Whitehouse" and the initial "J" are repeated several times. Other random writings are not legible. On the second page, preceding the first daily entry is the following: "Joseph Whitehouse's Journal Commencing at River deboise 14th May 1804.— it being a Minute relation of the various transaction[s] and occurrences which took place dureing a Voiage of [*blank*] years from the United States to the Pacific Ocean through the interior of the conti[nent of] North America—. under the directions of Capt. Meriwether Lewis & Capt. W Clark, and patronised by the Government of the U States. The individuals who composed the party engaged to essay the dificuelties, dangers fatigues of this enterprise with the Said Officers; Consists of the persons whoes Names are here-unto anexed— Viz: George Drewyer to act as Interpreter and Hunter; John Ordway, Nathl. Pryor, Charles Floyd & Patric Gass Sergts. John Shields, William Bratten, John Colter, Hugh Hall, John Collins, Joseph Field, Reuben Field, Silas Goodrich, Alexander Willard, William Werner, John Potts, Thomas Procter Howard, [Pe]ter Wiser, George Gibson, George Shannon, John B. Thompson, Richard Windser, [Rob]ert Frazer, Hugh McNeal, Peter Crusatt, Francis Labeech, & Joseph White[house;] also Capt. Clarks Black Man York—. At the Mandans Tousant Shabono Indian woman & child joined as interpreter & interpretis to the Snake Indians." It appears that Clark wrote the portion that begins with the words "under the directions of," to the end. This material was probably written sometime during the winter of 1804–5 while the party was at Fort Mandan or perhaps afterwards. The writing on the pages is from end-to-end, as in a stenographer's notebook, rather than side-to-side, as in a conventional book.

2. Referring to the Hebrew land of Goshen (Genesis 46, 47) and alluding to a place of goodness and plenty. Whitehouse may be using Goshen as a generic term for the surrounding neighborhood.

3. For the composition of the party at this time, see Appendix A, vol. 1.

4. The keelboat (perhaps Whitehouse's "batteaux") is discussed at Lewis's entry for August 30, 1803, and the pirogues at the entries for September 4, 1803, and May 13, 1804.

5. The party's small, swivel-mounted cannon, discussed at Clark's entry for May 29, 1804.

6. Near the mouth of Coldwater Creek, St. Charles County, Missouri, a little above the town of Fort Bellefontaine.

7. The first entry in Whitehouse's fair copy (see Introduction to this volume). The fair copy will be the second entry for each day's account unless otherwise indicated. Preceding this entry are several pages of introductory material beginning with a single page as follows:

Voyage
From Saint Louis, in the Territory of Louisiana and on the River Mississippi across the Continent of North America, by way of the River Mesouri, to the Pacific or Western Ocean; in the Years, 1803, 4, 5 & 1806, under the directions of Captain Merriweather

Lewis, and Captain William Clark, and patronised by the Government of the United States, with a description of the Countries through which they passed; taken from actual survey. Illustrated with Maps, with an account of the Latitude [*blank*] of the most noted places on the Mesouri and Columbia Rivers, by.

Joseph Whitehouse

To The Citizens of the United States.

This Volume is inscribed, by their fellow Citizen, and devoted Servant,

Joseph Whitehouse

[Next comes a blank page and then the following preface]

Preface

On presenting this Volume to my fellow Citizens, it is not necessary to enter into particular account of this Voyage; but I trust that the generous public, will make such allowances as they shall think fit, to one who has never before presented himself to them in the character of an Author; for which the course and occupations of my life; has by no means qualified me, being much better calculated to perform the Voyage (arduous as it might be) than to write an account of it; however it is now offered to the Public, with the submission that becomes me.   I was led at an early period of my life to enter into the Army of the United States, by views I had to acquire Military knowledge, & to be acquainted with the Country in which I was born; and accordingly was somewhat gratified by being ordered (shortly after I joined the Service) to Kaskaskias Village, in the Illinois Country.—   I there, from frequent conversations, I had with Traders; whose traffic was with the Indians, residing on the Mesouri River, contemplated that there might be a practibility of penetrating across the Continent of North America, to the Pacific Ocean by way of the Mesouri River, but found from the most perfect account that I could collect from any of them; did not extend beyond the Mandan Nation, who inhabited on the same River Mesouri, which lays in 47° 24′ 12 North Latitude; the Countries beyond that place, being utterly unknown to them, and even to the Indians inhabiting that Country.

I had been at Kaskaskia Village some time, when I was informed That His Excellency Thomas Jefferson Esquire, President of the United States, had appointed Captain Meriweather Lewis, and Captain William Clark, to take the command of a party of Continental Troops, and Volunteers; in order to explore the Mesouri River; and find out its source; and to find (if possible) by that rout a passage to the Pacific ocean.—   I was fortunate in being chosen one of the party of Continental Troops by them, which contributed much to quicken the execution of my favorite project, and of satisfying my own ambition.   The dangers I have encounter'd, and the toils I have suffered, have found their recompence, nor will the many and tedious days, or the gloomy and inclement nights that I have passed, have been passed in vain.—   This Voyage I hope has settled the dubious point respecting the Source of the great Rivers Mesouri, and Columbia; and I trust that it has set that long agitated question at rest, in regard to a passage being across the Continent of North America, to the Pacific Ocean, and the Northern boundary of Louisiana.—

In this Voyage I furnished myself with books, and also got from Captains Lewis and Clark, every information that lay in their power, in order to compleat and make my Journal correct; and part of my Journals were kept by one of them when I was on a fataigue party.— This was done by them, in case of any great accident happening to the party, so that if any of them should return to the United States, or their Journals fall into the hands of any civiliz'd Nation, that the grand object of our discovery's might not be defeated. The object being accomplished, it lays with you to determine the practibility of a commercial communication across the continent of North America, between the Atlantic and Pacific Oceans which is proved by my Journal.— Nor do I hesitate to declare, my decided opinion, that very great, and essential advantages, may be derived; by extending our Trade, from one Sea, to the other.

The very great advantages of the fur trade, from that hitherto unknown Country, both by ascending the Mesouri River, and by way of the Columbia River to the Pacific ocean, will I trust prove Interesting to a Nation, whose general policy, is blended with, and whose prosperity is supported by the persuits of commerce.— It will also qualify the reader, to pursue the succeeding Voyages, with superior intelligence and satisfaction.— This Voyage will not I fear afford the variety, that may be expected from it; and that which it offers to the Eye, is not of a nature to be effectually transferred to the Page; Mountains and Valleys, the vast Priaries; the wide spreading forests, the lakes and Rivers, on both sides of the Rocky Mountains, succeed each other in general description;

The permanent Villages, both on the Rivers Mesouri, and Columbia; and the Inhabitants in general, with bands of wandering Indians, are the only people, whom I shall introduce to the acquaintance of my readers.— The Buffalo, the white Bear; the Elk, the Antelope, the mountain Goat, & the Beaver; are mostly so familiar to the Naturalists, and are so frequently described, that a bare mention of them, as they enliven'd the landscapes, or were hunted for food; with a cursory account of the soil, the course of the Rivers, and their various produce, is all that can reasonably be expected from me.— The toil of our Navigation to the source of the Mesouri, was incessant; and often times extreme, and in our progress over the Rocky Mountains, with the Burthens on our shoulders; which aggravated the Toils of our march, and added to the wearisomeness of our way, adding to which the extreme dangers we encounter'd in descending the River Columbia at a season of the Year, that not even the Natives of the soil would attempt; I hope will convince my readers, that Manly fortitude and perseverance was our only guide.—

Though the events, which compose my Journal, may have little in itself to strike the imagination of those who love to be astonished; nevertheless, when it is consider'd, that we explored those Waters, which had never before borne any other Vessell, than the Canoe of the Savage; and traversed those Forests and plains, where no American Citizen, or European had ever before presented themselves, to the Eye of its swarthy natives; when to these considerations, are added, the Important objects which were pursued; with the dangers that were encounter'd, and the difficulties that were surmounted to attain them; this work will, I flatter myself, be found to excite an interest, and conciliate regard, in the minds of those who peruse it.— I hope the generous public, will indulge me, by believing; that I have laid before them, only whatever I saw, (or were seen by Captains Lewis or Clark) with the impression of the moment; that it was told by them, or presented itself to me, and have never allowed myself to wander into conjecture, but have given as full, and exact account of the Country, and other transactions, that occur'd in the Country, that we passed through, as my abilities would allow. I cannot in justice to myself omit saying, that the manly, and soldier-like behaviour; and enterprizing abilities; of both Captain Lewis, and Captain Clark, claim my utmost gratitude: and the humanity shown at all times by them, to those under their command, on this perilous and important Voyage of discovery; I hope will ever fill the breasts of Men who were under their command with the <will> same, and make their characters be esteem'd by the American people, and mankind in general; and convince the generous Public, that the President of the United States, did not misplace his judgment, when he appointed them to the command of this party on discovery; which is of so great a magnitude and utility, to the United States and mankind in general.—

I am not a candidate for literary fame, at the same time, I cannot but indulge the hope, that this volume, with all its imperfections, will not be thought unworthy the attention of the scientific Geographer; and that by unfolding Countries; hitherto unexplored, and which I presume, may be considered as a part belonging to the United States, it will be received as a faithful tribute to the prosperity of my Country.

Saint Louis   Joseph Whitehouse
December 10th 1806

[Then on a new page comes the following list of party members]

The Individuals who composed the party, engaged to essay the difficulties; dangers and fataigues of this enterprize with Captain Merryweather Lewis, and Captain William Clark, consisted of the persons, whose names are hereunto annexed. Viz—

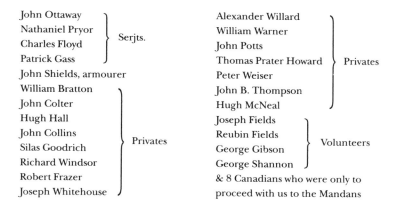

John Ottaway		Alexander Willard	
Nathaniel Pryor	Serjts.	William Warner	
Charles Floyd		John Potts	
Patrick Gass		Thomas Prater Howard	Privates
John Shields, armourer		Peter Weiser	
William Bratton		John B. Thompson	
John Colter		Hugh McNeal	
Hugh Hall		Joseph Fields	
John Collins	Privates	Reubin Fields	
Silas Goodrich		George Gibson	Volunteers
Richard Windsor		George Shannon	
Robert Frazer		& 8 Canadians who were only to	
Joseph Whitehouse		proceed with us to the Mandans	

Peter Crusatt ⎫ Canadians &
Francis Labeech ⎰ Volunteers,
   George Drewer, to act as Indian Interpreter and Hunter &
   Captain William Clark's Black Man, York,
   And at the Mandan Nation we were joined by Tousant Shabono (a canadian) and his Indian Woman, with a Child; this Indian Woman who was employed, as Interpreter to the Snake Nation of Indians.—

[Then comes a blank page and on a new page the heading for the daily entries and a first entry for November 17, 1803, after which begin daily entries from May 14, 1804]

Journal

Of a Voyage across the continent of North America, to the Western; or Pacific Ocean.

1803 novemr 17th   We embarked at 9 o'Clock this morning from Saint Louis (in the Territory of Louisiana) on board of a boat, belonging to The United States, for the River Dubois (or Wood River Indiana Territory,) having all hands that is mention'd in the former page belonging to our party on board, and several articles provided to make us comfortable <with us> during the Winter, which we intend staying at Wood River & remaining untill the River Mesouri should be free from Ice.   We arrived at the place pointed out by Captains Lewis & Clark at 5 o'Clock P. M. the distance being 20 miles; and the course of the Mississippi River: being N by East.—

The River Dubois (or Wood River) is a small River; laying on the East side of the Mississippi, and empties itself into the same.—   The Town of Saint Louis from which we took our departure; is situated on the West bank of the River Mississippi; and contains about 200 houses, built in the french fashion; and <lies> is situated under a hill and <is> lays in the form of an oblong Square.   The street runs paralel with the River; and cross at right Angles,—   and are Narrow; and most of the lots are picketted in.   The only public building is a Chapel, which is by no means elegant.—   On the west side of the Town are four Towers, built in a circular form, one of which is occupied at present by the American Troops as a fort; and also a half moon battery which stands on hill a short distance from the bank of the River at the North end of the Town.—

The land adjoining the Town for several miles is level and chiefly priaries, and very thinly settled.   The chief of the Inhabitants are canadian french, and a few families of Americans.   The River Mississippi opposite Saint Louis is about one Mile wide, has a large sand barr on the East side, and an Island laying <on> opposite to the South end of the Town, the banks of the River lays mostly high, and the waters are <mostly> muddy, as high up the River Mississippi to where the confluence of that River, and the River Mesouri commences.—   This Town lies in Latitude 38° 43′ North.—

   8. Pirogues.

Tuesday 15th May 1804. hard rain. we Set out eairly. the current Swift, & water muddy. passed Islands & Some inhabitants &c. the after part of the day proved pleasant. [w]e Camped on the North Side.—[1]

Tuesday May 15th   This morning early we set sail, in a hard Rain, the current of the River, being very swift, and water muddy; passed some Islands, with some Inhabitants on them; the latter part of the day proved clear; and in the Evening we encamped on the North side of the River.—

1. About five miles downstream from St. Charles, St. Charles County, Missouri.

[Wedn]esday 16th May 1804. a clear morning. Set out [early] and proceeded on verry well. about 2 oclock P. M. [we ar]rived at St Charls.[1] and passed the evening with a [gr]eat deal of Satisfaction, all chearful and in good Spirits. this place is an old french village Situated on the North Side of the Missourie and are dressy polite people and Roman Catholicks.—

Wednesday May 16th   We set out this morning, having clear weather, and proceeded on very well, about 2 oClock P. M we arrived at Saint Charles, where we passed the Evening with a great deal of satisfaction, and chearfulness, and all our men appeared to be in good spirits.

We shall waite here for Captain Lewis, who is to meet us from Saint Louis <here>;— Saint Charles is a Village settled by French Inhabitants. It is a handsome situation, laying on the North side of the River contains about 80 Houses, built in the french fashion, and has a small Roman Catholic Chapel. its Inhabitants are chiefly canadian french; who are chiefly concerned & employed by others Trading with the Indians who reside on the River Mesouri, and other Rivers that empty into it. The land adjoining it appear to be hilly, but the soil is good and fitting for Agriculture.—

Saint Charles lies in Latitude 38° 54' 39 North & 19 Miles from the Mouth of the Mesouri River,

1. St. Charles, St. Charles County, Missouri.

9

Thursday 17th May 1804.   a pleasant morning.   we are waiting here the arival of Capt. Lewis.   the evening rainy.

Thursday May 17th   A pleasant morning.   We are still here waiting the arrival of Captain Lewis; in the Evening we had some Rain.—

Friday 18th May 1804.   a fair morning.   we bought some acceseries &c. for the voiage.   passed the evening verry agreeable dancing with the french ladies, &c—

Friday May 18th   This morning very pleasant, part of this day we were employ'd, procuring necessary's for our Voyage; in the Evening we were amused at a Ball, which was attended by a number of the French ladies, who were remarkably fond of dancing.

Saturday 19th May 1804.   a rainy wet morning.   Capt. Lewis and Some of the officers from St. Louis arived here this afternoon.[1]   we made ready for a Start &c—

Saturday May 19th   This Morning proved Rainey & wet, Captain Lewis, and some officers from Saint Louis, arrived here in the afternoon; all hands were employed in getting every thing ready to start the remainder of the day.—

1. Lewis actually arrived the next day with U.S. Army officers Amos Stoddard and Stephen Worrell; see Lewis's entry.

Sunday 20th May 1804.   Several of the party went to church, which the french call Mass, and Saw their way of performing &c.—

Sunday may 20th   This day several of our party went to the Chapel, where Mass was said by the Priest, which was a novelty to them.—

Monday 21st May 1804.   Some rainy.   we took on board Some more provision bread &c. about 4 oClock P. M we Set out from this place. fired our bow peace[1] and gave three cheers, and proceeded on in good heart, about [*blank*] miles and Camped[2] on the North Side. 2 frenchman went back to the village. two of our men[3] Stayed at St. Charls in order to come on with the horses

Monday May 21st This morning we had some Rain, part of this day was employed in taking in Provisions &ca.— about 4 oClock P. M. we took our departure from Saint Charles, (a number of the Inhabitants had assembled to see us set off) we fired our Swivel, from the Bow of our boat; and gave them three Cheers, which they returned; we then proceeded up the River about 3 Miles, and came to, on the North side of said River where we encamped. We sent two of our hands (Canadians) back to Saint Charles, in Order to bring on two of our Men, that were left with horses at that place. We found the current of the River very rapid, the Banks steep, & the bottom very miry. The course of the River running due West from its mouth this place. The country lying level, and very fertile.—

1. The swivel cannon again.
2. About three miles southwest of St. Charles, St. Charles County, Missouri.
3. George Drouillard and Alexander Willard.

Tuesday 22nd May 1804[1] a fair morning. we Set out eairly proceeded on verry well passed canom[2] Creek on the Stard Several Indians came to us this evening. Gave us some venison

Tuesday May 22nd This morning being fair, we set out early and proceeded on very well. We passed Bonhom Creek, laying on the South side of the River, in the Evening, several Indians came to where we encamped, & behaved very friendly, and gave us some Venison. The course of the River still being nearly West, and the current rapid.—

1. Whitehouse may have written "4" over "6" for the year. See his entry of May 27.
2. Whitehouse means Bonhomme Creek, St. Louis County, Missouri, but he has it on the wrong side. It is correct in the fair copy.

Wednesday 23rd May 1804.[1]   a fair morning.   we Set out 6 oClock A. m. and proceeded on verry well.   passed Some Inhabitants called boons Settlement.[2]   passd. a noted [p]lace called cave tavern in a clift of rocks on South Side, which is 120 feet long 20 perpinticular high [*illegible*] us   inspected our arms and camped.

Wednesday May 23rd   We embarked this morning at 6 oClock, having fair weather, and proceeded on very well, and passed some Plantations, which is called Boons settlement lying on the North side of the River.   This settlement was made by Colonel Daniel Boone, the person who first discover'd Kentucky, & who was residing at this place, with a number of his family and friends.—[3]

Wednesday May 23rd   A pleasant Morning & We proceed on our Voyage, and crossed the River to the So. side and passed by a noted place which is called Cave Tavern, which is in a Clift of Rocks, 120 feet long, and 20 feet perpendicular, laying on the South side of the River; In the evening our officers inspected our Arms and accoutrements.

1. The first entry for this day is from the original journal; the fair copy has two entries for the day.

2. Boone's Settlement, near present Matson, St. Charles County, Missouri, named for Daniel Boone. See Clark's entry for this date.

3. This is the clearest statement in any of the journals that Boone was actually in residence at his settlement at the time the party passed by. None of the journals, including this one, indicates that they actually met him, which is odd since he already had the slightly exaggerated reputation of the man who "first discover'd Kentucky." Perhaps Whitehouse's scribe elaborated unjustifiably on Whitehouse's information.

[Thu]rsday 24th May 1804.   a fair morning.   we Set out eirily and proceeded on as usal   passd. timbred land on each Side   Current of the river Swift   Camped[1] on the South Side.

Thursday May 24th   We started early this morning, having fair weather; and proceeded on as usual.   Passed a country that appeared to be well timbered, on both sides of the River. The current of the River still being strong, and our course nearly West, in the evening we encamped on the south side of the River, the banks of which was high.

1. About four or five miles below Washington, Franklin County, Missouri.

Friday 25th May 1804. we Set out eairly passed a Smal river on the Stard. Side.[1] the Soil of this part of the country rich. towards evening we arived at a french village called St. Johns,[2] on the Stard. Side a boat came here loaded with fur & Skins had been a long destance up the River tradeing with the Savages &c we Camped near this Small village this is the last Settlement of white people on this River.

Friday May 25th This morning we set out early, passed a small River on the North side, the name unknown, The soil appeared very rich, towards evening we arrived at a French Village called Saint Johns or Charette on the North side of the River. We passed (River Boef)[3] shortly after our arrival at this place, a boat arrived laden with Furrs and peltry (deer Skins) which was returning from a Trading Voyage, the persons who were on board of it having been a great distance, up the Mesouri River; trading with the Indians. This small Village, is the last settlement of white people on this River; we encamped near it— The course of the River being <still> West by South

1. Contrary to other writers who note a river on the opposite side, Dubois Creek, Franklin County, Missouri.

2. La Charette, Warren County, Missouri; called St. John from the Spanish fort located there earlier.

3. River au Boeuf (Rivière aux Boeufs or Buffalo River) in Franklin County, which Clark reports passing on May 26. See Clark's entries of May 25 and 26, 1804.

Saturday 26th May 1804.[1] a fair morning. we Set out eairly Some Thunder and rain, towards evening we passd. a creek called otter Creek[2] on the N. Side.—

Saturday May 26th   We set out early this morning, the weather being fine
and clear, towards evening we had some Rain and Thunder.   We passed a
Creek laying on the North side of the River, called Otter Creek.   The current still running rapid.—

1. Whitehouse may have written "4" over "6" for the year. See the next entry.

2. Loutre River, Montgomery County, Missouri, across from Hermann; Clark says they
passed it the next day, but all the enlisted men's journals disagree.

Sunday 27th May 1806.[1]   a fair morning.   we Set out eairly.   passed a
creek called ash Creek,[2] on the N. Side   high clifts on the South Side.   proceeded on   in the afternoon we arived at the Mouth of Gasganade River[3]
on South Side, and camped on an Island opposite the mouth of Sd. River.—

Sunday May 27th   This morning we set out early, having fine weather,
passed a creek, called Ash Creek, laying on the North side of the River.   On
the south side of the River lay high Clifts.   we proceeded on, and in the
afternoon we arrived at the Mouth of the Gasconade River; laying on the
south side of the Mesouri.   We encamped on an Island opposite the Mouth
of said River.   The Gasconade River lies in Latitude 38° 44′ 35 North, and
course of the River Mesouri being still nearly West.   The Gasconade River
is 104 Miles from the River due De Bois (or Wood River) & lies in Latitude
38° 44′ 35S North.[4]

1. There is no ready explanation for Whitehouse using this later date. It seems inconceiv-
able that he would be rewriting the journal in 1806 and get his dates confused.

2. Probably Frame, or Frene, Creek, at Hermann, Gasconade County, Missouri.

3. Gasconade River at Gasconade, Gasconade County.

4. The latitude and mileage do not appear in the original version of Whitehouse's journal,
but they agree with Clark's figures; see Clark's Field Notes entry for August 17, 1804. The
sentence appears to have been crowded in between entries.

Monday 28th May 1804.   a pleasant morning.   Several men out a hunting.   the Latidude at this place is 38° 44′ 3 5–10th   as I was a hunting this
day I came across a cave on the South Side or fork of a river about 100 yards
from the River.   I went a 100 yards under ground.   had no light in my hand

if I had, I Should have gone further   their was a Small Spring in it.   it is the
most remarkable cave I ever Saw, in my travels.   I returnd to the River
found the boad had gone on and had left the french perogue for me.   I
called   they came across for me, and went to camp   took din[ner] and
procd. on   the barge had been gone abt. 2 hours.   we went about 2 miles
and Camped for the night.

Monday May 28th   This morning being fair I went out hunting with several of our Men, for the day; and on my route I discover'd a Cave on the
south side or fork of a small River, about 100 Yards from said fork.   I entered the Cave and proceeded about 100 Yards under the ground, and
found from light which came from the <top> Mouth of the Cave a small
spring in it.   I think it one of the most remarkable Caves I ever saw in my
travels.   I should have proceeded further into the Cave, but it being dark
towards the further end, and having no light, I was forced to return.—   On
my arriving at the River I found that Captains Lewis and Clark had proceeded on with the Boat, and had left a pettiauger and some hands waiting
for me.   On my hailing them, they came across for me.   We then proceeded to camp, and took dinner, after which we proceeded on with the
Pettiauger, the Barge having been gone about two hours, we followed on
about two hours; and encamped for that night.

Tuesday May 29th[1]   This morning being clear we pursued on with the
Pettyauger, and in the Evening overtook the boat, we encamped[2] on the
North side of the River.   The course of the River running still <due> West
by South.—

1. This is the fair copy entry; the original version of Whitehouse's journal has no entry for
this date.
2. According to John Ordway and Patrick Gass, they encamped on the south side, in Gasconade County, Missouri.

Wednesday 30th May 1804.   a fair morning.   we Set out eirily and proceeded on   about noon began to rain.   we passed a creek on the S. Side
called rush creek.[1]   procd. on   passed fine bottoms of timbered land on

each Side.   passd. a River on N. Side called little muddy River,[2] and panther River[3] on S. Side   a large Island opposite the mouth.

Wednesday May 30th   We set off early this morning, the weather being fair; we proceeded on 'till noon when it began to rain, we passed by a Creek laying on the South side of the River, called Rush Creek, and saw a fine bottom of Timber'd land, lying on both sides of the River, we passed a River called little Muddy River, lying on the North side, and a River called Panther River on the South side, having a large Island lying opposite its mouth and encamped here this evening.

   1. Called Rest Creek by Clark in his Field Notes; now Greasy Creek, at the town of Chamois, Osage County, Missouri.
   2. Evidently Muddy Creek, Callaway County, Missouri.
   3. Ordway's Panther Creek and Clark and Gass's Grinestone Creek, evidently Deer Creek, Osage County, Missouri.

Thursday 31st May 1804.   a fair morning.   we Set out as usal and prceedd. on[1]   met a perogue in which was a french man and 2 Indians on board.   their loading was beaver Skins and other peltry.   high wind, R. Fields killed a deer.[2]

Thursday May 31st   This morning being fair, we started early as usual, and proceeded on, we were met by a pettyauger having on board a french Man and two Indians; she was loaded with beaver Skins and peltry.—   The wind blowing hard we came too.   one of our Men named Reubin Fields killed a deer, we encamped here this evening.—

   1. All the other journal keepers indicate that the party remained in camp this day because of high winds. It is hard to account for this discrepancy if Whitehouse was actually keeping this journal at the time.
   2. Probably white-tailed deer, *Odocoileus virginianus.*

Friday 1st June 1804.   a pleasant morning.   we Set out eairly and proceeded on   passed a River on the N. Side called big muddy,[1] the bottoms low.   passd. a creek called beaver creek[2] on the S. Side.

Friday June 1st   We set off early this morning, the weather being pleasant, and passed a River on the North side called Big muddy; the bottom land laying low on the Mesouri, we passed a Creek called beaver creek, lying on the South side of the River, and encamp'd at the Mouth of the Grand Osage River[3]

1. Probably Auxvasse River, Callaway County, Missouri.
2. Presumably the Bear Creek of the other journals, which is probably Loose Creek, Osage County, Missouri.
3. Osage River, on the Osage–Cole county line, Missouri.

Saturday 2nd June 1804.   our officers lay by this day for observations.   4 men went out a hunting.   about 12 oC. they came in had killed 4 deer.   we now lay at the Grand osage River which comes in on the South Side which is a handsome River 397 yards wide   the Missourie is at this place 875 yards wide.   we fell Some trees in the point to open a place for observations

Saturday June 2nd   This day we lay by to get an Observation.   four of our Men went a hunting; about 12 oClock they returned, and had killed 4 deer, we still now lay at the Grand Osage River; which comes in on the South side of the Mesouri, it is a handsome River 397 Yards wide and the Mesouri River at this place is 875 Yards wide

We had a number of hands employed in felling Trees at the point of the Grand Osage River, to open a place in order to take an observation.

Sunday 3rd June 1804.   a fair morning.   Several men out a hunting. our officers takes observations &c.—[1]

Sunday June 3rd   This day being clear, several of the Men was sent out a hunting; Captain Lewis & Captain Clark observ'd, and found the Mouth of the Grand Osage River, to be in Latitude 38° 31 6 North.

1. Whitehouse fails to mention that the party moved several miles upstream this day. They encamped at Moreau River, Cole County, Missouri, east of Jefferson City.

Monday 4th June 1804. a fair morning. we branded Several trees &c.[1] in the afternoon we Set out and proceeded about 4 miles and Camped[2] at the [mouth] of a creek on S. Side.

Monday June 4th We started early this morning; Fair weather, Captains Lewis & Clark had several Trees branded, with their Names and proceeded on about 4 Miles, & encamped at the Mouth of a Creek laying on the South side of the River, The Name of this Creek was unknown to any of our party.—

1. The only one who mentions this act, Whitehouse gives no reason for the branding. It may have been done with Lewis's branding iron; see Lewis's entry for June 10, 1805.

2. Near "Mine Hill," present Sugar Loaf Rock, northwestern Cole County, Missouri. The nearby creek may have been Clark's "Zoncar," later Meadow Creek, Cole County.

Tuesday 5th June 1804.[1] a fair morning. we Set out eairly and proceeded on passed a creek[2] on the South Side and Camped[3] on the Same Side.—

Tuesday June 5th We embarked early this Morning & proceeded on our Voyage, and passed a Creek lying on the South side of the River, the name unknown, in the evening we encamped on the same side of the River, our course being still West by South

1. Following this entry are two pages of random writing mostly impossible to decipher. On the first is a column of notations which read

Joseph Whitehouse
much no much
434
860
1665
[8? *net.* wt.?]
9
[Joseph Whitehouse?]

On the next page are the words "Joseph Whitehouse" and a number of other writings, mostly illegible.

2. Rock Creek or Mud Creek, Cole County, Missouri.

3. In Boone County, Missouri, across from the present town of Sandy Hook, Moniteau County, Missouri.

[W]ednesday 6th June 1804. we Set out eairly and proceeded on passed a creek called led creek[1] on S. Side. passed a creek on N. Side called little good woman creek. the country is good Soil rich and well timbred &c. Camped[2] on the North Side.—

Wednesday June 6th We set out early this morning, and proceeded on, & passed a Creek called Lead Creek, laying on the South side of the River; also passed another Creek, called little good Woman Creek, The soil during this days travel appeared rich, and the Country well timbered, in the Evening we encamped on the North side of the River,

1. All the other journals indicate that they passed Lead Creek (Gass's Mine Creek, present Rock Creek or Mud Creek, Cole County, Missouri) on June 5. The same is true of Little Good Women Creek (present Bonne Femme Creek, Boone County, Missouri).

2. In Boone County, probably a little downstream from the point where Interstate Highway 70 crosses the Missouri.

Thursday 7th June 1804. the hunters and Capt. Lewis went out to a buffaloe lick two miles. Saw this Salt Spring, but no buffaloe. on N. E. Side of the Missourie up the Monetuie river[1] in a timbred country. fine bottons along each Side of the River, under brush thick.[2] Killd 3 Rattel Snakes[3] of Different Sorts at a large rock Close by the latter river after roed. 10 miles Campd. at the Mouth of Creek namd the <Old> Good woman[4] N. E. Side of the Missurie Our daily hunters[5] met us there with three Bears,[6] One Old famel & her two Cubbs brought By G. Drewyer—

Thursday June 7th This morning Captain Lewis & the hunters went to a Buffalo lick, two Miles from the River, and had a view of a Salt spring, but found no Buffalo,

Captain Lewis & the hunters proceeded to the Moniture River, (which lays on the North East side of the Mesouri River,) were they found a well timber'd country, having fine bottoms with rich soil, and along the River on each side of it, found thick brush; On their route they kill'd 3 Rattle snakes near a large Rock, close to the said River, we proceeded with the boat 10 Miles, and encamped at the Mouth of a Creek, call the good Woman Creek lying on the North east side of the Mesouri, where we were met by the party that went hunting; One of which, (G Drewer,) kill'd a She Bear, and her two Cubbs & brought them to the opposite side of the River where we were encamped at.—

1. Moniteau Creek, which meets the Missouri at Rocheport, on the Howard–Boone county line, Missouri.

2. Beginning with the next sentence a new, unknown writer takes over. In his edition, Reuben Gold Thwaites designated the writer as No. 2 to distinguish him from Whitehouse, whom he labeled No. 1, and from a final unknown hand which he called No. 3. We continue this convenient terminology.

3. Probably timber rattlesnake, *Crotalus horridus.*

4. Bonne Femme Creek, Howard County, Missouri.

5. Drouillard and John Newman.

6. Black bear, *Ursus americanus.*

Friday 8th   Got on our way at the usal hour   had strong Watter to Goe throug   <We had> the white pierogue had hard Crossing the River to bring the Meat from the hunters, Druyer Killd 5 deer before 12 Oclock. met two Connooes loaded with furr from the Zotte River[1] neer the Mandens. Got to the <imun> Amens River[2] at three Oclock but did not remain at it any times   Roed. 16 mile

Thursday June 8th   We started early this Morning, and found the current of the River very strong against us, we sent a Pettiauger to bring the bear meat to the boat, but the hands had very great difficulty in crossing the River to us.   The hunters being left, they proceeded a hunting; and one of them (G Drewer) killed five deer by 12 oClock A. M.   We proceeded on and met with Two canoes loaded with Furr, which had come from Zotto River, near the Zotto[3] nation.   At 3 oClock P. M. got to the River L'mine or lead River and remained there but a short time.   We proceeded on & encamped[4] on the North side of the River Mesouri, the distance come this day being 16 Miles

1. Evidently No. 2's effort to write Rivière des Sioux, the present Big Sioux River on the Iowa–South Dakota border, which the other journal keepers indicate was the stream mentioned, although it was not near the Mandans.

2. No. 2's attempt at Mine River, present Lamine River, Cooper County, Missouri.

3. "Zotto" and "L'mine" in the next sentence are written over erasures. In the second instance apparently over the word "Amens," as in the original notebook.

4. Clark and Ordway say they camped on an island, perhaps one of the two later called Arrow Rock Island, near the Saline–Cooper county line, Missouri.

Satery 9   Got on our way at the usal hour   roed. 7 miles   Stopd to take dinner at the End of a large Island above the arrow prarie   the distance from the latter to the River Charrotte River[1] is 14 miles   the hunters did Not Come <in> as the Storm was Great [*illegible, crossed out*]   the peirouge Could not Cross for them   Roed 15 Miles—

Saturday June 9th   This morning we got under way at the usual hour, and rowed 7 Miles, when we took up in order to dine; which we did at the point of a large Island,[2] above a place called the Arrow Priari, This Island lies distant from Charotto River 14 Miles.

The day proving stormy, we were obliged to waite for our hunters who were on the opposite side of the River, and it being unsafe to venture across in the Pettiauger for them.   we encamped on this Island, the distance come this day being 15 Miles

1. Chariton River, Chariton County, Missouri.

2. There may be some confusion here with the campsite of the previous day. The camp today was on an island somewhat above Richland Creek and probably below later Bluff Port, Howard County, Missouri.

Sunday 10   We got to the Charrotte River at 2 Oclock   Waited the Arrival of the hunters there <in>   Sufferd. by the Musquitoes On the N. E Side The Bigg Charrottoe is 100 Yds. at the mouth.   The little[1] comees in to it at the Distance of 300 Yds. apart its Brenth at the mouth is 50 yds. Broad Swem the horses and ferried the men across   had hard watter   Campd.[2] On the Charrotte prarie   Roed 13 Miles—

Sunday June 10th   We embark'd early this morning and proceeded on. at 2 o'Clock we arrived at the River Charotto lying on the North side of the River Mesouri, where we came too; and waited for the arrival of our Hunters, We encamped on the North East side of the Island for a while, but found the

Musqitoes so troublesome that we had to embark again.   The big Charotto
River is 100 Yards wide at its mouth.   The little Charotto River empties itself
into it, at about 300 Yards distance above it and is 50 Yards wide at its mouth.
We had great difficulty in swimming the horses, which the hunters had with
them (which was brought by them from Saint Charles) to the Island & getting them on board, we sent the Pettiauger for the hunters, who came on
board the boat, we proceeded on and went as far as the Charoto Priari,
where we encamp'd.   The wind blowing hard, distance come this day 13
Miles.—

    1. Little Chariton River joins the Chariton a little above the latter's mouth in Chariton
County, Missouri.
    2. About five miles above the Chariton River, in northeast Saline County, Missouri.

Monday 11th   the wind blew So strong in the morning that the Commanding Officer halted there that day   Drewyer Killd two bears & One buck
there Halted—

Monday June 11th   This morning we landed the horses on the banks of
the River; (it blowing very hard), the officers concluded staying here this day.
The Hunters went out a hunting and returned in the Evening with Two
Bears, and a Buck deer that they killed.—

Tusday 12   Left the Charrottoe Perarie and Saild. for the Grand River.
Met with 7 peirogues.   Loaded with peltry for Captn Chatto[1] in St Louis
Our men of Each Craft Exchangd. Blankets for Buffalow Robes & Mockisons
Sent One of Our Men Belonging to the white pierouge back that Belongd.
to Captn Stodders Company of Artilery[2]   Incampd within <thr> two miles
of the three point Island[3]   Roed 7 Miles that day—

Tuesday June 12th   This Morning early we set off from the Charotto Priari, with a fair wind and fine weather, all hands being well and in high spirits;
we found the current of the River still running strong, but are in hopes of
soon getting to the Grand River.   At 10 oClock A. M. met 7 Pettiaugers,

loaded with Peltry, belonging to Captain Choteau of Saint Louis. our Men exchanged with those belonging to the Pettiaugers, some blankets for Buffalo Robes, & Mockasins; we put on board the Pettiaugers, one Man that we had with us, belonging to Captain Stoddards company of Artillery, who is going to Saint Louis, in the Evening we encamped two Miles from an Island called the three point Island; the distance we came this day, being 7 Miles

1. René Auguste Chouteau or Jean Pierre Chouteau; no one else mentions that these men were Chouteau employees.

2. No other journal keeper mentions this event. The man was a member of Captain Stoddard's artillery company, from which several men were assigned to the expedition. He may have been John Robertson, or Robinson. See Clark's entries for this day, and Appendix A, vol. 2.

3. Not mentioned by any other journal keeper. A nameless triangular island appears on later maps in the right location on the Saline County, Missouri, side of the river. They camped in south-central Chariton County, Missouri.

Wendy 13th Got On Our way at the three point Island Or the falling <Do> Banks whare all hands Breakfasted belonging to the three Crafts— On the Oppisite Shore S. W. Side neer two or about 2 Oclock the Barge Struck a Sandbar She Keeld On her labord the Sand being Quick Vanquishd Suddently from <her> Under her the Currant Being Rappid Neerly Swept the men of their legs while Bearing her up from Sinquing. Got to the Grand River[1] at three Oclock our hunters met us there with a bear and Some Venison Incampd. there Roed 14 Miles this venison is [nice?][2]

Wednesday June 13th This Morning we set out early from the three point Island, we proceeded on till about 2 oClock P. M. on the South west side of the River, our Boat struck on a sand barr; she grounded on her larbourd side, the place being a quicksand and the current running strong. The sand vanquish'd quick from under her, & so suddenly; that the Men on the deck were nearly swept off their legs, whilst they were bearing the boat up from sinking, At 3 o'Clock P. M. we arrived at the Mouth of the grand River, where we was met by the hunters we had sent out; who brought with them a Bear and some Venison which they had killed. The Mesouri River

running from the North[3] West.   We encamp'd at this place, having rowed
14 Miles this day.—

Grand River lays in Latitude 38° 47' 54 North—

1. Grand River forms the boundary between Carroll and Chariton counties, Missouri.
2. This last sentence appears to be in the hand of No. 3.
3. "North" is written over "South."

Thursday 14   Got under way at the Grand River   Roed 3 miles and Got
in to a Byoe at the End of Sd Byoe Came to the main River—[1]   the River
Rose   the wrack Run Rappidly   we had to S[t]rike Streat Across the River
and the boat with the Other Crafts took the Sand bar   with much dificuelty
Got them of.   Got on through many Deficeultys.   Roe 6 Miles.   Incampd.
Neer the Willow praraie[2]

Thursday June 14th   We embark'd this morning from Grand River, and
proceeded on 3 Miles, and got into a Byo, the end of which Byo, entered
into the main River.   This day the River rose, and the wrack run rapidly.
we were forced to cross the River, in doing of which, the Boat, and the craft
that we had with us, struck on a Sand barr, we had much difficulty in getting
them off.   This day we met with many difficulties, owing to the raising of the
River and the fataigue we underwent was exessive.   We encamped near the
willow Priari, having Rowed only 6 Miles.—

1. Two blank pages follow but with no apparent break in the writing.
2. One of many instances in which Whitehouse applies a place-name used by no other
journal keeper. The camp was in Carroll County, Missouri, nearly opposite present Miami.

Friday 15   Got on Our way at the willow prarie   the wind S. E fresh   We
Crouded Sail and Saild 16 miles   Campd at the Indian Settlement namd.
little Zoe prarie[1]   the hunters met us with four bears And three deer   the
party drank a Drachm of whisky and Roe on—

Friday June 15th   This morning we left Willow point (or Willow Priari,[)]
with a fair Wind from the South east, and in the evening encamped at an

Old deserted Indian settlement (formerly belonging to the Caw Nation[)],[2] called the little Zoe Priari, where we were met by our hunters, who had kill'd four Bears and Three Deer, The Captains order'd a dram of whiskey, to be served to each man.   We had during this day, crouded all Sail and the distance we run being 16 Miles.—

1. The Gumbo Point site, an old Missouri village, in Saline County, Missouri.
2. Referring to the Kaw, or Kansa, Indians, but the site is generally considered a Missouri village.

Saturdy 16th   Got on our way at the little town Zoe peraraie   this perara is Extencive   from the Banks of the River Runs a Vast number of miles from the River back   the Wind Rose   we Saild 10 Miles   Got in Strong water In the Evening   towed the boat by cutting the timber off the Banks   Got On Successfully   Campd. at the Riffel Island[1] whare the water Rolld. Over in Quick Sand

Saturday June 16th   We left the little Indian town called the Zoe, early this morning; this Town is situated on a Priari of the same Name, This Priari is very large it running from the banks of the River many miles, back, The wind rose from the South East; and we set all our Sails, we found the current running very Strong   towards the evening, the wind lull'd & died away.   we then Towed the boat, and had much difficulty, being forced to cut the Timber down on the banks of the River to pass along it.—

We proceeded on towing our Boat 'till the evening with success, when we encamp'd at an Iland called the Riffel Island, were we saw the water rolling over the Quick sands in the River very violently   We sail'd & towed 10 Miles this day,

1. The other journalists say they camped on the north side of the river, in Carroll County, Missouri, and no one mentions Riffel Island. Whitehouse may be referring to the later Thomas Island.

Sunday 17th   Got on Our [way]   Roed One Mile And Incampd. and Made 20 Oars & 600 feet of Roap at the Roap Walk Camp—[1]

Sunday June 17th   This morning we embark'd early and proceeded on rowing for one Miles.   we then encamped; the remainder of the day all hands were employed in making Oars, and Ropes, the latter were made out of bear Skins, we made this day 20 Oars & 600 feet of Rope, the place we called Rope walk Camp.

1. Only Whitehouse gives the camp a name; it was in Carroll County, Missouri, about a mile above the previous camp.

Monday 18th   In the fore noon thunder and Litning Came On after a Rapid Rain   Got fair and finish Roaps & And Oars—   the hunters Killd. four deer and Colter one large Bare On the west Side of the River—

Monday June 18th   We remain'd here this day, in the forenoon of which we had severe thunder & lightning after which succeeded a Violent rain, in the afternoon it cleared up, and all hands were employed in finishing the Oars & Ropes.   toward evening our hunters came to us having killed four deer and one large Bear, on the South[1] side of the River.—

1. "South" is written over an erasure, perhaps "North."

Tusday 19   Got on Our way at the Roap walk Camp perarie   the day was Clear   a Sharp wind Arose   Saild. 12 Miles   Campd. at neer the River Taboe,[1] it Running N. E. the Breadth of it at the Mouth is 50 Yds. at the Mouth

Tuesday June 19   This morning we started early, from the Rope walk camp Priari, the weather being fine & clear, about 9 oClock A. M. a good Brees sprung up from the South East, We set sail, and in the evening encamped near the River Taboe, This River runs North East to its head the breadth of it at its Mouth is 50 Yards, The distance we rowed and Sailed this day being 12 Miles.—

1. Clark indicates that they camped a few miles past Tabo Creek, still in Lafayette County, Missouri.

Wendy 20th   Rain came on as we was a goeing to start in the morning Shortly after Got fair   the hunters[1] Came to the bank of the River.   the[y] Killd. a bear brought the Skin   left the Meat as it was poor   the Currant was Strong   towd Our boat Untill we Came to the head of the Strong watter Island whare the watter run So Rappid that the men of the french Peirouge Could not make headway by Roeing Or poleing   the[y] had to jumpd. out and push her through the water   Incampd On the point of and Islanand Calld. Strong water point[2]   Roed. 12 Miles

Wednesday June 20th   This morning as we were preparing to start a Rain came on which detained us, for some time, in about an hour the weather got clear, and our hunters who had crossed the River, early this morning came to the opposite bank of the River having killed a bear, but it proving very poor they brought only the Skin with them, the Meat being unfit for use, we started having our boat to tow, the current of the River being so strong that we found it impossible either to Row or pole her.   We proceeded on 'till we came to the head of strong Water Island, where the River ran so strong, that the Canadians who were in a Pettiauger could make no headway either by Rowing or poling, but were forced to jump into the River and push her through the water, We encamped on the point of an Island called strong Water point.   We towed our boat 12 Miles this day.

1. Apparently John Shields and John Collins, but Clark says only that they had not joined the party for two nights and were spotted on shore. Nobody else mentions these hunters on this date.

2. Apparently on Wolf Island, below Wellington, Lafayette County, Missouri.

Thursday 21st   Got on our way at the Strong water Point   the water was Strong   likeways had to towe the Cheif part of the day to the 3 Islands Calld. the 3 mills[1] whare the water Runs Rapidly   Campd. at the head of them Roed 12 Miles   the hunters Came in with One deer & One turky and a bear Skin

Thursday June 21st   We got under way from strong water point, being obliged to tow the boat, the Current setting so strong against us, we continued towing the greatest part of the day 'till we arrived at three Islands, called the three Mills where the water still run rapidly.— We encamped at the head of the three Islands, shortly after our hunters came to us, having One deer, One Turky,[2] and the Skins of the bear that they kill'd the day before. The distance we came this day being 12 Miles.—

1. No other journal keeper mentions the three islands, although Charles Floyd notes a single island where the current was very strong. They may be the islands at the point of Camden Bend, Ray County, Missouri (see Clark's entries).

2. Wild turkey, *Meleagris gallopavo.*

Friday 22nd   the Rain came on Rapidly in the <night> morning   Interupd our Starting at the usal hour.   the day Cleard Up at 7 Oclock   the two latter days was the hotist that has been Seen Or felt a long time.   the water was Strong with the heat of the day which made the times disagreeble to the party.   G. Drewyer Killd a large Male Bare weighd Neer 5 hundred Wt. Our hunters Came in which had been Absent from the 19th Inst. the[y] had part of One deer girkd with them   their names is J. Sheilds & Collins   Incampd[1] at the fire perarie   Roed 12 Miles—

Friday June 22nd   This morning we were detained from starting by a heavy Rain which continued till 7 oClock A. M   The weather proved excessive hot, as it was the two succeeding days, & being by far the warmest weather that we met with for a long time.

The current running very strong against us, and having to tow the boat it can hardly be imagined the fataigue that we underwent, We came too and Encamped at a place called the fire Priari, shortly after our hunters came to us, George Drewyer one of our hunters who had been absent from the 19th instant joined us having a large he bear with him which he had killed which weigh'd near five hundred weight, and part of a deer the flesh of which he had jerked.— We Towed 12 Miles this day.—

1. See Clark's entry for this date for a discussion of the difficulties of locating this camp.

Saterdy 23rd   Got on Our way at the fire prarie at day light   passd the River Calld painter Creek[1]   the wind Arose and blew a head of us renderd our days Work mighty hard for the hands of Each Craft   Saild. Only 3 miles Incampd[2] at the head of a Island namd. painter Island   the hunters Came In with two deer & One fish the[y] shot   Captn. Clark Could not Get aboard the wind blew So Strong   G. Drewyr went Out and Kill 2 deers and one Bare befor Night which made four deer and One bare Kill in all that day

Saturday June 23rd   We embarked from the Fire Priari at day light, and passed a Creek called painters Creek, the wind arose and blew ahead of us, which render'd our towing the boat extreme difficult & fataigueing; we proceeded on only three Miles, and encamped at the head of an Island called Painters Island, the hunters came in to us, having two deer and one fish they had shot.   It blew so hard that Captain Clark who was on shore could not come off to us.— George Drewyer, one of the hunters went out again, and killed two deer and one Bear; which he brought to us.

1. "Painter" here means "panther," the mountain lion, but Clark refers to passing Tiger River, today's Crooked River, Ray County, Missouri, and the "Isle of Panthers" (Whitehouse's "painter Island") on June 19.

2. In the vicinity of Sibley, Jackson County, Missouri.

Sunday 24   Got on Our way at [*blank*] and Crossd. the River to the west Shore   at 12 oclock we Stopd to Girk our meat on account of the weather being [so?] warm, passd the River Calld the Straw Hill,[1] On the west Side <the Lan> Runing N. E. by E   high land On Each Side of the River, N[o] Indians has Apeard On our Rout Yet   the hunters Killd 8 deer one of which from a board the white peerouge on her way   Roed 13 Miles   Incampd at hard Scrable perara[2]

Sunday June 24th   We embarked early this morning and crossed the River to the So West shore, at 12 oClock A. M. we stopped to Jerk our meat, the weather being so warm that we were afraid it would spoil, at 3 o'Clock P. M. we got under way, and passed a River called the Straw Hill river, lying on the So West side of the Mesouri.   This River runs North East by East The land on both sides of this River lying very high.—

We met with no Indians as yet on our rout, excepting those in the Canoe near Charette   our hunters returned to us in the evening with 8 deer they had kill'd this day.   We encamped at a Priari called hard scrabble Priari, we having Rowed 13 Miles this day.—

1. Another version of Hay, or Hay Cabin, Creek, now Little Blue River, Jackson County, Missouri.

2. The camp was in Jackson County, above Missouri City; only Whitehouse gives this name for the location. "Hardscrabble" means a hard struggle, or scramble, for existence; it was used to describe poor farm land, as a "hardscrabble farm," but Floyd describes the area as "Good first Rate Land."

Monday 25   Got on our way at hard Scrable Perarie   passd two Creeks the One Calld. la beane[1] and the other Rowling Creek—[2]   S. W. S[ide]   a litle above the latter two wolves appeard On Shore   A man from on board of the white Peiroug went ashore Shot One of them   On the E side is high land and well timberd   the hills puts in neer the River—   Roed 14 Miles— Incampd on a small Island   the hunters—[3]

Monday June 25th   This morning early we left hard scrabble priari, and passed two creeks in about one Mile distance from where we started; the first called Labeane and the other rowling Creek laying on the So. side their courses being to their heads South west by South, a small distance above the latter creek, we saw two Wolves, on the shore; one of our Men went a shore from on board the pettiauger, and shot one of them.   The land on the North side of the River lays high & is well Timber'd.   Several hills running near the River, the current still running strong.   in the Evening we came too, and encamped on a small Island called hunters Island, the distance we rowed this day being 14 Miles.—

1. Evidently Sugar Creek, Jackson County, Missouri, and perhaps named for François M. Benoit (see Clark's entry for this day).

2. Not mentioned by the other journal keepers. Perhaps it is a much distorted version of Coal Creek, or of the French name which Clark gives as "Chabonea," and which Nicholas Biddle gives as "Charbon" in his edition of the journals. That stream is perhaps present Sleepy Branch, Jackson County, Missouri. However, "Rolling Creek" may be meant.

3. Given as "Hunters Island" in the fair copy, another place-name used only by Whitehouse. The island was evidently opposite Sugar Creek, Jackson County.

Tusday 26th the morning was Clear the water was Strong at the head of the Island we Campd on Got to the E. Shore, and towed Our boat by Cutting <our> the timber of the Banks the day Got mighty hot Saw 3 deer Swiming Down the River the white peerogue took after them Killd. the three One of whom Sunk as Soon it Got Shot in the head Got the Other two Brought them Up to the Barge— G Druery Killd 8 deer that day <Roed> took them on board 2 miles before we Reachd the River de-Caugh[1] at Sun Set Roed 10 Miles—

Tuesday June 26th This morning being fine weather we embark'd early, and found the water running very strong at the head of the Island that we encamped on, we crossed the River to the North side, where we were oblig'd to Tow our boat the water running so strong against us, this was attended with a great deal of labour, being forced to cut the Timber off the bank in order to pass along it with the Tow rope, The day proving extreamly warm which still added to our fataigue; we saw three deer swimming down the River; The Men in the Pettyauger went after them, they killed them all; but one that was shot through the head, sunk, they then returned with the other two,

We proceeded on our Voyage about 2 Miles when George Drewer one of our hunters came to the River having killed 8 deer & brought them with him, we then took him on board, and proceeded on and encamped at the River decaugh at sunset, having towed the Boat 10 Miles.—

1. Perhaps meaning Kaw, for the Kansas River; the camp was in present Kansas City, Wyandotte County, Kansas.

Wendy 27th halted at the above mentiond River <in the> Nixt morning <Halt> Cleard. off the point and formd a temperery brest work or piqct— Least the Savages would Attempt Comeing in the Night the Sd. River de Caugh as the[y] take the tittle from it I was Informd by One of Our Men that traded Up the River that 300 <hund> Warriers lives in One Village Up the River About 50 leagues—[1] Latd. 38D 31M 13S N this River lies in the head of it lies S. W— Halted—

Wednesday June 27th   We halted this day at the above mention'd place and in the morning all hands were employed in clearing the point of said River from Trees.   we then form'd a temporary breast work with pickets, in order to defend ourselves against the Indians, fearing that they might make an attack on us in the Night.   The Captains were inform'd by one of the Canadians who were with us, and who had traded up that River, that 300 Warriors lives at a Village up the said River, about 50 Leagues; The head of this River lies Southwest, this information we received from the same person, The Captains took an Observation and found the Mouth of said River to lye in Latitude 38° 31′ 13 North.—

1. This sentence is intended to explain that the Kaw, or Kansa, Indians took their name from the river, although the reverse is probably the case.

Thursday 28   halted at the river de Caugh   Meassurd the Breadth of it is 230¼ Yds.   a little farder is four hundred Do.—   the hunters[1] Kill five deer one woolf[2] and Catchd an other about five Months old   Kept it for three days Cut it's rope   Got away.

Thursday June 28th   We continued at the River Decaugh, and were employ'd measuring the width of this River   it measur'd at the mouth 230¼ Yards, and a small distance up it 400 Yards, The hunters returned with five deer and one wolf they had killed, and a Young wolf which they catch'd; we kept this for three days when it cut the Rope which tied it, & made its escape.

1. Including Reubin and Joseph Field.
2. Gray wolf, *Canis lupus.*

Friday 29   Rested Untill 4 Oclock P. M   Started On Our journey   Roed. five 5 miles   Campd. at woolf Creek—[1]

Friday June 29th   We continued still at the River Decaugh untill 4 o'Clock P. M. and then started on our Voyage   we rowed 5 Miles and encamped at a Creek call'd Wolf Creek.—

1. Another place-name given only by Whitehouse; possibly Line Creek, Platte County, Missouri.

Saterday 30   Got on our way at day light   the water Was Strong the land high on Each Side   the deer was plentifull on the Sand beech as we passd along   all sorts of fowls   likeway the woolves and Bears Every day   Roed 12 Miles—

June 30th Saturday   This morning at day light we embark'd and proceeded on our Voyage, found the current setting strong against us, The land on both sides of the River lies high, We perceived the Deer in abundance on the Land beaches, as we passed along, likewise Bears & Wolves, <with> and abundance of Wild fowl.   we encamped[1] on the Bank of the River, having rowed 12 Miles this day—

1. In the vicinity of the village of Wolcott, Wyandotte County, Kansas.

July 1st Sunday   the water was Strong all day   passd a Number of Islands to the labourd   Roed 12¼ Miles   the hunters did not Come up to Us that day—

Sunday July 1st   We embarked early this morning, the current set strong against us this day; passed a number of Islands lying on the South side of the River, our Hunters did not come up to us this day.   We encamp'd on an Island call'd Green Island,[1] distance that we rowed this day being 12¼ Miles.—

1. Only Whitehouse gives this name for what was probably later Leavenworth Island, opposite Leavenworth, Leavenworth County, Kansas.

Monday 2nd   Got on Our way at Green Island at 4 Oclock P. M., the water was Strong   passd a prarie on the west S. at Sd place Crossing the [river] at Sd. place the Boat Swong the [*page torn*]   Exerted them selves mighty well [*page torn*]   off halted and got a mast [*page torn*]   the Barge   Roed. 10½ Miles [*page torn*]   the head of Ordaways[1] [*page torn*]

Monday July 2nd   This morning we left Green Island, at 4 oClock A. M.[2] Found the water to run very strong against us   we passed a Priari lying on the So West side of the River, we crossed the River at this Priari, and in so doing the boat swung and got aground, but by the exertion of the Men she got off.   we halted and got a Mast for our boat & We encamped in the Evening at the head of Ordaways Island, having rowed this day 10½ Miles.

1. Ordway's Island, as the fair copy makes clear, but no one else, including Ordway, uses the name. Evidently this is Clark's "Wau-car-ba war-con-da" Island, probably later Kickapoo Island, north of Fort Leavenworth, Leavenworth County, Kansas. The camp was near Weston, Platte County, Missouri.

2. There is an erasure on the "A," but it is clearly that letter.

Tusday 3rd[1]   Got on our way [*page torn*]   Island oposite the [*page torn*] Wind Rose   Saild. [*page torn*]   Lat 38° 31 13 N.

Tuesday July 3rd   We started from Ordaways Island, opposite to a place called the French Garrison.[2]   The wind being in our favour, and blowing a good Breeze, The hunters this day killed 3 deer.   We encamp'd[3] in the Evening, having Sailed 14 Miles this day.—   Latitude of Ordaways Island being 38° 31′ 13 North

1. Following this entry on a badly torn page is a blank page, but there is no apparent break in the writing.

2. Undoubtedly the "old trading place" mentioned by Ordway and Gass.

3. In Atchison County, Kansas, somewhat above Oak Mills.

Wendy 4   Got on our way at Green point at the Usal hour   the wind being favourable and the water being Good Roed on Successfully   the day mighty hot when we went to toe   the Sand [s]Calded Our [feet]   Some fled from the Rope   had to put on Our Mockisons.   within the River Calld Independance[1] found a Gray horse on the W. Side <Roed our>   Roed 16 Miles   Incampd on a Perarie namd Old town deCaugh—[2]

Wednesday July 4th   This morning we started Early from green point or Ordways Island[3] having a fair wind, and the water being good, we rowed on successfully.   this day proved very warm.   we left off rowing and went to Towing the boat, but the sand was so hot, that it scalded <out> our feet, some of the Men left the tow rope, and had to put on their Mockasins to keep their feet from being burnt, we passed a River which we called Indep128 pendance, where we found a Gray horse on the So. West side of said River. we came as far as a Priari, call'd Old town de Caugh, where we encamped, the distance being 16 Miles—

1. Independence Creek on the Atchison–Doniphan county line, Kansas. See Clark's entry for this day for a discussion of the confusion between this creek and the one the party called Fourth of July Creek.

2. Clearly the Kansa village noted by Clark and Gass, although only Whitehouse uses this name. The site is at Doniphan, Doniphan County, Kansas (see Clark's entry).

3. A clear error by the copyist, since they left what Whitehouse calls Ordway's Island on July 3.

Thursdy 5   Got on our way   Roed. a mile Up the prarie   Crossd the River with the white horse and left him with the others that the hunters had on the E. Shore   Roed. 10 Miles   Incampd at the Rock Prarie—[1]

Thursday July 5th   We started early this morning, and rowed one Mile on our way; and took in the white horse and crossed the River with him, and landed him with the other horses on the No. East shore where the hunters had left them, and Encamp'd in the evening at the Rock Priari, distance come this day being 10 Miles

1. Yet another place-name given only by Whitehouse. The place is in Doniphan County, Kansas, some miles northeast of Doniphan.

Fridy 6   Got on Our way at the Usal hour at the Rock Prarie   the water was tolarably Good.   the land a little distance from the River Hilly prarie. had Good Sailing   Roed 15 Miles   Campd. at a prarie Calld. the bald hills—[1]

Friday July 6th   This morning we started at the usual hour, from the Rock priari, the water was tolerable good, The land a little distance from the River was hilly Priaries.   We encamp'd at a Priari called the Bald hills.   We had good sailing this day the distance being 15 Miles—

1. Once again Whitehouse uses a place-name given by no one else. Here there may be some confusion with the "Bald-pated Prairie" on the Missouri–Iowa state line, which the party reached on July 16. The camp was perhaps at Peter's Creek, Doniphan County, Kansas, near St. Joseph, Buchanan County, Missouri, on the opposite side.

Saterdy 7   Got under way about Sun Rise   Six Miles from whare we Started Came to the most beautifull prarie On the E. S. Whare Nature formd Some battryes And Read Outs[1]   the hills putts in Neer the River   A Quarter of mile <from the River> to the N. E of Sd. prarie a rock on the Bank of the River about 320 feet from the Surface of the watter high to the top thereoff. after passing Sd. place towards the Evening a man Espyd. a wolf lying a Sleep with the Noise of the Oars Roeing he awoke Stood to know what was a comeing   Captn. Lewis shot at him Wounded the Animal, Colter likeways, Killd him   it was thought he was mad when the first <Ball> Bawl Struck him he Snapd. at his hind part   Roed. 15 Miles.   Incampd.—[2]

Saturday July 7th   We left the Priari at sun rise, and proceeded on Six Miles, when we passed a most beautiful Priari, lying on the No. East side of the River, where Nature had formed some batterys and Redoubts, by Hills, which put in near to the River.—

On the bank of the River, about one quarter of a Mile North east of the Priari is a rock <which lies on the bank of the River,> and is 320 feet high from the surface of the Water to the top of it, we left this rock and towards evening, one of our men espied a Wolf laying a sleep on the shore, as we approached towards him, the noise of our Oars awoke him, he stood there to see what was coming, when Captain Lewis shot at him, and struck him with a Ball, the Wolf then acted as if mad snapping continually at his hind parts.   The Captain order'd one Colter to fire at him, which he did, and killed him.—   In the Evening we encamped on the bank of the River, having rowed 15 Miles this day.—

1. "Redoubts," as in the fair copy.
2. A little upstream from St. Joseph, Buchanan County, Missouri.

Sunday 8th   the wind rose before we started and blew fair with us   Saild. Chiefly for the space of Eight hours   we Came to Small River Calld little

Nan doughe,— In Indian tounge, Inglish little woody River,[1] it lieing in latude 39D 39M 22S ⁷⁄₁₀₀ an Island to the S. S On Our W. S. a bear apeared but Could not be Shot Made his alopement we Got to the River Nandouie Roed. 15 Miles Incamd. at the head of a large Island—

Sunday July 8th This morning we embark'd early with a fair wind, and sail'd for 8 hours, when we came to a small River called Little Nan doughe, in the Indian language, which is in english little wood River, it lying by observation taken by Captains Lewis & Clark in Latitude 39° 39′ 22 ⁷⁄₁₀₀ North. there is an Island lying on the South side of the River, & on the So. West side, a bear was seen & being pursued by one of our hands, it made its escape, we proceeded on, and arrived at the River Nandoucee, and encamped at the head of a large Island, the distance we came this day being 15 Miles.—

1. Only Whitehouse gives this explanation of the name of the Nodaway River, the boundary between Holt and Andrew counties, Missouri; see note at Clark's entry for an alternative interpretation.

Monday 9 Sat out the Usal hour of Day light Rain Came on Raind the Most part of the day the hunters did not Come in We Rod 12 Miles at piettet River de louce or woolf River—[1] Incampd. it lies on the W. S. the Mouth is about 20 yds. B. the hunters Came <in> did not Come in

Monday July 9th We set off early this morning, shortly after we had started a Rain came on, which continued most part of the day.—
We proceed on our Voyage and arrived at a River called Petit River De louce, or Little Wolf River, the mouth of which is 20 Yards wide. This River lies on the So West side of the River Mesouri, our hunters that were out, did not come to us this day, The distance we rowed this day being 12 Miles.

1. Wolf Creek, Doniphan County, Kansas.

Tusday 10 Got On Our way at woolf River at Sun Rise the water was Strong the Morning was Clear. On the E. S. of the River whare Stopd to take breakfast the willd. Rice[1] was pleanty Groeing on the bank of the

River, Straberyes,[2] Rosies,[3] Red And white   Roed 11 Miles   Campd.[4] at [*blank*]   the hunters Came in   brought 2 deer with them—

Tuesday July 10th   This morning at Sunrise we got under way from Little Wolf River, we found the current still setting strong against us, & very hard rowing to stem it, we encamped for a while to refresh ourselves at 8 oClock A. M.; we found here wild Rice, strawberry's and Red & white Roses <and Strawberry's> growing along the bank of the River, at 10 oClock A. M. we proceeded on, and in the evening encamped on the bank of the River where our hunters came in to us, having 2 Deer with them which they had killed. We rowed this day 11 Miles.—

    1. No one else mentions wild rice, but Clark and Ordway note wild rye, probably Canada wildrye, *Elymus canadensis* L.

    2. Wild strawberry, *Fragaria virginiana* var. *illinoensis* (Prince) Gray.

    3. An unknown rose, *Rosa* sp.

    4. In Holt County, Missouri, near the Nebraska–Kansas boundary on the opposite shore.

Wedndy. 11   Got Under way at an Early hour   It appeard. like rain but cleard up   passd Some Islands to the E. of us   Got to Grande, mo, haugh[1] at Eleven Oclock   Halted that day and Next—   Roed 4½ Miles—

Wednesday July 11th   We embarked early this morning having cloudy weather & appearance of Rain, at 10 oClock A. M. the Clouds dispers'd and the weather became clear, we passed by some Islands which lay to the No East of us, and got to the Grand na Mahaws River about 11 oClock A. M. which is a noted place, & halted there this day distance come being 4½ Miles. The Grand na Mahaw River lies on the South side & is 35 Yds. wide at its mouth

    1. Big Nemaha River, Richardson County, Nebraska, just above the Nebraska–Kansas line.

Thursday. 12th   Rested at the above mentiond place   found a pybold horse on the E. S.   the hunters Came in brought 4 deer with them— Captn Lewis took the altude as follows Latd 39D 55MN.

Thursday July 12th   We remained here this day, on the No. East side of the River, we found a horse of pybald colour, our hunters came to us, having brought with them 4 deer which they had kill'd.   Captain Lewis took an observation; (having a clear Horizon,) & found this place to lie in Latitude 39° 55′ 56 North.—

Friday 13   Got under way Early and Swim the horses across a Creek Tar Kia,[1] for the hunters   the wind Rose   pass Several Islands Is On Our labourd.   Saild [21?] Miles.   Campd.[2] On the little Sandy Isle Oppesite the Hurrican prarie—[3]

Friday July 13th   This morning we set out early, and swam the horses across a Creek called Tar Kia, for the hunters.   The wind rose, and we passed several Islands on our South side, We sail'd 2½[4] Miles & encamped on an Island called little sandy Island, opposite the hurricane Priari.—

1. Tarkio, or Big Tarkio, River, reaching the Missouri in Holt County, Missouri.
2. Probably in eastern Richardson County, Nebraska.
3. Once again Whitehouse uses a name given by no one else; the reference may be to the violent wind of the next day, which Floyd calls "a Dredfulle hard Storme."
4. An error for 20½.

Saty 14   the Rain Came on before we left Camp with a Smart wind that Inragd the watter to Such a degree that all hands had to Get in the Watter to keep up the boat—   Roed on after the Storm was over 10 Miles

Saturday July 14th   This morning before we embarked a heavy Rain came on, with a hard wind; which occasioned the River to run in high Waves, & to so great a degree, that all hands had to get into the Water to keep up the boat.   The Storm abated about 10 oClock A. M. and we preceeded & encamp'd[1] on the River bank distance come this day being 10 Miles

1. Near the Nemaha–Richardson county line, Nebraska.

Sundy 15   the Morning was foggy   had to wait Untill it went off   Passd. the River namd. Nishnay Baton[1] at 3 Oclock passd. the little Mohaugh[2] Got to Camp[3] on the Mohaugh prarie.   Roed. 11 Miles

Sunday July 15th   The morning being foggy, we had to waite 'till it cleared away, at 9 o'Clock A. M. we set off, and passed a River called Nishna Balon, at 3 oClock P. M. passed the little Mahaw River; and encamped at the Mahaw Priari, having rowed 11 Miles this day—   The little Mahaw River lies on the South side of the Mesouri.—

1. The Nishnabotna River, which everyone else says they passed the previous day.
2. Little Nemaha River, Nemaha County, Nebraska.
3. In Nemaha County, somewhat above present Nemaha.

Monday 16   The morning was Clear   The water Strong   the wind rose had Good Sailing   passd. a number of Islands to the labourd.   Seen Some Elk[1] on the E. Shore as we passd. the prarie   Roed. 20 Miles   Campd. on the Mohaugh prarie[2]

Monday July 16   This morning we started early, the weather being fine & Clear, and the wind in our favour we set all our Sails, we passed a number of Islands laying on the South side of the River, and saw a number of Elk on the No. East shore feeding on the Priari, in the Evening we encamp'd on the Mahaw Priari, having Sailed 20 Miles this day.—

1. Elk, or wapiti, *Cervis elaphus.*
2. In this instance it is Bald-pated Prairie, Fremont County, Iowa, near present Waubonsie State Park.

Tusdy[1] 17   Halted on the latter mention prarie Neer the Bald pated hills took an altitude of the meriedian Latd. 40 29 54 $\frac{5}{10}$ N   Go Druier[2] Brought in 3 deer in the Evening

Tuesday July 17th   This day being fine and clear, we staid at the Mahaw priari, at a place called the Bald pated hills, Captains Lewis & Clark both took Observations, and found it to lay in Latitude 40° 29" 54 North, one of our hunters (George Drewer) who had went out hunting this morning, returned in the Evening, having killed 3 deer which he brought in with him.—

1. Apparently written over the word Thursday.
2. Another variant of Drouillard's name.

Wendy 18   the Morning was Clear   Got under way at day light   the wind blew fair   Saild. 13 miles Before Dinner.   passd. an Iron oar Mine[1] on the Bank of the River on the W. S.—   wint 22 Miles—   the hunters brough 2 deer in with them

Wednesday July 18th   This morning being clear, we got under way at day light, with a fair wind, and sailed 13 Miles before Noon, we passed a Mine of Iron Ore, laying on the bank of the River on the So. West side.   The hunters brought us in this evening 2 Deer which they kill'd.   We encamped[2] on the bank of the River, having Sail'd this day 22 Miles—

1. No one else suggests that actual mining operations had been carried on here; the reference is to the iron ore deposits near present Nebraska City, Otoe County, Nebraska.
2. In Otoe County, a little south of Nebraska City.

Thursday 19th   Got on under way   the Morning was Clear   passd. 4 Islands to our Stabourd   as we came along Shore there was two large Cat fish had hold of Each other Could not get off   one of the french men Shot the two the first Shot.[1]   On the W. Shore at Butter run,[2] the men pulld a Great Quantity of wild Cherrys[3]   put them in the Barrel of whisky.   Roed. 12 Miles   Campd. on an Island neer the River Calld. the Crying Water—[4]

Thursday July 19th   We got under Way this morning, having clear weather, and passed 4 Islands on our way, laying on the No. East Side of the River, as we passed along the Shore we espy'd two of the largest siz'd catfish, which had hold of each other, One of the Canadian french Men, shot at and kill'd one of them on the So. Western side of the River & wounded the other, which we got also, we landed & found a great quantity of Wild cherries, we gather'd a Quantity of them, which we put into a barrell of Whiskey, we proceeded on at 3 oClock P. M. <we proceeded on> & encamped on an Island called the crying Island, & near a River call'd the crying Water, distance come this day 12 miles.—

1. Only Whitehouse mentions this incident; perhaps the fish were channel catfish, *Ictalurus punctatus.*

2. Yet another name mentioned only by Whitehouse; probably either North Table Creek or South Table Creek, both entering the Missouri at Nebraska City, Otoe County, Nebraska.

3. Probably choke cherry, *Prunus virginiana* L., as indicated by Gass.

4. Probably in Fremont County, Iowa, two or three miles above Nebraska City, and below Weeping Water Creek, Otoe County, Nebraska.

Friday 20th   Got on our way at an Early hour.   Came up to the creek Calld. Crying water   Breakfasted In the Mouth of the breanth there of is 20 Yds. at the mouth   On the W. S. Under bald hill.[1]   at one ocLock Came to a Large Open preaarie neare the River PLate   it hie Land and Rich, and Some groves of TimBer.   a freash Bres of wind   Come fare and we SaLed we Came to Iland cross under   an lest night the hunt kiLed 2 deare   Camp[2] nere the Read Blufe   Rowd 17 miLe—

Friday July 20th 1804   This morning early we embarked <at an early hour> & came up to a Creek called the crying Water, the breadth of this creek at its mouth is 20 Yards wide lying on the So. Side of the River.   At the So West side under a bald hill at One o'Clock came to a large open Priari, near the River Plate; the land lies high at this place, and is very rich; having some Groves of large timber, we continued rowing till towards Evening, and encamped on an Island.   The hunters came to us having killed 2 Deer. This day we rowed 17 Miles—

1. After this point begins the writing of No. 3, the most difficult of all to read. The writing runs to the middle of the next entry.

2. In Cass County, Nebraska, a little above Spring Creek

Santday 21   got on oer way at an [*blank*]   the wind Come fare   [we?] Come [4] miles and Eat oer Breakfast.   the wind Seased Bloing   a reamark hiLL tow hundrerd foot hie from the warter   Come to the River opLate[1] at one ocCLock   this River On the west Side of the Mesury   a fine preare [our clear?]   on the mouths of the PLate [in the?] [*illegible*] [are?] a very Strong

Streame   it Baks the Mussiry over [*illegible*] Land on the West Side and 1 2 ILand.[2]   The wedth of the Great River Platt at its mouth across the bars is about ¾ of a mile, but further up we are told by a Frenchman[3] who lived 2 <Seasons> years up this River that it does not rise 4 feet, but Spreads 3 miles in Some places.   we passed a creek called Pappeo R.[4]   praries are between the 2 Rivers.   we camped on the S. S.   G. Drewyer joined us with 4 Deer he Killed.

Saturday July 21st   We embarked from the Island   got underway, and the wind came fair, we sail'd 4 Miles and came too, and breakfasted; we embarked again at 8 oClock A. M, we proceeded on rowing the boat, the wind having (died away)   we came to a remarkable hill, laying on the Water side which measur'd 200 feet from the surface of the Water & we arrived at the River Plate at one o'Clock P. M.   The River Plate lies on the South side of the Mesouri River; it is a beautiful River, and joining it, on both sides is a fine priari.   the stream of this River runs strong at its mouth.   The width of this River at its mouth is about three Quarters of a Mile.   it has several Bars at that place.   This River in some places, not far distant from its mouth spreads 3 Miles <in some places> & the water is clear   We proceeded on, & passed a Creek called Pappes Creek lying on So side priaris lays between the River platt & this Creek.   We encamped on the South side.   one of our hunters brought in 4 Deer he had killed

1. The Platte River reaches the Missouri between Cass and Sarpy counties, Nebraska.
2. Here ends the writing of No. 3, marking the return to Whitehouse's hand.
3. François Labiche or Pierre Cruzatte, more likely the latter.
4. Papillion, or Big Papillion, Creek, Sarpy County, meeting the Missouri about a mile north of the mouth of the Platte.

Sunday July 22d 1804.   we Set out eairly to find Some good place for observations &c. for Incamping.   we passd. a creek on the N. S. called Musquetoe Creek.[1]   came 1 2 miles & camped.[2]   cut & cleaned a place for encamping pitched our tents built bowereys &c,—

Sunday July 22nd   This morning we embarked early <this morning> & proceeded on, in Order to find a place suitable to take an observation, we passed a creek, lying on the North side of the River, called Musketo Creek, we <encamped> landed, and cleared a place for encamping. we pitched our Tents & built a Bowrey.

The distance we came this day being 12 Miles

1. Still Mosquito Creek, Pottawattamie County, Iowa.
2. At the party's Camp White Catfish, near the Mills–Pottawattamie county line, Iowa.

Monday July 23rd 1804. a clear morning   G. Drevyer & St. Peter[1] Set out to go to the Zotoe & Paunie[2] village 45 miles to Invite them to come to our camp for Certian purposes &c— we hoisted the american Collours on the Bank   The Latidude at this place is 41D 3m 19S ¾ North.   one of the hunters killed 2 Deer to day—

Monday July 23rd   We remaind here this day in Order to get an Observation, the weather being fine & clear   The commanding officers sent George Drewer & a frenchman named St. Peter to the Zotoe & pawne Villages, distance 45 Miles, in order to invite the Indians inhabiting those Villages, to come to our Camp, in order to hold a Council with them.   We hoisted the American Colours on the bank of the River, and Captain Lewis and Clark took an observation, and found this place to lay in Latitude 41° 3′ 19s North, we named this place White catfish Camp, one of our hunters killed 2 Deer this day which he brought into our Camp.—

1. Apparently Cruzatte, with terminology used also by Ordway.
2. Whitehouse's spelling of Oto and Pawnee.

Tuesday July 24th 1804.   Some rain this morning   4 men went to makeing ores for the Batteaux.—

Tuesday July 24th   We remained here this day, and had some Rain in the morning; 4 of our Men were sent out to make Oars for the Boat.   we employ'd ourselves in overhawling sundry Articles which we had in the Boat.—

Wednesday July 25th 1804.   a pleasant morning.   Som men out hunting. G. Drewyer & St. peter Returned found no Indians, they were in the praries hunting the Buffelow.—   Collins killed 2 Deer   Jo. F. 1 Turkey.

Wednesday July 25th   We still remain'd at same place, waiting the arrival of George Drewyer & St. Peter from the Zoto & Pawne Villages, about 3 oClock P. M. they return'd, having been at those Villages but had found no Indians.   they having all gone into the Priaries in order to hunt the Buffaloe.—

Our hunters returned in the evening, having killed 2 deer & one Turkey.—

Thursday July 26th 1804.   pleasant morning   Some men out hunting. G. Drewyer killed 2 Deer & 1 Turkey,—   the later part of the day the [wind] hard from the South   a Great many Beaver[1] caught at this place by the party.—

Thursday July 26th   This morning, we had pleasant weather, one of our hunters went out hunting, & returned; having kill'd & brought in with him 2 Deer & one Turkey, the latter part of the day, the Wind blew hard from the South, our people went out to hunt beaver, and caught near this place a large number of them.—

1. The American beaver, *Castor canadensis.*

Friday July 27th 1804.   cloudy morning   the Boat made ready to Start. we Set out about 1 oClock   proceeded along.   high wood land on S. S. G Shannon killed one Deer to day.   we passed a prarie on The S. S.   we passd. many sand bars, the River very crooked; came about 15 miles & Camped on a bank of a high prarie,[1] among a Grove of Cotten wood.[2]   the 2 men who were with the horses did not join us to night.

Friday July 27th   The morning being Cloudy, we were employed getting the boat ready to start; we set out about 10 o'Clock A. M. and proceeded on, the land on the South side of the River, being covr'd with Forests, and appear'd very rich,—   We passed a Priari, laying on the South side of the River where we saw number of Deer & bear.   The River is very Crooked in this days route, we encamped on a Creek, near which is a high Priari, & along the bank of the River found a Grove of cottonwood Trees, the Two Men that

45

had the horses for bringing in Game, did not return to us, One of our Hunters came in & brought a deer he had killed with him.—

1. Within the limits of Omaha, Douglas County, Nebraska, in the vicinity of the Douglas Street Bridge (Interstate 480).

2. Cottonwood, *Populus deltoides* Marsh.

Saturday July 28th 1804. cloudy morning. we Set out eairly proced on past a high Bottom prarie on N. S. Some Timber on the Ridge back of those praries above the Bottom prarie the hills make in close to the River verry high & Steep. we passd. the mouth of a Small Creek on N. S. named Round Knob Creek.[1] the wind Blew hard from N. E. G. Drewyer joined us at 11 oC with one Deer.[2] we Came to a hi CLift or Buut one hun[dred] feet[3] the Barge Struck a Sand Bare on the Side of the River on the Star Bord S. inCampe on the north Side of the [river] at the foot of a iLand CaLd the BLuf iLand[4] we Rowed 10 Miles that day. the hunterers Comin and Brought one indian with [them &c?][5]

Saturday July 28th The morning still continued Cloudy, we set out early, and passed a high bottom Priari on the North side; having on the back side of them high ridges with Trees growing on them. above the bottom Priari the hills make in close to the River; and are very high and steep, we passed the Mouth of a Creek, laying on the North side of the River, which is called knob Creek, the wind blowing hard from the North East.— One of our hunters came to us having One deer which he had killed, with him.—

This hunter came to us opposite a remarkable high hill laying on the North side of the River, we took the meat on board, and proceeded on one Mile, when the boat struck a sand barr, on her larbourd Side, and all hands were obliged to jump out in the Water to prevent her from sinking, (the place the boat Grounded on being quick sand) with much difficulty we got her off, we then proceeded one Mile, & encamp'd at the point of an Island, laying on the South side of the River.— One of our hunters came in and brought an Indian with him of the Zoto Nation distance come this day 10 Miles.—

1. Ordway also uses this name, Clark calls it Indian Knob Creek, and Floyd has it as Beaver Creek; it is probably Pigeon Creek, Pottawattamie County, Iowa.

2. After this begins the writing of No. 3.

3. The bluff at Council Bluffs, Pottawattamie County, Iowa, which Clark noted as the first high ground on that side of the river above Nodaway River.

4. This name is not given by any other party member, but obviously derives from the bluffs on the Douglas County, Nebraska, side of the river, near the campsite, if not that in Pottawattamie County, Iowa.

5. In the fair copy Whitehouse says he was a "Zoto" (Oto), but Clark calls him a Missouri Indian.

Sunday 29   the Morning was Rany   the indian and LiBerty¹ went to the nation to Bring the rest of them to a treaty   the hunter Come to us at 12 CLock with Some EaLk meat and one deare   the Camp² was near the Same Praerie Land   Some groves of timBer weL wartered   I Cut my [*illegible*] on the 27   had to Lay By my ower   the Cout was one inch and half Long WiLard Left his tommehake weare we Camped on the night of the 28 Instan [*illegible words*]   we Came to the Grean Prarie   it [is] very hansom   the hils Com in near the river   th[ere] Come in smale Creak on the West Sd of the river   Cald it Potts Creak about 20 yds at the Mouth.³   Roed 11½   Campd.⁴ on the E. S.—   Joseph fields Shot a Brareowe⁵   he is the form of a dog. his colour is Gray his talents on the four feet is 1½ Inch long his picture never was Seen by any of the party before.

Sunday July 29th   This morning was rainey, we started at sunrise.   Captain Lewis sent the Zoto Indian that had come to us the day before; and a Canadian named Liberty; to the Zoto nation; to bring the Warriors and chiefs to Council Bluff, in order to hold a treaty with them, The Canadian Liberty never returned to us, this put the Captains much at a loss to know what had become of him, fearing the Indians had killed him.—

We rowed 11 Miles this day & encamp'd on the South side of the River

1. La Liberté, who asserted his own liberty by deserting the expedition; see Appendix A, vol. 2, and Clark's entry for this day.

2. A nearly illegible word, but "Camp" is the most likely interpretation. An alternate reading would be "Cowes," but they would have to be buffalo, and no one else mentions them this day.

3. No. 3 appears to stop writing here. No. 2 begins with the next sentence and continues until August 18. Pott's Creek is Boyer River, Pottawatamie County, Iowa.

4. Apparently in Pottawattamie County, somewhat above the Washington–Douglas county line, Nebraska, on the opposite side.

5. From the French *blaireau,* for the badger, *Taxidea taxus,* but the others indicate it was killed the next day. See Clark's entry for July 30.

Mondy July 30th   Sat out at an Early hour to find a place of Incampment to wait for le barty & the Zottoe Indians to form A Treaty with them   Come to a place of Incampt. about Eigh Oclock On the W. S. in a piece of woods Cloase to a high Bank whare No. 2 walkd. On; from Surface of the water it is neerly 100 feet in hight.[1]   Roed 4 Miles & haltd there

Monday July 30th   We set out at an early hour, in order to find a place in order to form our encampment; and to waite for the Frenchman, (Liberty) and the Zoto Indian who we had sent to the Zoto nation returning.   about 8 o'Clock A. M. we came too, on the So West side of the River, close to a high bank, where some of our Men went on Shore, this place; was cover'd with woods,

We measur'd the heighth, of the bank from the surface of the water, which was 100 feet high.—   One of our hunters brought in an animal which he had shot, which the Canadians, who were with us called a Brareowe, this animal was formed like a dog, of a Grey colour, the nails on his fore feet being 1½ Inches long, his head long and pecked;[2] none of the party but this Canadian had never seen such an animal before, and it was a novelty among us, we encamped at this place having come 4 Miles this day.—

1. The party's Council Bluff, near the town of Fort Calhoun, Washington County, Nebraska.

2. Perhaps "peaked" is meant.

Tusday July 31   the Morning was Clear   G. Dreuier Catched a young beavour   kept him for a pet; Joseph fields, and his brother lost the horses when the[y] went to bring whome a deer that the Sd Joseph shot on the Evening of the 30th Inst[1]

Tuesday July 31st   We formed our encampment this day at the above mention'd place; having fine clear weather, One of our hunters caught a Young beaver, which he kept for a pet, Two of our hunters went out, & took horses with them, in order to bring in a deer, that they had shot in the evening of the 30th instant; They returned in the Evening, having lost the horses.—

1. Clark says that the Field brothers brought in the beaver kit and that Drouillard killed the buck; Ordway and Gass agree with Whitehouse.

Wendy August 1st   the Morning was Clear   G. Druire & Colter went to look for the horses that was lost on the 30th of last month; G. Gibson was Sent back One Days Journey to See if the Indians came there with Liberty that was Sent for them to come to a Treaty with Captn. Lewis & Wm. Clark at the Camp of the Brareowes—[1]   Shields Kill One Deer   Gibson returnd but did not see liberty or the Indians there

Wednesday August 1st   This morning was clear, we remain'd still at our encampment; the Captains sent two of our hunters out, in Order to hunt for the two horses that was lost; and one Man who was to proceed one days Journey back, in order to see if the Zoto Indians, had come with the frenchman Liberty, in Order to hold a treaty with them.—   We named this place, the Camp of Brareowes the name of the unknown animal that we had brought to us by our Hunters.—

Two of our hunters returned, with one deer they had kill'd, but had not seen Liberty or the Zoto Indians on their route.—

1. Whitehouse, along with Ordway, uses this name for the Council Bluff camp.

Thursday 2nd   G. Druier & Colter Returnd   found the horses   Killd. an Elk—.   Brought It to Camp   12 of the Zottoe Indians Arivd. at Our Camp Calld. the Council Bluffs, or the Brarareham prarie; at the Hour of P. M 7 Oclock   No buissness was don. the commanding officer Orderd them plenty of Provisions.   <No buisness was Excuited the>   Halted.

Thursday August 2nd   We remain'd still at the Camp of Brareowes.   the men that we had sent out to hunt the horses returned, having found them, & brought an Elk which they had killed with them.   at 7 oClock A. M. the Zoto Indians arrived at our Camp, which the Captains had alter'd the name of, to that of Council Bluffs, or the Brareoham Priari.— no business with the Indians commenced this day, the number of Zoto Indians that arrived were 12, the remainder of the Warriors, Chiefs, and hunters of that nation having not returned from hunting Buffaloes in the Priaries.—   The commanding officers order'd them plenty of Provisions.   They are a handsome stout well made set of Indians & have good open Countenances, and are of a light brown colour, and have long black hair, which they do wear without cutting; and they all use paint in order to compleat their dress.—

Friday 3rd   the morning was <clear> foggy   the Indians Beheavd. well while Incampd. Neer our party   Captn. Lewis Brought them to a treaty after the hour of 9 Oclock—   there was Six of the Zottoe Cheifs & Six of the Missueriees;   he gave 3 of the head chiefs a Meaddle[1] Each; and the Other three Commissions in the Name of the president of the U. S.   the[y] was well Content With what the[y] Recd.   the Officer Commanding Gave Each of the privates[2] Some Small presents   which made them all on an Eaqual Satisfactory Atonement for their Visit.   the[y] was well Content in the presence of their two fathers, which was M. Lewis & Wm. Clark do.   when the Articles was Opend Out the[y] Said as long as the <San> french had traded with [them] the[y] Never Gave them as much as a Knife for Nothing   Got underway in the Evening   Saild 5 miles—

Friday August 3d   This morning was foggy, the Indians had behaved themselves well in their encampment which lay near ours.—   At 9 o'Clock Captains Lewis & Clark held a treaty with those Indians.   There was Six Chiefs of the Zoto nation, and Six of the Mesouri Chiefs, Captain Lewis gave to three of the heads Chiefs, each a Medal, and the other three Chiefs Commissions, in the name of the President of the United States, they all seemed well content with what they received, The commanding officer, (Captain Lewis) gave each of the others (to whom he had given Commissions) some small presents, which gave general satisfaction— & they consider'd that they were well paid for their Visit.—

They told Captain Lewis & Captain Clark (which was Interpreted <George Drewyer> by a frenchman we had with us our Interpreter) that they were well contented with what their fathers, (meaning them had gave them) when the articles was deliver'd, they mentioned, that as long as the french Traders, had traded with them that they had never even gave them as much as a knife, without receiving something from them for it.— They staid with us till 5 oClock P. M. when we got under way, and sail'd 5 Miles and encamped[3] on the West bank of the River.—

The Latitude of Council bluff is in 41° 17' north Latitude

1. Presenting medals to Indian dignitaries was a long-standing custom. Lewis and Clark carried medals of various sizes and inscriptions. The most common displayed the profile of President Jefferson on one side, while the reverse showed clasped hands and crossed tomahawk and pipe.

2. Probably meaning the non-ranking Indian warriors.

3. Some miles south of Blair, Washington County, Nebraska, but perhaps on the opposite side in Harrison County, Iowa.

Saturday Augst 4th   The morning was Clear   passd. Several Indian Old Camps On the W. S.   one was Calld. the hat as the Indian died there namd the hat[1]   Campd.[2] on the East Side   Roaed 17 ms.—

Saturday August 4th   This morning we set off early, having fine Clear weather, and passed several old Indian Camps lying on the So West side of the River, which were called the hat, it being the name of an Indian, who had died there of that name; in the Evening we encamped on the No. East side of the River, having rowed 17 Miles this day

1. Another piece of information provided only by Whitehouse; the site would be in Washington County, Nebraska, in the vicinity of present Blair.

2. Northeast of Blair, in either Washington County, Nebraska, or Harrison County, Iowa.

Sunday 5   Nothing Extraordinary happned that day   Road 16 miles Campd.[1] On the S. S   Read deserted from our party—[2]

Sunday August 5th   We started early this morning and proceeded on rowing 16 Miles, we encamped on the South side of the River in the Evening.—
One of our Men named Read, deserted from our party this Morning—

1. In Harrison County, Iowa, nearly opposite the Burt–Washington county line, Nebraska.
2. Moses B. Reed had left on August 4, but this was no doubt the day they realized he was
not coming back.

Monday 6th   the morning was fair   got under way at Sun Rise   passd.
an Island to the L. S.   Roaed 12 miles before Dinner.   the hunters[1]
brought 3 deer to the River   Campd[2] on the sd: S.   Roaed 18¾ Miles—

Monday August 6   This morning being fair, we got under way at Sunrise,
and passed an Island lying on the So. West side of the River, we rowed 12
Miles by Dinner, the hunters brought 3 deer to the River   we encamp'd on
the So West side of the River in the evening having row'd 18¾ Miles this
day.—

1. Including Drouillard.
2. In Harrison County, Iowa, about halfway between Soldier and Little Sioux rivers.

Tusday Augt. 7th   the Morning Clear   the party Sonsisted of 4 their
names first G. Druier, R. fields, Bratton, and William[1] that was Sent after
Ms. Read that Deserted in Latd 41 17 00 N.   Nothing Else happend. Extraordinary this day.—

Tuesday August 7th   This day we remained at same place   Captain Lewis
sent out 4 Men to find Read who had deserted from us, This place is a
Priari, and the land lays level & is very rich; nothing extraordinary happen'd
this day.—

1. Actually François Labiche, whom Clark occasionally called William.

Wendsy Augt 8th   Captn M. Lewis Shot a pillican[1]   the Bagg that it carried its drink in containd. 5 Gallons of water by Measure   after we passd the

pillican Island there was better than 5 or 6000 of them flying   the[y] Kept bfore Us one day   Roaed 19 Miles   Campd.[2] On the E. S.

Wednesday August 8th   We embark'd early this morning, and proceeded on Rowing; Captain Lewis shot a Pelican, the bag which it carried its drink in, held five Gallons by measure, we passed an Island, called the Pelican Island where we saw a very considerable number of Pelicans flying, they kept flying before us the whole of this day, in the Evening we encamp'd on the bank of the River on the North[3] side, having rowed 19 Miles this day.—

  1. American white pelican, *Pelecanus erythrorhynchos.*
  2. Probably in southwest Monona County, Iowa, a little above the Harrison County line. A river shift may have placed the site in Burt County, Nebraska.
  3. "North" is written over "South."

Thursday Augt 9th   the Morning was foggy   Cleard Up at 8 Oclock   the Wind blew south   had Good Sailing for better than 14 Miles—   Camped[1] On the E. S.   Roaed & Saild 20 miles

Thursday August 9th   This morning we set out in a fog which cleared up at 8 oClock A. M.   the Wind blew from the South; we set sail & went 14 Miles, when the wind died away, we then took to our Oars and rowed.   in the evening we encamped on the North[2] side of the River having rowed & Sailed 20 Miles this day.—

  1. In Harrison County, Iowa, a mile or so south of Onawa.
  2. "North" is again written over "South."

Friday 10   the morning was Clear   the musquitoes was mighty trouble-some Untill The Sun rose to Some hight.   Campd.[1] On the E. S.   Roaed 24 mils

Friday August 10th   We set out early this morning.   We found the Mus-ketoes very troublesome untill the Sun rose to some heighth, when they quit-ted us, the wind being fair we Sail'd the greatest part of this day.   We encamped in the Evening on the North[2] side of the River having rowed & sail'd 24 Miles.—

1. In Monona County, Iowa, across the river and a few miles above the Thurston–Burt county line, Nebraska.

2. Again written over "South."

Sateday Augt 11   Rain Came On at the hour of 3 Oclock A. M.   a heavy wind blew after—   the Crafts got under way at 6 Oclock favourd. With a South Wind, Passd. a bluff whare the Black bird[1] the late King of the Mahars was buried 4 years ago   the Officers took a flagg with them and assended the hill which was 300 feet higher than the water   left the white flagg on a pole Stuck on his Grave.   Road 18 Miles on the E. S.[2]

Saturday August 11th   At 3 o'Clock this morning we had a rain, which was very heavy, which was immediately succeeded with a smart breeze from the South.   at 6 oClock we set sail, and passed a bluff where the Black bird, the late king of the Mahaws was buried about 4 Years before, the officers landed a small distance above the bluff, and took with them a White Flag, and ascended the Hill which was 300 feet higher than the surface of the water, and placed the flag which they had fix'd on a long pole stuck in the grave.   At 10 oClock A. M the officers embarked again   We proceeded on & in the Evening encamped on the North[3] side of the River.   The distance we sail'd this day being 18 Miles—

1. Blackbird, chief of the Omahas, was buried on Blackbird Hill, Thurston County, Nebraska.

2. Due to changes in the course of the Missouri, the campsite would be in the vicinity of Badger Lake, Monona County, Iowa.

3. Again written over "South."

Sunday Augt 12th   the Morning was fair a Sharp Breese of wind Blew from the South   Sald. 21 Miles from 12 Oclock the 11th to 12 Oclock this day and Gaind. 914[1] yards on a direct Cource.   Camped[2] on the W. S. <roe> 21 Miles—

Sunday August 12th   This morning we Started early with a fair wind from the South, We found by one o'Clock P. M. that we had sailed 21 Miles from 12 oClock the 11th to 12 o'Clock, this day and only gained 914 Yards on our direct course.—

We continued Sailing 'till the evening and encamped on the South side of the River, having Sailed 21 Miles this day.—

   1. Clark has 973 yards, Gass 974.
   2. In either Monona or Woodbury County, Iowa, near the county line.

Monday Augt. 13th   Arived. at the fish camp Neer the Mahars Village[1] at 4 oclock this day   the Commanding Officer Sent a Serjt. & 4 Men with a white flagg, to the Village to Invite them to Come to a treaty, but the[y] found no Indians at the Village   Returnd. Nixt day after 12 Oclock—

Monday August 13th   We embarked early this morning and continued on, at 4 oClock P. M we arrived at a Camp, near the Mahaw Village when the commanding Officer, sent a Serjeant and four Men, with a White flag to the village, to Invite them to come to a Treaty.—

The Serjeant & party proceeded on to the Mahaw Village but found no Indians there, we continued here this day, waiting for their return.—

   1. The Omaha village was named Tonwontonga, or Big Village, and was located in Dakota County, Nebraska, about one mile north of Homer. The camp was in Dakota County, or in Woodbury County, Iowa, a few miles south of Dakota City, Nebraska.

Tusday 14th   the day was fair and pleasant   Some of the men Went a hunting   Returnd found no Game—

Tuesday August 14th   This day we had pleasant weather   we still continued at the same place, about one o'Clock P. M. the Hunters went out but returned without any Game.—

Wendy 15   Captn. <Lewis> Clark and Some of the men went a fishing to a pond One mile from the River[1]   the[y] had Good Success   the[y] Catchd 386 fish—

Wednesday August 15th   We continued at this place this day.   Captain
Clark and some of the Men went out fishing to a pond, which lay one Mile
from the River, and met with good success they caught 386 fish of different
kinds

1. The pond appears on *Atlas* map 16.

Thursday Augst. 16   Captn. Lewis went out the Nixt day with his party
and Returned with 709 fish Neerly 200 pike fish[1] amongst them—

Thursday August 16th   This morning fine & clear, Captain Lewis went
out with his party a fishing at the above pond, and towards Evening they
returned having caught 709 fish of different kinds nearly 200 of which were
pike.—

1. Northern pike, *Esox lucius.*

Friday Augt. 17th   the weather was fine   the men Ocepyed their time in
Cam[p] Repairing their Arms, and Cloathing.   LueBash returned By himself   Lost the Party and came to Camp with measige   Santdy 18[1]

Friday August 17th   We remained still at same place, the men were employed repairing their Arms, and Cloathing; La'Beech <or> our Interpreter
in the Evening came by himself to us and informed our Officers, that he had
left the Zoto head chief, called the Pettit Wallow,[2] & 12 of his Chiefs & Warriors with Read, who had deserted from us, 6 Miles from our Camp, and told
our Captains, if any of the Mahaw Indians were with us, we should remain
still, but if none of them were then among us, to fire off our <Cannon>
Swivel, the Zoto Indians being at Warr with the Mahaws.—[3]

1. From "LueBash" on, the writing appears to be in the hand of No. 3.

2. Petit Voleur, or Little Thief; see Clark's entry for August 3, 1804.

3. Whitehouse seems to imply that the Otos did not wish to meet the Omahas, which is
contrary to Clark's implication in his note for this day.

Saturday 18th Augt.[1]   G. Drewyer & the other 2 men Returned & Brought with them M. Reed the Deserter, likewise the pettevaliar the Big chief of the Zottous & another called the Big horse, a frenchman & 7 of the warriers &c— they all came for the purpose of treating & making friends with the Mahars, &c   M. Reed tried & towards evening he Recd. his punishment, the chiefs Sorry to have him punished &c.   La Liberty has not returned.   it is expected that he has deserted.—

Saturday August 18th   We fired off our Cannon as a signal for the Indians & We remained still at same place, G. Drewyer, and two other Men who had been sent out in search of Reade who had deserted returned; having brought the deserter with them, they likewise were accompanied by Pettis <ahar.> Wallow, the big chief of the Zoto Indians, also another Indian of the same Nation called the Big horse, and a frenchman 7 Indian Warriors, and a number of Indians all of the same tribe <of Indians.>   They came in Order, to holde council & have a treaty with Captain Lewis & Captain Clarke, and to make a lasting peace with them, in behalf of the United States.   In the Evening M Read was tried by a Court Marshall, and sentenc'd <was> to <have> be punish'd by whipping him.   The Indians were all concerned at seeing Read receive his punishment, and seemed truly sorry.—   The Men that was sent after Read, could gain no Inteillgence of the frenchman called Liberty; and the commanding officers expect he has deserted.—

1. With this entry the writing of No. 1 begins again.

Sunday 19th   the Indians all appear to be friendly   at 9 oClock the Captains read a long Speech to them & Counseled with them, & Gave one a medal & the others they Gave commissions, & Some Small preasants &c   we Gave them provisions while they Remained with us.   Sergt. Floyd Taken verry ill this morning with a collick.—

Sunday August 19th   We still remained at this place, in order to hold a treaty with the Indians who are here, These Indians appear to be very friendly towards us, At 9 oClock A. M. Captain Lewis deliver'd them a long

Speech (which was Interpreted to them by <Drewyer> a frenchman our Interpreter,[)]¹ and gave the head Chief a Medal, and to the other Chiefs, he gave Commissions; and presents were distributed among the whole of them. We supplied them with Provisions plentifully whilst they remained with us. in the Evening they left our Camp, being well pleased, One of our Serjeants named Floyd, was taken Ill of a Cholic this morning

1. Perhaps Labiche; see the fair copy entry of August 17.

Monday 2oth we Set out eairly this morning under a gentle breeze from the S. E. the Indians all Set out for to return to their village, we Sailed on verry well till noon when we landed for to take Dinner. Sergeant Charles Floyd expired directly after we landed. he was layed out in the most decent manner possable. we proceded on to the first hills on N. S. where we halted and dug a Grave on the top of a round knob & buried the desed with the honours of war.¹ the funeral Serrymony performed &c— we named this hill Sgt. Floyd's Bluff we then proceeded on to a Creek on the Same Side which we named Sgt. Floyds Creek.²

Monday August 2oth We embarked early this morning with a gentle breeze from the South East, the Indians who had encamped a small distance from us, also set out to return to their Villages. We continued sailing on very well 'till noon, when we landed to take dinner.— shortly after one of our Serjeants Charles Floyd expired; we laid him out in the most decent manner possible. We then proceeded on to the first hills, which lay on the North side of the River, where we halted and dug a Grave on the Top of a high round Nob; and Interred him, with all the honors of Warr.— and had a funeral Sermon preach'd over him. we named this Hill Serjeant Floyds bluff. The disease which occasion'd his death, was a Bilious cholic,³ which baffled all medical aid, that Captain Lewis could administer, We proceeded on to a Creek, lying on the same side of the River, which we named Serjeant Floyds Creek, and encamped

1. At Sioux City, Woodbury County, Iowa.
2. Floyd River, Woodbury County.

58

3. Gass, on August 19, describes it as "a violent colick"; both descriptions would fit the symptoms of appendicitis that might have been observed.

Tuesday August 21st 1804.   we Set out eairly this morning under a hard Breeze from the South.   we passed the mouth of the Grand River Souix [1] close abo. a high Bluff on N. S.   we came 20 odd miles & camped [2] on S. S.—

Tuesday August 21st   We set out early this morning with a stiff breeze from the South, and pass'd the Mouth of the Grand River Souix; which is close to a high bluff, which lays on the North side of the River, we saild 21 Miles this day and encamped on the South side of the River.—   The Country here is very Rich Priari land, having very high Grass on it; and at the farther side from the River, it has some Trees growing on it & affords a pleasant view.—

1. Big Sioux River forms the Iowa–South Dakota boundary.
2. In Union County, South Dakota, south of present Jefferson, and probably on the north side of Lake Goodenough, the apparent 1804 bed of the Missouri.

Wednesday 22nd Augt. 1804.   we Set off eairly   the current Swift.   the [wind] hard from the South.   we passed a ceedar Bluff on the South Side in which we found Some kinds of minral Substance, the 2 men who had been with the horses joined us [1]   had killed 2 Deer we pasd. an allum Stone clift on the S. S.   we camped [2] at a prarie on the N. S.   we See a great deal of Elk Sign &c

Wednesday August 22nd   This morning we set out early, and found the current running very Strong against us, the Wind blowing from the South, we passed under a bluff lying on the south side of the River, and some of our Men landed from the Pettiauger, they found some kind of mineral substance, but its qualities appear'd to be utterly unknown to us, The Men that had the Horses came to the bank of the River, having killed 2 Deer, which we took on board,—   we then proceeded on, and passed an Alum stone Clift, laying on the South side of the River, we proceeded on, & in the Evening we encamped at a Priari which lay on the North side, where we saw a great many Tracts & signs of Elk.—

1. Evidently Reubin Field and George Shannon, but Clark refers to Field's return with the horses the next day and says nothing about Shannon's return.

2. Probably in Union County, South Dakota, a little south of the present community of Elk Point.

Thursday 23rd   we Set off eairly   2 men went on Shore hunting.   passed round a bend   Capt. Clark walked on Shore a Short time and killed a fat Buck.   we halted to take Breakfast.   2 Elk Swam across the River close abv. the Boat   we wounded boath of them   Jo. Fields came to the Boat had killed a Bull Buffelow.[1]   Capt. Lewis & 10 men of the party went out & Brought it to the Boat.   John Collins killed a faun.   the 2 men on the S. S. who had been with the horses came to the Boat with 2 Deer—   we halted in a bend to dine   the wind verry hard so we jurked our meat &c.   the wind fell towards evening   we proceeded on till dark & camped[2] on the S. S.—

Thursday August 23rd   We set off very early this morning, having previous to our departure sent 2 Men out a hunting; and Captain Clark walked along the Banks of the River, we proceeded on rowing, and passed round a bend of the River, a short time after passing this bend Captain Clark shot a buck Deer which was very fat, we halted with the boat & took Captain Clark on board, likewise the Buck; we proceeded on a small distance, and landed to take breakfast, whilst we were breakfasting 2 Elk swam across the River close above the Boat, <one> Some of our hands shot at them, & wounded them both, & we got them, One of hands that we had sent out this morning returned, he having shot a Buffalo Bull.

Captain Clark and Ten Men went out in order to bring the Buffalo to the boat, which they did, One of our Men killed a fawn, which he brought likewise to us, The Men who were on the South side of the River with the horses came to us, having 2 deer which they had shot, We proceeded on and halted in a bend of the River to dine, The wind blowing hard we Jerked our Meat & overhauled several articles on board the boat.   towards evening the wind died away, We Proceeded on 'till dark, when we encamped on the South side of the River,—

1. The first buffalo, *Bison bison,* actually killed by the party. See Clark's entry for this date for the slight confusion about which Field brother actually shot it.

2. In Dixon County, Nebraska, or Clay County, South Dakota.

Friday 24th   Some Small Showers of rain last night   we Set off about Sun rise.   we passed rugged Bluffs on the S. S. where we found Some red berreys which they call Rabbit berrys.[1]   we passed a handsom prarie on N. S.   in this prarie we are informed that their is a high hill which they call the hill of little Devills.[2]   we passed the mouth of a large Creek on N. S. called white Stone River[3] which is abt. 50 yards wide & extends a Great distance in to the Countrey, we Camped on the S. S. of the Missouri.—[4]

Friday August 24th   We had some showers of Rain during the night.   we set off about sun rise and passed a ragged bluff laying on the South side of the River, where we found some Berries, which is called Rabbit berries.— We passed a handsome Priari, laying on the North side of the River, not far from the Priari, is a high hill, which is called little Devil, we likewise passed a large Creek, lying on the North side call'd white stone River, which is 50 Yards wide at its mouth, and runs a great distance in the Country.   in the evening we encamped on the South side of the Mesouri River,

1. Buffaloberry, *Shepherdia argentea* (Pursh) Nutt.
2. Spirit Mound, Clay County, South Dakota, about eight miles north of Vermillion. See Clark's entries for the day for the beliefs that gave rise to the name Whitehouse gives it.
3. Vermillion River, reaching the Missouri in Clay County, southeast of the town of Vermillion.
4. Because of river shifts, probably in Clay County, a little west of Vermillion.

Saturday 25th   2 men of the party caught 9 nine cat fish[1] last night, 5 of them verry large, Capt. Lewis & Clark & 10[2] more of the party went back to See the hill of little Devils.   the Boat waited till Eleven oClock & then went on.

Saturday August 25th   We remained here part of this day   some of our Men caught Nine Cat fish.   5 of them was very large, weighing on an average each 100 lbs.   Captain Lewis & Captain Clark with 10 Men, went back to take a view of the Hill, called the little Devil, we waited for them till 11 o'Clock when they returned.[3]   We proceeded on, and in the Evening encamped on the North side of the River.—

1. Perhaps channel catfish.

2. According to Clark, the men were Drouillard, Ordway, Shields, Joseph Field, John Colter, William E. Bratton, "Cane" (perhaps *engagé* Cann), Labiche, Richard Warfington, Robert Frazer, and perhaps York.

3. In fact, the captains' party did not return to the main group until the next day; this seems a clear case of Whitehouse's scribe misinterpreting the original journal entry.

Sunday 26th   the Boat detained this morning to Jurk an Elk which Shannon killed, abt. 9 oClock the party returned to the Boat much fatigued   they informd us that their was nothing but Birds to be Seen & that it is about nine miles from the Missouri & a handsom round hill in a mence large prarie. they Saw a Great many Buffelow from the hill.   they were all most famished for water &c—   we proceeded on   passed a white clay Bluff on S. S.   we found a large plumb orched[1] in a prarie N. S.   we Camped on a large Sand bar N. S. opposite a Creek called pet arck or little Bow where their was formerly an Indian village.—[2]

Sunday August 26th   This day we remain'd at the place that we encamp'd the precing Evening, we employ'd ourselves in Order to Jerk the Meat of an Elk, which one of our hands shot early this morning, about 9 oClock A. M. our hunting party[3] returned to the Boat much fataigued, having seen nothing on their Route but Birds, they mention'd that about 9 Miles from the Mesouri, they saw a handsome round hill and a very large Priari, They saw a number of Buffalo from the Top of the hill, The Men were almost famished for want of Water.   We proceeded on, and passed a white Clay bluff, lying on the South side of the River, and a Plumb Orchard in a Priari on the North side, We encamped in the Evening <we encamped> on a Sand barr, which was very large lying on the North side of the River, opposite to a Creek called pittarc or little bow, where there was formerly an Indian village

1. The day before, Clark noted the abundance of plums, including the common wild plum, *Prunus americana* Marsh., and big-tree plum, *P. mexicana* Wats.

2. Bow Creek, Cedar County, Nebraska; "pet arck" is Whitehouse's version of the French *petit arc*, "little bow." On the village, see Clark's entry for this day. The camp was in Clay County, South Dakota.

3. This is the captains' party which the day before the copyist had said returned that day.

Monday 27th   G. Drewyer came to us this morning   2 men Sent out for to hunt the horses.   we Set out at Sun rise under a gentle Breeze from the S. E.   we proceeded on   passed a chalk Bluff on S. S.   in this Bluff is Mineral Substance &c—   we passed the Mouth of a large Creek called River Jaque[1] on the N. S.   here we Saw 3 Indians[2] they informed us that their Camp was near & Sergt. pryor & 2 men went[3]   we then proceeded on until dark & camped[4] on a large Sand beach on the N. Side.

Monday August 27th   This morning early George Drewyer our hunter came to us, two of our Men were sent out to hunt the horses, We set out at sunrise, with a gentle breese from the South East, and proceeded on, we passed a Chalk bluff, laying on the South side of the River; this bluff had also Mineral substance on it.   We proceeded on, and passed the Mouth of a large Creek, called the River Jacque, lying on the North side of the River. Here we met with 3 Indians, who informed us that their Camp lay near us. Captain Lewis sent Serjeant Pryor & 2 Men to find them out & bring them to us.—   We proceeded on our way with the boat &ca till dark, and encamped on a large Sand barr, lying on the North side of the River—

1. James River, Yankton County, South Dakota.
2. The Indians were Yankton Sioux, the first plains nomads the party had met.
3. Pierre Dorion, Sr., and another Frenchman accompanied Nathaniel Pryor.
4. In Yankton County, between the mouth of the James River and the town of Yankton.

Tuesday 28th   we Set off eairly under a fine Breeze from S. E.   we passed high praries on N. S. handsome & ascending graddually from the river   at 2 oClock P m. the wind Blew hard from the S. W.   the <canoe> pearogue got a hole Broke in to hir by dashing a gainst a Snag, So that they had to begin to unload, but they Stoped the Water from comming in by Stopping in one thing & another.   So we went across the river on the South Side and camped[1] to wait the arival of the Indians &c—   in order to counsel with them &c—   a flag pole raisd   this place is below a large Island & Sand bar below a hill & Bluff on the S. S. in a handsome Bottom & Groves of oak[2] Timber, &c—

Tuesday August 28th We set off early this morning with a fine Breeze from the South East; and all Sail set. we proceeded on and passed some Priaries which lies high, they lie on the North side of the River, they appear very beautiful ascending gradually from the River, about 2 o'Clock P. M. the Wind blew hard from the South West the boat plunging, had a hole broke in her by running against a Snag, so that we were obliged to put ashore, and had begun to unload her, but fortunately we got the hole stop'd We crossed the River to the South side and encamped, to waite the arrival of our Men, which we had sent to find out the Indian Camp the day before; in order to hold a treaty with them, We here raised a Pole in order to hoist our flagg.— This place lies below a large Island, and a sand barr and bluff & is below a hill, on the South side of the River.— There is also a handsome bottom near it, with Groves of fine white Oak Timber growing on it.

1. Below Gavins Point Dam, Cedar County, Nebraska.
2. An unknown oak, *Quercus* sp.

Wednesday 29th a hard Storm arose from the N. W. last night abt. 8 oC—of wind & rain. cloudy morning, Some Thunder, colter Sent on with Some provision for to hunt Shannon & the horses &c. the pearogue repaired the men make a Towing line out of our Elk Skins. we have pleanty of fine cat fish which the party catch in the Missouri River, in the afternoon Sergt. pryor & the 2 men returned brot with them 60 Indians of the Souix nation they appeared to be friendly. they camped on the opposite Shore we carried them over Some provisions & capt Lewis Sent them Tobacco &c— Sergt. pryor informed us that their Town was abt. 9 miles from the Missouri, and consisted of 40 lodges, and built with dressed Buffelow Skins &c— painted different coulers &c— G. Drewyer killed one Deer to day—

Wednesday August 29th We had this night a hard Storm from the Northwest, accompanied with Thunder lightning & Rain, in the morning, a Man was sent out with some provisions, in Order to hunt the Men who were with the horses. We set about repairing the Boat, which we compleated— The men were employed making a Tow line out of Elk skins, and catching of fish. they catch'd a great quantity of Cat fish in the River Mesouri, which afforded us an excellent dinner. In the afternoon Serjeant Pryor & the two Men returned, having with them Sixty Indians of the Souix nation; they appear'd very friendly— They are a handsome well made set of Indians, are about the middle stature, and do not cutt their hair as most the Savages in this part does.—[1] They encamped on the opposite shore to where we were. The commanding officers sent them Provisions & Tobacco.— Serjeant Pryor informed us, that their Town lay about 9 Miles from the Mesouri River, and consisted of 40 Lodges, and that their habitations were coverd with Buffalo skins & painted with different Colours.— One of the hunters return'd in the Evening with a deer he had killed.—

1. Apparently a reference to the roached hairstyle of the men of several tribes of the Missouri River.

Thursday 30th   the fog is So thick on the river this morning that we could not See across the river, untill late in the morning.   about 9 oClock the Indians was brought across the river in our pearogue   our Captains counseled with them read a Speech to them, & made 5 of them chiefs & Gave them all Some Marchandize &c— &c— they Received them verry thankfully divided them out among themselves, & play on their juze harps, Sung &c.   they Boys Shot with their Bows and arrows for Beeds and appeared to be merry, and behaved well among our parte[y].— Capt. Lewis Shot his air gun   told them that their was medician in hir & that She would doe Great execution, they were all amazed at the curiosity, & as Soon as he had Shot a fiew times they all ran hastily to See the Ball holes in the tree   they Shouted aloud at the Site of the execution She would doe &c.   The Captains Gave them provisions &c.   as Soon as it was dark a fire was made   a drum was repaired among them.   the young men painted themselves different ways. Some with their faces all white others with their faces part white round their forehead, & breasts &c— then they commenced dancing in curious manner to us.   their was a party that Sung and kept time with the drumm.   they all danced or all their young men espacilly.   they Gave a houp before they commenced dancing, they would dance around the fire for Some time and then houp, & then [r]est a fiew minutes.   one of the warrirs would git up in the centre with his arms & point towards the different nations, & make a

Speech, telling what he had done, how many he had killed & how many horses he had Stole &c— all this make them Great men & fine warrirs, the <greater> Larger rogues the best men &c or the Bravest men & them that kills most gets the greatest honoured among them.

Thursday August 30th   This morning was so foggy that we could not see across the River, untill it was late, about 9 o'Clock A. M. the Indians were brought across the River in a pettyauger.   Our Captains held a council with them & deliver'd a speech to them, (which was interpreted by a frenchmen) [1]   our Captains made 5 of them chiefs, and gave them medals, On the Talk being finish'd, they gave them all presents of Goods & they thankfully receiv'd them

They put all the presents that they got, together, and divided them among their whole party equally.—   The Indians after the goods were divided, was very merry; they play'd on the Jews harps & danced for us for Beads that we gave them.—   they behaved well to us.—   The Indian Boys shot with their Bows for some small trifles we gave them.—   After they had finished dancing Captain Lewis took his Air Gun and shot her off, and by the Interpreter, told them that there was medicine in her, and that she could do very great execution, They all stood amazed at this curiosity; Captain Lewis discharged the Air Gun several times, and the Indians ran hastily to see <if to see> the holes that the Balls had made which was discharged from it.   at finding the Balls had entered the Tree, they shouted a loud at the sight and the Execution that was done surprized them exceedingly.—   The shooting with the Air Gun being over, the Indians were supplied with Provisions.   As soon as dark set in, and a drum was prepared among them, The Young Indian Men painted themselves in different ways.   some of them painted their faces all over with white paint, others painted half their faces, and round their foreheads & breasts with white paint also, when they had finish'd painting they then commenced their dancing, in a curious manner before us; one party of them sung & kept time with the drum, whilst the remainder of them danced, especially the Young men commencing their dancing by a loud Whoop which they gave.—

The Indians continued to dance round the fire some time, and then would stop & whoop.   in a few minutes after some one of their Warriors would get up in the Centre, where all their Warriors stood with his Arms; and point towards where the different Indian nations lived, and make a speech, telling what feats he had done, how many he had killed, & how many Horses he had stole from them &ca   all of which among these Indians, make them great Men, and Warriors; and much esteem'd by their nation.   The dance being finish'd the Indians retir'd to their Camp.—

1. The word "frenchman" is written over an illegible erasure, perhaps the name of the interpreter.

Friday 31st   a pleasant morning.

Friday August 31st   This morning we had pleasant Weather.   The Indians sett off for their Towns early & crossed the River; taking a friendly leave of us all, The Indians were of the Soioux Nation, and Tribe of Debois-B-ruly, or the Burning Woods.—[1]
The Council Bluff lies in Latitude 41° 17' North

1. A passable translation of Bois Brulé; however, these people were in fact Yankton Sioux.

Septm. 1[1]   the morning was rainy   got under way at the Calmit bluff   at that place Captn. Lewis & Clark Held a treaty with the tribe of the Deboughbruley or the Burning wood

Saturday September 1st   This morning being rainey, we left Council Bluff,[2] where we had held a treaty, and proceeded rowing till the evening when we encamped[3] on the bank of the River on the North side.—

1. This entry is apparently in the hand of No. 2.
2. Calumet Bluff, which the copyist has evidently confused with the Council Bluff where the party met with the Otos and Missouris; see July 30.
3. On Bon Homme Island, Bon Homme County, South Dakota.

Sunday 2nd Sept. 1804.   a hard Storm of wind and rain last night which lasted about 2 hours, cloudy this morning   we Set off eairly   three men out hunting.[1]   the hunters killed three Elk.   we halted at 8 oC on the S. S.

where their was an ancient fortification in the form of a half moon[2] it appeared that one Side had washed into the river. Capt. Clark took the dimentions of it. the wind high from the North So that we were obliged to lay too at a high prarie[3] where we found plumbs & Grapes[4] a pleanty—

Sunday September 2nd   Last night we had a hard Storm of Wind, accompanied with Rain, which was very heavy. it lasted for near 2 hours   we set off early this morning having cloudy weather, Three of our Men went a hunting & Return'd to us, having killed 3 Elk, which they brought to us.—

We came too with our boat at 8 o'Clock A. M. on the South side of the River, near where the remains of an Ancient fortification stood, it was in the form of a half Moon, and had the appearance of once being very Strong, One side of it had washed into the River.   Captain Clark took the dimensions of it   being 1¾ Miles in length 600 Yards wide in the Center.—   The wind raising & blowing hard from the North, we proceeded on but a small distance, and came too at a high Priari, where we found Plumbs & Grapes in great abundance

1. Drouillard, Reubin Field, and Collins.
2. The entire party believed these natural sand ridges opposite Bon Homme Island in Knox County, Nebraska, to be man-made fortifications; see Clark's detailed survey of this day.
3. In Bon Homme County, South Dakota.
4. Perhaps river-bank grape, *Vitis riparia* Michx.

Monday 3rd Sept.[1]   cool and pleasant this morning; we Set off at Sun rise passed yallow Bluff & many beaver Signs   we passed a Chalk Bluff   we passed plumb Creek on the N. S.[2]   Camped[3] on the S. S.

Monday September 3rd   We this morning took a new Mast on board, which some of the hands had made the preceding day, and set out at Sun rise, and passed by a Yellow bluff, where was a great many signs of beaver, We also passed by a Chalk bluff, laying on the North side of the River; and in the Evening we encamped on the South side of the River.—

1. Several pages have been removed at the point where this entry crosses two pages. No break in the writing is apparent.

2. Probably Emmanuel Creek, Bon Homme County, South Dakota.

3. In Knox County, Nebraska, probably near the western boundary of the Santee Sioux Indian Reservation.

Tuesday 4th Sept. Set off eairly. proceded on found Some plumbs. passd. white panit Creek¹ on the S. S. we Sailed fast, we passed the Mouth of Big Rapid River² on S. S. Saw an Indian raft at a Cdeeder Bottom abo. the Mo. of Rapid River. G. Drewyer killed a Turky we looked for tracks of Shannon but could not See whether he had passd or not.

Tuesday September 4th We set off early this morning and proceeded on, & found some plumbs, we passed a Creek called plumb creek, lying on the South side of the River, the wind blowing fresh, we sett all our Sails & proceed on Sailing fast, We passed the Mouth of the big Rapid River, lying on the South side; we passed by an Indian Raft near a bottom, above the Mouth of rapid River; we sent to see if the Tracts of one of our Man named Shannon, who had been missing from us some days, but they could discover no signs of his having passed that way.—

We continued on till evening and encamped³ on the South side of the River—

1. Bazile Creek, Knox County, Nebraska.

2. Niobrara River, meeting the Missouri in Knox County.

3. Above the mouth of the Niobrara, in Knox County, in or near present Niobrara State Park.

Wednesday 5th Sept. we took a ceed[er] mast on board Some hunters out we Sailed on passed Goat creek¹ on N. S. where the Beaver had made a damm across the mouth of it. we passed handsome Minneral Springs on the N. S. the hunters killed 2 Elk & a Deer.

Wednesday Septemr 5th This morning we sent out our Hunters, and then set sail, we passed by a Creek called Goat Creek, lying on the North side of the River, where the Beaver, had made a Dam, across the mouth of it. We passed a handsome Mineral spring, lying on the North side of the River, In the Evening our hunters returned, having kill'd 2 Elk and one Deer, which they brought to us, We encamped[2] on the North side of the River on its bank.—

1. Chouteau Creek, between Bon Homme and Charles Mix counties, South Dakota.
2. On an island between Charles Mix County, South Dakota, and Knox County, Nebraska.

Thursday 6th Sept. a cloudy morning.— Several hunters out hunting. colter joined us had not found Shannon. the hunters killed 1 Buffalow one Elk 3 Deer one woolf 1 Deer & four Turkies. Camped[1] on N. S.

Thursday Septemr 6th We started early this morning, it being cloudy weather; We sent out our hunters, in the Evening they returned; but had not found Shannon, the Man who was Missing; they brought in with them, One Buffalo, One Elk, three deer, One Wolf & four Turkies, we encamped on the North side of the River.—

1. In Charles Mix County, South Dakota, a little below the Knox–Boyd county line in Nebraska, opposite.

Friday 7th Sept. 1805.[1] a clear morning we Set off eairly. one of the hunters killed a prarie dogg[2] & Sd. he Saw a village of them we halted the Capt. went out with [10?] men and drounded out one & took it alive & kept it. it is a curious annimal much like a little dog, & live in holes all in a compact place like a village.

Friday Septemr. 7th This morning being clear we set off early, One of our Hunters returned, having killed an animal & brought in with him, which he called a Priari dog, and mentioned, that he had seen a large number of them, which had their habitations lying together, We halted, Captain Lewis went on shore with 4 Men, to hunt for those Animals. Captain Lewis & the men proceeded on, & went to the place where they catched one of the Priari dogs, and brought it alive to the Boat,— It is much in resemblance of a small Dog, These animals live in holes, which is cover'd with compact Clay & are regularly placed, & has the resemblance of a Village. We continued at the place we had halted at, and encamped.—[3]

1. Again Whitehouse gets the year wrong.

2. The party adopted the French traders' designation *chien*, or dog, for the prairie dog, *Cynomys ludovicianus*, a rodent.

3. Near the Nebraska–South Dakota state line.

Saturday 8th Sept.   a pleasant morning.   we Set off eairly.   G. Drewyer joined with the horses had killed 2 Elk a faun Deer and caught 2 large beaver we passed an old Trading house on N. S.[1]   capt. Clark walkd on Shore & killed a faun Deer 3 Turkies & a Squerrell.[2]

Saturday September 8th   This morning we had fine pleasant weather, One of our hunters came in, and brought the horses, he had with him & 2 Elk, & four deer which he had killed, and two large Beaver which he caught in a Trap.   We set off early, and passed an old trading house, lying on the North side of the River.   Captain Clark, who had went out a hunting this Morning, returned in a short time, with the other hunters having kill'd 2 Buffalo, and One Deer, We passed several small Creeks, and encamped[3] on the South side of the River in the Evening.—

1. Where Jean Baptiste Truteau wintered in 1794–95, some thirty miles above the mouth of the Niobrara River, in Charles Mix County, South Dakota.

2. Clark says it was a fox squirrel, *Sciurus niger*.

3. Apparently on later Chicot, or Strehlow, Island, on the Gregory–Charles Mix county line, South Dakota.

Sunday 9th Sept.   we Set off eairly.   Saw Several Gangs of Buffalow on the Side hills on S. S.   Capt. Clark walked on Shore   passed Several creeks.[1]   G. Drewyer killed a Deer.   R. Fields killed a Buffalow.   Capt. Clark killed a Bufalow.

Sunday September 9th   We sett off early this morning, and saw several Gangs of Buffalo which were on the side of some Hills, laying on the South side, of the River.   Captain Clark walked on shore & passed several Creeks. We proceeded on, & encamp'd[2] on the South side of the River in the Evening.—

1. Including Spring, Pease, and Campbell creeks, in Charles Mix County, South Dakota.
2. In Gregory County, South Dakota, opposite Stony Point on the opposite shore.

Monday 10th Sept. 1804. a foggy morning. we Set off eairly. proceeded on. we Saw a ruck of Bones on the Bank S. S. which appeared to be the Bones of a monstrous large fish[1] the Back Bone is 45 feet long. the hunters killed three Buffalow & a Deer

Monday September 10th This morning was foggy, we set out early, and proceeded on; we landed and saw lying on the banks on the South side of the River, the Bones of a monstrous large Fish, the back bone of which measured, forty five feet long. our hunters returned, having killed 3 Buffalo, and one deer. We encamp'd[2] on the South side of the River on the bank.—

1. A pleiosaur, an aquatic dinosaur of the Mesozoic era.
2. On Pocahontas, or Toehead, Island, between Gregory and Charles Mix counties, South Dakota.

Tuesday 11th Sept. 1804. Set out an eairly hour Clear morning & fare wind. proceeded on passed an Isld. covd with timber. high hills and prarie Saw a man coming down to the bank horseback near. we came to Shore and found it was Shannon that had been with the horses. he had been absent 16 days and 12 of them he had Eat nothing but Grapes. the reason was his balls ran Short. the hills commenced close on both Sides of the river. Capt. Clark, Sergt. Ordway & Sergt. Pryor went out to hunt this morning [came] to us heree. had killed 2 Elk 4 Deer and one porkapine.[1] one of the horses which Shannon had with him Gave out & he left him 7 days ago. we proceeded on rained verry hard passed black bluffs on the S. S. R. Fields went with the horse as we have only the one now the rain continued untill 7 oClock in the evening. Camped[2] on the South Side.—

Tuesday September 11th We set out this morning at an early hour, with a fair wind & pleasant weather; and proceeded sailing on. we passed an Island, which was cover'd with Timber, and a Priari, having some high hills on it.— We passed on, and saw a Man coming down to the Bank of the

River on horse back; We put the Boat to the shore, and found it was the Man, (Shannon) who had been missing, and was with the horses, he had been absent 16 days, 12 of which; he had nothing to subsist on but Grapes, the reason of which was, that his Balls had given out, The hills at this place ran close to the River, on both sides of it; Captain Clark & 2 Serjeants who had went out a hunting, early this morning; came to us here, They had with them 2 Elk, 4 deer and a porcupine which they had killed. One of the horses which Shannon had with him, had gave out, and he had left him 7 days before he joind us, We proceeded on & it began to rain[3] very hard, and passed some black bluffs, lying on the South side of the River.— The Rain continued untill 7 o'Clock in the evening. We sent one Man with the horse (the only one that we had left) to go along the shore and we encamped on the South side of the River.—

1. The porcupine is *Erethizon dorsatum,* in this case perhaps *E. d. epixanthum,* the yellow-haired porcupine, a subspecies.

2. A little south of the Lyman–Gregory county line, South Dakota.

3. The words "began to rain" are written over an illegible erasure.

Wednesday 12 Sept. 1804[1]   Clouday.   R. Fields continued on with the horse.   passed a long range of black bluffs on the S. S. and an Island covered with timber.   that is all the wood that is to be Seen at this place.   all the country is hills and praries.   at 12 oclock Capt. Clark Newman and Sergt. Gass went a hunting.   those in the barge had a Great deal of trouble to Git along the Sand bars, their was So many and the current So rapid that we did not come more than 4 miles.   Camped[2] after dark on the S Side.

Wednesday Septemr 12th   This morning Cloudy, the Man who had the horse on shore, continued on with him.   We set out about 8 o'clock A. M. and passed a long range of black bluffs, lying on the South side of the River; and an Island covered with timber, which is the only place here that had wood on it.   The country here being Priaries and hills.   At 12 oClock A. M. Captain Clarke and two of our Serjeants landed, in order to go a hunting. The Men who were in the barge, had a great deal of trouble to get her along, their being so many sand Barrs in the way, and the current running, so rapid against us, so that we did not come more than 4 Miles this day. We came too after dark, & encamped on the South side of the River,

1. Whitehouse again may have written "4" over "6" for the year.
2. In Brule County, South Dakota.

Thursday 13th Sept. 1804 cloudy and hard rain. G. Drewyer caught 4 beaver last night high wind, passed a creek on S. S and range of black bluffs. three of the party went out to hunt and has not returned yet. Camped[1] on the N. S.—

Thursday Septemr 13th We started early this morning it being Cloudy and some Rain, One of our Men (G drewyer the Hunter) caught four Beaver in the Traps overnight, The wind blew hard. we passed <the> a Creek, lying on the South side of the River, and a range of black bluffs, Captain Clark & the two Men who went hunting Yesterday,[2] had not yet return'd We proceeded on, and encamped on the North side of the River

1. In Brule County, South Dakota.
2. Apparently Whitehouse wrote this entry on the next day; Ordway, Pryor, and Shannon went out hunting this day, September 13, and did not return until the next day. See Ordway's entries for those dates.

Friday 14th Sept. 1804. a foggy morning, a cloudy day and Some rain the water is So Shallow that we had to waid & hall the barge over the Sand bars. at 8 oClock we halted for to take breakfast. the 3 men who went a hunting yesterday joined us here. the hills and praries are pleasant but barron. G. Drewyer caught 3 beaver last night the Musquitoes are troublesom. passd. black bluffs on the S. Side and an Island which had Som timber on it. passed a creek on South Side.[1] the hunters killed a goat and a hare.[2] the Goat was killed by Capt Clark & the first that was Seen by the party on the Missourie—

Friday September 14th This morning we had a great fog, on its going off, it was Cloudy & we had some Rain, We set off, and found the Water so shallow, that we had to go into it—and to haul the Boat over the Sand Barrs, at 8 oClock A. M. we stopped the Boat to breakfast; Captain Clark & the two Men who went a hunting, returned to us here.— The Country here, is hilly and Priaries.— which appear to be barren land; but is tolerably pleasant, One of our hunters caught during last night 3 Beavers in his traps, We proceeded on, and passed some black Bluffs lying on the South side of the River, and two Islands lying on the same side, which were cover'd with Timber, we also passed a Creek which lay on the same side of the River; Captain Clark shot a Goat and a hare, which they brought to us.— and all our hunters join'd us in the Evening, this was the first Goat that was seen by any of our party since we enter'd the Mesouri We encamped on the South side of the River at dark.—

1. Bull Creek, Lyman County, South Dakota; they camped just below its mouth.

2. Pronghorn, *Antilocapra americana*, were seen as early as September 3 but were not fully described by the captains until this day. The hare is a white-tailed jackrabbit, *Lepus townsendii.*

Saturday the 15th Sept. we Set off eirily a cloudy morning. Collins went with the horse. we passed a creek on the S. Side named Shannons creek[1] and black bluffs on N. S. passed white River[2] on the S. Side Sergt. Gass & R. Fields went up white River Some distance. they found it to be a handsom river and a handsom country. 12 miles up this R. it is 150 yds. wide the current and coulour is like the Missourie R.

Saturday September 15th We sett off early this morning the weather being cloudy, we proceeded on, and passed a Creek lying on the South side of the River, which Captain Lewis named Shannons Creek, and some black bluffs on the North side of the River,

We continued on our Voyage, and passed White River, lying on the South side of the River Mesouri.— Two of our Men were order'd to go up White River & to View it, They proceeded up it 12 Miles, and returned. they found the River to be a handsome one, & an Elegant Country lying on both sides of it. its width 150 Yards, the current running Strong, & the Water (like the Mesouri,) muddy. We encamp'd in the Evening on the South side of the River on its bank.—

1. Bull Creek, Lyman County, South Dakota, where Shannon had camped for several days while lost.
2. White River reaches the Missouri in Lyman County.

Sunday 16th Sept. 1804. we Set off eairly and proceeded on   passed the mouth of White River on the S. Side—   Came 4 miles and Camped at a beautiful bottom wood with thin timber named pleasant Camp.[1]   I went out a hunting and Several more of the party, thier was a nomber of buffaloe Elk Deer Goats & one magpy[2] killed this day.   Sergt. Gass & R. Fields returned. had killed 3 Deer—

Sunday Septemr 16   We set off early this morning, and proceeded on 4 Miles, and encamp'd at a beautiful bottom cover'd thinly with Timber; which we named pleasant Camp.   I went with several of our party out a hunting, We saw large numbers of Buffalo, Elk deer & Goats, but they were very Shy.— One of the party Shot a buffalo, which we got.—   The party that had went to View White River, also brought in 3 Deer that they had killed

1. On September 17, Clark called it "Plumb Camp"; returning to it on August 26, 1806, he used Whitehouse's name. It was near Oacoma, Lyman County, South Dakota; the party remained here until September 18.
2. Black-billed magpie, *Pica pica.*

Monday 17th Sept. 1804.   Capt. Lewis and Several more of the party went out a hunting.   they came in had killed 13 common Deer 2 black taild Deer[1] 1 Goat & 3 Buffaloe   the Goats in this is different from the Goats in the States   they have much longer ears and courser hair.   Drewyer caught 1 beaver.   killed a prarie wolf.[2]   these wolves are larger than a fox—

Monday Septemr 17th   We remained at Pleasant Camp, and Early this morning, Captain Lewis, and several of the party went out hunting, They returned in the afternoon, having killed 13 common deer, 2 black <Color'd> Tail'd deer, 8 Goats, and 3 Buffalo.   The Goats are not like those in the United States, they having much larger Ears & Coarser hair,—   One of our hunters returned in the Evening, having catch'd 1 Beaver in his Trap &

killed a Priari Wolf, The Priari Wolfes are not so large as those in the United States, being very little bigger than a Fox.—

1. Mule deer, *Odocoileus hemionus;* the captains gave it its common name.
2. Coyote, *Canis latrans.*

Tuesday 18th Sept. we Set off from camp pleasant a clear day. passed timbered land on the S. S. hills and prarie on the N. S. passd. an Isd. and a Great nomber of Sand bars. Capt. Lewis in his yesterdays hunt killed a bird not common in the States a bird of pray resembling the Europian magpy. <as> Capt. Clark Drewyer & jo Fields killed 11 deer and one wolf we Camped[1] before night in order to jerk our meat on the S. Side Fields did not join us this night.—

September 18th Tuesday We set off from Pleasant Camp[2] early this morning, having Clear & pleasant weather; we proceeded on, and passed by fine timber'd land, lying on the South side of the River, the land on the North side being hilly Priaries. we met with a great number of Sand Barrs, and an Island lying on the North side of the River, Captain Lewis kill'd in his hunt Yesterday, a bird, which is uncommon in the United States It was a Bird of Prey, and had some resemblance of the Magpie.— The hunters who had went out early this Morning return'd to us; having killed 11 deer, and one Wolf, which was brought to us. We encamped in the afternoon on the South side of the River, in order to Jerk the meat which had been kill'd these two days,

1. A few miles northeast of Oacoma, Lyman County, South Dakota.
2. "Pleasant Camp" appears to be written over an erasure.

Wednesday 19th Sept. we Set off eairly. a clear day. we passed handsom large bottoms on Each Side covered with timber Jo. Fields killed a black tailed Deer & hung it up on the bank of the river. Capt. Clark & 2 men went out to hunt on N. S. at noon we Saw Some buffaloe Swimming the river. we Stoped and Killed 2 of them. proceeded on Capt. Lewis and Drewyer went to hunt on an Island opposit to this Isld. comes in River

called the Souix pass over of the three Rivers.[1]   at the upper end of the
Same Isd. comes in a creek called Elm Creek[2]   up the bluffs abt 2 miles
comes in another Creek called wash creek.   Capt. Lewis and Drewyer Came
to the Boat again.   about 2 miles we passd another Creek called night
Creek,[3] at which place we Camped on the South Side.   Here Drewyer came
to us had killed 2 deer of the black tald kind.—

Wednesday September 19th   We set out early this morning having fine
Clear weather.—   We passed some fine bottoms of land, lying on each side
of the River, well covered with Timber, One of our hunters killed a black
Tailed deer, and hung it on the bank of the River, we put too, and took it
aboard, At Noon, Captain Clark and two of our men went out a hunting on
the North side of the River.—

At noon, we saw some buffalo swimming across the River; we stopped the
boat, and shot 2 of them, which we took on board and proceeded on.—
Captain Lewis and George Drewyer went out to hunt on an Island, opposite
to which Island, is a River called the Souix Passover, of the Three Rivers; at
the upper end of the same Island, comes in a Creek, called Elm Creek, up
the Bluffs about 2 Miles, we paesed a Creek called Wash Creek.—   Captain
Lewis & George Drewyer came to the boat, we proceeded on two Miles; and
passed another Creek, called Night Creek; lying on the South side of the
River, at which place we encamped, George Drewyer return'd to us, having
kill'd 2 deer of the black tail'd kind

1. The "three rivers" are Crow, Elm (or Wolf), and Campbell creeks, behind Des Lauriens
Island, all in Buffalo County, South Dakota.

2. See Clark's entry this day about creek names. Elm Creek may be Good Soldier Creek or
Counselor (Camel) Creek, Lyman County, South Dakota.

3. Another source of confusion; Night Creek may be Counselor (Camel) Creek or Fish
(Brule) Creek, in Lyman County.

Thursday 20th Sept.   Set off eairly   a clear day & fair wind.   passed handsom riseing prarie on N Side and a bottom covered with timber on the S.
Side.   Capt. Clark walked on Shore.   Drewyer and Shields went across a
point withe the horse about 2 miles which was 30 miles round by water,
which is called the Grand bend of the missourie.[1]   at one oClock we halted

to dine.   Capt. Lewis and R. Fields went a hunting.   at 2 oC we proceeded on   passed a long range of bluffs on N. S. of a dark coulour.   out of those and others of the Same kind is where the missourie Gets its muddy colour for this Earth melts like Sugar, and every rain that comes they wash down and the rapidness of the current keeps continualy mixing through the water all the way to the mouth of the Mississippi.   at 7 oC. we Camped² on a large Sand beach on N. S.   here boath the Captains and R. Fields joined us.   had killed 2 Goats and 2 deer   at 1 oClock at night the bank began to fall in So fast we had to raise all hands and go on one mile further before we could Camp.   then crossed the river & Camped again.

Thursday Septemr. 20th   We set off early this morning, having fine weather, we passed 2 Priaries, lying on the North side of the River, and a fine bottom of land, cover'd with timber, lying on the South side.   Captain Clarke walked along shore, two of our Men went with the horse across a point about 2 Miles, which is 36 Miles round it by Water.—   This is the place called the Great bend of the Mesouri River, at 1 o'Clock P. M we halted to dine.   At 2 oClock P. M Captain Lewis, and some of the Men went hunting We proceeded on, and passed a long range of bluffs, lying on the North side of the River, these bluffs were of a black Colour; from those and others of the same kind, it is supposed that the Water of the Mesouri river, derives its muddy colour; the black Mud lying on those black bluffs, melting like Snow at every Rain, and runs rapidly into the River; The current at this place runs very Rapid, so that it keeps the muddy Water, from those bluffs, continually mixing with the Water of the River, adding to which the falling in of the banks of the River, is thought the sole cause, of the Mesouri being muddy from its Mouth upwards.—   at 7 oClock P. M. we encamped on a large sand beach, lying on the North side of the River.—   we were joined shortly after, by both our Captains & one of the Men, they had killed 2 Goats and 2 Deer which they brought with them.—   At 10 o'Clock P. M. (night,) the Bank of the River on the side we were encamped began to fall in, It fell in so fast, that Captains Lewis & Clark, thought it dangerous to continue at our encampment, They order'd all the hands to their Oars, and we proceeded on One Mile and crossed the River before we could find a place fit to encamp upon, where we again Encamped.—

1. The Big Bend of the Missouri River, enclosing land in Lyman County, South Dakota.
2. In Hughes County, South Dakota.

Friday 21st Sept. Set off eairly   a clear day.   proceeded on 4 miles [passed] the bluffs on the [South Side] and came to the End of the bend where it is not more than 2 miles across to our Camp of the 19th Inst. after a journey of 35 miles.   we proceeded on   passed black bluffs on S. S. and handsom plains on N. S.   passd. a ceeder bottom on S. S. and bluffs on the N. Side   passed a creek on the S. S   called Tylors creek.[1]   Camped[2] on the N. Side—

Friday Septemr. 21st   We embarked early this morning, having fine pleasant weather, & proceeded on 4 Miles, we passed some black bluffs, lying on the South side of the River; We proceeded on and passed the end of the great Bend, of the Mesouri River; which we found to be 35 Miles round, and only two Miles across it, from the commencement of it, which we left the 19th instant; we continued on our way, & passed some other Black bluffs, also lying on the South side, and some handsome plains lying on the North side of the River, and some handsome bottoms of land, with fine cedar growing on them; these lay on the South side of the River, the bluffs still continuing as we passed on the North side, We also pass'd a Creek, lying on the So side of the River, called Tylors Creek, and in the Evening, we encamped on the North side of the River

1. Medicine Creek, Lyman County, South Dakota.
2. In Hughes County, South Dakota.

Saturday 22nd Sept. Set off eairly   a foggy morning.   passed Some timber on S. S. high plains on N. S.   about 3 oC we passed a ceeder Isld. one of the 3 Sister where Mr. Louesell had built a fort of ceeder.[1]   it is pickeded in 65 or 70 feet Square a Sentery box at the 2 angles corners   the pickets are 13½ feet above Ground.   in this Square he built a house 45½ by 32½ feet divided into 4 equal parts, one for a common hall one to trade in and one for a famaly house.   opposite this Drewyer & Shields came to us with the horse.   they had killed Several deer and one white wolf.   passed a creek & Isl. of the 3 Sisters   proceeded on   passed an old Indian Camp where we found Some of their dog poles, they answer us for Setting poles. the reason that they are called dog poles is that they tye them to their dogs & they hall their baggage &c. from one Camp to another.[2] we Camped[3] on the N. S.

Saturday Septemr 22nd   This morning we sett out early, having some fog, about 8 oClock A. M. the fog cleared away, and we passed by some Timbered land, lying on the south side, and high plains lying on the North side of the River; about 3 o'Clock P. M. we passed an Island, called Cedar Island, which is one of the Islands call'd the Sisters   On this Island <is> stood a Fort, built by a Monsieur Louselle, This Fort <is> was picketted   The pickets being of red Cedar 13½ feet high, and <is> was built in the form of a square; the length of each side being 70 feet, and had a Centry Box at the two Angles corners, In the Center of this square stood a house, 45½ by 22½ feet, which was divided equally, into four appartments.   The one appartment being occupied as a common Hall, one as a Store for trading with the Indians, one as a lodging Room, and the other for Cooking in &ca. by Monsieur Louselle at the time he resided there.—   The situation of this Fort <is> was a handsome one it commanding a <handsome> most delightful View of the River & the land lying on both sides of it for a considerable distance and had some beautiful Groves of Cedar, and other Trees on it The Island is 1½ Miles in length and the soil very rich.—   The two Hunters that were out joined us here, having the horse with them.—   the Horse was loaded with several carcases deer they had killed <and the White> and a White Wolf Skin the wolf <skin also which> one of them Shot.—   We proceeded on, and passed a Creek, and another of the Sister Islands; and also passed an Indian camp where some, of <the> Our Men landed, they found some poles, which the Indians call dog poles, These poles the Indians tie to their dogs & they hawl their baggage on them, from one Camp to another as they Remove.—   We brought too, and took the Men & poles on board, (they answering us for setting poles for the boat).—and proceeded on, and in the Evening encamped on the North side of the River on its bank

1. Régis Loisel built Fort aux Cedres in 1800, or perhaps two years later, for the Sioux trade. It was on later Dorion Island No. 2, Lyman County, South Dakota, but the site was not precisely determined before the island was inundated by Big Bend Reservoir.

81

2. A dog travois, used extensively by the Plains Indians before the introduction of the horse, and to some extent afterward.

3. In Hughes County, South Dakota, nearly opposite the mouth of Loiselle Creek (see Clark's entry for this date).

Sunday 23rd Sept. we Set out eairly a clear morning. passed Some timber on the N. S. high land on the S. S. passed a creek on the N. S. called Smoak creek.[1] R. Fields went out to hunt we passed Elk Island at the lower end of the long reach. a handsom bottom on the N. S. and barron hills on the S. Side. At 6 oC in the evening we Seen 4 Indians on the S. S. we Camped[2] on the N. S. and three of them Swam over to us they belonged to the Souix nation. they Informed us that their was more of their nation not far off we Set them back over the river again R. Fields joined us here had killed one Goat.

Sunday Septemr 23d We set out early this morning, having fine clear weather, we passed by some bottom land on the North side, cover'd with heavy Timber, and high land lying on the South side of the River which appear'd to be very rich & the Soil black, we also passed a Creek lying on the North side of the River, called smoak creek, here we stop'd the boat; and sent out one of our Men to hunt; we proceeded on <and passed on to> our way till we arrived at an Island call'd Elk Island, which lies at the lower end of a long reach, it having a handsome bottom of land on it which runs its whole length, Elk Island lies on the North side of the River, and on the South side <is> lay barren Hills, In the Evening we saw four Indians on the South side of the River; We came too, & encamped on the North side, shortly after we had encamped, three of those Indians, swam the River over to us, they belonged to the Soux Nation. They informed us by our Interpreter, that there was more of their nation, not farr off, from where we were encamped We put the Indians again across the River in our pettyauger where we met with one of our Hunters, who had killed a Goat which he brought with him.—

1. Chapelle Creek, Hughes County, South Dakota.
2. In Hughes County, just below the mouth of Antelope Creek on the opposite side.

Monday 24th Sept.   Set off eairly   passed a Small creek[1] on the S. Side about 3 oClock Coulter came up the bank and told us that he had went on an Island this morning, and while he was their the Indians Stole the horse, he had killed 2 Elk   one perogue Stopd. to dress & take them on board. we saw 5 Indians on the bank but we could not understand them nor them us.   we ankred the boat out in the river to wait for the perogues.   one came up   we then proceeded on to the mouth of the Teton River[2] on the S. Side where we ankered out 100 yards from Shore and all the men remained on board except the Guard & the cooks.   we had one frenchman[3] on board who could Speak a little of their language.   they told us that their chiefs would come to See us tomorrow.   they Sayd that if their young men had taken the horse they would Git him again.   these are a band of the Souix nation called the Tetons.[4]   those 5 we Saw on Shore Stayed all night.

Monday September 24th   This morning we set off early, & passed a small Creek, lying on the South side of the River, About 3 oClock P. M. One of our Men named Coulter, that was out a hunting, came to the bank of the River, and informed Captain Lewis that he had been On an Iland to hunt this morning; and while he was there, some Indians had stole the Horse he had left on the shore, he had killed 2 Elk, Captain Lewis order'd one of the Pettyaugers to stop, and take them on board.   in a short time after, 5 Indians came to the bank of the River, they spoke to us in their language, but none on board of the boat could understand them, neither could they be made to understand what we said to them.— We anchor'd the Boat out in the River, to waite for the Pettyaugers that were a distance behind us.   after waiting some time, <one> they came up to us, We weighed our Anchor, and proceeded on, till we arrived at the Teton River; which lies on the South side of the River Mesouri.   we anchor'd the boat out, opposite the Mouth of the Teton River, at about 100 Yards distance from the Shore, & all the Men re-main'd on board, except the Guard & the Cooks, We had among the french Canadians that were with us, One Man that could speak, and understand a little of the language, that was Spoken to us by those 5 Indians, that came to the bank of the River; by him we learnt that they said their Chiefs, would come and see us tomorrow; and added, if their Young Men had taken the

Horse, they would get him for us again.— These Indians are a Band of the Souix Nation called the Tetons. Those 5 Indians came, and staid on the Shore opposite the boat all this Night.—

1. Antelope Creek, Stanley County, South Dakota.
2. Bad River, Stanley County, opposite Pierre.
3. Probably Cruzatte or Labiche, speaking Omaha.
4. Teton Sioux; see Clark's entry for this date.

Chapter Fifty-Six

Winter at the Knife River

September 25, 1804–April 6, 1805

Tuesday 25th Sept.   We delayed to wait for the Indian chiefs and warries to come which we expected.   about 10 OClock they came about 50 in nomber.   our officers made three of them chiefs,[1] and Gave them meddels & Some presents.   5[2] of them came on board & Stayed a long time.   Capt. Clark and Some men took them to Shore in a perogue.   the Indians did not incline to let us Go on any further up the river.   they held the cable of the perogue and Said that they wanted one perogue at least to Stay as they were poor.   Capt. Clark insisted on Going on board but they resisted for a long time.   they Sd. they had Soldiers on Shore as well as he had on board. Capt. Clark told them that he had men and medican on board that would kill 20 Such nations in one day.[3]   they then began to be Still and only wished that we would Stop at their lodges untill their women & children would see us.   4 of them came on board again, & we proceeded on 1 mile and ankered out at the lower point of an Island in the middle of the river.[4]   the 4 Indians stayed with us all night.

Tuesday Septemr 25th   We waited at an Anchor this morning, in expectation of the Indian Chiefs and Warriors arrival here.   about 10 o'Clock A M they came to the bank of the River, there was fifty in number; our officers went on shore to them, where they held a Council, and made three of them Chiefs, and gave them Medals, and some presents.   five of those Indians came on board the boat, and staid a considerable time; they were curious in examing our boat, having never seen one of the kind before— Our Captain returned on board, fearing some treachery from those Savages.— Captain Clarke and some of the Men went on Shore afterwards in one of the Pettyaugers.— He found that the Indians inclined not to let us pass any further up the Mesouri; on his going to leave the Shore, a number of them held to the Cable of the Pettyauger, saying, they wanted one of the Pettyaugers to stay behind with them, as they were poor. Captain Clark insisted on going on board, but they resisted him for a long time— they told Captain Clarke, that they had Soldiers on shore, as well as he had Soldiers on board his Canoes; Captain Clarke then told them that he had Men and Medecine on board the boat, & Pettyaugers, that would kill twenty such nations in a day.— They then began to be still, and only said, they wished that we would stop at their lodges, untill their Women & chlldren could see us & our boats.—

Four of the Indians came on board of our boat, and we proceeded on one Mile; and Anchor'd the Boat & Pettyaugers out in the River, at the lower point of an Island, which lay in the middle of the River. Those Indians that came on board the boat staid with us this Night.—

1. Black Buffalo, Buffalo Medicine, and Partisan.

2. The chiefs named above and probably Warzingo and Second Bear (see Clark's entry), but perhaps some unnamed "soldiers."

3. Clark says only that "I felt my Self warm & Spoke in very positive terms."

4. The captains called it Bad Humored Island, for obvious reasons. It is probably later Marion Island, Stanley County, South Dakota, opposite Pierre.

Wednesday 26th Sept. we Set off eairly   proceeded on 4 miles   all the way on the S. Shore was covered with Savages.[1]   at 10 oClock we came to where the whole band had formed a circle of their lodges & pitched in the best order possable.   we ankered out about 100 Yards from Shore.[2]   Capt. Lewis the 4 chiefs & 4 or 5 men went on Shore.   the natives appeared peacable & kind.   Capt. Lewis came on board & Capt. Clark went out.   when the Indians Saw the officers comming they Spread a buffaloe Robe on the Ground and they Set down on it, then it was taken up by 4 warries and carried to the Grand chiefs lodge.   they killed Several fat dogs which they call the best meat that ever was.   at night the women assembled and danced untill 11 oC. at night.   then our officers came on board and 2 chiefs with them.

Wednesday Septemr 26th   We set out early this morning, and proceeded on four Miles.—   as we passed along, the South shore was covered with Indians, at 10 o'Clock we came to where the whole band of these Savages,[1] had their lodges.   They were placed in the form of a Circle, and pitched in the best order possible, We anchor'd our boat, & Pettyaugers 100 Yards from the Shore.—

Captain Lewis, the four Indian chiefs that had staid aboard of <us> our boat; & five of our Men shortly after went ashore, in one of the Pettyaugers. The Indians met them, and behaved very peacable, and kind to them.   In a short time Captain Lewis returned, with the Men on board.—   Captain Lewis and Captain Clark in about an hour, went on Shore again, when the Indians perceived our officers coming; they spread a buffalo Robe on the ground, and our Officers at landing set down on it.   The Robe was then taken hold of, by four of their Warriors, and they were carried to the Grand Chiefs lodge, where they remain'd till an entertainment was prepar'd for them.   <The Indians killed several> this consisted of several of their fattest dogs which the Indians had killed & which they Roasted, esteeming dogs flesh, as the best of Meat, which they had served up to our Captains, and their Warriors & chiefs.—   As soon as night had set in, the Indian Women assembled, and commenced dancing, which lasted 'till about eleven o'Clock P. M. (at night,) when our Captains came on board, and brought two of their chiefs with them.—

1.   The word "Savages" is written over "Indians."
2.   In Stanley County, South Dakota, about four miles north of Fort Pierre.

Thursday 27th Sept. 1804.   we Stayed here this day.   Capt Lewis and Some of the party went over to See the Indians Camps.   their lodges are about 80 in nomber and contain about 10 Souls Each, the most of them women and children.   the women are employed dressing buffaloe hides for to make themselves cloathing and to make their lodges &c.   they are or appear as yet to be the most freendly people I ever Saw but they will Steal and plunder if they can git an oppertunity. they are verry dirty the vessels they carry their water in is the pouch of their game which they kill and in the Same manner that they take them out of the animel. they gave us different kinds of victules to eat. Some of it I never Saw the like before.[1] about 15 days ago they had a battle with the Mahars. they killed 65 men and took 25 women prisoners. they took the 65 of the Mahars Sculps and had them hung on Small poles, which ther women held in their hands when they danced. we Saw them have one dance this evening. they kept it up untill one oclock dancing round a fire about 80 of them in nomber. they had drums and whistles for musick. they danced war dances round the fire which was curious to us. when we came on board an axedant happened by running the perogue across the bow of the boat and broke our cable and lost our anker all hands was raised and roed the barge to Shore. the Sav-ages ran down to know what was the matter. we told them they Said that they came to our assistance we thanked them for Showing their good will but kept on our guard all night for fear they would turn our enimies themselves.—

Thursday Septemr 27th We remain'd at same place at Anchor this day, Captain Lewis & some of our party went ashore to see the Indian Encamp-ment; and carried the two Indian Chiefs with him.— Their encampment consisted of Eighty lodges, in number; and contained ten Souls in each, the most part of them Women and Children, The women were employed dress-ing Buffalo hides, to make themselves Cloathing, and to make their lodges, they appear'd to be the most friendly people I had ever seen as Savages, but they will steal and plunder if they can get an opportunity to do so; They are very dirty in regard to the Vessells that they carry their Water in.— This being the Paunch of the Animals they kill, and Water is put into it, in the same condition, as it is taken from the Animal.— They gave us Victuals to eat, which was different from what we had ever before seen or tasted, as I was one of the party that came ashore with Captain Lewis, I had an opportunity of seeing what I have here mention'd in regard to these Indians— They inform'd Captain Lewis (by the frenchman our Interpreter) that fifteen days before this time, that they had a battle with the Mahaw Indians, and that they had killed Sixty five of their Men and had taken Twenty five of their Women

Prisoners, who was then here   they took the Scalps off those 65 Mahaws, <which they had there with them> and had them hung on small Poles, which the Women held in their hand, when they danced the evening before, This Evening they commenced dancing again, which they continued to do till one oClock in the morning, there was about 80 of them, & they danced round a fire, and had a drum made out of a hollow piece of wood with a Skin stretch'd over it & some whistles of their own making for music.—   They danced their Warr dance, which was a curiosity to us—   We put off from the Shore, to go on board the boat; when the Pettyauger running across the Bow of the boat, broke the Cable of the boat, & we lost her Anchor.—   This caused all the hands to be roused, and the Oars to be manned immediately, which being done, the Boat was rowed towards the Shore, The Indians observing the Boat coming to the shore, where they was; got alarmed.   numbers of them came to the bank of the River, and enquired, what was the matter;   They were told by our Interpreter the cause; at which they seem'd satisfied, and said, that they came to assist us.   The Interpreter thanked them for showing their good will.—

Our officers fearing the treachery of these Indians, kept up a strong guard this night, not wishing to lay it in the power of these Indians to do us any injury, as the boat lay under the bank of the River & fasten'd to a Stake with the remainder of the Cable.—

1. Clark's entry of September 26 mentions pemmican, dog, and "ground potatoe" (perhaps Indian potato, ground nut, *Apios americana* Medic.).

Friday 28th Sept. 1804.   we draged the river in hopes to find our anker but it was in vain.   about 9 oClock we went to Set off   Some of the chiefs was then on board and concluded to go a little ways with us.   when we were about to Shove off a nomber of warries on Shore caught hold of our cable and another whiped of[f] the children   the women went off also   only about 60 warries on the edge of the bank and we jest under the bank.   Some of them had fire arms and the rest had Good bows and arrows ready for war. the consequence had like to have been bad as Capt. Lewis was near cutting the cable with his Sword and giving orders for the party to fire on them. then the chiefs went out and Spoke to them.   they Said if we would Give

them a carrit of tobacco they would loose the rope.   we gave them tobacco.
the chief after Some hesitation loosed the rope himself.   we then Set of[f]
under a fine breese of wind.   passed high land on N. S. & bottom on S. S.
Saw an Indian[1] comming up the Shore.   we hoisted a white flag, and a red
flag for peace or war, and was determined to fight our way, if we could not
Go without.   Capt. Lewis Got into a perogue and went on Shore to See what
the Indian wished brought him on board.   he Informed us that 300 more
of Savages had arived at the village they wished us to Stop and talk with them,
but we did not Stop.   he remained on board.   about Sunset we ankered out
near a Small Sand bar in the middle of the river for to Stay all night.[2]

Friday September 28th   This morning the hands were all employed, (excepting the Guard) in dragging for our Anchor and Cable; but without any
success, about 9 oClock A. M. we went to sett off.   some of the Indian Chiefs
was then on board of the boat, and concluded to go a little way with us, We
then proceeded to shove off the boat, a number of their Warriors who were
on the shore caught fast hold of the Cable, one of their Warriors drove off
their Women and Children from the Boat, Whilst about Sixty of their Warriors stood on the Edge of the bank of the River; and our boat lay just under
the bank of it.   The Warriors were all Arm'd some of them had fire Arms,
and the remainder Bows & Arrows, they appeared all ready for Warr, which
would have been attended with dangerous consequences to us, they having
such a superiority to us in regard to Number.—   Captain Lewis was going
to cut the Cable of the Boat with his sword; and to give Orders for our party,
to fire on the Indians.   When their chiefs who were on board the Boat; went
out and spoke to them, they told our Officers that if they would give the
Warriors that held the Rope, a few Carrots of Tobacco; that they would loose
the Rope.   The Officer then threw <a> some Carrotts of tobacco among
them, and they left the Rope and ran to get it, One of the Chiefs which had
been on board, the boat after some hesitation loosed the Cable.—
    We then set out with a fair breeze of Wind, and passed some high land,
lying on the North side of the River; and fine bottoms of land, lying on the
South side of the River, We proceeded on, when we espied an Indian coming
running up the Shore, the Officers order'd a White flag, and one of Red to
be hoisted, as a sign to the Indians, that we were either for peace, or Warr;

they being determined if we could not proceed on without fighting, that it should be the case; but if possible, to get on peacably;   Captain Lewis got on board one of the Pettyaugers, and proceeded to shore, to see what the Indian wanted, and to gain what information; he could from him, respecting the intention of the Indians toward us; Captain Lewis soon returned, and brought the Indian on board with him;—

This Indian told the Officers, that Three hundred more Indians, had arrived at the Village, that we had just left; and that they wished us to stop, and have a talk with them.— and that he had come to us, for that purpose; Our officers proceeded on with the Boat & Pettyaugers, not wishing to have any further connection with such a banditti of Villains.— The Indian remained on board the boat with us, at Sun set we anchor'd the Boat & Pettyaugers out near a Sand Barr, lying in the middle of the River; Where we remained 'till the morning— The Tribe of the Teton Indians are part of the Soix Nation, they inhabit on both sides & near the Mesouri River.   They are a fierce looking Sett of Savages, & chiefly delight in Warr, plundering &ca.— they are stout well made Indians and their Women are in general handsome, If I may be allowed to judge from those which I saw in the lodges that we left Yesterday.—

1. Buffalo Medicine.

2. About three miles above Oahe Dam, between Hughes and Stanley counties, South Dakota; the area is now inundated by the reservoir.

Saturday 29th Sept. *1804.*   we Set off eairly.   proceeded on   passed bluffs on S. S.   Saw Several Indians on Shore 1 or 2 of the brave men as they called themselves, wanted Some tobacco.   the Officers gave them 2 carrits of tobacco but told them that we Should not Stop untill we Got to the RickRee I.[1] Nations.   passed an old village[2] on S. S. where the Ricka-Rees had lived 5 years ago, had raised corn beans [peas and Simblins?][3] Camped[4] on a Sand beach on the S. Side.—

Saturday Septemr. 29th   We set off early this morning, having fine clear Weather, and passed by several Bluffs lying on the South side of the River, we saw several Indians on the shore as we passed along, One or two of them, (brave Men as they called themselves,) told the Officers that they wanted some Tobacco, The officers gave them two Carrots of Tobacco, and told them, that we should not stop 'till we got to the Rickoree nation, We proceeded on, and passed an old Indian Village, lying on the South side of the River; where the Rickorees had lived five Years before; and we were inform'd by one of the frenchmen, that was with us, that they had raised Corn, Beans, pease & Simblins at that place, We proceeded on, and encamped in the Evening, on a Sand Beach lying on the South side of the River.—

1. Arikara Indians.

2. An Arikara village on Chantier Creek, Stanley County, South Dakota, believed to have been abandoned about 1794.

3. The peas could be Indian potato, or hog peanut, *Amphicarpa bracteata* (L.) Fern. Simlins are summer squashes.

4. Clark says they camped on an island, which would be between Stanley and Sully counties, South Dakota, about three and one-half miles above Chantier Creek.

Sunday 30th Sept. 1804. Set off eairly. a cloudy morning. we proceeded on Saw a Great nomber of Indians on the S. S. comming down the river. we halted a fiew minutes and Gave them Some tobacco & Spoke a fiew words to them, and went on under a fine breeze of wind towards night the waves ran & our boat rocked So that it Skared our old Indian which was on board He was afraid to go any further with us, and went out on Shore in order to return to his nation. we Camped[1] on the N. S. of the river.—

Sunday Septemr 30 We set off early this morning, having cloudy weather, We proceeded on, & saw a great number of Indians, on the South side of the River; Running down to the River, The Officers stopped the boat a few minutes, and gave them some Tobacco, The Interpreter[2] spoke a few Words to them; they belonging to the Souix nation; which is by farr the most numerous Tribe of Indians, that Inhabit along the Mesouri, We proceeded on with a favourable breeze of Wind, towards evening, the Waves ran very high, and our boat Rocked exceedingly—

The Indian who was on board the boat, was so much frightened at the boat rocking,— that he requested to be put on shore; being afraid to venture any further with us.—

We landed this Indian on the shore, after the Officers had made him some presents, and he took a friendly leave of us and returned towards his nation— We proceeded on 'till Evening, and encamped on a Bank lying on the North side of the River.—

1. Either on Cheyenne Island, just below the mouth of Cheyenne River, or on the nearby shore of Sully County, South Dakota.
2. Perhaps Cruzatte, who spoke the Omaha language and perhaps a little Teton Sioux or Lakota.

Monday 1st October 1804. Set off eairly. a cloudy morning fare wind. we Sailed on rapidly. at 9 oClock we passed dog River[1] which comes in on S. S. we Camped[2] on a Sand bar in the middle of the river, a french trador[3] came to us from the S. Shore.

Monday October 1st This morning we started Early, the weather being cloudy, and a fair Wind, we hoisted all sail and made great headway, At 9 o'Clock A. M. we passed Chien or Dog River, which emties itself into the Mesouri, on the South side of that River; We encamped on a Sand barr; in the middle of the River; at which place, a french Trader came to us from the South shore, and staid with us all night he being one of a party, who was with Louselle & had left him; he left us early in the next morning with his Canoe

1. Cheyenne River, Stanley County, South Dakota. Whitehouse, like the other members of the party, confuses "Cheyenne" and the French *chien*, or dog.
2. In Dewey County, South Dakota, a few miles above Cheyenne River.
3. Jean Vallé, a trader from Ste. Genevieve, Missouri, or a young employee of his.

Tuesday 2 October 1804. Set off eairly. proceeded on. passed a range of black bluffs on N. S. and a large bottom on S. S. about 2 oClock we discovered a nomber of Indians on the hills on N. S. one of them came down on the bank of the river & fired off his Gun and cryed out. we hardly new his meaning but we held ourselves in rediness in case they Should attack us we were determined to fight or dye. proceeded on passed a Creek[1] on the S. S. Camped[2] on a Sand bar in the middle of the river.

Tuesday October 2nd   We set off early this morning, and proceeded on, and passed a range of black bluffs, lying on the North side, and a large bottom on the South side of the River; about 2 oClock P. M. we discovered a number of Indians, on the hills on the North side of the River, One of those Indians came on the bank of the River, and fired off his Gun, and hallowed to us.   We hardly knew his meaning, but stood in readiness, in case <they> any of these Savages should attackt us, Our Officers being determin'd to proceed on our Voyage, at the risque of their lives, and the Men determin'd to support them in the attempt

We proceeded on, and passed a Creek lying on the South side of the River, and in the evening we encamped on a Sand barr, lying in the middle of the River—

1. Besides Whitehouse, only Gass mentions this stream, probably the one that appears on *Atlas* map 24, opposite the party's Caution Island, later Plum Island. It would be in Dewey County, South Dakota, and is now inundated by Oahe Reservoir.

2. Just above Plum Island, between Sully and Dewey counties, South Dakota.

Wednesday 3rd Oct. 1804   a cloudy morning, and Some rain   We Set off at ½ past 7 oClock, proceeded on   at 1 2 oClock the wind blew So hard down the river that we Delayed untill 3 oC. then proceeded on   passed a long range of dark Couloured bluffs on S. S. bottom & Some timber on the N. S. Camped[1] on the South Side.—

Wednesday October 3d   This morning it was cloudy, attended with some Rain, We sett of at half past 7 oClock and proceeded on, the Wind blowing hard down the River from the West; We came too at 9 oClock A. M, and lay by 'till 3 o'Clock P. M.   We then proceeded on, and passed a long range of dark colour'd bluffs, lying on the South side and bottoms covered with heavy Timber lying on the North side of the River.   In the Evening, we encamped on the South side of the River.

1. Near the Potter–Sully county line, South Dakota; see Clark's entry for a discussion of the problems with this day's courses.

Thursday 4 Oct. 1804. Set off eairly. at 9 oClock we halted for breakfast an Indian Swam the river & came to us. proceeded on passed a creek on S. S. called Teed creek[1] Camped on the upper point of an Island.[2]

Thursday October 4th We set out early this morning, at 9 o'Clock A. M. We stopp'd to take our break fast, soon after, an Indian swam the River, and came to us; We proceeded on, and passed a Creek, lying on the South side of the River, called Teel Creek, and in the Evening, we encamped on the upper point of an Island

1. Or "Teel" Creek, as in the fair copy. It is Stove (perhaps actually Stone), or Cherry, Creek, Dewey County, South Dakota.
2. Later Dolphees, or Lafferty, Island, between Dewey and Potter counties, South Dakota.

Friday 5th Oct. 1804.[1] Set off eairly Some whight frost last night. the day clear and pleasant. about 11 oClock we Saw Some Goats Swimming the river. one of our hunters Shot 4 of them. passed a creek on the N. S. called hidden Creek.[2] we killed a prarie wolf Swimming in the river passed a creek on the S. S. called whight Goat creek.[3] Camped[4] on the S. Side.

Friday October 5th This morning we had a White frost, we set out early, the day being clear & pleasant; we proceeded on about 11 o'Clock A. M. we saw some Goats swimming the River, one of our Hunters pursued them in a Pettyauger & killed four of them, which was brought on board— We continued on, and passed a Creek, lying on the North side of the River called hidden creek Shortly after we saw a Priari Wolf swimming across the River, which One of the Men Shot & we got on board—
We proceeded on, and passed a Creek, lying on the South side of the River, called white Goat Creek, and encamped in the Evening on the South side of the River—

1. The "4" in 1804 is written over either a "5" or "6."
2. Little Cheyenne River, or Cheyenne Creek, Potter County, South Dakota.
3. If this is Whitehouse's hand, and it appears no different from other writing of the jour-

nalist designated No. 1, he has misspelled "white." Clark called it White Brant Creek, a name it retained until late in the nineteenth century; it is now Swift Bird Creek, Dewey County, South Dakota.

4. In Potter County.

Saturday 6th Oct. Set off eairly. clear & pleasant. about 11 oC we were passing a bottom covered with timber on the S. S. 2 of our hunters went out and killed 1 Elk. in this bottom a band of the Rick a rees lived last winter. they left a nomber of round huts covered with earth, and Some water crafts made out of buffaloe hides.[1] proceeded on passed a creek[2] on the S. S. we Camped[3] on a Sand beach on N. S.

Saturday October 6th We set off early this morning, having clear pleasant Weather and continued on 'till 11 oClock A. M. and passing by a bottom covered with heavy Timber, one of our Hunters went on shore, and killed an Elk in this bottom, where we found a Band of the Rick ARees Indians had lived, during the last Winter, They had left a number of round huts, which was cover'd with Earth, and some Water Crafts made out of buffalo Hides—

We stopped and took the Man & Elk on board, and proceeded on, and passed a Creek lying on the South side of the River, and in the Evening We encamped on the bank lying on the North side of the River.—

1. Bullboats, buffalo hides stretched over a hemispherical frame.

2. Mentioned by Gass and Ordway, but not by Clark; perhaps Four Bears Creek, Dewey County, South Dakota.

3. At Swan Creek, Walworth County, South Dakota.

Sunday 7th *Oct. 1804.* we Set off eairly. a clear day. passed a creek on the N. S. Goodrich[1] and a Small River[2] on the S. S. called Sir war about 90 yards wide. at the mouth of this River is a wintering camp of the Rickarees having about 60 lodges. we Saw 2 of the Souix indians on the N. S. Capt. Clark killed a Deer and a brarow. we Camped[3] on the N. S. opposite the head of an Island.—

Sunday October 7th This morning we had clear weather. We set out Early and passed a Creek lying on the North side of the River, and a small

River lying on the South side of the same, this River is called Sirawa, and is about 70 Yards wide at its Mouth.— At the Mouth of this River <is> We saw, a Wintering Camp of the Rick a Rees Indians, containing about 60 lodges; We saw two of the Souix Indians on the North side of the River. Captain Clark went on Shore on the South side of the River, & killed one deer and a brarerow which was brought on board. We encamped on the North side of the River, opposite the head of an Island.—

1. No one else attaches Silas Goodrich's name to Clark's Otter Creek, now Swan Creek, Walworth County, South Dakota.

2. Moreau River, Dewey County, South Dakota.

3. Just above Blue Blanket Island, Walworth County, near Mobridge.

Monday 8th Oct. 1804   we Set off eairly, a pleasant morning.   we passed a run on the S. S. called Slate run.[1]   proceeded on   about 12 oClock we passed the mouth of Marroppy River.[2]   we came to the upper end of an Island[3] where one band of the Rick a rees live.   we camped[4] above the Isd on the S. S.

Monday October 8th   We set off early this morning, having pleasant Weather, we passed a Run of water lying on the south side of the River called Slatt Run, and proceeded on, about 12 o'Clock A. M we passed the Mouth of the Marrapy River, and came to the upper end of an Island, where One band of the Rick a Rees Indians lived, and Encamped above the Island on the South side of the River.—

1. Deadman Creek, Corson County, South Dakota.

2. Clark's Maropa River is present Oak Creek, Corson County. Gass and Ordway, however, seem to confuse it with Clark's "We tar hoo," the Grand River, also in Corson County, a little below Oak Creek. Whitehouse does not give enough detail for us to be sure whether or not he repeats this confusion.

3. Later Ashley Island, site of an Arikara village.

4. In Corson County, between Oak (or Rampart) Creek and Fisher (or Cathead) Creek.

Tuesday 9th Oct. 1804.   a Stormy day.   we delayed here all day in order to counsel with this nation   their is 2 frenchmen[1] lives with the natives. they all appear to us verry friendly.—

Tuesday October 9th   This day we had Stormy weather, we lay by, in Order to hold a Councill with the Rick a Ree Indians, Two frenchmen who reside among them, who came to us, and appear very friendly to us & stay'd during the night in our Camp

1. Pierre-Antoine Tabeau, a trader, and either Joseph Gravelines or Joseph Garreau, interpreters.

Wednesday 10th Oct. 1804.[1]   our officers held a counsel with the natives and gave them Some presents.

Wednesday October 10th   This morning some of our Men, with the Two frenchmen that stayed with us during last night, went off to the Indian Village, they found <there to be> that Village to contain 60 lodges in number, forming 16 Square <in> the whole forming a Circle of about 30 feet <they are>   These lodges were about Six feet high—   The lodges are constructed by laying poles from One fork to the other, and the whole is laid on, in the like manner and they had cover'd the Tops of them over with Willows and Grass, and a thick Coat of mud over all, and had left <in> a hole in the Top which served for a chimney—and a place for a door, at the entry place.—   The<ir> labour is chiefly performed by their Squaws, The Men returned, with three bands of the Rick a Rees, being the whole Nation; and our Officers held a treaty with them on the bank of the River, and made them some presents, And gave them a talk, which they received & seemed highly pleased & They went back to their Villages in the Evening—

1. This entry in the original version and those for October 11–15 have large "X"s crossed through them.

Thursday 11th Oct. 1804.   about 12 oClock the natives came to our camp & Gave us Some corn beans & Squashes & wished our officers to Speak a good word for them at the Mandans, for they Said they wished to make peace.

Thursday October 11th   This day at 12 o'Clock the Indians came to our Camp, and brought to us some Corn, Beans and squashes; They requested of our officers, by their Interpreter, to speak a good word for them to the Mandan Nation of Indians, as they wished to make a peace with them, which our Officers agreed to do.   they mention'd, that they wished to be at peace with all Nations.   At One o'Clock we proceeded on our Voyage, and passed a Creek[1] lying on the South side of the River 20 Yards wide.   about 4 oClock P. M. We came to the Village of the Rick A Rees, they had a Flag hoisted which Captain Lewis had given them the day before.   Their Village is built in a Priari, on the South side of the River, in the same manner that the other Villages were built.   We encamped[2] this night on the South side of the River.—

1. Possibly Clark's Kakawissassa Creek, later Cathead Creek, now Fisher Creek, Corson County, South Dakota.
2. In Campbell County, South Dakota.

Friday 12th Oct. 1804.   about 12 oclock we Set off.   one of the natives went with us, to go as far as the Mandans.   we Camped[1] on the N. S. of the River—

Friday October 12th   This morning we had pleasant weather, the Indians that had been with us, the last Evening, we found had stole one of our Axes, about 2 o'Clock P. M. we set off, one of the Indians came to the Boat & embarked with us, We proceeded on till 4 oClock P. M. and encamped on the North side of the River, We had been encamped but a short time, when some Indians came to the opposite side of the River and called to us, to bring them over.   One of the Pettyaugers was sent, and brought them, they remain'd with us during the Night.—

1. In Campbell County, South Dakota.

Saturday 13th Oct. 1804.   we Set off eairly clouday, about 12 oclock it rained some.   we halted 2 hours.   then proceeded on untill dark and camped[1] on the N. S.

Saturday October 13th   We set out early this morning, the weather being Cloudy, we passed a River, called Pond River[2] lying on the North side of the

Mesouri. it is 50 Yards wide at its mouth where one of the Rick a Ree Squaws we had on board the boat left us, three Indians still remain'd with us at 12 oClock A. M. we had some Rain we stopped with the Crafts for two hours, & then proceeded on till dark & Encamped on the North side of the River—

1. In Campbell County, South Dakota, about a mile south of the North Dakota state line.

2. The name reflects its supposed origin in a nearby small lake; it is Clark's Stone Idol Creek, now Spring, or Hermaphrodite, Creek, Campbell County.

Sunday 14th Oct. 1804. cloudy. Some rain. we Set off eairly, proceeded on passed a creek on the S. S.[1] campd.[2] on the N. S. nothing else extraordinary hapened this day.

Sunday October 14th We sett off Early this morning and had some Rain, we proceeded on, & passed some bottoms of fine land, lying on the South side of the River, it continued raining all this day, We encamped on the North side of the River

1. They called this stream Piaheto, or Eagle's Feather, Creek, after an Arikara chief, presumably the one who accompanied them. It is now Bald Head Creek, Corson County, South Dakota.

2. In Emmons County, North Dakota, their first camp in that state, roughly opposite Fire Heart Butte.

Monday 15th Oct. 1804.[1] rained all last night. we Set off eairly.

Monday October 15th[2] We set off early this morning, it having rained the whole of last night; and proceeded on, and passed along about two Miles, where we met a party of the Rick a Ree Indians returning to their Villages, We put to the Shore, and they gave us some deer & buffalo Meat, We proceeded on, and passed a Creek[3] lying on the South side of the River, where there was a Camp of Rick a Ree Indians.—

This is the last Camp of Rick a Ree Indians we expect to see, they were a hunting party— There was in this Camp, about 30 Indians; as we put too to them, they behaved very friendly, they gave us plenty of Meat & we encamp'd near them this Night.—

1. Following this entry in the original version there is a gap in the writing until November 1 where a new writer begins, the person designated No. 2. There are no missing pages; in fact, this entry ends on one side of a sheet and the entry of November 1 begins on the back of the same sheet.

2. Above this entry in the fair copy is a pointing hand; its significance is unknown.

3. Probably either Long Soldier or Porcupine Creek, Sioux County, North Dakota.

Tuesday October 16th[1]   We set out early this morning, and passed a Creek[2] lying on the South side of the River, we continued on 'till the afternoon, when we saw a hunting party of the Rick aRee Indians, who were shooting at a flock of Goats, which were in the River; Some of our Men from One of the boats shot 3 of them which they got on board, We proceeded on, and in the Evening we Encamped[3] on the South side of the River

1. As a result of a gap in the original, the single entries for the period October 16–31 are from the fair copy.

2. Probably Clark's Girl Creek, either Porcupine or Battle Creek, Sioux County, North Dakota.

3. In Sioux County, some two miles above the mouth of Beaver Creek.

Wednesday October 17th   This morning Early we set out, (having sent some of our Men out a hunting) the Wind blowing hard against us at West, so that it occasion'd our getting on slowly, part of the day, The River running strong against us.   We came too, & Encamped[1] on the South side of the River in the Evening; part of the Men return'd to us, having killed 6 deer, which they brought to us, One of the hunting party did come to us this Night.—

1. A mile or two south of the entrance of Cannonball River, Sioux County, North Dakota.

Thursday October 18th   We set out early, and proceeded on about 2 Miles, where we met 2 frenchmen[1] in a Canoe, who informed our Officers, that they had been up at the Mandan Nation, Trapping Beaver, and on their return, that they were robbed, by a party of the Mandan Indians, who had taken their Traps & furrs from them; <and that> as they were returning back to the Rick a Ree nation   The owner of the Traps & fur, was one of the french men that we had with us, (Monsier Gravellin)   The two frenchmen returned with us, being in hopes to Recover their Traps & fur from the Indians—

We proceeded on, and passed a small River, lying on the South side of the River; which is called Cannon Ball River,[2] when we put too, and sent several of our Men out a hunting.   we went on, and passed a Creek,[3] lying on the North side of the River, called fish Creek, we continued on, and encamped[4] on the South side of the River.—   Our hunters all came to us, having with them 6 deer, 4 Goats, 3 Elks, and one pelican that they had killed.—   The mouth of the River bullet or Cannon ball River, lies in Latitude 46° 29′ N

1. One of them was perhaps Francis Fleury *dit* Grenier, an employee of Gravelines. For further discussion see Clark's entry of this date.
2. Cannonball River is on the border between Sioux and Morton counties, North Dakota.
3. Long Lake, or Badger Creek, Emmons County, North Dakota.
4. In Morton County, a little above Rice Creek.

Friday October 19th   This morning being clear, we sent our Hunters out, and proceeded on our Voyage with a fair Wind; we passed a Creek, lying on the South side of the River, as we passed along we saw a great quantity of Buffalo, Elk, and deer in gangs, We came too in the Evening, and encamped[1] on the North side of the River, our hunters returned, and brought with them 3 Elk & 7 deer—which they had killed this day

1. The site is not certain, but probably in Morton County, North Dakota, a few miles above the town of Huff.

Saturday October 20th   We set off early this morning, having pleasant Weather; and passed a Creek,[1] lying on the North side of the River 20 Yards wide at its mouth, we proceeded on, & passed a River[2] the name unknown and an Island lying on the South side, The land along the River being Rich bottoms, covered with heavy Timber, on both sides of the River, and a great number of Buffaloes, feeding on the Sides of the Hills.—   on the South side of the River   We proceeded on, and in the Evening we encamped[3] on the South side of the River, Our hunters who had went out this morning returned to us, having killed 14 deer 1 Goat and a Wolf, and had wounded a White or brown Bear,[4] which was the first that they had seen, since we enter'd the Mesouri River, They brought in with them the Deer, Goat, and Wolf to our Camp.—

1. Probably Clark's Shepherd's Creek, modern Apple Creek, Burleigh County, North Dakota.

2. Little Heart River, Morton County, North Dakota.

3. About five miles south of present Mandan, Morton County, within Fort Lincoln State Park and nearly opposite Bismarck.

4. Cruzatte had the party's first encounter with the grizzly bear, *Ursus horribilis.*

Sunday October 21st   Last night we had rainy disagreeable Weather, We set out early this morning, Shortly after we had some Snow, we passed a small River, lying on the South side of the Mesouri, called Chief Charet.[1]   We proceeded on till Evening, & encamped[2] on the South side of the River.— Our hunters came to us, having killed a Buffalo, and One Otter[3] which they brought to our Camp

1. One of the more interesting spellings for the Arikara name for the Heart River. See Clark's entry for this day.

2. In or near present Mandan, Morton County, North Dakota.

3. River otter, *Lutra canadensis.*

Monday October 22d   This morning was Cold & Cloudy, We set off about 9 oClock A. M.   we passed on, and saw Eleven of the Souix Indians coming down the River in Canoes, from the Mandan Nation, at One oClock P. M. the weather cleared off and became pleasant   In the Evening we encamped[1] on the South side of the River.—

1. Probably in southeast Oliver County, North Dakota, a little above the Morton County line.

Tuesday October 23d   We set out early this morning.   about 8 oClock it began to snow, we proceeded on, and passed by some Indian Cabbins, which the frenchmen that was with us, informed that they were robbed of their Traps & peltry at, and also pas'd some Rich bottoms cover'd with Timber lying on both sides of the River, this evening, we encamped[1] in a bottom, lying on the South side of the River, which was cover'd with heavy timber, where we found a great quantity of Berries called Rabbit Berries.[2]—

1. Near Sanger, Oliver County, North Dakota.
2. Buffaloberry again.

Wednesday October 24th   This morning was Cloudy, we set off early as usual.   at 9 o'Clock A. M. it began to rain, we stopped the Boat and Petty-augers for about one hour, and then proceeded on, at 12 oClock A. M., we came too, were a party of Indians belonging to the Mandan Nation were hunting, we halted about two hours with them, and then proceeded on our Voyage, 'till the Evening and Encamped[1] on the North side of the River, where five Indians of the Mandan Natlon came to us.—

1. About two miles below Washburn, McLean County, North Dakota.

Thursday October 25   We set off early this morning, having a fair Wind & pleasant Weather, and proceeded on, we saw a number of Indians, walking and Riding along the Shore on the North side of the River, We proceeded on, and in the Evening we encamped[1] on the South side of the River.—

1. In the vicinity of later Fort Clark, in either Oliver or McLean counties, North Dakota, depending on river shifts.

Friday October 26th   This morning we had clear & pleasant Weather, We set off early, at 10 oClock we came too, where a party of the Mandan Indians were hunting, & they were encamped in a River bottom which was cover'd with heavy Timber, on the South side of the River,—   We found with those Indians an Irishman[1] that belonged to the Northwest Company of Traders. We stop'ed with those Indians about one hour, and then proceeded on our way 'till Night, and encamped,[2] on the South side of the River, Some of the Mandan Indians who we found a hunting this day came and staid with us this night

1. Hugh McCracken was apparently an independent trader. See Clark's entry for this day.
2. About half a mile below the Mandan village of Mitutanka (see next entry), perhaps in McLean County, North Dakota, rather than Mercer County, due to later river shifts.

Saturday October 27th   We had pleasant weather, and we set out early, and proceeded on our Voyage.   at 7 o'Clock A. M. we came to the first Village of the Mandan nation of Indians,[1] This Village contain'd between 50 & 60 lodges, built in the same form that the Rick A Ree Indian lodges were built, and is situated on a high plain, which <is> lay on the South side of the Mesouri River,—   The Mandan Indians are in general Stout, well made Men; and they are the lighest coulour'd Indians I ever saw, We stopped at this Village about 2 hours, and then proceeded on, about one Mile above the 2nd Village of the Mandans, and encamped on a lage Sand beach, near a bottom covered with Timber, The officers had encamped here in Order to hold a Council with the Mandan nation & the Gross Vaunter & Water Soix[2] nation of Indians who all reside near each other, and are friendly to one another, These Indians do not bury their deceas'd as the other nations living on the Mesouri do, The manner in which they treat them, is by placing them on a high Scaffold, wrapped up in Buffalo Robes, we saw Several of their deceased placed on Scaffolds, and was inform'd of it being their custom by the Interpreters among us.—   It was about 11 o'Clock A. M., when we arrived at this place, the distance from where we enter'd the Mouth of the Mesouri River being 1,610 Miles.—

1. Mitutanka village, Clark's Matootonha, but known to archaeologists as the Deapolis site, Mercer County, North Dakota.
2. Another interesting variation by Whitehouse or his scribe. The writer is using the French term *Gros Ventres*, "big bellies," who were also called Watersoons (spelled variously); they are Hidatsas.

Sunday October 28th   This morning, we had fine clear weather, which continued the whole day, the wind commenced blowing and blew so hard, that we could not sit in Council with the Savages, The officers had the Flag of the United States hoisted, which continued flying the whole of this day & we remain'd still at our encampment on the Beach

Monday October 29th   This morning we had fine clear weather.   some of the Head Chiefs and Warriors of the Mandan Indians & the Gross Vaunters & Water Souix Chiefs came to our Encampment, in Order to hold a Council with our Officers.   At 11 oClock A. M. the Council commenced, and One of our Swivels was fired off—

Our officers then took the Chiefs of the Indians by the hand, and Captain Lewis <made> deliver'd a Speech to them, all, which lasted some time, and was Interpreted by our Interpreter to them,—   at which they seemed highly pleased   The Council being over, he gave presents among them of Goods & Cloathing and to each Nation he gave an American Flag, he also gave to the Mandan Chiefs a Steel Corn Mill, and by Interpreter explained the use of it, in grinding of Corn, instead of pounding it, which was the only way they had of making Corn Meal.—   In the Evening the Indians left our Camp and seemed well pleased

Tuesday October 30th   This day we had clear & pleasant weather, the Officers were waiting for an answer to some requests, that they had made to the Indians Yesterday.—   Captain Clark, and several of our Men went in a Pettyauger up the River about 6 Miles to an Island in Order to look out a place for our Quarters during the winter, At 5 o'Clock P. M. he returned and found that the Island would not answer for that purpose, we still remain'd at our Encampment on the Sand beach.—

Wednesday October 31st   This morning we had fine pleasant Weather, the Indians not having sent our Officers an answer to their request yet. about 12 o'Clock A. M. Captain Clark and several of our Men went down to the Second <Town> Village of the Mandan Indians,[1] The head Chiefs of this Village gave Captain Clark between 9 & 10 bushels of Indian Corn and some Buffalo Robes, and behaved to him very friendly.—

The Men that went with Captain Clark found among the Indians at this Village, Corn, Beans, Simlins, and many kind of Garden Vegetables, They & the Rick a Ree nation are the only Indians that we saw that cultivated the Earth, that reside on the Mesouri River.—[2]   Their Village consisted of about 200 Lodges built in the manner, that the Rick a Ree build their

lodges.— This Village we supposed contained 1500 Souls. they were Gov-
ern'd by a Chief called the Black Cat, They behaved extreamly kind to the
party, and the only animal that was among them, was some horses, which are
stout servicable Animals, This Village <is> was situated, on a large high
plain, and they plant in a Bottom lying below it and to appearance are a very
Industrious sett of people,

   1. Ruptáre, McLean County, North Dakota, called the Black Cat site after the village chief
of Lewis and Clark's time.
   2. The Otos, Missouris, Omahas, and Poncas all practiced agriculture, but either the party
did not meet them or Whitehouse did not see their villages.

November thur. 1st 1804.[1]   the wind blew So fresh from the South that
we Could not Get Under Way <In> at the time appointed as the Officers
Intended falling down the [*crossed out, illegible*] the river before two Oclock
P. M., to the place that they wishd. to build a fort.   at dark we arivd. with the
boat and Peirouges 9½ Miles <bel> Below the 2nd vilage of Mandans at a
piece of woods On the N. E. Side whare we Commend. building the fort.—[2]

November 1st Thursday   This morning, we had the Wind blowing hard
from the South, that we could not set off at the time appointed; our Officers
having agreed on, to return down the River, before 2 o'Clock P. M., to a
place that they had concluded on, to build a Fort; at 3 oClock we set of, and
arrived at the place at dark; with the boat and Pettyaugers.   This place lies
9½ Miles below the 2nd village of the Mandan Nation, and <is> lay in a
piece of Woodland, lying on the North side of the River Mesouri, and lies in
Latitude 47° 21′ North.—

   1. Here resumes in the original version the daily entries, now in the hand of No. 2.
   2. They did not actually reach the Fort Mandan site until the next day. The camp for this
day was between that site and Mitutanka village, McLean County, North Dakota.

Friday 2nd November   Began the works of the fort[1]   the weather Continued pleasant for 14 days during which time all the men at Camp Ocepied
thair time dilligentntly in Building their huts and got them Made Comfer-
table in that time to live in—

Friday November 2d   This morning we began to build the Fort, having pleasant weather for 14 days, during which time all hands were busily employed in building of Huts to winter in, they compleated them in that time and made them comfortable to live in.—

1. This day they reached the site of Fort Mandan, McLean County, North Dakota, some fourteen miles west of Washburn, where they would remain until April 7, 1805. The actual site has been washed away by the Missouri.

Saturday 3rd[1]   a party of hunters was Sent down the river with a Peirogue to Bring the meat whome, in the[y] Remaind 15 days, and On the 18th Inst the[y] had good Success   the[y] Killd. 34 deers 10 Elks and 5 Buffelows, in all they had Upwards of 20 hundred Wt.   Nothing Else happnd. Extraordinary—

Untill the 30th Inst. a messenger from the mandans Came to the fort to Inform Our Officers that a hunting party of theirs was Robed by the Sues & Rees,[2] Indians, on the 27th last, of Eight horses and their meat that they had Killd, & Killd One of their men and wounded two Others

the[y] Applyd. for Some Assistance from the fort which Captn. Lewis & Clark Readly granted them.   Twenty Men turnd Out Volentary Under the Command of Captn. Clark out of the fort to goe to fight the Sues   the Guard Set us Across the Missourie at Eleven Oclock at the fort   the Captn. formd. his men On the S. W Side of the river Missourie and told them off in Sections, from the right, and Sent out a Noncommissiond. Officer and a file of men on Each flank to Reconitere the woods at the distance of neerly One hundred Yds. from the head of Company.   After a march of 6 miles we Arivd. at the first Village of mandans, with our two Interprators One of the mandans & one of the Grosvauinties,[3] thinking to be Reignd. forsd. [reinforced] by a party of Each Nation With a Detachment from the <Watoonse> Watesoons Nation like-ways, as they and Groce Vaunties, are Nigh Neighbours to the Mandans Nation   but after we Arivd. At the Village the Cheifs of Both Nations Concluded not to goe to fight as the weather was Cold and the Snow Upwards of 18 Inches Deep on the Ground, before Spring Nixt.

   The Captn. & the party halted two hours at the Village   he told the Cheifs and Warieres of the Mandans that he and his Men was on the Ground Ready to Assist them And the[y] Should See that Him and his Men Could fight.

After Some little Conversation with the Savages, we took Our leave of them and Started for the fort   we Crossd. the river between the first & Second Village On the Ise And Came whome to the fort   Arivd. at dark   the Evening was Cold.   Each Drank Some Good Spirits After which Revivd. Us <much> Very Much And Retird. to Our Rooms Each—

Saturday Novemr. 3d   A party of hunters was this day sent down the River. they carried with them a Pettyauger to bring what Meat they killid on their hunt; they remained down the River a hunting 15 days, and on the 18th November they returned, having had good success in hunting, they brought with them 34 deer, 10 Elk, and 5 buffaloes all weighing 2,000 lbs as near as we could guess.—

Nothing happened extraordinary till the 30th day of November (instant) when an Express arrived from the 2nd Mandan Village, at our Fort; who informed our Officers that a hunting party of theirs was robbed, by the Sues & Rees Indians on the 27th of last Month of Eight horses, and all their meat, & that they had killed one of their Men, and wounded two others, and applied to <the> Our Officers for some assistance from the fort which the Officers readily granted to them.   Twenty of our Men immediately turned out Volunteers, under the Command of Captain Clark to go against those Indians, (the Sues) and the Guard at the Fort set us across the River.— Captain Clark formed his Men on the South West side of the River Mesouri on their landing; and told them off in Sections from the right, and sent a file of Men and a Non commission'd Officer on each flank, to reconitre the Woods, at the distance of nearly 100 Yards from the head of the Company.— After we had marched about 6 Miles, we arriv'd at the first Village of the Mandan Indians, with our Two Interpreters, One for the Mandans & the other for the Grovanters Captain Clark thinking that he would be reinforced by a party, from each nation, and a detatchment from the Watesoons a part of the Nation, who are neighbours to the Mandan Nation, and their friends.—   On our arrival at the Village, the chiefs of both nations, concluded, not to go to fight those Indians with us, they saying the Weather was cold, and the Snow was deep, (being upwards of 18 Inches on the Ground,) and that they should put it off, 'till the next spring—   The Captain halted the party two hours at this Village.   he told the Chief and Warriors of the

Mandan Nation; that he and his Men was on the ground and was ready to assist them, and that they should see that he and his Men could fight.— After the Captain had some more conversation with those Indians, we all took our leave of them, and started for the Fort, we recrossed the River on the ice.— between the first and Second Villages of the Mandan Indians, and came to the Fort, where we arrived at dark. this Evening, being very cold, the Officers had some Whiskey served out to the Men that was on the March which revived them much, & they all Retired to their Huts.—

1. Here the writer summarizes the events for the remainder of the month as it is also given in the fair copy.
2. Sioux and Arikaras.
3. *Gros Ventres,* that is, the Hidatsas.

December 1st Nothing hapend Extraordinary Continued Picquiting in the huts—

December 1st Saturday This day, all our Men, were employ'd in procuring pickets, and picketting in our Fort which the Officers were determined to have made Strong.

2nd[1] the Big white a Cheif of the mandans Came to Our fort in the Morning to Inform Us that the Buffelow was Close to us a Comeing in[2] Captn Lewis and 15 Men turnd. Out to Shoot them the[y] killd 10, And the Indians Killd. 50 the two Captains Lewis & Clark took it in turn day about with a party Each day to goe a hunting And had Great Success until the 15th Inst. that the Buffelow got neerly twenty miles off Captn Clark and his party Returned On the Morning of the 16th[3] Inst. but Could find no game But two deer, the[y] Slept in the woods all night Some Snow fell that made the Air warmir On the Night of the 15th Inst—

Sunday December 2nd Sunday 16th This morning the Big white chief came to our Encampment, he being a head Chief of the Mandan Indians, and informed Our Officers, that the Buffalo were in gangs, close to us, coming from the Priaries, in order to get into the River bottoms, which they always do, when the Snow is on the Ground, in Order to get Buds of Trees, and Grass which is at all times are to be found in the River bottoms, to feed on.— Captain Lewis and fifteen of the Men went out to hunt them— they returned in about 3 hours, having killed Ten Buffalo which was brought to the Fort.— They fell in with a large party of the Mandan Indians on their route, who was also going to hunt Buffalo; the Indians accompanied Captain Lewis, and his party; and had great success, they kill'd 50 Buffalo that day.— From this day to the 15th instant, our Officers took it by turns, with a party of our Men to go out hunting, and met with very great success.— On the 15th instant, they found that the Buffalo had got nearly twenty Miles off from our Fort.— Captain Clark, and his party returned on the Morning of the 16th instant with only two Deer, the Buffalo being entirely gone.— They had remain'd all night in the Woods, & some Snow falling that night (15th instant) the Weather became more moderate, it being extremely Cold the three preceeding days.—

1. In this entry and in the fair copy the writers summarize the events until December 17, where writer No. 1 (presumably Whitehouse) resumes.

2. Clark and Ordway say Big White actually gave this news to the party on December 7.

3. Actually on December 15, according to Clark and Ordway.

Monday 17 Decr. a cold day. Sergt. Gass fixed a horse Sled for one of the N. W. Compy. tradors to go to thier forts with.[1] Some of the Mandans come & Informed us that the buffaloe had come near the River again.—

Monday decemr 17th This day was clear and cold weather. One of our Serjeants fixed a horse sled, for one of the North west traders, a number of that Company Traders being in the two Villages of the Mandan Nation. They trafficed with the natives for Furr, Peltry & Buffalo hides to a very considerable amount, in the afternoon some Mandan Indians arrived at our Camp, and informed our officers, that the Buffaloes had returned near the River again—

1. The trader was probably Hugh Heney; the forts were the North West Company posts on the Assiniboine River in Saskatchewan and Manitoba.

Tuesday 18th Decr. 1804 a verry cold day. 8 of the party went out to hunt, but Saw nothing but Some goats. the N. W. Compy. tradors Set of this morning notwithstanding the coldness of the weather.

Tuesday Decemr 18th This day we had very Cold weather, A party of our Men went out hunting, but saw nothing of the Game kind, but some Goats. The North West Traders left us this morning, having come to take their leave of our Officers and Men, and proceeded on their Journey notwithstanding the coldness of the weather—

Wednesday 19th Decr. 180[5?]. a clear pleasant day. we began to Set up the pickets of our fort.

Wednesday decemr 19th We had clear weather & a pleasant day, all the Men were employed in setting up the pickets of the fort.—

Thursday 20th Decr. 1804[1] a quite warm day. the Snow melted fast. we continued on our work as usal.

Thursday Decemr 20th This day we had moderate weather, the Snow melting fast. the Men were all employed picketting the fort as usual.—

Thursday Decemr 20th[2] The weather continued still moderate our men were still employ'd picketting in, the Fort.—

1. Whitehouse appears to have placed a "4" over a "6" here.
2. A second entry for the day in the fair copy.

Friday 21st Decr. Still pleasant and warm. we continued on our work as usal &c.

Friday Decemr. 21st We had still pleasant Weather, and the Snow continued melting all the Men were employed at fixing up the Pickets as usual.—

Saturday 22nd Dec. 1804   a clear pleasant warm day   a great nomber of the natives came to the fort with corn beans and moccasons to trade.   they take any trifling thing in exchange viz. old Shirts buttons knives awls &c &c.

Saturday decemr 22nd   This day we had fine pleasant weather   in the morning a number of the Natives came to our Fort, and brought with them, some Corn Beans, and moccosins, to Trade with us.—   They exchanged those articles, for old Shirts, buttons, knives &ca. and went away in the Evening seemingly well pleased with their Trade.—

Sunday 23rd Decr. 1804   a clear pleasant day.   we continued our work Setting up the pickets &c.

Sunday Decemr 23d   The weather still continued pleasant   all the Men was still employed setting up the Pickets round the fort.—

Monday 24 Decr. 1805.[1]   Some Snow fell this morning.   about 10 oC cleared off   a fair day.   we finished our fortifycation.   in the evening our Captains contributed to the party Some flour pepper dryed apples &c. to celebrate the Chrisstmas.

Monday decemr 24th   This morning we had some Snow, at about 10 o'Clock A. M. <as> it cleared away, and we had fair weather the remainder of the day, the Men finished picketting in the Fort,—   and made it compleat.—   In the Evening our Officers distributed among the party, flour— dried apples, pepper &ca. that they might celebrate Christmass

1. Whitehouse anticipates the new year.

Tuesday 25th Decr. 1804.[1]   we ushred in the morning with a discharge of the Swivvel, and one round of Small arms of all the party.   then another from the Swivel.   then Capt. Clark presented a glass of brandy to each man of the party.   we hoisted the american flag and each man had another Glass of brandy.   the men prepared one of the rooms and commenced dancing.

at 10 oC. we had another glass of brandy, at one a gun was fired as a Signal for diner. half past two another gun was fired to assemble at the dance, and So we kept it up in a jovel manner untill Eight oC. at night, all without the compy. of the female Seck, except three Squaws[2] the Intreptirs wives and they took no part with us only to look on. agreeable to the officers request the natives all Stayed at their villages all day.—

Tuesday Decemr 25th This morning being Christmass, the day was announced by the discharge of our Swivels, and one Round from our small arms of the whole company; about 7 o'Clock A. M. we fired our Swivels again, when Captain Clark came out of his quarters, and presented a Glass of Brandy to each Man of our party.— He then ordered the American Flag to be hoisted, which being done; he presented them again with another Glass of brandy.— The Men then prepared one of the Rooms, and commenced dancing, we having with us Two Violins & plenty of Musicans in our party.—

At 10 o'Clock A. M. the whole of the party were again served with another Glass brandy they continued dancing 'till 1 o'Clock P. M. when our Cannon was fir'd off, as a signal for dinner, at half an hour past 2 oClock P. M. we fired off our Cannon, and repaired to the Room to dance, which they continued at till 8 o'Clock P. M. There was none of the Mandans, Excepting 3 Squaws our Interpreters Wives at the Fort, the Officer having requested the Natives, to stay in their Towns, which they complied with, the Officers this day named our Fort, Fort Mandan,—

1. From this date until December 31 there is a gap in Whitehouse's writing in both the original journal and the fair copy.

2. Toussaint Charbonneau's two Shoshone wives, one being Sacagawea, and the wife of René Jusseaume.

Monday 31st Decr. 1804[1] nothing particular occured Since christmas but we live in peace and tranquillity in our fort, visited dayly by the natives with Supplys of corn &c.

Monday decemr 31st We had no event of any consequence happened from the 25th Instant to this day, The natives came into our Fort daily, &

brought, Corn, Beans & dried Squashes, in with them   these they exchanged with our party, for some trifles.   the weather continued pleasant &
the Air Serene.—

The Fort which we built here & which we named Fort Mandan,[2] is situated
on the North East side of the Mesouri River.   It <is> was built in a triangular form, with its base fronting the same, had a platform on the No. Side 12
feet high with Pickets on it, six feet, and a Room of 12 feet square, the under
part serving as a Storehouse for provisions &ca.   the three sides were 60 feet
in length each, & picketted on the front side only, with pickets of 18 feet
long & the houses which we resided in lay on the So West side & the Smith
& Armourer Workshop was at the South point of the Fort.

1. About the lower one-third of the page is blank after this entry, and the next entry,
January 1, 1805, begins at the top of the next page, the reverse of the sheet.

2. Only Gass, on November 3, 1804, provides such detailed information on Fort Mandan
and this paragraph is markedly different than his account. Perhaps Whitehouse gave verbal
detail to the copyist.

January 1st 1805.   Tuesday.   2 Guns was discharged from the Swivel to
celebrate the new year, a round of Small arms immediately after by each man
of the party, a Glass of old ardent Spirits was given.   a short time after Capt.
Clark gave another.   about 10 oClock one of the Intrepters & one half of
the party went up to the 1st village of Mandans[1] by their request to dance.
Some time after Capt. Clark and 3 more men Came up also.   the day was
warm and pleasant.   in the afternoon Capt. Lewis Gave another glass.   in
the evening Capt. Clark & Some of the party came home & Some Stayed all
night.

January 1st Tuesday   This being the first day of the Year, we Early this
morning fired off our Swivels twice, and immediately after, fired a Volley of
small Arms, in honor of the day.—   Captain Lewis gave each of the party a
Glass of spirit, which was a short time after, repeated by Captain Clark, about
10 o'Clock A. M. One of our Interpreters, and one half of the Men of our
party; went up to the first Village of the Mandan Nation, by request of their
Chiefs, to dance, they having a desire to see our manner of dancing.   The
party had not been long arrived at this Village, when Captain Clarke and

three more of the Men arrived.— The Men commenced dancing, which the Natives much admir'd, frequently signifying their approbation by a Whoop they gave, In the evening Captain Clark and some of the Men returned, and part of the Men staid all Night at the Village—

1. Mitutanka.

Wednesday 2nd Jany. 1805. Some Snow fell this morning. the rest of the men came from the village, about 10 oClock Capt. Lewis & the rest of the party who had not been went up to the 2nd village,[1] we danced and amused our Selves the greater part of the [day] which pleased the natives &c. in the evening the most of the men returned home. the natives keep their horses in their lodges with themselves every cold night dureing the winter Season & feed them on nothing but the branches of cotton wood which they cut off the Bark, which is Sweet & good. they live on it & look tollarably well.

Wednesday January 2d This morning we had some Snow, our Men that had remained at the Indian Village last night returned; About 10 o'Clock A. M. Captain Lewis, and the remainder of our party, that had staid at the Fort, went up to the 2nd Indian Village of the Mandan nation, the party arrived at the Village where they danced, and amused themselves the greater part of the day.— This pleas'd the Inhabitants of this Village exceedingly.— In the Evening the party returned to the Fort.—

The Mandan Indians in this Second Village had a number of horses, which they keep in their lodges with them, every Cold night during the Winter; they feed the Horses on branches of the Cotton wood trees which is Sweet as well as the bark of the same Tree which they Eat, and subsist on, looking in tolerable good Order

1. Ruptáre.

Thursday 3rd Jany. 1805 Some buffalow came near our fort, 9 men went out but killed none of them. one of the men killed a butiful white hair[1] which is common in this country.

Thursday January 3d   This morning some Buffalo came near our fort, the officers sent out 9 Men to hunt them, they returned but had killed none, One of the hunters killed a beautiful white hare, which is common in this Country.—

1. Probably a white-tailed jackrabbit.

Friday 4th Jany. 1805. the weather is not as cold as it was Some time past. Some hunters went out & 3 of Stayed out all night, the rest came home. had killed one Small buffalow.   in the evening it got verry cold and the wind blew verry hard all night.

Friday January 4th   This morning Clear, and the weather was moderate, to what it had been some days past, Our officers sent out the Hunters, they all returned but 3 who remained out all night, The hunters that returned, had killed one Small Buffalo, which they brought to the Fort.—   In the Evening, the weather grew very cold and the Wind blew hard from the N. West all night—

Saturday 5th Jany. 1805.[1] a cloudy cold day.   the 3 hunters which who went down the river a hunting on the 4th Inst. returned on the 7th Inst. they informed us that they had nothing the 2 first days to eat only one wolf which they killed.   they informed us that it eat very well.   they killed after that 4 Deer & 2 wolves.   the weather continued verry Cold.   nothing else remarkable hapened, Since the 5th Instant.—

Saturday 5th Sunday 6 Monday 7 Tuesday 8 January   These 4 days we had Cloudy, Cold weather   The three Hunters that was out from 4th instant returned on 7th instant, they informed us that they had nothing to eat the first two days, excepting a Wolf, which they had killed, they said it eat very well, they kill'd after that 4 deer & 2 Wolves, which they brought to the Fort.—

The Weather continuing very Cold—

1. A short summary of events until the next entry, January 9, with no gaps in the notebook.

Wednesday 9th Jany. 1805.[1]   2 unexperienced hunters went out to day, the day proved to be very cold & Stormey, one of them returned to the fort about 8 oClock in the evening with one of his feet frost bit.   the other Stayed out all night.   in they morning Some men were going for them expecting they were froze, but they came in before they started well & hearty.   Some of the Natives went in the prarie a hunting, in the evening as they were returning one of them gave out.   they left him behind.   Some of his friends or his father went after him expecting to find him a Corps, but after they left him he came too So that he changed his position to the woods, & broke branches to lye on, So his life was Spared, but his feet was froze verry bad.   they got him to our fort.   Capt. Lewis doctered him.   Some hunters went out the Same evening & Stayed out all night.

Wednesday & Thursday Janry 9 & 10th   This day we had severe cold weather, in the morning 2 of our Men that were unexperienc'd in hunting, went out, in pursuit of Game, one of these Men did not return to the Fort till 8 o'Clock P. M.   the other staid out all night, On the 10th The weather still continued to be extremely Cold and Stormy, The Officers had some of our party preparing to go in search of the Man, who Staid out all night, beleiving from the severity of the weather that he had been froze to death,— but fortunately he returned to the Fort, before they had started in good health.—   Some of the Natives came to our Fort, bringing with them one of their Nation, that was frost bitten—   They told the Officers, that they had went out on the 9th instant into the Priari to hunt, & had this Indian with them, but the weather was so Cold that he gave out, and they were forced to leave him behind.—   Some of his friends with his father went out this morning, in search of him, expecting to have found him froze to death.—   On their arrival at the place, that they had left him they found that he had come too, and had walked to where there was thick Woods, & broke some branches off the Trees, on which they found him lying <on>, His feet was very much bit by the frost, but his life was Spared.   Captain Lewis afforded this Indian what medical Aid lay in his power.—   Some of our hunters went hunting and staid out all Night.—

1. A separate entry for January 10 is missing in the original version, but the events of the day seem to be included here.

Friday 11th Jany. 1805. 2 of the hunters came to the fort   had killed 3 Elk & dressed them & took the meat to their Camp.   Some other of the hunters went lower & down the river.

Friday Janry. 11th   This day the weather still continued Cold & the Air very thin; about Noon 2 of the hunters that went out to hunt Yesterday returned to the Fort, they brought with them, 2 Elk which they had killed, some of those hunters that were out with them had went further down the River in quest of Game.—

Saturday 12th Jany. 1805. a clear cold day.   Some of the men went down for the meat with a Slide   two more hunters went out to day.—

Saturday January 12th   The weather still continued clear and cold; the officers sent some of the party, for meat down the River, they took a Slide with them to bring it on.—   Two more of our hunters went out to hunt this day.—

Sunday 13th Jany. 1805. continues clear & cold.   a number of the natives went down the river to hunt, with our men.   in the evening one of our Intrepters[1] & a frenchman returned who had been up the river Some time to a nation of Indians called the osnaboins[2] after fur &c   their guide got froze so that they had to leave him their, & they got their faces frost bit So that the Skin came off.   this nation live near the rockey mountains, about 180–90 miles from this place

Sunday January 13th   The weather still continues clear & Cold, a number of the Natives, went from the Fort down the River to hunt with our Men who was there.—   In the Evening one of our Interpreters & a frenchman, came to the Fort, they had been gone up the River some time, and had went to a Nation of Indians called the Oznabone Nation to Trade for furr &ca., They inform'd us that the Guide who went with them, had got so bad frost bitten, that the whole of the skin came off.—   They told our Officers that the Oznabone nation; have their Village near the Rocky Mountains, and between 180 & 190 Miles distant from this place, by land—

1. Charbonneau.
2. Assiniboine Indians.

Monday 14th Jany. 1805. Some Snow fell this morning. 6 more hunters went out to join the rest a nomber of the natives went out also, in the evening one of the hunters[1] that went out first Came to the fort, he informed us that they had killed one buffaloe a wolf & 2 porkapines, & I got my feet So froze that I could not walk to the fort.

Monday Janry 14th   This morning we had some Snow, the Officers sent out 6 more of the Hunters to join those that were out, they were accompanied by a number of the Natives.— In the Evening one of the hunters that went out with the first party a hunting returned to the Fort, he informed us that the party he was with, had killed One Buffalo, One Wolf and 2 Porcupines, and that one of the party had his feet so frost bitten that he could not return to the Fort.—

1. Shannon.

Tuesday 15th Jany. 1805.   warm to what it has been.   the man who went to the fort yesterday, Came down with 2 horses after me & Some meat, the day kept warm & pleasant.—

Tuesday January 15th   This day the weather had moderated considerable, the Man who arrived Yesterday at the Fort, was sent down with 2 horses (which was procured from the Mandan Village) after the Man that was frost bitten, and to bring up some Meat from the Hunters.—

Wednesday 16th Jany. 1805.   quite warm for the time a year & pleasant the Snow melted fast.   I Came to the fort & 2 more men with me   my feet got Some easier.—

Wednesday January 16th   This day the weather was warm and pleasant, for this season of the Year, and the snow melted fast.— In the Evening the Man return'd to the Fort, bringing the Man that he went after and one other of the hunting party & some deer & buffalo Meat.— The Man that was frost bitten informed us that he felt much easier than he had done, since he was frost bitten

Thursday 17th Jany. 1805. about 3 oC. this morning the wind began to blow from the North & began to freeze. continued cold & the wind the Same course all day.

Thursday January 17th This morning about 3 o'Clock the Wind began to blow from the North, & freeze which continued all this day, the Weather being very Cold—

Friday 18th Jany. 1805. clear cold weather 2 of our hunters came in had killed 4 Deer 4 wolves and one brarow. 2 men[1] who belonged to the N. W. Compy. that trades at the grossvauntares villages came to our fort, this day they told us that these animals we called Braroes are a Specie of the Badgers, which are common in Europe.—

Friday Janry. 18th This day we had clear cold Weather, about 12 o'Clock A. M. two of our Hunters came to the Fort, & informed us, that they had killed 4 deer 4 Wolves, and a Brarerow, In the afternoon two Men, belonging to the North West company of Traders came to the Fort also, they had come from the Gross Vaunters Village, they informed us, that The North West company, had Men employ'd trading at that Nation.— They told us that the Animals which are called the Brarerows, were a Specie of the Badger, which they said were common in Europe.—

1. François-Antoine Larocque and Charles McKenzie, according to Clark; see Clark's entry for November 27, 1804.

Saturday 19th Jany. 1805. 2 men Sent with three horses down the River for meat to the hunting Camps, which is about 30 miles distant from the Fort the way they go on the Ice.—

Saturday January l9th The weather continued Cold and Clear, Our Officers sent two of the Men, with three horses down the River, to the hunting

Camps for meat,—the distance being about 30 Miles from the Fort, They proceeded on the Ice the River being fast froze over for some time past.—

Sunday 20th Jany. 1805.[1]   Some men went up to the villages. they informed us that they all used them verry well.   gave them pleanty to eat, & when they had done eating they gave a bowl of victuls to a buflows head which they worshiped, & Sd. Eat this So that the live ones may come in that we may git a Supply of meat.[2]   Some of them & indeed the most of them have Strange & uncommon Ideas, but verry Ignorant of our forms & customs, but quick & Sensible in their own way & in their own conceit &c &c.

Sunday Janry 20th   We still continued to have clear cold weather. some of our Men went up to the 1st Mandan Indian Village, on their return they informd us, that they had been well used by the Indians of that Town, and that they had given them, plenty to eat, of buffalo Meat, beans, & pounded Corn boil'd.—

They informed us, that after they had finish'd eating <they> That the Mandan Indians put a quantity of the same Victuals into a Woodin Bowl. they then brought forward the Head of a buffalo, which they fell down & Worshipped, and then set before it, the Bowl of Victuals, and said (as our Interpreter who was with us told us) Eat this, and tell the live Buffaloes, to come in to us, so that we may get plenty of Buffalo meat to Eat.— They let this Bowl remain before the head of the buffalo, 'till our Men left their Village.— The party who was at this Village also say that those Indians, possess very strange and uncommon Ideas of things in general, They are very Ignorant, and have no Ideas of our forms & customs, neither in regard to our Worship or the Deity &ca.

They are Indians of very Quick apprehension, of anything in their way; and Conceited in themselves to a fault.— This they judged from the <first> answers, they gave to questions they asked <by> <from> them; the whole of which was told to our Men, by the Interpreter that they took with them from the Fort,—

1. About the lower one-third of this page is blank after the entry. A new entry, May 1, 1805, begins at the top of the next page; there seem to be no sheets missing from the notebook at this point. The fair copy provides entries for the missing days but has some gaps itself.

2. Gass and Whitehouse both describe this religious practice and seem to have understood its purpose, which was to placate the spirit of the buffalo and cause the animals to come near and offer themselves as food.

Monday January 21st[1]   The weather still continued Clear and Cold, the two Men that was sent to the hunting Camp returned to the Fort, having the three horses loaded with Elk meat and Venison, they returned on the Ice on the River.—

1. From this point until May 1, 1805, only the fair copy survives of Whitehouse's journal.

Tuesday Janry. 22d   This day all our Men who were at the fort was employed to cut the Ice in order to get the boat & Pettyaugers out of the River, in the night we had a heavy fall of Snow, which made it difficult to work in the Ice for some days.—

Wednesday 23d January   We had a continuation of Snow the greater part of this day, on its leaving off, it continued Cold to the 30th Instant, all hands during this time were employed at work on the boat & Pettyaugers to get them free from the Ice, and hawled Stones on a Sled which they made warm in a fire, in order to thaw the Ice from about the said Crafts, when the Stones were put into the fire, they would not stand the heat of the fire but all of them broke, so that their labour was lost.

Thursday January 31st   This morning we had a fresh wind from the N West, and the weather Cold, five of our hunters went out, and took two horses with them, in Order to hunt.   In the afternoon it got warm & pleasant weather.—

Friday February 1st   This morning we had pleasant weather.   about 11 o'Clock A. M. our Hunters came to the Fort, they had killed a number of Elk and Deer,—   One of our Men went out a small distance, and Shott a deer which he brought to the Fort, he then went out again and kill'd another Deer which he likewise brought into the Fort.

Sunday February 3d   This day we had Clear cold weather, nothing of consequence happened at the Fort worth mentioning.—

Monday February 4th   This day we had Clear weather but cold, Captain Clarke took eighteen Men of our party,[1] and set out to go down the River to hunt, they proceeded 20 Miles down the River[2] but found no game

1. It is not clear whether Whitehouse was with this party, since the fair copy, our only version of his journal here, never refers to him in the first person. He summarizes the events of Clark's trip in an entry or two as does Gass, who was with Clark.
2. Clark's party camped in the vicinity of Mandan Island, four or five miles below Washburn and a little above Sanger; the camp may have been on the island, in McLean County on the east side of the river, or in Oliver County on the west, all in North Dakota.

Tuesday February 5th   We had fair Weather, nothing material happend in the Fort, Captain Clark and his party still proceeded on down the River, and met with some Indian camps on their way,[1] That party killed 3 deer this day

1. Probably some of the abandoned earthlodge villages below Mandan Island, McLean County, North Dakota.

Wednesday February 6th   This day was clear & pleasant Weather, nothing material happen'd at the Fort.— Captain Clark and his Men, proceeded still on[1] hunting & kill'd 7 more Deer, on the 7th Instant Captain Clark and his party halted in a large bottom,[2] lying on the South side of the River, the hunters went out, and killed 10 Elk and 18 deer at that place, they were then 40 Miles distant from the Fort, as near as they could reckon.— They there built a pen, to preserve their Meat in from the Wolves; & other Animals.— The Wolves at that place were very numerous and Ravenous.— Captain Clark then proceeded a small distance further down the River, and encamped.—[3] On Saturday the 9th instant Captain Clark returned towards the Fort,[4] the hunters kill'd some Elk and deer on the Route that day, Captain Clark, and his party proceeded on their Route to the Fort the 10th & 11th instant[5] and on the 12th instant they came to us all being well.— nothing material happen'd at the Fort from the 7th instant to this 12th Instant worth mentioning

1. They camped near the mouth of Square Butte Creek (Clark's Hunting Creek), Oliver County, North Dakota, a little below the Morton County line.

2. Clark seems to indicate that they stayed in camp at Square Butte Creek this day, Gass seems to say they moved, and Whitehouse is ambiguous, although the phrasing would be more consistent with a move.

3. Clark's account makes it clear that on February 8 they moved a few miles downriver, built the pen, then moved down and camped opposite the mouth of Heart River, in or near present Bismarck, Burleigh County, North Dakota. See Clark's entry of February 13, 1805.

4. The hunting party apparently camped at one of the old earthlodge villages between Fort Mandan and Heart River. Clark says they were about forty miles below the fort.

5. On February 11 they seem to have camped at one of the abandoned villages below Mandan Island, McLean County.

Wednesday February 13th   This day clear & pleasant weather.— The blacksmith[1] was employed shoeing the horses, in Order to go and fetch to the Fort, the meat, that was killed by Captain Clark and his party.—

1. Shields.

Thursday February 14th   This morning we had clear weather but pleasant.— The officers sent 4 Men[1] with 3 Horses and two Sleds (the horses being procur'd from the North West company's Traders) to bring the Meat, left by Captain Clark, and his party to the Fort; They set out on the Ice and proceeded on about 25 Miles, when they halted to water their horses, at a place in the River, that was open near a piece of Timber'd Land, where there was a Warr path, part of the Souix Nation being hidden in that place, waiting to plunder & murder any that might pass by them, that were not of their own nation, The Savages rushed out of this piece of Woods, and Ran towards our four Men Whooping and Shouting as they came, (the Men not having finish'd watering their horses) there being near 120 of those Savages, they then surrounded our Men, and took away the three horses, but offered no Violence then to them, One of these Savages returned back to one of our Men one of the horses, The Man to whom the Indian returned the horse gave that Indian some Corn bread, and divided another loaf of Corn bread, among them, giving their Chief that was with them a large Share.— These Savages took the two other horses, and two knives from them, they then formed a half-Circle round them and held a consultation, the result of which, was that they should be murder'd by their party; which would certainly have been the case; had not two of their Warriors opposed them, and would not agree to its being done, the Savages then set the <three> four Men at liberty, to go to the fort, These Savages proceeded down the River, to the Rick a Ree nation, and told them what they had done, they likewise informed the Pawne Indians [2] of the same, This was told to Captain Lewis (by a frenchman [3] who lived among the pawne Indians and was there, when this set of Indians, arrived at that Village,) <at our Fort some short time afterwards>.— <being the 28th instant>.— The party that was robbed by the Indians returned to the Fort, at 12 o'Clock the same night, they were very much fataigued. They immediately on their arrival, gave information to our Officers. The Officers immediately called on the party for 20 Volunteers, to off early in the Morning, in pursuit of those Robbers.— Twenty immediately of them volunteered their Service, and prepar'd themselves to be in readiness by day light.—

1. Drouillard, Frazer, Goodrich, and Newman.
2. Pawnee (spelled variously) was a name the party sometimes used for the Arikaras; the two tribes spoke related Caddoan languages.
3. Gravelines; see Clark's entry for February 28, 1805.

Friday February 15 This morning we had fine Clear weather, At day light, Captain Lewis & the party of our Men [1] under his command<ed> left the Fort, in pursuit of those Savages, that had robbed our Men, they proceeded on, and marched 30 Miles that day, without being able to overtake them; that Party encamped [2] on the North side of the River Mesouri for that night, in a thick Wood.— Nothing worth relating happen'd at the Fort this day.—

1. Once again, it is not clear from the fair copy whether Whitehouse was with Lewis's party. However, this account is the most detailed description of the foray, even more so than Ordway's.
2. At an abandoned Indian village in Oliver County, North Dakota.

Saturday Febry. 16th We had a fine Clear day, the weather being moderate.— Captain Lewis and the party under his command left their encampment at day light, in pursuit of the Savages.— They continued on their March, untill 11 oClock A. M. when they arrived at the Point of Woods laying on the South side of the Mesouri River, Captain Lewis halted his Men at this place and sent out a Spy to find if any Indians were to be seen, The Spy return'd in a short time, and informed Captain Lewis, that he had perceived a Smoak on the opposite side of the River.   The Captain and party immediately crossed the Mesouri, to the opposite shore on the Ice, a small distance above, where the smoak was seen, On landing, the Men were formed in two divisions.   The Captain taking the Command of the right Wing, and the left wing he gave the Command of to one of our Serjeants, who was order'd to march in another Circular direction to what he was to march, with those which he commanded, in Order that both parties when they met, would be able to surround the fire from whence the Smoak issued.—

Captain Lewis gave Orders to the Serjeant, that on hearing the Sound of a horn, the left Wing, would join the right with all the speed possible.— Both parties then advanced towards where the smoak was, and perceived the fire, and found that those Savages, that they were in pursuit of, were gone, they having encamped (where we found the fire) the Night before, They burnt the Huts & meat that Captain Clark had left at that place, They found from Tracts, that those Savages had left the River, and had taken through the Priari, down along the River bank.—   Captain Lewis & his party joined by those that was under the command of the Serjeant, proceeded on their pursuit this day, but without success, In the Evening they encamped on the South Side of the River Mesouri.—

Sunday February 17th   The weather continued Clear & moderate, Captain Clarke sent out the hunters from the fort hunting, they met with great success, killing a great quantity of Elk and deer, they continued hunting and on the 18th instant they had as much meat as loaded two Sleds, One of which was drawn by 16 Men, and the other by the horse which the Savages, had return'd to one of our Men, when they robbed them.—   They brought the Sleds loaded with the Meat up the River on the Ice, it still being froze over the Mesouri, & the Ice very thick & strong.—

Tuesday & Wednesday 19th & 20th february   We had fine clear moderate weather for these two days, nothing material occur'd, Captain Lewis & the party under his command having not yet returned to the Fort.—

Thursday February 21st   This day the weather still continued Clear & pleasant, In the afternoon Captain Lewis, and the party under his Command arrived at the Fort, They were very much fataigued.   They brought with them, abundance of meat that they had killed on their return.—

Friday Febry 22d   We had still Clear, pleasant weather; Captain Lewis & party rested themselves this day, being still fataigued

Saturday February 23d   The weather still continued fine and Clear, all our party were employ'd in cutting the Ice from round the Boat & Pettyaugers.   at one o'Clock we got one of the Pettyaugers out of the Ice on Shore.—

Sunday february 24th   We had pleasant weather.   all our party were still employed in cutting the Ice round the Boat & pettyauger   we succeeded, and got out both the Boat & pettyauger on the Bank of the River at the Fort, and clear of danger, when the Ice broke up in the River.—

Monday febry 25th   This day was Clear & pleasant.   the Men were still employ'd at fixing the boat & Pettyaugers, which they compleated

Tuesday Febry 26th   The weather continued still clear & fine; the Men were employed in getting the Tools in Order for making pettyaugers[1]
The officers set 16 Men to work to make 4 Pettyaugers in the afternoon

1. Here, dugout canoes rather than pirogues.

Wednesday febry 27th   We have still fine weather; the Men were employed cutting wood for to burn Coal, and falling of large Trees for to make Pettyaugers.   The natives (Indians) came to our Fort, to get our Men to do some work for them,[1] and brought with them some Corn to pay for it—

1. Perhaps to make tomahawks. See Clark's entry for January 28, 1805, and Lewis's for February 5. But see also Whitehouse's entry of March 1, 1805.

Thursday February 28th   This morning the weather cold but towards Noon it moderated   The Natives still continuing to come into the Fort, bringing with them Corn to pay for work they got done by our Men, they behaving very well.—

Friday March 1st   The men employed to build the Pettyaugers, continued their work   the Natives still continue to bring in Corn for work they want done, which is chiefly getting their Guns repaired by our Blacksmiths the weather continued Clear & Cold—

Saturday March 2nd   This day we had fine Clear weather.   the Men are all employed in Cutting, wood, and Repairing & mending their Cloathes, dressing Deer & Elk Skins & making of mockasins &ca.—

Sunday March 3d[1]   This day we had Clear cold weather; the party were all employ'd untill the 20th instant, in making of ropes out of Buffalo, and Elk skins, burning of Coal for the Armourer & Blacksmiths, working on the new Pettyaugers &ca.—   They finished the Pettyaugers during that time, and had them brought down to the bank of the River, but was prevented bringing them near the Fort, the Ice preventing it.   The Officers placed a Guard of 3 Men at the new Pettyaugers, in order to prevent the Indians from doing any damage to them.—   The weather continued Clear & pleasant during this time

1. Whitehouse's copyist fails to note that on March 16 Whitehouse had an incident with one of the locals. Clark writes, "one Indian much displeased with whitehouse for Strikeing his hand when eating with a Spoon for behaveing badly."

Thursday March 21st   This day we had still, pleasant Weather, nothing occur'd worth mentioning

Friday March 22d   We had some Rain this morning, but it continued but a short time, the weather being cloudy & cold.

Saturday March 23d   This morning we had Snow.—   towards Noon it ceased, and the weather moderated and became pleasant.—   In the Evening it grew Cold & froze during the Night

Sunday 24th Monday 25 March   We had pleasant Weather during these two days, continuing to freeze in the Evenings

Tuesday March 26th   This day we had moderate weather, and the Ice broke up, The Men were employed in conveying the Pettyaugers from where they were built, to the Fort, which they accomplish'd

Wednesday March 27th   This day we had pleasant weather, the Men were employed in getting the Crafts in order to proceed on our Voyage—

Thursday March 28th   This day was blustering which continued the whole day.—

Friday March 29th   We had all this day high winds, but the Air was not so cold, as it had been for several days past.   nothing new occurred worth mentioning

Saturday 30th Sunday 31st March   We had the first of these days, high wind, but not cold, the other fine Clear warm weather.—

Monday April 1st   This morning we had some rain, which lasted about 2 hours & clear'd up Cool, all our party was employed in putting the Boat & Pettyaugers into the River, which they Effected.—

Tuesday April 2nd   This day the weather was cold & in the fore part of the day it froze.   The latter part we had Blustry weather—

Wednesday April 4th   This day was Clear, & pleasant weather.   All our Men were employed in preparing the lading for the Boat & Pettyaugers; nothing material happen'd this day.—

Thursday 4th Friday 5th Saturday 6 April   We had fine Clear weather during these days, And all our Men were employed in loading the Crafts, which they compleated on the 6th instant   Our officers had concluded to start on our Voyage this morning, (6th instant) and every thing necessary was in readiness, when a Messinger arrived at the Fort, from the Mandan Villages, he informed our Officers, that the Rick a Ree nation of Indians, was then on their way, to make Peace, with their Nation.— Captain Lewis concluded to stay that day, in order to know if the Messenger told the truth.   In the Evening ten of the Rick a Ree Indians came to our Fort, being on their way to the Treaty.—

Chapter Fifty-Seven

Great Falls
of the Missouri

April 7–July 14, 1805

Sunday April 7th   This day we had fair weather,— in the morning the Rick a Rees chief[1] came to the Fort, on a Visit to our Officers; he informed them, that the Chiefs of their Nation, was ready to descend the River in our boat, in Order to pay a Visit to the President of the United States.   At half past 4 o'Clock P. M; we all embark'd, in our large Canoes and left Fort Mandan, on our way for the Pacific Ocean.—   The boat sett off, Under the command of Corporal Warfington with a Command[2] on board for Saint Louis at same time on board of which was sent the deserter Read   we proceeded on and encamped,[3] on the North side of the Mesouri River, opposite to the first Village of the Mandan Nation.—

This Village lies on the South side of the River and contains 300 Lodges. the land adjoining it is Priaries, which gradually rise from the River, the Soil is very rich, producing Indian Corn, pumpkins, Squashes & beans in abundance

The Natives have large fields, which they cultivate and which produces plentifully, They have likewise Gardens, which they plant & have several kinds of Garden Vegetables in it, such as Lettuce, Mustard &ca   they have likewise growing in their Gardens, Gooseberrys,[4] which is superior in Size, to any in the United States & Currants of different kinds.—   They are in general peaceable well disposed people—and have less of the Savage nature in them, than any Indians we met with on the Mesouri River.

They are of a very light Colour, the Men are very well featur'd and Stout; the Women are in general handsome; this Town or Village Contains from the best calculation we could make 2,000 Inhabitants,[5] they are Governed by a Chief called the Big White and the Indians here live to a very old age, numbers being 100 Years old.—

1. Kakawita, or Raven Man, an Arikara chief; see Clark's entry for the date.
2. For the names of members of the return party, see Lewis's entry for this day.
3. Opposite Mitutanka, McLean County, North Dakota, about three miles below Stanton.
4. An unknown gooseberry, *Ribes* sp.
5. An exaggeration since Clark counts about 1,250 people in both Mandan villages. See Clark's "Estimate of Eastern Indians" in vol. 3.

Monday April 8th   This day we had clear weather, the Wind blowing fresh from the Northwest.   we proceeded on our Voyage, and passed the 2nd Mandan Village,[1] and a River lying on the South side of the Mesouri called the River de Cutto,[2] which is 20 Yards wide at its mouth, We passed in the afternoon <a> Villages[3] Inhabited by a nation of Indians called the Big belly's, or Gross Vounters, which also lies on the South Side of the Mesouri River, We proceeded on and encamped[4] on the North side of the River on its bank, having come 14 Miles this day.—

The second Village of the Mandan Indians lies on the North side of the River mesouri, it is situated on a Priari, of a vast extent, the Soil of which appears to be exceeding Rich and productive.—   The Natives have large fields, which they Cultivate, and plant the same as those of the first Village, They have among them a number of fine horses, and are very expert in managing them in riding, The Inhabitants of this Village are in Colour and form the same as those of the first Village, This village contains 200 Lodges and by the best calculation 1500 Souls, and is Governed by a Chief who is called Black Cat as before mention'd

1. Ruptáre (Black Cat site), McLean County, North Dakota.
2. Knife River, McLean County. The French word for "knife" attemped here is *le couteau*.

3. The three Hidatsa villages along the Knife River, Mahawha (Amahami site), Metaharta (Sakakawea site), and Menetarra (Big Hidatsa site).

4. In McLean County, a mile or so below Garrison Dam.

Tuesday April 9th   This day Clear & pleasant weather, We set out early this morning, and proceeded on; at 10 o'Clock A. M we passed a small River[1] the Name unknown, lying on the North Side of the Mesouri.   The banks of the River not being so high gave us an opportunity of seeing the Country which appear'd to be a mixture of Priaries & Wood land, in the Evening we encamped[2] on the North side of the Mesouri, distance this day come being 22 Miles.—

1. The party's Miry Creek, now Snake Creek, McLean County, North Dakota.

2. In McLean County, North Dakota, above Douglas Creek and a few miles southeast of Garrison.

Wednesday April 10th   We set off at day light, and passed a party of the Big belly or Gross Vaunters Indians hunting on the South side of the River, We proceeded on 'till Evening & encamped[1] on the North side of the River, distance come this day 17 Miles.—

1. Just above the later site of Fort Berthold, McLean County, North Dakota.

Thursday April 11th   We set off at day light, this morning, the weather being Cool, about 10 oClock A. M, We passed another party of Gross Vaunters or Big belly Indians a hunting also, on the South side of the River, we proceeded on, and Encamped[1] in the Evening on the North side of the River having rowed 20 Miles this day.—

1. In McLean County, North Dakota, a few miles below the mouth of the Little Missouri River.

Friday April 12th   This morning we had pleasant Weather, we started early and proceeded on our way till 11 oClock A. M., when we arrived at the Little Mesouri River,[1] which lies on the South side of the great River Mesouri. its width at its mouth is 150 Yards, the Water <that runs from> in it is

Muddy, & its current runs strong, Our hunters went out hunting, but met with but little success.— The Country here is chiefly Priaries and lies level, we encamped here, having come 7 Miles this day— The Mouth of the little Mesouri lies in Latitude 47° 31′ 26 North—

1. The mouth of the Little Missouri River may have shifted over the years; it is now in McLean County, North Dakota.

Saturday April 13th   We set out at day light this morning, having a fair wind from the Eastward, we sailed the greater part of this day, The land, being all Priaries that we passed.   in the Evening we encamped[1] on the North side of the Mesouri having come 24½ Miles this day.—

1. In Mountrail County, North Dakota, in what was once called Fort Maneury Bend, now inundated by Garrison Reservoir.

Sunday April 14th   This morning we set out early and proceeded on the Banks of the River being high, & part cover'd with Woods.   In the Evening we encamped[1] on the South side of the River—distance come this day 16 Miles.—

1. In Mountrail County, North Dakota, opposite and a little above the mouth of Bear Den Creek.

Monday April 15th   We set off this Morning, having a fresh breeze from the N-East   about 8 o'Clock it veered round to the South East, and blew moderately.—   We proceeded on, and passed a small River, and a Creek;[1] lying both on the North side of the River, and encamped[2] in the Evening, on the bank of the River on the North side.—

1. Whitehouse adds a second stream that no one else has. The river is Little Knife River.
2. In McKenzie County, North Dakota, a site now inundated by Garrison Reservoir.

Tuesay April 16th   This morning we started early on our Voyage.   The Weather was Cool and clear; we proceeded on with all Sails set, having a fine breeze from the South East, We encamped[1] in the Evening on the South side of the Mesouri, having sail'd 27 Miles this day.—

> 1. In McKenzie County, North Dakota, a little above Beaver Creek on the opposite side.

Wednesday April 17th   We got underway at the usual hour of day light, we proceeded on, and passed a high bluff to a sand barr, and a beautifull Priari, which put in near the River, likewise a Creek[1] that Runs a North Course under the Bluffs, and a small distance further passed two Creeks[2] lying on the same Side of the River; and one Creek[3] lying on the South side.—   We encamped[4] on the South side of the River, having come 26 Miles this day

> 1. No one else seems to mention this stream, but since it is apparently on the north side, it may be later Beaver Creek, Mountrail County, North Dakota.
> 2. Presumably the two creeks on the north side mentioned by Gass, the first Hall's Strand Creek, later Tobacco Creek, the second perhaps later Garden Creek, both in Mountrail County.
> 3. Apparently later Clark Creek, in McKenzie County, North Dakota.
> 4. In McKenzie County.

Thursday April 18th   This morning Clear pleasant weather, We set off Early, having the wind from the South   the water in the River was at a stand in regard to its depth, In the Evening we encamped[1] on the North side of the River, having come 15 Miles this day.—   In the night the dew fell, which was what we had not seen for a long time.—

> 1. In Williams County, North Dakota, where they remained until April 20.

Friday April 19th   This morning we had the Weather dark and Cloudy.— the Wind blowing hard from the North   the Water still at a stand, we remained here this day, the wind blowing so hard that we could make no head way.—

Saturday April 20th   We got under way at daylight, and proceeded on our way 6 Miles, the wind blew so fresh from the North, that we could make no headway, we came too and encamped[1] on the North side of the River.—

> 1. In Williams County, North Dakota.

Sunday April 20th[1]   This morning we had pleasant Weather, in the night we had a frost, we sett out early, the Wind blowing from the Northwest.   the Water in the River fell one Inch   We proceeded on, and passed the River called Le Tear Black,[2] lying on the South side of the Mesouri, and Encamped on the North side of the River Mesouri, having went 16 Miles this day.

1. The day is corrected from Saturday, but the date was not changed to April 21. The next entry should be April 22, a Monday as noted.

2. Since this is a misdated entry for April 21, Whitehouse is referring to the party's supposed White Earth River, in French *La Terre Blanche.* For the correct identification see the next day's entry. There are a number of course, distance, and campsite errors in these entries.

Monday April 21st[1]   We got under way at the usual hour, and passed another branch of the River La Tear Black,[2] the Wind blew from the N East and the Water fell 2 Inches in the River, We went 9 Miles this day & encamped[3] on the North Side of the River.—

1. It is not altogether clear whether this is the entry of April 21 or 22, since there is an apparently misdated entry for the previous day and none for the twenty-second.

2. The party's White Earth River is not the present stream of that name, which they passed on April 16. This is Little Muddy River, Williams County, North Dakota.

3. Whether this is April 21 or 22, the camp is placed on the wrong side of the River. That of April 21 is in McKenzie County, North Dakota, nearly opposite present Williston. The camp of the next day is also in McKenzie County, a few miles above the previous one.

Tuesday April 23rd[1]   This morning, we had Clear weather and set off at the usual hour,—   (Early)   We proceeded on about 3 Miles, when the Wind blew so fresh, that we had to come too, it being a head Wind from the North west.—   We stopped for about two hours, & Captain Clark, and some of our Men went out hunting; We then proceeded <then> on our Voyage, & passed the finest thickets of Wood & level priaries, that we had seen, since we left the Mandan Nation, In the Evening, we came too, and Encamped[2] on the North side of the Mesouri River, having come 15 Miles this day.— Captain Clark & the party that went with him hunting, joined us some short time after, having kill'd that day 3 large Male Deer, and a Buffalo Calf, which they brought to the Camp—

1. When compared with other journals, this appears to be the true entry for April 23.
2. In Williams County, North Dakota, where they remained until April 25.

Wednesday April 24th   This day we had Clear weather; but the Wind still blowing from the North West (ahead Wind) that we lay by, at the place we encamped the last night.   A party of our Men were sent out a hunting. They returned in the Evening, they had met with great succees, having kill'd a considerable number of Buffalo, Elk and Deer, one of the party brought in with him 6 Young Wolves,[1] which he caught.—   The Country where we encamped, is a Rich & level land, being priaries with some Wood land, lying on the back of them.—   The growth of the Wood land being chiefly Cotton Wood, Walnut[2] & Wild Cherry.—   all very large sized.—

1. According to the captains these were wolves "of the small kind," that is, coyotes.
2. No one else mentions walnuts, and the party is too far north to see this species. It is not clear what Whitehouse saw.

Thursday April 25th   We set off early this morning, having fine Clear weather; about 11 oClock A. M. we had to come too, on account of the Wind being a head & blowing hard, Captain Lewis and 4 of our Men left us, having set out by land, in Order to go to the Mouth of the River roshjone;[1] which lies higher up the Mesouri; & to where the confluence of both these great Rivers are.—   They took with them, Mathematical Instruments, in order to assertain the Latitude of the River Roshjone, and were to waite there for our arrival.—   We proceeded on our Voyage at 10 o'Clock A. M. and went on till Evening, passing as we went along, fine level Priaries & some small Skirts of wood land, running close to the Bank of the River, We encamped[2] on the South side of the River, having gone 13 Miles this day.—   The dew at this place never falls; and it seldom Rains, this we were told, by an Indian Women that was with us, that embark'd on board one of the Pettyaugers at the Mandan Nation with a frenchman her husband as our Interpreters to the Snake Indians.—[3]

1. The *Roche Jaune,* in French, or Yellowstone.
2. In Williams County, North Dakota, in the vicinity of Glass Bluffs on the opposite side.
3. Shoshone Indians, Sacagawea's people.

Friday April 26th   This morning we had fine Clear weather, and set off on our Voyage Early; and proceeded on till 12 oClock A. M, having went 10 Miles, and arrived at the River's mouth called Roshjone,[1] where we came too, in Order to wait for Captain Lewis and his party.— who had not arrived yet here, Captain Clark shortly after our arrival here, sent a party out a hunting, and directed them to proceed up to the Point of the River Roshjone; and then proceeded to assertain the Width of both Rivers at this place.— <he> they found on measuring these Rivers, that the River Mesouri was 337 Yards wide; and very deep; and the River Roshjone at its mouth, 97 Yards wide, and continued the same width for a considerable distance up it.— The River Roshjone is a Shallow River, the water in it is Clear and its current rapid.— The mouth of this River is 1,888 Miles, from the mouth of the Mesouri River, and 279 Miles from Fort Mandan.   The Country here is Priaries, and some thickets of Trees, the land appears very rich & fertile.—   In the Evening we were Joined by Captain Lewis and his party.— They had killed several buffaloes, Antelopes, and Deer; which they brought with them and a Buffalo Calf alive, which had followed them 7 or 8 Miles, it being common for the Buffalo Calves, when separated from their dams, to follow the hunters.—

The party that Captain Clark had sent out hunting returned; bringing with them, a number of Buffalo Calves which they had killed— The game at this season of the year being poor, the flesh of the Buffalo Calves, was a welcome supply to us, they being in general in good Order, and in Taste very & [*illegible, crossed out*] like Veal <much like it as well as> and had much the resemblance of Veal in its appearance, We found a great many signs of Beaver in the bottoms on both Rivers.— The place that we encamped in this Evening; <is> was a handsome point, lying on the South side of the River Roshjone

The River Roshjone at its mouth on the South side of, it lays in Latitude 48° North

1. The Yellowstone River meets the Missouri in McKenzie County, North Dakota, just east of the Montana state line.

Saturday April 27th   We were delayed overhawling the Loads on board the pettyaugers till about 9 o'Clock A. M.   The weather being clear and pleasant; when we proceeded on our Voyage, and passed a handsome Priari, lying on the South side of the Mesouri River, in which lay a handsome Pond of Water, this Pond was wide and very long, One of our Hunters that was out Yesterday in formed us, that at the upper end of it, that it was almost cover'd with Geese,[1] Swans[2] & other Water fowl, We stopped at One o'Clock A. M. to dine in a bottom, cover'd with Cotton wood Trees, lying on the North side of the River, shortly after the Wind blew so hard a head, from the Westward that we were delayed from starting till 4 o'Clock P. M. we then got underway, and in the Evening, we encamped[3] on the South side of the River Mesouri, having had a strong current against us, we came only 8 Miles this day.—

1. Probably the Canada goose, *Branta canadensis*.

2. Either trumpeter swan, *Cygnus buccinator,* or tundra (also whistling) swan, *C. columbianus.*

3. The party's first camp in Montana, in Roosevelt County, about a mile below and opposite the village of Nohly, Richland County.

Sunday April 28th   This day we had fine clear weather & pleasant, we set out Early in the morning; and proceeded on till 9 o'Clock A. M. when we stopped to break fast, under a high bluff lying on the South side of the River, about 15 Miles, above the Mouth of the River Roshjone, We found that the banks of the River Mesouri, was not so high, as it was lower down this River; and that the Sand barrs, lay generally in the middle of this River; The land as we passed along, appears to lay more level than what we had passed for several days past, but very Rich & fertile   We encamped[1] in the Evening, in a handsome bottom, on which there was Cotton wood Trees growing.— The bottoms are not so large in general here, as below, and the Timber not so plenty.—   We came 24 Miles this day & the place we encamp'd on <lies> lay on the South side of the River Mesouri.—

1. In Roosevelt County, Montana, near Otis Creek, opposite in Richland County.

Monday April 29th   We set out Early as usual this morning, and proceeded on; and passed in the forenoon, some very high bluffs, being much higher, than any that we had seen, since we entered the Mesouri River.   On the Top of one of the highest of those Bluffs, we saw the Animal called the Ibex, or mountain Sheep,[1] they were in a large Flock.—

This animal is about the size of a large Buck deer,— the Colour Grey, and has hair coarse & like that of a Goat, it ears small and its body lengthy, the horns like that of a Ram, (sheep) but four times as large. They are very nimble, and generally are to be found on high Mountains and Bluffs, and are very Shy, and difficult to be come at.— The Indian women that was with us, inform'd us that those animals were very common to be found On the Rocky mountains.— Captain Lewis, and one of the hunters, went out a hunting for a short time, and killed a Bear[2] which they brought to the Pettyaugers This Bear was of a Yellow brownish colour, and had prodigious large Claws, and <are> is what is called the White Bear by the Natives; We continued on our Voyage, & in the Evening, we encamp'd[3] on the bank of a River, which emtied itself into the Mesouri on the North side, which is 70 Yards wide & by our Officers called Martha's River, having come 25 Miles this day.

1. Bighorn sheep, *Ovis canadensis;* see Lewis's entry of April 26 for a possible subspecies.
2. Their first actual specimen of a grizzly bear, from which Lewis wrote the first scientific description.
3. In Roosevelt County, Montana, just above Big Muddy Creek, the party's Martha's River, which Clark named "in honor to the selebrated M. F.," a woman whose identity remains a mystery.

Tuesday April 30th We set out early this morning, having fine pleasant Weather. we proceeded on, and passed by a most beautiful Country, being Priaries lying on both sides of the River, which rise <greatly> gradually from the banks of <the River,> it and the Soil very rich, In the afternoon we stopped and encamped[1] on the North side of the River, Captain Lewis shortly after we encamped, went out a hunting, and killed a large Elk, in a bottom, near to where we had encamped,— which was brought to our Camp, the distance we went this day being 24 Miles.—

1. In the vicinity of Brockton, Richland County, Montana.

Wednesday 1st day of May 1805.[1] a clear pleasant morning but cold. we Set off at Sun rise, the wind from the East. we Sailed Some. we passed high bluffs & round knobs on the S. S. and bottoms of timber on each Side of the River. the hills in general are not So high as they have been below, the country more pleasant, and the timber more pleanty. about 12 oClock the wind rose So high that we were oblidged to halt in a bottom of timber on the South Side. one cannoe lay on the opposite Shore & could not cross. I and one more was in the cannoe and ware obledged to lay out all night without any blanket. it being verry cold I Suffered verry much. Some of the party went out to hunt. they killed one buffaloe one Deer 2 beaver and one Goose. the party camped[2] opposite to where I lay all night the man who was with me killd a Deer. (came only 10 miles to day)

Wednesday May 1st   We set off at day light this morning, the weather being cool and pleasant, and the Wind blowing from the Eastward, we proceeded on Sailing, and passed some high bluffs, and round Nobs,— lying on the South side of the River; and bottoms of fine land lying on both sides of the River, covered with Timber, the hills being not so high as those below, The country appearing more pleasant, and Timber'd land more plenty; At 12 o'Clock A. M. we came too, (the wind being so high) and Stopped in a bottom of Timber'd lands, lying on the South side of the River,— One of our Canoes stopping on the opposite side of the River, on account of the Wind, where she lay all night, the Men in it suffering much, on account of the Cold; Some of the party went out hunting, and killed One Buffalo, One deer, 2 Beaver, and a Goose; The Men that was with the Canoe killed a Deer.— we encamped at this place having come 15 Miles this day.—

    1. Entries in Whitehouse's original version of his journal resume.
    2. The party camped in the vicinity of later Elkhorn Point, Roosevelt County, Montana. Whitehouse and his unnamed companion were opposite in Richland County.

Thursday 2nd May 1805.   at day light it began to Snow & blow So that we did not Set off this morning. Some men went out to hunt. Killed Some buffaloe & Some Deer. one of the party killd two beaver last night. the men who was out a hunting found Several peaces of red cloath at an Indian camp, where we expect they left last Winter for a Sacrifice to their maker as that is their form of worship, as they have Some knowledge of the Supreme being, and any thing above their comprihention they call, big medicine.

about 3 oC the wind abated & quit Snowing.   we Set off.   proceeded on. the [wind] had shifted & blew from the west.   the Snow lay on the Edge of the Sand beaches where the wind blew it against the bank about 12 Inches Deep but their was not more than about one Inch on a level.   Capt Clark & one of the party[1] Shot 3 beaver on the South Shore.   the air verry cold.   we Camped[2] on the N. S. at a handsom bottom partly covered with timber. came mes. 5 miles to day.

Thursday May 2nd   At day light this morning it began to Snow <with> & we had a hard Wind, we lay by the fore part of the day, some of our party went out to hunt, they killed some Buffalo Calves, and Deer; and caught some Beaver in their Traps, which they brought to our Camp, The hunting party found several pieces of red Cloth, at an Indian Camp; which we expect the Indians had left there, the last winter, as a Sacrafice to their maker, the Indian woman mention'd is the custom when they break up their encampment, & which shows that they have some knowledge of the supreme being, The Indians generally call every thing beyond their comprehension Medecine; and are fearfull of it.—   This we learnt from the Indians at the Mandan Villages.—   about 3 o'Clock P. M the Wind abated, and it quitted snowing.—   We sett off, and proceeded on our Voyage—the wind having shifted to the Westward, and the snow lying on the Sand Bars edge, (where the wind blew the snow against the bank,) and it, lay 12 Inches deep <it> but was not <being> more than one Inch on the level ground.—   As we proceeded on our way, Captain Clark and one of the party shot 3 Beaver on the South shore, The Air was cold during the whole of this day.   In the Evening we encamped on the North side of the River; in a bottom nearly covered with Timber.

1. Drouillard, according to Clark.
2. In Richland County, Montana, in the vicinity of the crossing of Montana Highway 251.

Friday 3rd May 1805.   clear but verry cold for this month.   we Set off about 7 oC & proceeded on   the Standing water was froze over in places, & froze to our poles as we were working along.   a white frost last night.   the Ground is covered with Snow.   the wind rose high from the west.   we halted about one oC. at a bottom covd. with timber on the N. S.   Capt Clark who

walked on Shore Since morning came to us had killed an Elk near   Some
men went & brought it in.   one man went a Short distance along the bank
and Shot a beaver.   we have Saw Great Sign of beaver all day.   the wind
cold & high.   we proceeded on   Saw a Great many buffaloe on the ridges
& plains.   the Snow is all gone this evening.   passed large bottoms & plains
in the course of the day but no high hills.   passed a creek on the S. S.[1]
Came 20 miles and Camped[2] in a bottom on the N. S.   as we were a landing
it being after dark Got the Irons broke off the red perogue, which the rudder
hung on.   we passed a creek towards evening on the N. S. which came in at
a sandbar.   I forgot it.

Friday May 3rd   This morning we had Clear weather, but very Cold for
the Season; We set out about 7 oClock A. M. and proceeded on, the Standing
water froze last night, and the Water froze to our Setting poles, as we worked
the Pettyaugers along, We had a severe white frost last night, and the ground
cover'd with Snow,—   The wind rose & blew hard from the West, We
stopped at 1 o'Clock P. M. in a bottom cover'd with Timber which lay on the
North side of the River   Captain Clark who had walked on Shore since
Morning, came to us here; he had killed an Elk, and & party of Men were
sent for it, and they brought it to us, one of our party, went a small distance,
along the shore of the River; and shot a beaver, we saw great signs of beaver
this day, the wind continued Cold, during the whole of this day, We proceeded on at 3 o'Clock P. M. and saw a great number of Buffalo, on the
Ridges & in the plains, In the Evening, the Snow had all melted away; we
passed some large bottoms & plains during the course of this day; but saw no
high hills, we likewise passed a Creek, lying on the South side of the River,
We came too, and encamped in a bottom on the North side of the River.   As
We were landing it being after dark, we got the Irons broke off the <ridge
poles> rudder, of one of the Pettyaugers.   Just before it was dark, we passed
a Creek, lying on the South side of the River, which came into the River at a
Sand barr.—   We came 20 Miles this day.—

1. Like Ordway and Gass, Whitehouse appears to have reversed the location of the two
streams passed this day. The first, the captains' Porcupine River, present Poplar River in
Roosevelt County, Montana, is on the north. Next, on the south, is their 2000 Mile Creek,

now Red Water River, McCone County. The fair copy compounds the error by putting both on the south side.

2. In McCone County, Montana, three or four miles above Poplar, Roosevelt County.

Saturday 4th May 1805. clear & pleasant. we delayed Some time to mend the rudder which Got broke last night. we Set off about 9 Oclock, and proceeded on. passed large bottoms covered with timber on each Side and Smoth high plains back from the River. at a 11 oC. we passed the mouth of a Creek[1] which came in on S. Side of the Missourie. proceeded on passed a beautiful plain on the N. S. where we Saw large Gangs of buffaloe Elk & Cabberee or Goats. Camped[2] in a bottom on the N. S. Came 22 miles to day. we killed two Deer today.

Saturday May 4th   This morning we had clear, pleasant Weather, we delayed some time, to mend the Rudder Irons broke last night; We set off, and proceeded on our Voyage at 9 oClock A. M. and passed some bottoms cover'd with timber, and high plains, lying on both sides of the River.   At 11 o'Clock A. M. we passed by the Mouth of a creek, that came in on the South side of the River, we proceeded on & passed a beautiful plain lying on the North side of the River.—

We saw in this plain, large Gangs of Buffalo, Elk, & Goats; our hunters that went out this Morning kill'd two Deer, which they brought to the bank of the River, and we took them in.—   We encamped in the Evening in a bottom lying on the North side of the River, having come this day 22 Miles.—

1. Probably Antelope, or later Nickwall, Creek, McCone County, Montana.
2. In Roosevelt County, Montana.

Sunday 5th May 1805. Clear and pleasant. we Set off eairly. one of the hunters lay on the S. S. last night, joined us at breakfast time   had killed two buffaloe Calfs. we proceeded on. Saw buffaloe Elk Deer & goats on each side of the River. passed bottoms and plains on each side. at 12 oC. we Saw 4 bair on a Sand beach on S. S. passed a handsom large plain on the N. S. we halted to dine on the South Side at a bottom of timber. our officers Gave out to the party a half a Gill of ardent Spirits. we Saw buffaloe and flocks of Goats. Jo. Fields verry Sick.[1] we proceeded on. towards evening, we killed a verry large bair in the River. the Natives call it white but it is of a light brown coulour the measuer of the brown bair is as follows. round the head is three-feet 5 Inches, do the neck 3 feet 11 Inches, do the breast 5 feet 10½ Inches. also round the middle of the arm one foot 11 inches. the length from the nose to the extremity of the hind toe is 8 feet 7½ Inches. the length of tallons 4 feet ¾ Inches. his teeth or tuskes were allmost worn out. the toe nales ware worn Short. when we got him to Shore we halted for the night on the N. S.[2] dressed the sd. brown bair found a fish in him, which he had caught & eat. we rendred out about 6 Gallons of Greese and did not render only a part of it he was not fat but reckened to be about 600 weight as he was killed. one of the hunters went out and killed an elk & Saw another bair nearly of the Same discription. Came 16 miles this day.

Sunday May 5th We had a Clear and pleasant weather, We set out Early this morning, and proceeded on our Voyage; we stoped at 8 o'Clock in Order to break fast on the South side of the River, where we were join'd by one of our hunters who had laid out on that shore all night, he had killed two buffalo calves which were brought to us— At 9 oClock A. M we set out again and proceeded on; and saw Buffalo, Elk, & deer in gangs in the Priaries, & Goats in large flocks on the Hills on both sides of the River, and some bottom lands, likewise lying on both sides of the River, At 12 o'Clock A. M. we saw 4 Bear on a Sand beach which lay on the South side of the River, and passed some handsome plains lying on the North side, At one o'Clock P. M the party halted to dine, in a bottom of Timber'd land lying on the South shore, here our Officers gave each Man of the party, half a Gill of Ardent Spirits, at this place we saw flocks of Goats & Gangs of Buffalo in abundance on both sides of the River.— One of our party named <Shield> John Fields, was taken very Sick at this place.— At 3 oClock P. M. we got under way, and proceeded on 'till towards Evening, and saw a very large bear in the River.—

The Men who belonged to the party, that was on board the foremost Pettyauger, shot at; and killed this bear; and got him near the shore on the North side of the River, he was one of those called by the Natives, the white bear, altho' his Colour was a light brown.— As he was by far the largest of the kind, we had seen, Our officers on their arrival; had his dimensions taken which were as follows.— Round the head three feet 5 Inches, Round the neck, Three feet 11 Inches; Round the breast five feet 10½ Inches, Round the middle of the Arm (or fore foot) One foot 11 Inches, The length of this animal from the Nose to the extremity of his hind Claws 8 ft. 7½ Inches His Talons 5 Inches, his Tushes were all nearly worn off, and his Nails on the fore feet, worn short, The Officers order'd the Pettyaugers to put too at this place and we encamp'd in Order to Skin and cut up this bear & get it on the Shore, it nearly took our whole party to hawl him up <which lay> on the North side of the River, in a bottom covered with Timber,— We dressed this huge animal & found in him a large fish which was fresh & which we supposed he had caught & eat at the time our Men shot him, We got from part of the fat taken out of this Bear, Six Gallons of oil, when melted, he was not so very fat, but at the nearest calculation weigh'd Six hundred pounds Nett weight— One of our hunters went out a hunting, and killed an Elk, which was brought to our Camp, he mention'd that he had seen on his Route, another Bear, of the same kind, as the One we had killed, and full as large.— The distance that we come this day was 16 Miles.—

1. See Lewis's entry for May 4 for Field's symptoms and treatment.

2. In McCone County, Montana, southeast of Wolf Point. Shifts of the river have placed the site on the opposite side.

Monday 6th May 1805. clear pleasant and warm. the wind from the East. we Sailed on verry well. Caught two beaver last night. Saw a brown bair Swim the River before us. about 2 oC. we halted to dine at a handsom bottom covered with timber on the N. S. Capt. Clark killed an Elk, a light Sprinkling of rain, but did not last long. passed a bluff on S. S. and Some hills also. high plains & bottoms on the N. Side and on the S. S. Came about 27 miles in all this day, and Camped[1] in a bottom of timber on the S. Side. the bottoms is all trod up by the Game, and different paths in all directions &c—

Monday May 6th We had this morning the weather pleasant, and Warm, and a fair wind from the East, We set out early, and proceeded on with our

Sails set, some of the party during last night caught 2 Beaver, about 2 hours after we started we saw a brown Bear swimming the River before us   About 2 o'Clock P. M, we halted to dine at a handsome bottom, covered with Timber lying on the North side of the River.   Captain Clark went out here a hunting, and killed an Elk which was brought by our Men to us.—   We proceeded on our Voyage, at 4 o'Clock P. M; and passed a Bluff lying on the south side of the River, and some hills on the same side, & bottoms & high plains also lying on the South side—   We had sprinkling rain fell this afternoon but it lasted but for a short time.—   In the Evening we came too; and encamped in a bottom cover'd with Timber lying on the South side of the River, This bottom as well as that we dined at was much trod with Game of different kinds, and they had made fair paths in them in different directions—

1. In McCone County, Montana, a few miles southwest of Oswego.

Tuesday 7th May 1805. clear and pleasant. we Set off eairly. the wind rose from the East. we Sailed on untill about 12 oC.   the wind rose So high that one of the cannoes filled with water   we got it Safe to Shore, and halted for the wind to abate on the S. Side   Some men went out to hunt.   two beaver was caught by Some of the men last night and Shot five[1] more at this place. about 4 oC. we Set off and proceeded on verry well.   passed handsom plains and bottoms on N. S.   rough hills & ridges & bottoms on the S. S. Saw large gangs of buffaloe on each Side of the River.   Came 15½ miles to day, & Camped[2] on the S. S.   Capt. Clark and one hunter killed two buffaloe, which we found to be good meat to Eat.

Tuesday May 7th   This day the weather Clear & pleasant, we set off early, Shortly after the wind blew from the East, we set our Sails, and continued on, Sailing till about 1́2 oClock A. M. at which time the wind rose so high, that one of our Canoes filled with water, we got the Canoe to the shore, and stopped on the South shore for the wind to abate, some of the party caught 2 Beaver during last night, a party of our Men went out to hunt.   They shot five more Beaver at this place.   About 4 oClock P. M. we set out again and proceeded on, and passed by some handsome plains; & bottoms lying on the

North side, and Rough hills, ridges & bottoms on the South side of the River, We saw large Gangs of Buffalo as we passed on both sides of the River.   In the Evening we stopped and encamped on the South side of the River— Captain Clark who had went out hunting from the place we stopped at this day; returned to us here, with one of the hunters, they had killed 2 Buffalo, which was brought to our Camp, they were in good order and their flesh good eating.—

    1. The word "five" is written over "two."

    2. In either McCone or Valley County, Montana, depending on shifts in the river, a few miles southwest of Fraser.

Wednesday 8th May 1805. we Set off eairly. clouded up and rained Some the current Swift. we proceeded on under a fine breeze from the East, 20 miles by about 1 oClock then we passed the mouth of a River[1] on N. S. about 200 yards wide and verry deep. it is 2100 miles from the mouth of the Missourie R. to the mouth of this River. we named this River Scolding or milk River.— we halted on the point above the mouth to dine. Some men went a Short distance up this River. one of them killed a deer. about 2 oC we proceeded on passed handsom bottoms thinly covered with timber on the River and high beautiful high plains on the N. S. and River hills on the S. S. Came 27 miles this day and Camped[2] on a timbred bottom on the S. S. one man killd. a beaver. we Saw a Great deal of beaver Sign all Sorts of Game on each Side R.

Wednesday May 8th   We set off early this morning, shortly after the weather Clouded up and rained; we found the current of the River to run very strong against us; we proceeded on, and set our Sails, having a fine breeze of wind blowing from the East; we came 20 Miles by 10 o'Clock A. M. not withstanding we had so strong a current against us,— and passed a River which emties itself into the Mesouri lying on the North side, this River <is> was about 200 Yards wide at its mouth, and <is> very deep. The mouth of this River is 2,100 Miles distant from the Mouth of the Mesouri River, Our Officers gave this River the name, Scalding Milk River.—[3] We halted at a point above the Mouth of this River to dine, where Some of our party went a short distance up this River, and killed a deer which they brought to us.—

The party that went up Scalding Milk river mentioned, that the River continued its breadth and depth as high up as where they had been—the Water Clear, and deep; the banks tolerably high, and the land very rich, and the country fertile, being partly Priaries and some Skirts of woodland.— At 2 o'Clock P. M. we proceeded on our Voyage, and passed some handsome River bottoms, thinly cover'd with Timber, and beautiful high plains, lying on the North side of the River; and hills lying along the River on the South side.— We came too in the Evening, and encamped in a bottom with Timber; lying on the South side of the River   One of our party shortly after we encamped, went out a hunting, and killed One beaver, We have this day seen vast Signs of all kind of Game on both sides of the River, and beaver in particular, We came this day 27 Miles—

1. Milk River, reaching the Missouri in Valley County, Montana, still bears the name the captains gave it.

2. Probably in Valley County, a mile or two above Fort Peck Dam.

3. This is the copyist's attempt to understand Whitehouse's "Scolding or milk River," which is in fact derived from the captains' correct conclusion that the Milk was the "River Which Scolds at All Others," of which the Indians had told them at Fort Mandan.

Thursday 9th *May 1805.* clear and pleasant.   we Set off at Sun rise and proceeded on   about 9 oC. we halted to take breakfast in a beautiful Smoth bottom thinly or partly covred with timber on the S. S.   Capt. Clark killed two deer.   the Game is getting So pleanty and tame in this country that Some of the men has went up near enofe to club them out of their way. about one oC. we passed the mouth of a large River[1] which came in on the S. S.   it is at high water mark about 437 yards wide, but the water at this Season of the year Sinques in the quick Sand So that their is none to be Seen at the mouth.   this River is called [*blank*]   we halted to dine.   Some of the party killed two buffaloe.   proceeded on   passed large bottoms covred with timber on each Side of the River   Saw large gangs of buffaloe and elk on the Side of the hills in the bottoms and on the plains.   Came 25 miles to day and Camped[2] at the mouth of a creek (named warners River) on the

N. S.   Saw great deal of beaver Sign in the course of the day.   the country for Several days back is pleasant, the Soil good, & the Game pleanty

Thursday May 9th   This morning we had Clear pleasant Weather, we set out at sunrise, and proceeded on 'till about 9 o'Clock A. M. and came too, at a fine beautiful smooth bottom, thinly cover'd with Timber; where we breakfasted.—   Captain Clark here left us and went out a hunting, with some of the party.—   they returned in a short time, having killed two deer, which they brought to us, The men informed us, that the Buffalo were so numerous and tame at a small distance from us, that some of them, went up near enough to strike them with Clubs, but were so poor as not to be fit for use.—

About 1 o'Clock P. M. we proceeded on, and passed the Mouth of a large River, that came in on the South side of the Mesouri, it was by measurement 437 Yards wide, but the water at this season of the Year, had sunk so much in it, that it was entirely dry at its mouth, This River <is called> was named by our Officers dry River   We halted to dine a small distance, above this River, and some of our party went out and killed two Buffalo, which <they> some of our party brought in with them to us, they were in tolerable good Order.—   We proceeded on our Voyage at 3 oClock P. M. and passed large bottoms covered with timber; lying on each side of the River; and saw large Gangs of Buffalo; and Elk on the side of the hills & in the bottoms and plains, on both sides of the River.   We halted in the Evening at the Mouth of a large Creek or River which Our Officers named Warners River, lying on the North side of the Mesouri, during this days travel we saw great signs of beaver, which has been the same for these several days past; we had pleasant weather, the Soil good, and game continues to be very plenty.—

1. The party's Big Dry River, still called Big Dry Fork, or Creek, in McCone and Garfield counties, Montana.

2. A few miles above the town of Fort Peck, Valley County, Montana. "Warners River," present Duck Creek, was named for William Werner of the party.

Friday 10th May 1805.   clear and cold.   we Set of[f] about Sun rise and proceeded on.   the wind rose from the N. W.   came about 4 miles and halted[1] for the wind to abate at a bottom covred with timber on the S. S. where the beaver had eat down considerable of a peace of Small timber Several of the party went out to hunt   the wind rose high   Some Squawls of rain.   one of the men caught a nomber of fish.   the hunters killed 1 fat buffaloe 4 beaver and 3 Deer.   Some of them Saw Some mooce Deer[2] which was much larger than the common deer.   our officers Inspected our arms &c.   Camped here for the night.

Friday May 10th   We had clear and pleasant weather, and set out at Sunrise, and proceeded on, when the wind rose from the North west, we went on about 4 Miles, and halted for the Wind to abate, it blowing fresh; the place that we halted at, was in a bottom covered with Timber, lying on the South side of the River, where the Beaver had cut down a considerable quantity of small Trees.—   Some of our party, went out to hunt, and one of them to fish, The wind rose considerably high, accompanied with Squalls of Rain.—

The Man who went a fishing met with great success, and caught a number of fish, The hunters returned to us, having killed One buffalo, which was in good order, 3 deer and four beaver which they brought to us.—   The hunters mentioned that they had seen some Moose deer, which they said was <much> considerably larger than the common deer.   Our Officers inspected our Arms & We encamped at this place this night

1. In either Garfield or Valley County, Montana, on a site now inundated by Fort Peck Reservoir.

2. Ordway also identifies them as moose. It is probably a mistake for mule deer.

Saturday 11th May 1805.   a clear cold morning, a white frost last night. Some of the party caught 2 beaver last night.   we Set off eairly, and proceeded on   passed black bluffs on the S. S. and hills on each Side partly covred with low ceeder.   we Saw large gangs of buffaloe in the bottoms on Each Side of the River.   towards evening one of the party[1] wounted a brown bair, and was chased by it to the perogues.   Several hunters went to his assistance and killed it   it was nearly of the Same discription as the other we killed Several days ago.   we fount it fat and good meat.   Capt. Clark who walked on Shore killed 2 buffaloe and 2 deer.   (one beaver also)   one of the men killd. another buffaloe. we Saw hills on the N. S. partly covred with pitch pine[2] the first we have Seen. the country begins to be hilley and broken, but verry rich Soil the bottoms on the River chiefly covred with cottonwood timber, which is filled with Game Some Smoth plains under the hills covred with wild hysop.[3] we came 17 miles and Camped[4] on the South Side before night on account of dressing the bair, which detained us untill night &c. passed 2 or 3 Small runs to day, &c

Saturday May 11th We had a white frost last night, and this morning was Clear & cold, some of our party, during the night, caught 2 Beaver, We set off early, and proceeded on, & passed some black bluffs, lying on the South side of the River, and hills on both sides of the River, partly covered with low Cedar Trees growing on them,— and saw large gangs of Buffalo, in the bottoms on each side of the River,— towards the Evening, one of our party that went out hunting wounded a Brown Bear, The animal was so fierce, that he chased the hunter, to where our Pettyaugers lay. Several of our hunters went to his assistance, and killed it.— This Bear was nearly in size, the same as the one I have before described, which we had killed in the River, some days past, but much fatter,— and its flesh good meat Captain Clark, & some hunters who had walked on shore since Morning, with some of our party, came to us here; They had killed 3 Buffalo, 2 deer, and One beaver and a party was sent to bring them to the Pettyaugers.— We saw here some hills lying on the North side of the River, partly covered with Pitch pine Trees, which were the first of the kind we had seen since we entered the River Mesouri, The Country here begins to be hilly and broken; but the Soil very rich, The bottoms on the River are chiefly cover'd with Cotton wood and is filled with game.— There is some plains lying under the hills at this place, which is covered with wild hysop,— We stopped at the place where we <put out> took in, the hunter, who had wounded the Bear, and en-camped, it being on the South side of the River on the bank,— in Order to dress the Bear & preserve the meat that was killed this day, which kept us employed till Night

1. Bratton.
2. Ponderosa pine, *Pinus ponderosa* Laws.

3. Probably big sagebrush, *Artemisia tridentata* Nutt.

4. In Garfield County, Montana, on a site now inundated by Fort Peck Reservoir.

Sunday 12th May 1805. a clear pleasant warm morning. we Set off Soon after Sunrise and proceeded on. passed the pitch pine hills on the N. S. one of the hunters killed a deer in a bottom on the S. S. Capt. Clark killed a beaver in the River. passed a Small River[1] on the N. S. the wind rose high from the N. W. we halted[2] about one oC. to dine on the S. S. opposite the lower point of an Island covred with willows in the middle of the River. the wind detained us the remainder of the day. Some men went out hunting & killed Some Elk & Deer. Camped for the night. had come [*blank*] miles this day. Squwls of rain this evening. &c.

Sunday May 12th We had a clear, pleasant warm morning and set off soon after sunrise; and passed some hills, having pitch pine growing on them, lying on the North side of the River; one of our hunters that was out, killed a deer in a bottom, which lay on the South side of the River, Captain Clark as we passed on, killed a Beaver as it was swimming in the River, We proceeded on, and passed a small River, lying on the North side of the Mesouri, here the Wind rose from the North West, and blew hard.— About One o'Clock, we stopped to dine, on the South side of the River; opposite to the lower point of an Island, cover'd with Willows. This Iland lies in the middle of the River Mesouri,

The wind continuing to blow hard, detained us here the remainder of the day,— A party of our Men went out hunting, and killed some Elk and deer, which they brought into our Camp, In the Evening we had some squalls of Rain. We encamp'd having come 10 Miles this day.—

1. Perhaps Seventh Point Coulee, Valley County, Montana.

2. Where they camped, on a site in Garfield County, Montana, now inundated by Fort Peck Reservoir.

Monday 13th May 1805. the wind blew hard all last night. Some rain high wind and Squawls of rain this morning, So that we did not Set off eairly. Some men went out hunting and killed Several Elk and deer. about 2 oC. p. m. the weather cleared off pleasant. the wind abated and we Set off

Some of the hunters had not returned. we proceeded on   the current Swift   passed hills on each Side which make near the River only the bottoms on the points & in the bends.   came 9 miles and Camped[1] in a bottom on S. S.   the hunters joined us one of them had wounded a white or brown bear.   we passed a creek at the lower end of this bottom, the Current verry Swift in the Missourie.   came about 9 miles this day.

Monday May 13th   The wind continued blowing hard all last night, and this morning, we had Squalls of rain, & high wind, which occasioned our not setting off Early,—   some of our Men went out hunting, and killed several Elk and deer—   about 2 o'Clock P. M. the weather cleared off & became pleasant, and the wind abated.—   We then set off and proceeded on our Voyage, (some of the hunters that went out this morning had not returned to us,) the current of the River running very swift, we passed some hills, which make in, near to the River, the bottom land being only on the points, and in the bends of the River, We came 9 Miles, and encamped in a bottom, lying on the South side of the River   At the lower end of this bottom <is> Run a large creek, Our hunters joined us here with the game that they had killed, One of the hunters had wounded a brown bear, but he did not get him, The current running very Strong in the Mesouri at this place—

1. In Garfield County, Montana, a mile or two above Crooked Creek.

Tuesday 14th May 1805.   a hard white frost last night.   our mocasons froze near the fire.   a clear and pleasant morning.   we Set off at Sun rise and proceeded on   passed the mouth of a large creek[1] on N. S. named [*blank*] and a Small willow Island abo. the mouth of Sd creek.   we Saw verry large gangs of buffaloe, on N. S.   high rough black hills on each Side of the River.   Some Spots of pitch pine on the hills on each Side of the River. about 1 oC. we halted to dine at timbred bottom on the S. S.   Capt. Clark killed a buffaloe   about 2 oC. we proceeded.   (we had passed the mouth of a large creek[2] this fore noon on S. S.   Sergt. Gass Saw Some banks of Snow on the N. Side of Some hills.)   about 4 oClock P. M. we passed the mouth of a large creek[3] on S. S. 100 yards wide at high water mark.   we proceeded on   at 5 oC. we Saw a verry large brown bear on the hills on S. S.   Six men went from the cannoes to kill him   they fired at him and only wounded him he took after them and chased 2 men in to a cannoe.   they Shoved off in the River and fired at him   Some of the men on Shore wounded him worse he then chased one man down a Steep bank in to the River and was near gitting hold of him, but he kept up Stream So that the bear could not git up to him.   one of the men on Shore Shot the bear in the head, which killed him dead after having nine balls Shot in him.   we got him to Shore and butchered him.   his feet was nine Inches across the ball, and 13 in length, nearly of the Same description of the first we killed only much larger   his nales was Seven Inches long &c.   the two captains ware out on Shore after a verry large gang of buffaloe.   the white perogue of the captains hoisted Sail as the wind blew fair.   a violent Storm of wind arose from a black cloud in the N. W.   the wind shifted in N. W. and took the Sail of a Sudden and had it not been for the eairning [awning] and mast She would have turned up Side down.   She filled ful of water   with much trouble they got her to Shore and unloaded hir.   found that the most of the loading was wet   the Medicine Spoiled or damaged very much   Some of the paper and nearly all the books got wet, but not altogether Spoiled.   we opened all the loading, on the bank and Camped[4] at a bottom covred with timber on the N. S.   our officers gave each man a draghm of ardent Spirits, Came 18½ miles this day.— (1 man wounded another bear).

Tuesday May 14th   We had last night hard white frost, so that our Moccasins froze near the fire, the morning was clear and pleasant, We set off at sunrise, and proceeded on our Voyage; and passed a large Creek lying on the North side of the River which our Officers named Whitehouses Creek, opposite to this Creek, we passed a small Island covered with Willows, we saw this day very large gangs of buffalo,—   On the North side of the River, as we passed along; we saw high rough black hills, lying on both sides of the river, About one o'Clock we halted to dine in a bottom, lying on the South side of the River, Captain Clark went out at this place to hunt, and killed a Buffalo, which was brought to us, about 2 o'Clock P. M. we set out; (We passed this forenoon, the Mouth of a large Creek lying on the South side of the Mesouri, 100 Yards wide at high water mark) and Serjeant Gass who was out hunting, saw some Banks of snow, on hills, lying on the North side of the River.—   at

4 oClock P. M. we passed another large Creek on the South side of the River also about 100 Yards wide, and saw a very large Brown bear on the hills, Six of our Men went from one of the Canoes in order to kill him, They came near and fired at him, and only wounded the Animal.— The bear on being wounded, took after the party and followed 2 of the Men so close that they took into one of our Canoes, and shoved her off from the Shore. The Men in the Canoe discharged their Guns, as well as those Men on Shore at this bear, & wounded him again, and he then took after one of those Men who was on the Shore, and chased him down a steep bank, into the River, and was near getting hold of him. The Man who was chased by the Bear, kept going up the Stream of the River, so that the bear could not overtake him.— One of the Men on the Shore, shot the bear through the head, which killed him— We had shot nine balls into this bear, before we killed him, The Men then got him to the Shore where they butcher'd him— The feet of this bear was Nine Inches across the balls, and thirteen Inches in length,— differing only from the first large bear that we killed, in having <toe> larger Nails; these being 7 Inches long.— Our two Captains had gone ashore, after a very large Gang of buffalo that they had seen; when the Men on board of the Pettyauger that the Captains went in, hoisted Sail, (the Wind being fair) and set off; shortly after a Violent Storm came from a black Cloud, which lay in the Northwest, and the Wind shifting suddenly to that point; took the Pettyauger aback and had it not have been for the Awning & Mast, she must have turned upside down, The Pettyauger filled full of Water, and with much trouble they got her to the shore—and unloaded her, We found that the most part of her loading was wet, the Medicine damaj'd, & part of it Spoiled—

We also found some of the papers, and books had got wet, but not so much as to be spoiled.— The Men that was with the Craft were all employed in unloading the Pettyauger, and opening the loading, in Order to dry it.— We encamped in a bottom of timber lying on the North side of the River. Our officers came to us, and the Men that were out, One of which had wounded a brown bear, We came 18½ Miles this day.—

1. Probably the party's Gibson's Creek (after expedition member George Gibson), now Sutherland Creek, Valley County, Montana. Unaccountably, the copyist calls it "Whitehouses Creek."

2. Probably their Stick Lodge Creek, now Hell Creek, Garfield County, Montana.

3. The party's Brown Bear Defeated Creek, present Snow Creek, Garfield County.

4. In Valley County, a few miles above Snow Creek, on a site now inundated by Fort Peck Reservoir.

Wednesday 15th May 1805. cloudy. we delayed to dry the goods which was wet, opened them but Soon had to cover them again for a Shower of rain which lasted about one hour, then we opened them again. Several men out a hunting, they all returned towards evening. had killed one buffaloe 7 Deer and 4 beaver. Stayed here all day & dressed Skins &c.

Wednesday May 15th This morning we had Cloudy weather. We delayed here to dry the Goods, that got wet Yesterday.— they were all opened but we had to cover them again soon, A Shower of rain coming on, which lasted about One hour, when it cleared off.— The Goods were all opened again to dry, several of our Men <Some of our party> went out hunting this morning, and all returned towards Evening, they had killed one Buffalo 7 deer & 4 Beaver. We staid here this day some of the party were employed in dressing Skins &ca.

Thursday 16th May 1805. a heavy diew last night a clear pleasant morning. we opened the goods &c. in order to get them dry before we packed them up. Some of the men wounded a large panther[1] in this bottom, as he was coverring up a deer which he had killed not long before. about 12 oClock Sergt Ordway killed a cabberree or antelope, a Specie of our goats. one of the party killed another which was mired in the mud. about one oC. we packed up our goods and loaded the officers perogue. about 3 oClock P. M. we set off and proceeded on. passed high broken hills & round knobs on each Side of the River and narrow bottoms. passed a Small willow Island near the N. S. we halted a fiew minutes at a bottom on N. S. and killed 2 buffaloe, 3 Deer and one buffaloe calf. Camped[2] on the S. S. at a bottom covered with timber. came 7 miles to day.

Thursday May 16th · A heavy dew fell last night, but a pleasant Clear morning. All hands were employed, in opening the Goods, to get them thoroughly dried before we packet them up again,— Some of the Men after they had finished opening the Goods, went a hunting.— they wounded a large Panther, in the bottom which we were encamped in, as he was covering up a deer which he had killed a short time before.— About 2 o'Clock P. M. One of our Serjeants killed a Caberree or Antelope, which is a specie of the Goat kind, and another of the party killed another of the same kind, that was fast mired in the Mud,— About One oClock P. M. we packed up all our Goods, and loaded the Officers pettyauger, At 3 o'Clock P. M we set off, and passed high broken hills, & high Nobs which lay on each side of the River, and narrow bottoms, and a small Island having Willows growing on it lying on the North side of the River, We halted a few minutes at a bottom on the North side of the River, when some of our party went out and killed, 2 buffalo, One buffalo Calf, and three deer, which were brought to our Pettyaugers We proceeded on, and Encamped in a bottom cover'd with timber; lying on the South side of the River, having come 7 Miles this day.—

1. Mountain lion, *Felis concolor.*

2. In Garfield County, Montana, on a site now inundated by Fort Peck Reservoir; see Lewis's entry for further discussion of this campsite.

Friday 17th May 1805. a clear pleasant morning. we Set off eairly and proceeded on. passed high broken whiteish couloured hills, which wash by rain, and make close to the River on each Side, the bottoms high and narrow. Some Spots of pitch pine on and between the hills on each Side, but the cottonwood gits Scarser. we Saw large gangs of Elk, but a fiew buffaloe. Saw a number of geese and goslings on the river about 2 oC. we halted to dine at a Small bottom on S. S. where there was Some old Indian Camps. about 3 oC. P. M. we proceeded on towards evening we killed a brown bear, the first femal that we killed we passed a creek[1] on the S. S., & verry high rough naked hills on each Side all this day. we Came 20¼ miles and Camped[2] on a narrow plain on the South Side— (killed 2 Elk)

Friday May 17th A Clear pleasant morning, We set off early, and proceeded on our Voyage, and passed by high, broken whitish colour'd hills, on each side of the River, here the Cotton wood was scarce, The hills which we passed wash by the Rain, and they make close in <close> to the River on both sides of it. the bottoms lay high, and are narrow, Some spots of pitch pine, <and> growing between the hills on both sides of the River,—

We saw large gangs of Elk, and but a few Buffalo this day, we also saw a number of Geese and goslins in the River, about 2 o'Clock we halted to dine, at a small bottom on the South side of the River; where there was some old Indian Camps,— about 3 o'Clock we proceeded on our way, & towards Evening one of the party killed a brown bear, the first female brown bear that was killed by our party. — We proceeded on, and passed a Creek lying on the South side of the River; and we saw very high rough naked hills lying on both sides of the River all this day, We encamped in the Evening on a narrow plain, on the South side of the River, and One of our hunters brought to us 2 Elk he had killed, We came 20¼ Miles this day.—

1. Probably the party's Burnt Lodge Creek, now Seven Blackfoot Creek, Garfield County, Montana; see Lewis's entry this day about the confusion surrounding this stream.
2. In Garfield County, a little above the mouth of Seven Blackfoot Creek.

Saturday 18th May 1805. a clear warm morning. one of the party killed a rattle Snake.[1] another caught a beaver. about 7 oC. we Set out and proceeded on. passed Some narrow bottoms of timber & covered with rose bushes.[2] about 10 oC. clouded up and began to rain. we had Several Small Showers. about 12 oC Capt. Clark killed a fat deer. we halted to dine and dry our Selves at a large bottom covered with timber on N. S. this bottom is filled with buffaloe Elk Deer &c one of the party killed 2 Elk. another killed a beaver. about 2 we proceeded on the weather cleared up and we had a pleasant afternoon the River water is gitting clear and gravelly bottom &c. we came 19 miles and Camped[3] at a Smooth high bottom on S. S. N. B. (Capt. Clark killed three deer)

Saturday May 18th We had a fine warm morning, One of our party killed a rattle Snake of a large size and another caught a beaver, About 7 o'Clock we set out, and passed some narrow bottoms of timber, <and> covered with Rosebushes.— At 10 oClock A. M. it clouded up and began to rain; and we had small Showers. at 12 o'Clock A. M. Captain Clark went on shore, and killed a fat deer, We then halted to dine and to dry our Cloathes, at a large bottom covered with timber lying on the North side of the River. This bottom is filled with buffalo, elk, deer & other game, Two of our party killed 2 Elk and One beaver, About 2 o'Clock P. M We proceeded on our way, and the weather cleared up, and we had a pleasant afternoon, Here the Water of the Mesouri River, that had been muddy ever since we first entered it, began to get clear, and the bottom that was mud, is gravelly— Captain Clark who had been out a hunting joind us in the Evening; having killed 3 deer, which we took on board the Crafts, We encamped that Evening on a high smooth bottom, lying on the South side of the River, having come 19 Miles this day

1. Prairie rattlesnake, *Crotalus viridus viridus,* described by Lewis on May 17.
2. An unknown rose, *Rosa* sp.
3. In Garfield County, Montana, about two miles upstream from the Devils Creek Recreation Area; the area is now inundated by Fort Peck Reservoir.

Sunday 19th May 1805. a heavy diew fell last night. a clear pleasant morning. we Set off as usal and proceeded on. passed pitch pine hills on each Side of the river. about 10 oClock we killed a Small female brown bear on S. S. we took on board the meat & Skin and proceeded on. about 1 oC. we halted to dine at a bottom on the N. Side. Capt. Clark killed 3 Deer. about 2 we proceeded on passed a handsom willow Island near the N. S. of River. passed pitch pine & ceeder hills as usal, & bottoms of timber on each Side of the River. we Came about 18 Miles and Camped[1] at a bottom on the N. Side, where Capt. Lewis killed an Elk & Some of the men killed 3 Deer. Some of the hunters killed 3 beaver to day.—

Sunday May 19th   A heavy dew fell last night, and this morning was clear and pleasant, we set off early, as usual; and proceeded on, and passed on each side of the River, hills cover'd with Pitch pine, about 10 o'Clock A. M. some of our party killed a small female brown bear on the South side of the River, we stopped for a short time; and took on board the Meat, and Skin of this bear, we then proceeded on till about One o'Clock, when we halted to dine in a bottom laying on the North side of the River, Captain Clark who had been on shore hunting, join'd us here; having killed 3 Deer, which was brought to us, by a party sent after them,— At 2 o'Clock P. M we proceeded on our Voyage, and passed a handsome Island with Willows growing on it, lying on the North side of the River, & hills lying on both sides of the River; the growth on which was Pitch pine and Cedar, and fine bottoms of timber, we proceeded on till Evening, and encamped at a bottom lying on the North side of the River, Captain Lewis who had been out hunting with a party of our Men since we dined returned to us here having killed One Elk 3 deer and 3 Beaver.— We came 18 Miles this day.—

1. In either Phillips or Garfield County, Montana, at or near later Long Point, now inundated by Fort Peck Reservoir.

Monday 20th May 1805. a clear pleasant morning. we Set off as usal. one of the hunters caught a beaver last night. abt. nine oC. we passed the mouth of a Creek[1] on the S. S. and a handsom bottom of C. wood timber. one of the hunters killed a Deer another killed a beaver. we proceeded on passed pitch pine & ceeder hills on each Side River. about 11 oClock, we arived at the mouth of Mussell Shell River[2] on the S. S. this River is 110 yards wide and the Missourie 222 yards wide at this place, and 2271 miles from the mouth of the Missourie River. we encamped here on the point between the 2 rivers which is a large bottom covered with C. wood timber. we delayed here all day for observations &c. found the latitude 47° 24' North. the hunters killed at this place Eight Deer 4 Elk one woolf—and remained here all the afternoon & Camped for the night 2 men Stayed out hunting beaver all night. we came only 6 miles this morning.

Monday May 20th A Clear pleasant morning, we set off as usual, One of the hunters during last night caught a beaver; about 9 oClock A. M. We passed the Mouth of a Creek lying on the North side of the River, and a handsome bottom of Cotton Wood timber lying on the same side; We proceeded on our Voyage at about 11 o'Clock A. M. We arrived at the Mouth of a River named by our Officers Muscle shell River, lying on the South Side of the Mesouri, this River is 110 Yards wide at its mouth, and the Mesouri River; at this place 222 Yards wide; and the distance from the Mouth of the Mesouri River, to the Mouth of Muscle shell River 2,271 Miles We took up

Camp here, on a point situated between these two Rivers, in a large bottom Cover'd with Cotton wood, we halted here this day, Our Officers intending to ascertain the Latitude of this place, which they compleated and found it to lay in Latitude 47° 22′ North,—

The party that went out a hunting returned to us here, having killed 9 deer, one beaver, one Elk and one wolf Two of our hunters went out this night, and stayed out all night to trap beaver.— We came 6 Miles this morning—

1. The party's Blowing Fly Creek, later Squaw Creek, Garfield County, Montana.
2. Musselshell River, here dividing Garfield and Petroleum counties, still bears the party's name.

Tuesday 21st 1805. a clear pleasant morning. the 2 men returned who Stayed out all night had caught one beaver & killed a deer. they Swam across the Mussel Shell River before Sun rise. Soon after we Set off. another beaver was caught we proceeded on. passed timbred bottoms & hilly land on each Side, but the River hills are not So high, as they were for Some distance below. Some of the party yesterday discovered a high range of mountains[1] to the west, a long distance off. we Saw Some old Indian Camps in a timbred bottom on N. S. where Capt. Clark killed an Elk. about 1 oC. P. M. we halted to dine at a handsom timbred bottom on the South Shore. one of the hunters killed an Elk. the wind rose So high from the N. W. that we delayed about 2 hours and proceeded on passed bottoms & pine hills as usal. Came about 15 Miles and Camped[2] on a large Sand beach on N. S. one of the hunters killed a buffaloe another killed a beaver. the wind rose verry high Soon after we Camped, and made the Sand fly So that it was verry disagreeable. the most of the party moved back towards the hills.

Tuesday May 21st This morning we had clear and pleasant Weather; the Men that were out catching beaver returned this Morning at day light. they had bad success, having caught only one Beaver, however they kill'd a deer, both of which they brought to our Camp. We set out early, and passed bottoms covered with Timber, and hilly land lying on both sides of the River.

The Hills here are not so high, as they were below,— Some of our party that was out hunting Yesterday, reported that they had seen, a high ridge of Mountains, which lay to the West, but appeared to be a very great distance from them, We proceeded on, and passed by some Bottom land, lying on the North side of the River where we saw some Indian Camps, that were old; these Camps were surrounded with Cotton Wood Trees, <where> Captain Clark went on shore at that place, and killed an Elk, we shot a Beaver in the River, on our way here this day.— About 1 o'Clock P. M. we halted to dine in a bottom of Timber, lying on the South side of the River, where one of our hunters killed an Elk.— The wind rose here, to a very great height, from the North west so that we were forced to halt for two hours at that place.—

We proceeded on our Voyage about 3 o'Clock P. M and passed bottom land & Pine hills, lying on both sides of the River, and came about 5 Miles and encamped on a Sand beach, lying on the North side of the River, our hunters that were out, killed a Buffalo, and a Beaver which was brought to our Camp, Soon after we encamped, the Wind blew so very hard, and the sand flew so much; that it made the place disagreeable, that most of our party moved back to some hills not far distant from the River.—

    1. The Little Rocky Mountains, in Phillips and Blaine counties, Montana, which Clark saw on May 19.

    2. In Phillips County, at a site now inundated by Fort Peck Reservoir.

Wednesday 22nd May 1805. the wind blew hard all last night (caught 2 beaver last night) and continues blowing this morning, Cloudy. about 11 oC. A. M. the wind abated So that we Set off and proceeded on passed a Small Island near N. S. and one Near the S. Side. the River hills make near the River. passed black bluffs the pitch pine close along Sd. bluffs to the bank of the River. passed a Creek[1] on the N. S. we wounded a brown bear in the River. (abt. 2 oC. we) halted to dine at a handsom timbred bottom on the N. S. a cold chilly day. towards evening Some of the hunters killed a large brown bear. we Saved the Skin & greese. we Camped[2] on the N. S. Came 16½ Miles to day. Sergt. Ordway and one of the hunters killed a large buffaloe.

Wednesday May 22nd   The wind continued blowing hard, all last night which was the case in the Morning till about 11 o'Clock A. M. when it abated, We then set off, and proceeded on our Voyage; and passed Two small Islands, one laying near the North & the other near the South side of the River, the Hills making in, near the River, and black bluffs, [*crossed out, illegible*] with Pitch pine Trees growing close along those bluffs, to the bank of the River, We likewise passed a Creek lying on the North side of the River, where one of the Hunters that was out wounded a brown bear, but we did not get him— he was in the River and made his escape.—   At 2 o'Clock P. M. we stopped to dine at a Handsome piece of Timbered bottom land, lying on the North side of the River; the day was chilly and Cold, towards Evening some of our hunters killed a large brown Bear, which they brought to us, We halted here to Skin & get the Oil of this animal & One of our hunters killed a large Buffalo; We encamped on the North side of the River & came 16½ Miles this day.—

1. Grouse Creek to the party, now probably Beauchamp Creek, Phillips County, Montana.
2. In Phillips County, just below CK, or Kannuck, Creek, the party's Teapot Creek.

Thursday 23rd May 1805.   a cold frosty morning.   the Standing water was froze over.   we Set off at Sun rise and proceeded on.   one of the hunters who went on Some distance & Stayed out all [night] joined us, had killed 5 deer.

we passed bottoms   killed [*blank*] Deer in Sd. bottoms   passed pitch pine hills on each Side of the River.   passed Several Small Islands in the River. about 2 oC. P. M. we halted and made fire to dine at a timbred bottom on N. S.   one of the hunters took his rifle & bullitt pouch on Shore   the fire broke out into the woods, and burned up his shot pouch powder horn & the stalk of his rifle.   about 3 oC we proceeded on   passed pine hills as usal. towards evening we killed a brown bear in the river but he Sank in under a large drift of wood So that we could not git it.   we Came 28 miles to day and Camped[1] at a timbred bottom on the N. S.   Some of the party discovered high Mountains[2] to the west of us a long distance or as far off as their eyes could extend L. S.[3]

Thursday May 21st[4]   We had a cold frosty morning.   the standing water was froze over, and cover'd with Ice, We set off on our Voyage at Sun rise, and proceeded on, Some of the Hunters that had went on some distance before us, stopped on the bank of the River to waite for us, they had killed 5 deer, which we stopped and took on board; We proceeded on, and passed some bottom land, (& some of our party killed some Deer in them;) and Saw hills having pitch pine growing on them, on both sides of the River, and several small Islands, About 2 oClock P. M. we halted to dine, and kindled a fire in a bottom on the North side of the River, when one of our hunters took his Rifle, and bullet pouch on shore, the fire caught in the Woods, and burned up his shot pouch, powder horn and stock of his Rifle—.   About 3 o'Clock P. M. we proceeded on, and passed some Hills with pine growth on them lying on both sides of the River, towards Evening, some of the party killed a brown bear, as he was swimming in the River; but he sunk in under a large drift of Wood, so that we could not get him out.—   We encamped at a bottom, Covered with timber lying on the North side of the River where some of our party discovered, some very high Mountains, lying to the West-ward of us, at a very great distance running to the Northward as far as their sight could Extend   We came 28 Miles this day.—

1. A little below the mouth of Rock (their North Mountain) Creek, Fergus County, Montana.

2. The Little Rocky Mountains.

3. The last two letters appear to be "L. S.," but the Little Rockies are to the north. "L. S.," larboard (or south side in this instance), is uncharacteristic usage by Whitehouse.

4. An error by the copyist, the entry is clearly for May 23.

Friday 24th May 1805.   clear & pleasant.   we Set off as usal, & and pro-ceeded on   passed Several Creeks[1] & Several Small Islands in the river passed pitch pine hills & timbred bottoms on each Side.   about 3 oClock P. M. we halted to dine at a Small & narrow bottom covered with timber on N. S.   Capt. Clark who walked on Shore had killed a fat buffaloe   Some of the party went for the meat, high black bluffs on the S. S. & a large Creek[2] which came in a Short distance below.   the wind from the S. E. So that we Sailed Some part of the time   about 4 we proceeded on.   2 canoes waited for the five men to come with the meat.   Came 24¾ miles to day and

Camped[3] at a bottom covered with c. wood timber which the leaves were dead. they had been killed by the frost. the 2 Canoes & 6 men Stayed behind all night. we Saw a nomber of old Indian Camps in the bottoms near the River.

Friday May 24th This morning we had Clear pleasant weather, We sett of early, and proceeded on our Voyage, we passed several Creeks, & small Islands lying in the middle of the River, and bottoms and hills with pitch pine growing on them on both sides.— At 3 o'Clock P. M. we halted to dine at a small narrow bottom, covered with Timber lying on the North side of the River; Captain Clark, who walked along shore, killed a fat buffalo, some of our party was sent to bring the Meat to us. we proceeded on, and passed high black bluffs, lying on the South side of the River, & a large Creek, which came in, just below them.— The wind began to blow from the South east, and we set all Sail.— leaving 2 Pettyaugers behind, to waite for the five men that had went for the Buffalo meat.— At 4 o'Clock P. M. we encamped at a bottom, covered with Cotton wood timber, lying on the North side of the River.— The leaves of these Trees were killed by the frost, The Men that went for the Meat, did not return to us this night, we saw a number of old Indian Camps lying in the River bottoms.— on both sides of it

1. Including the captains' North Mountain Creek, now Rock Creek, Phillips County, Montana, and their Little Dog Creek, after a prairie dog village on the other side of the river, now Sand Creek, Fergus County.

2. Their South Mountain Creek, Fergus County, later known by that name or as Armells Creek.

3. In Fergus or Phillips County, some three miles above where U.S. Highway 191 crosses the Missouri.

Saturday 25th May 1805. a clear pleasant morning. we waited for the 2 Canoes to Come up. about 7 oC. they came. then we Set off and proceeded on. passed 2 creeks[1] on the N. S. and one large one[2] on the S. S. passed 2 Small Islands before noon about 12 oC we passed a large handsom large Island covered with handsom c. wood timber, near the N. S. Saw Several Eagles nests. passed high bluffs & knobs and hills partly covred with pitch pine timber on each Side of the R. the wind blew from the N. W. about 3 oClock we halted to dine on a beautiful level thin timbred Island near the N. S. of the River. Capt. Clark and one man who walked on Shore joined us had killed two Mountain Sheep, one a yew the other a ram. the ram had large horns which turned back of a gradual taper, they have the resemblence of our Sheep only fine brownish hair in Stead of wool. they were poor and not as large as the natives represented, but these are the first we have killed.

about 4 oC. P. M. we proceeded on the current has been verry Swift for Several days. we passed river hills as usal. passed Several Creeks in the course of the day. Came 18 miles to day and Camped[3] on the S. S. little above a high handsom Island in the river mostly prarie only a little large timber at the upper end of it. Gibson one of the hunters putt one of his Shoulders out of place to day but got it in again.

Saturday May 25th This morning we had clear & pleasant weather, we waited at our encampment for the 2 Canoes that had gone for Meat, to come up <at which> it was some time before they arrived, We then set off, and proceeded on our Voyage, and passed two Creeks, lying on the North side, and one large Creek lying on the South side of the River; we passed 2 Small Islands before 12 o'Clock, At 1 oClock we passed a large Island, covered with handsome Timber; lying near the North side of the River, were we saw several Eagles nests.— We proceeded on, and passed high bluffs, and Nobs and hills, partly cover'd with pitch pine lying on each side of the River.—

The wind shifted to the Northwest, but blew moderately.— About 3 o'Clock we halted to dine, on a beautiful level piece of land, thinly timbered, (being an Island,) lying near the North side of the River; Captain Clark who had walked on the Shore, having one of our party with him, since Early this morning joined us here, they had killed two mountain Sheep (or Ibex) a Ewe and a Ram, the ram had very large horns which turned back like those of a common Ram Sheep their make resembles that of the common Sheep, but had fine brownish Colour'd hair, instead of Wool, they were poor, They were not so large as the Natives had represented them to us to be; About 4 oClock P. M. we proceeded on the current of the River running very swift, (it being so for these several days past;) and we passed several hills lying near the River, in the Course of this day.— We encamped in the Evening, on the South side of the River, a little above a handsome Island, lying high, having some large Timber at the upper end of it, the remainder being Priari land.—

1. One of them is Antelope Creek, Phillips County, Montana.
2. Two Calf Creek, Fergus County, Montana.
3. In Fergus County, some five or six miles below the present Cow Island Landing Recreation Area and near the present Missouri ferry crossing.

Sunday 26th May 1805. a clear pleasant morning. we Set off eairly and proceeded on with the towing line under high bluffs which make near the River on each Side & are verry Steep & barron   Some Spots of pine, but the most of the knobs and river hills wash by rains.   passed high Clifts of Sand Stone on each Side.   passed Several Creeks[1] which appeared to be large, Some on each Side.   passed Several Small Islands in the river.   Some of the hunters killed 2 mountain Sheep or Ibex as Capt. Clark calls them which were running along in flocks where the bluffs were to appeerence nearly perpenticular   we Suppose they keep on high Steep clifts & bluffs & mountain[2] in order to keep out of the reach of other larger animals   they are verry Suple & run verry fast.   one of these Ibex which was killed today, had verry large horns.   the head & horns weighed 27 pounds, one of the hunters killed a hare which weighed 8½ pound   we proceeded on with the towing lines all day   towards evening we Came to a rapid place[3] in the river, where the hills made close on each Side & high clifts of rocks.   this rapid had considerable of a fall, which gave us Some trouble to git over our crafts but by towing & waiding in the water & holding the canoes from filling in the waves, we all got Safe over by dark, and Camped[4] on the S. Side below a Small prarie is at a Small bottom of timber where their was Several old Indian Camps.   Capt. Lewis & one of the hunters killed 2 buffloe.   we Came 22 miles this day.

Sunday May 26th   We had a Clear pleasant morning, & set off early; the stream running so strong, that we were forced to use the tow lines, in order to make headway, we passed under high bluffs lying near the River on both sides of it which <are> were very steep and barren; and some small spots of Pine Timber, here most of the knobs, & River hills Wash by the Rains into the River.—

We continued on our way, and passed high clifts, of sand stone lying on each side of the River, and several Creeks which appeared to be large on each side of the River also, and small Islands lying in the middle of it.— Some of our hunters that were out hunting killed 7 Mountain sheep (or Ibex) out of a flock, which were running on the top of the Clifts, which were to appearance very high; & perpendicular.— Those animals are rarely seen in any place, but on the Tops of high hills or Clifts, and it is said they use these places in Order to avoid the large beasts of prey.— They are very Subtle, nimble & Run very fast.— One of those Ibex or mounting Goats that was killed this day had very large horns, The upper Jaw of the head & horns, weighing Twenty Seven pounds, these animals were in good order, and their flesh <eat like> had the Taste of Mutton, One of our hunters killed a hare, which he brought to us, It weighed 8½ pounds.— We proceeded on, towing our Crafts, when we came to a rapid place in the River; where the hills made close in on both sides of it, and high Clifts of Rocks.— This rapid, had a considerable fall, and it gave us much trouble to pass through it.— This we accomplished with much labour, by Towing and wading in the Water, and holding the Crafts & preventing them filling with Water from the Waves, which ran high.— We all got safe over by dark with our Crafts, and encamped on the South side of the River, below an Island of priari land, at a Small bottom of Timber, where there was several old Indian Camps.— Captain Lewis and one of our party, killed 2 buffalo as they went along Shore, We came 22 Miles day.—

1. One is the captains' Windsor's Creek, after Richard Windsor of the party, now Cow Creek in Blaine County, Montana. Another is their Soft Shell Turtle Creek, now Bullwhacker Creek, Blaine County.

2. At this point of a page break in the entry it appears that two sheets have been cut out, but there is no break in the writing.

3. The party's Elk Fawn Rapids, now Bird Rapids.

4. In Fergus County, Montana, above the rapids.

Monday 27th May 1805. pleasant weather. the wind high from the N. W. about 10 oC. we Set off and proceeded on with the towing lines. the current verry Swift. passed a great nomber of rapid places. passed verry high Steep mountains and clifts Steep precipices.[1] these mountains appear to be a desert part of the country. they wash by rains, but a little rain in this part. no diews like other parts but barron broken rich Soil but too much of a desert to be inhabited, or cultivated. Some Spots of pitch & Spruce pine.[2] the game is Scarcer than it has been. no grass nor timber for them to live in, but what Ibex or Mountain Sheep, Elk deer &c live on what little grass their is in the vallies and narrow plains on river, which is covered with wild hysop rose bush & Some grass. Some different kinds of mint[3] along the Shore. Saw mussel[4] Shells also. the Shore is Stoney & gravvelly. no falling in banks but the creeks drive the earth and gravvel in Some distance in the river which causes the most of the hard riffles, which we have had all day and had to double man our perogues to git them over Safe. one mountain ram or Ibex killed to day. we Came 13 mes today, and Camped[5] at an old Indian Camp on the S. Side [of] River we are 800 & 10 miles from the Mandans, 2415 [from the mouth of the Missouri?]

[undated][6]

Remarks of Different places—

Latd of the Gasnage		38	15	57	N
Do	Gran zoe—	39	16	23	N
Do	rock pole	38	16	00	N
Do	the two Cherottors	38½	19	00	N
Do	Decough	38	31	13	N
	River plate	41	3	19¾	N
Do	Camp of the Brareow on Council Bluffs—	41	17	00	

From River Duboise—

To St Charles—   21 Miles by water

" Gasconade—   104   "   "   —

From River Duboise (*continued*)—

Unto the Osage River	138	"	"	.t
" Mine River	201	"	—	—
2 Charottoes Rivers	226—			
" Old village of Misuries	246—			
" Grand River	254—			
" Kanzies River	366—			
2nd Old Village of Kanzies—	433—			
" Nodoway River	481—			
" Grand Na, mahawr	511—			
" Bald pated prarie	570—			
Moute of plate River	632—			
Council Bluffs—	682—			
Little Scioux River	766—			
Mahars Village	870—			
The Mouth of the Big Souix River—	880—			
The Mouth of the river Jacque—	970—			
Grand Calumet Bluffs—	980—			
the River of rapid water—	1020—			
Ceeder Island—	1090—			
River White R—	1142—			
To the Island in the Big bend or Grand detorture of the Missouri River }	1183—			
round the Bend 30 miles—	1213—			
To the Ceeder Island above the Big Bend—	1235—			
To the Mouth of the Teton River—	1275—			
To the 1st Village of Rickierees—	1480—	1430		
To Mouth of the River Bullette—	1505—			
River Chiss-Che-tar above the old village of Mandans }	1550—			
Fort Mandans on the N. Side—	1600½			

Joseph Whitehouse

1600	1550	45	Bolet	
1550	1505	25	Rikeres	
50	45	50		
1505		120		
55			1600	
			1480	
			120	
			1600	
	1480	1183		
	1505	1142		
	25	41		
	00			
1480				
1275				
205	1275			
1480	1235			
	1240			
	22			
	1213			
	1183			
	30			

Latudes of the Different Remarkable Places

on the Missourie River of St. Charles—	38	54	39	N
Gasconade—	38	44	35	
Mo of the Osage River	38	31	6	
mo of the Grand River	38	47	54⁹⁄₁₀	
mo of the Kanzies River	39	5	25	
12 ms. above Dimond Isl.	39	9	38	

3 ms. below the [*crossed out*] 2nd Old Village of Kanzies	39	25	42	
mo. of the Nordaway—	39	39	22	
mo of Na mahaw—	39	55	56	
Good Isld.—	40	20	12	
Bald Pated Prarie	40	27	6	
white Catfish Camp—	41	3	19	
Council Bluff—	41	17	00	
Mo of Stone River or the little Sioux	41	42	34	
On the South Side whare the late King of the Mahars	42	1	3	N
Fish Camp Neer the Mahars Village August 14th 1804	42	13	41	
Septmb. 1 Calimet Bluffs opsite the Sues <Village> Lodges whare we met the Nation of the Sues	42	53	13—	
Ceeder Island Louesells Fort—	44	11	33—	
the Mouth of the Chien River—	44	19	36—	
Mouth of the Water-hoo River	45	39	5—	
the Mouth of the River bullette—	46	29	00—	
Fort Mandans on N. Side—	47	21	00—	
at the forks of Mariah—	47	24	12—	

Monday May 27th   This morning pleasant weather, but the wind high, from the Northwest, about 10 o'Clock A. M. we set out, and proceeded on our Voyage, towing the Craft, the current of the River running very Swift. We passed a number of rapid places, Steep mountains, Clifts and precipices.— This place appear'd to be a desert Country,— The hills washing by the Rains, No dews fall here, and it seldom Rains, The Soil is rich, but has the appearance of being too much a desert, ever to be Inhabited. The Game became scarcer here, than they have been for some time past, owing to their being no Grass, or Timber'd land for them to live in.— no Trees to be seen here, but a few Pitch pine & Spruce.— The Ibex, Elk & deer, being in the Valleys, & narrow plains below this on the River.— Those Valleys and plains are covered with wild hysop, Rose bushes, and some Grass.— some different kinds of wild mint grow along the Shore of the River, and Mussles are to be found in great abundance.— The land along the Shore is Stoney, & Gravelly; and no falling in banks.— The water that comes in here from the Creeks, runs so strong that it drives the Stones, and gravel, some distance into the River; which caused most of the hard Riffles, that we passed this day.— And we had to Man our Crafts doubly in order to get them over Safe.— One of our party kill'd a Mountain Sheep (Ibex,) this day; We came too and encamp'd where we found an old Indian Camp on the South side of the River, we are now 800 Miles above the Mandan Nation & 2,415 Miles from the mouth of the Mesouri River

1. The party was traveling through the Missouri River Breaks, Blaine and Fergus counties, Montana.

2. Douglas fir, *Pseudotsuga menziesii* (Mirb.) Franco.

3. Probably field mint, *Mentha arvenis* L.

4. Mussels could be from either the Margaritanidae or Unionidae family.

5. In Fergus County, near later McGarry Bar.

6. At the end of Whitehouse's entry of May 27 in the original version and partly running into it comes the following miscellaneous material. It consists of eight pages of mileage figures, latitude tables, and random scribbles, some illegible. The random scribbles, for the most part repetitions of Joseph Whitehouse's signature, are not given here. The tables and mileage figures are transcribed as fully as possible and may be compared with similar material in Clark's journals as published in vol. 3 of this edition. Whitehouse's notations are written upside down in the notebook and across the page as in a conventional book, rather than from top to bottom of the page as in a stenographer's notebook as is the practice with the narrative portion of the journal. The material is placed here reading from back to front in the notebook, which is the progression of the tables. The date of its composition is unknown, but Whitehouse does give the latitude of the Marias River where the party arrived on June 2. The entry of May 28 begins on a new page and section of the notebook. From here the pages are somewhat larger than the preceding section and are bound separately to the animal skin cover.

Tuesday 28th May 1805   a clear pleasant morning.   we Set off and proceeded on.   passed over hard riffles.   the Bluffs & clifts are high [*illegible*] as yesterday. abt 10 oC. Capt. Clark killed a mountain Sheep & [*illegible*] Deer. about noon we halted to dine near Some old Indian Camps. Some thunder & Small Showers of rain which lasted about 2 hours. we then proceeded on a pleasant afternoon. towards evening the hills began to git lower passed large bottoms, partly covered with c. wood timber. passed Several Islands 7 or 8 in the course of the day, Some of them handsom groves of timber on them. we passed a number of large Creeks[1] on each Side of the river, which force the Gravvel Stone from the hills in to the river. we Came 21½ miles & Camped[2] in a bottom of the river on the N. S. a large Creek came in on the opposite Shore. we Saw a gang of Elk in this bottom, & beaver Signs [*illegible*] the Shores. a large bottom on the S. Side. we found an Indians foot ball floating down the river & dog poles also.

Tuesday May 28th This morning we had clear and pleasant Weather, we set off and proceeded on our Voyage towing our Crafts. we passed some Riffles and Clifts, as those we passed by Yesterday, About 10 oClock A. M. Captain Clark killed a Mountain <Goat> Sheep or Ibex, about noon, we halted to dine, near some old Indian Camps, We had some thunder, and small showers of rain which lasted about 2 hours, We then proceeded on, and had a pleasant afternoon, towards evening the hills began to be lower, We proceeded on and passed by large bottoms partly covered with timber, and several Islands some of which had handsome Groves of timber on them, we passed a number of large Creeks, lying on each side of the River, which drove the Gravel into the River We encamped in a bottom lying on the River on the North side, opposite to the Mouth of a large Creek where we saw a Gang of Elk in the bottom, and signs of beaver on both Shores,— a large bottom of timber being on the South side of the River, here we found an Indian foot ball floating down the River, and Indian dog poles.— We came 21½ Miles this day.—

1. Including the party's Thompson's Creek, after John B. Thompson, now Birch Creek, which meanders the boundary between present Chouteau and Blaine counties, Montana, and meets the Missouri in Chouteau County.

2. In Chouteau County, near the Judith Landing Recreation Area, and opposite present Dog Creek, their Bull Creek, in Fergus County.

Wednesday 29th May 1805. Some clouday. a large buffloe Swam the river last night, and came out across one of the perogues & broke a blunderbuss,[1] & bent a rifle & came up the bank through the Camp & like to have tramped on Several of the men as they were a Sleep. we Set off as usal & proceeded on. passed the mouth of a large Creek or 2,[2] on the S. S. & bottoms of timber. about 10 oC. A. M. we passed a handsom bottom on the N. S. where about 100 lodges of Indians had lately been camped. we Suspect it was a nation called the blackfoot Indians which live back from the River, to the Northward. we got Some of their dog poles. we proceeded on passed over hard rifles which was So rapid that caused high waves for Some distance below. passed Several Creeks on each Side of the river. about one oC. P. M. we passed high Steep clifts of rocks on the N. S. where the natives had lately drove a gang of buffaloe off from the plains[3] they fell So far on the uneven Stone below that it killed them dead. they took what meat they wanted, & now the wolves & bears are feasting on the remains, which causes a horrid Smell. Capt. Clark killed a wolf with a Sphere[4] near that place. we Saw several brown bear on the mountains on the S. Side. about 3 oC. P. M. we passed the mouth of a large Creek or Small river[5] on S. S. we halted little above at a handsom bottom of timber on the N. S. began to rain, the wind rose high from N. W. So we Camped[6] for the night. Some of the hunters went out in the plains. they Soon returned & Said it Snowed & hailed on the hills back from the river. our officers gave each man a draughm of ardent Spirits. one of the hunters killed an Elk. hard rain this evening. we had come 18 miles to day through a Mountaneous desert Country. Saw a nomber of geese on the river. one man killed one of them.—

Wednesday May 29th We had Cloudy weather this morning, last night a Buffalo swam the River, and came out across one of the Pettyaugers, he passed over a Blunder buss, and trod on one of our Rifles which he bent, and came up the Bank, through our Camp, and had like to have trampled on several of our Men who were asleep, We set off this Morning at the usual hour, and proceeded on our Voyage and passed 2 large Creeks lying on the South side of the River, & large bottoms of Timber,

About 10 o'Clock A. M we passed a handsome bottom of land, lying on the South side of the River where stood about 100 lodges of Indians that had lately been encamped there; we expected it had been a nation of Indians called the Black foot Tribe, who reside back from the River, to the Northward, we landed and got some of their dog poles, for setting poles for our Crafts, We proceeded on and passed over some hard Riffles, which were so rapid, that it caused the Waves to run high, for some distance below, and passed several Creeks lying on both sides of the River, About 1 o'Clock P. M. we passed a high Clift of Rocks, lying on the North side of the River, where the Natives had lately drove a Gang of Buffalo, off, from the plains, Those Buffalo fell so far & the Uneveness of the Stones below; that it had killed a number of them, they had taken what Meat they wanted, and we saw Gangs of Wolves, & Bears, feasting on the remainder, The Indians had piled a large number of the Bones of the Buffalo & upwards 400 Horns, the putrified Meat caused a horred Stench, Captain Clarke killed a Wolf, with a Spear near that plece; We saw several brown bear on the Mountains on the South side of the River, About 3 o'Clock we passed the Mouth of a large Creek, or rather a small River, lying on the South side, We halted a little above at a handsome bottom of Timber, lying on the North side of the River, where it began to Rain & the Wind rose, & blew hard from the North West, At this place we took up our Encampment for the Night.—

Some of our hunters went out into the plains, but soon returned to us, and mentioned that it snowed, & hailed on the Hills back from the River; our Officers gave each of the party a dram of Ardent Spirit, One of those hunters killed an Elk, which was brought to our Camp, In the Evening we had rain, We had come this day 18 Miles through the Mountains, and a desert Country, We saw a number of Geese in the River this day, and One was shot by one of our party—

1. The party had two blunderbusses, which were heavy, swivel-mounted shoulder arms, generally used to fire buckshot for defense.

2. Judith River, Fergus County, Montana, named by Clark for his future wife, Julia Hancock, and Chip Creek, the party's Valley Creek, Chouteau County, Montana.

3. See Lewis's entry for the day on the question whether this was an actual buffalo jump.

4. The captain's espontoon.

5. The party's Slaughter River (now Arrow Creek), from the supposed buffalo jump, the boundary between Chouteau and Fergus counties.

6. At the Slaughter River Landing Recreation Area, Chouteau County.

Thursday 30th May 1805. Cloudy & rain, the wind high from the N. W. we delayed untill about 10 oC. then Set off, though disagreeable working. passed white Straight range of Clifts[1] on the S. S. proceeded on with the towing lines about 5 miles & halted to dine on the N. S. Some of the hunters Shot an Elk. cold chilly wind & rain. passed a Camp wher 29 lodges of the blackfoot Indians had lately been & left piles of mussel Shells at each fire. Came 8 miles. Camped[2] at a handsom narrow bottom covered with thin c. wood timber, where 50 or 60 lodges of Indians had lately been Camped. they were gone as we expect up the river. they left Several lodge poles & considerable of fire wood gathered. 2 of the hunters went across the river on the hill & killed 2 buffaloe.—

Thursday May 30th This morning we had the weather Cloudy and Rainey; & the wind blowing hard from the North west, We delayed setting off till 10 oClock A. M. the weather still being very disagreeable, & bad to Tow the Crafts; we then proceeded on our Voyage, and passed a white strait range of Clifts, lying on the South side of the River, we proceed still on, towing our Crafts about 5 Miles, when we halted to dine on the North side of the River; One of our hunters Shot an Elk, which was brought to us.— the weather still continued Cold & Chilly with some rain,— We set off about 2 o'Clock P. M. from the place that we dined at; and passed an Old Camp of 20 lodges, which the black foot Indians we supposed had lately left. they had left, piles of Muscle shells, at each fire, We came 8 Miles, and encamped at a handsome Narrow bottom, thinly covered with Cotton wood; where we found 60 lodges, that some Indians had lately left, and we expected had gone up the River Mesouri, Those Indians left several lodge poles, and a considerable quantity of fire Wood, which they had gather'd; 2 of our hunters went across the River to a hill, where they killed 2 Buffalo, which they brought to our Campe.—

1. The White Cliffs area of the Missouri River Breaks, Chouteau County, Montana.
2. In Chouteau County, nearly opposite the mouth of Sheep Shed Coulee.

Friday 31st May 1805. cloudy. we Set off as usal. the canoes crossed the river & the men went for the meat which was killed last night. one of the hunters killed an Elk. we proceeded on. abt. 11 oC. began to rain, rained moderately for Some time. we passed verry high clifts of rocks, halted <abt. noon> at 12 oC. to dine. our Captains gave each man a draughm of Spirits as it was wet. Capt. Lewis killed a fat buffaloe, & Some of the hunters killed 2 more but lost one of them in the river. abt 1 oC. we proceeded on passed high white clifts of rocks & Some pinecles which is 100 feet high from the Surface of the water. Some verry high black walls of Stone also on each Side of the river, which is curious to See. we Saw a brown bear on the N. S. Some of the hunters went out in order to kill it. passed Straight white clifts of rocks on the S. Side Came 17½ miles & Camped¹ at a handsom bottom covered with c. wood timber on the N. S. which was the first timber we Saw to day except a fiew Scatering trees along the Shore and a fiew ceeders on the hills. the current has been Swift all this day. the hunters came in at dark had killed 1 black taild. Deer 2 Ibex or mountain Sheep (rams) which had handsom large horns. we took care of the horns in order to take them back to the U. States. a pleasant evening. (one man Saw a large pond or Small lake, out in the plains on South Side)

Friday May 31st We had cloudy weather this morning, one of our Hunters went out Early this morning and killed an Elk which was brought to us.— We set off early and proceeded on our Voyage, still towing the Crafts; about 11 o'Clock A. M it began to rain, and rained moderately, for some time; We continued on, and passed some high Clifts of Rocks, lying on both sides of the River.— About 12 o'Clock A. M. we halted to dine, Our Officers gave each Man, a dram of Spirit, they being wet and Cold; Captain Lewis went out hunting, and killed a fat buffalo; and some of the Hunters that was out hunting killed 2 More of those Animals, but lost one of them in the River; the Buffalo being brought to us, about One o'Clock P. M. we proceeded on our Voyage, and passed high white Clifts of rocks, and some high pinnacles which was 100 feet high from the Surface of the Water, and some very high black Walls of Stone, lying on each side of the River, which appeared curious, We also saw a brown Bear, on the North side of the River; and some of our hunters went out in order to kill it, We went on and passed some straight white Clifts of rocks which lay on the South side of the River, The current of the River ran very strong, the whole of this day, The hunters returned to us in the Evening, they had killed 1 black Tailed deer, & 2 Ibex or mountain Sheep, They were 2 Rams and had handsome large Horns, those Horns the Officers, had taken care of, in Order to carry them back with us, to the United States.— One of our hunters mention'd of his having seen a very large lake, or pond, of water, on the South side of the River.—

In the Evening, the weather cleared off, and became pleasant; and we encamped, at a handsome bottom, covered with Cotton wood, Timber lying on the North side of the River; which was the first growth of timber, that we had seen this day; excepting a few scattering Trees, along the Shores, and a few Cedar Trees, which grew on the hills, We came this day 17½ Miles

1. Just above the mouth of Eagle Creek, the party's Stonewall Creek, in Chouteau County, Montana.

Saturday 1st June 1805. a clear pleasant morning we Set off eairly & proceeded on. passed Steep clifts of white rocks which had villages of little birds,[1] built along the projecting rocks. one of the party killed a Mountain ram or Ibex which had fine horns. we passed handsom bottoms of c. wood & box elder[2] timber on each Side. Saw old Indian Camps at a bottom on N. S. passed a Creek[3] on N. S. & Straight bluffs. passed Several Small Islands. about one oC. P. M. we passed a beautiful large Island covered with large & Small timber Saw Some Elk on it. the hills & bluffs are not So high on the river as they have been for Some time. about 2 oC. we halted to dine and air our goods &c. the wind rose from the S. E. the river bears to the South, handsom baron plains back from the river. we Saw Mountains a Short distance from the river on the N.S.[4] and on the S. S.[5] at a considerable distance up the river. about 3 oC. we proceeded on passed a Creek on the N. S. passed Several Islands covered with timber. passd. a Straight clift of rocks Steep from the Surface of the water about 100 feet perpinticular. passd handsom high plains on each Side. Came 24 miles & Camped[6] on the 7th Isld. a Small Island covered with timber. had passd. 2 little below

Saturday June 1st This morning we had Clear & pleasant Weather; we set off early, and proceeded on our Voyage, towing the Crafts as usual, and passed Steep Clifts of white Rock, which had a number of nests of some small birds built, along the projecting Rocks, as we pass'd.— One of our party, <killed> who was out hunting, killed a Mountain Sheep or Ibex, which had remarkable fine Horns.— We proceeded on and passed <a> some handsome bottoms of land, having Cotton Wood & Box Elder Timber on them, lying on both sides of the River; and saw some old Indian Camps, in a bottom, on the South side of the River, We also passed, a Creek lying on the North side, and Bluffs and several Small Islands.— About One o'Clock P. M. we passed a beautiful large Island, cover'd with large and small timber, and saw some Elk on it.— The Hills and bluffs, are not so high along the River, as they have been for several days past.— About 2 oClock P. M. we halted to dine, and to Air the Goods &ca. which were on board the Crafts, The wind rose here, and blew from the South East, the Course of the Mesouri running to the Southward, here we <was> saw Some Elk on the hills and Clifts.—

And there lies some handsome barren plains, which lay a small distance back from the River, We saw likewise here Mountains, which lay a short distance from the River, on the North side, and some Mountains, lying on the South side of the River, at a considerable distance up it. About 3 oClock P. M. we proceeded on our Voyage, and passed a Creek lying on the North side of the River; and some Islands, cover'd with Timber and a Strait Clift of Rocks, lying very steep from the Surface of the Water, they appeared to be 100 feet perpendicular, and some handsome plains, lying a small distance back, from the River on both sides of it.— We also passed 2 Islands which lay on each side of the River, We encamp'd in the Evening on the end of an Island, which was cover'd with timber, having come 24 Miles this day.—

1. Probably the cliff swallow, *Hirundo pyrrhonota,* mentioned by Lewis and Clark on May 31.

2. Boxelder, *Acer negundo* L.

3. The captains do not mention the streams noted by Gass and Whitehouse this day. This one may be Little Sandy Creek, Chouteau County, Montana.

4. The Bears Paw Mountains.

5. The Highwood Mountains.

6. On Boggs Island, Chouteau County.

Sunday 2nd June 1805. a clear pleasant morning. we Set off as usal & proceeded on. about 9 oC. Some of the hunters killed a buffalow and an

Elk. passed high bluffs on each Side, high plains, narrow bottoms and Islands. passed a creek[1] on the N. S. and one on the S. Side[2] about 12 oC. killed another Elk. about 1 oC. we halted to dine at a bottom of timber on the N. S. Some of the men killed another buffaloe. the wind high from the N. W. clouded up. the current is not So Swift yesterday & to day as it has been Some time past. we git along verry well with the towing lines. a Small Sprinkling of rain. about 2 oC. we proceeded on   passed Several Islands of cotton wood bluffs & high land   towards evening the hunters killed a yellow bear in a bottom of cotton wood on S. S. we Came 18 miles & Camped at a fork of the river.[3] we could not determine which was the Missourie. the hunters killed 6 Elk in all to day. we Saw a high mountain[4] to the west of us. one hunter man Shot a large beaver this evening.

Sunday June 2nd   A Clear pleasant morning, we set off early; and proceeded on our Voyage. About 9 o'Clock A. M. some of our hunters killed a buffalo, and an Elk, we proceeded on, and passed high bluffs lying on each side of the River, also high plains, narrow bottoms of land, & Islands, on both sides; and two Creeks, One on the North, and the other on the South side of the River, about 11 o'Clock A. M. one of our hunters killed another Elk, at 12 o'Clock A. M. we halted to dine on a bottom, lying on the North side of the River, Where one of our party killed a Buffalo, The wind blew hard from the North west at this place, and the Sky became Cloudy.—

The current of the Mesouris not running so swift, these two days past; as it had done for some time before; so that we made good head way, with towing the Crafts along,— about One o'Clock P M, we had some small sprinkling of rain— about 2 oClock P. M. we proceeded on, and passed several Islands, lying on both sides of the River; having Cotton wood on them.— and bluffs and high land.— towards evening, our hunters killed a Yellow Bear in a bottom, on the South side of the River, We encamped at a place where the Mesouri River forked, the officers being at a loss which fork was the Mesouri River, The Hunters that were out this day, returned to us, having killed 4 more Elk, and in the Evening one beaver,— We saw a high Mountain lying to our West. We came 18 Miles this day.—

1. Gass says there were two streams on the north, neither noticed by the captains; they are Spring and Sixmile coulees, in Chouteau County, Montana.

2. Also unmentioned by the captains, it is Crow Coulee, Chouteau County.

3. They had arrived at the confluence of the Marias and the Missouri rivers and camped in Chouteau County, opposite the mouth of the Marias, which was perhaps a mile below the present mouth. Lewis named the river after his cousin, Maria Wood.

4. Probably the Highwood Mountains, again.

Monday 3rd June 1805. a fair morning. we delayed untill 8 oClock then moved our Camp over to the point between the two rivers.[1] two Small canoes were unloaded and a Sergeant and 2 men I was one of them Sent in each up the 2 rivers[2] to See what discoveries they could make. Some men went out a hunting also. their is 3 Islands in the mo. left hand river, which is the largest & Swiftest river. Some men went out towards a mountain[3] covred with Snow to the South of this place. the Captains walked out on the high hills in the point they observed a level country to the foot of the mountain which lay South of this also a River[4] which falls in to the right hand fork about 1½ miles up from the mouth on the Lard Side. This little River discharges a great deal of water & contains as much cotton timber as either of the others. they Saw buffalow & antilopes, wild cherries[5] red & yallow berrys[6] goose berrys,[7] &c. abound in the river bottoms, prickley pairs on the high plains the Captains had a Meridian altitude & the Latitude produced was 47° 24″ 12″ North, the after part of the day proved cloudy. Capt. Clark measured the each River & found the one to the right hand to be 186 yards wide of water <& rapid> and the left hand fork 372 yards wide & rapid, the right hand fork falling the other at a Stand & clear. the right hand fork & the river which fall into it is couloured, and a little muddy. Several of the party complain of their feet being Sore by their walking in the Sand & cut by the Stones. we to be Sure have a hard time of it obligded to walk on Shore & haul the towing line and 9/10 of the time barefooted. in the evening the men all returned had been about 15 miles up each river but could not determine which was the Missourie, nor which would be our best course. our officers & all the men differ in their opinions which river to take. we expect the right hand fork would take us too far to the North, the left hand fork we expect heads in the mountains. however the officers conclude to leave the party here, and go by land with a Small party up each river, in order to find out which will be the best for us to take. the hunters killed 4 buffaloe 3 Elk 3 beaver & deer &c. the Capts Gave each man a dram of ardent Spirits.— I killed 2 Elk myself to day, as I was up the left fork as a Spye.—

Monday June 3rd   This morning we had fine and clear weather, we remained at our Camp untill 8 oClock A. M. when we removed over to a point lying between the Two Rivers, Two of our Crafts were unloaded, and a Serjeant and two Men embark'd in each of them, in Order to go up each of these Rivers to make discoveries; some Men were also sent out a hunting, & to make discoveries likewise; and some others of the party, went out towards a mountain covered with snow; lying to the Southward of the confluence of those 2 Rivers, 3 Islands lying in the River which lay the most Southermost, The River which lays to the Southward-most, is by far the <most> largest & Swiftest running River.—

Our Captains went out to some high hills, which lay in the point of those two Rivers, in Order to have a view of the Country, and make discoveries, They found that it was a level country to the foot of a mountains lying South of this place, and a River which fell into the North fork of these two Rivers, and that about One & a half Miles up from the Mouth of the Fork of the River lying most northerly, on the South side of that fork, that this little river emptied itself into it, and discharged a great quantity of water, and was equally covered on both sides of that River with Cotton wood Trees, which is the same with the forks of both these great Rivers; they likewise saw Buffalo, & antelopes in great plenty, and found Wild Cherries, red and Yellow berrys, Goose berries in abundance; and prickly pears growing on the high plains.— Our officers took an Observation here with their Mathematical Instruments, and found the Latitude to be 47° 24' 12s North, the afternoon of this day was Cloudy.— Captain Clark measured the width of each those Rivers, and found the North fork of the River measured 186 Yards of water; and the South fork measured 372 Yards of the same, & running rapidly, the Water in the North fork of the River falling; and that of the South at a stand, & clear, The right hand or North fork and the small River that empties itself into it Colour'd, and a little muddy.— Our party was complaining of their feet being very Sore Occssion'd by their walking in the sand & cut by the stones in towing our Crafts, a greater part of them being fatiauged & bare foot— but still determin'd to prosecute the Voyage under ev'ry difficulty.—   In the evening the Men that were sent out on discovery, and the hunters re-turned.— they reported that they had been fifteen Miles, up each of those Rivers, but they could not determine, which was the Mesouri River,— or which would be our best course to take, a Council was held by our Officers, and the opinion of our Men were all taken; but they differ'd in their Oppi-nions, and were at a loss which River to take, We expected that the right hand or North fork, Would take us too far to the Northward, and that the left hand or South fork, head in the Mountains.— The Officers came to a conclusion to leave the party here, and go with our hunters by land, up each River, in order to find out which will be our best course to pursue; in order to facilitate our Voyage.— The Hunters killed this day 4 Buffalo, 3 Elk, 8 Beaver, and some few Deer.— and one of the party that went up the South fork of the River on discovery, killed 2 Elk, the Game of all kinds being plenty on both these Rivers. Our Officers in the Evening gave each of the party a dram of Ardent spirits

1. In Chouteau County, Montana, below the present mouth of the Marias, where they remained until June 12 to determine which branch was the true Missouri.

2. Gass went up the Missouri with a party including Whitehouse, while Pryor and his party went up the Marias.

3. Perhaps the Highwood Mountains, again.

4. Teton River, a tributary of the Marias; the captains also called it Tansey River, after a plant growing on its banks.

5. Probably choke cherry.

6. The red berry is probably buffaloberry.

7. An unknown gooseberry.

Tuesday 4th June 1805. Capt. Lewis & 6 men[1] Set out to go up the Right hand fork. Capt. Clark & 5 more[2] Set out to go up the left hand fork. they intend to go about one day & a halfs walk up the rivers & See what discoveries they can make. Some of the men at camp killed 2 faun Elk close by the camp for the Skins, to dress. the day proved cloudy. a fiew drops of rain towards evening, & high cold wind from the N. E. 2 men who had been from camp a hunting returned had killed an Elk & a Deer, & had Set 2 traps for beaver. cloudy all day.—

Tuesday June 4th We remained this day at the place, we encamped at Yesterday; in the forks of the Rivers, The weather was Cloudy, Captain Lewis and Six hunters, set out to go up the North fork of the River; and Captain Clark and five hunters, also set out to go up the South fork, they intend going about One & a half days Journey up each River, in Order to make discoveries, and to ascertain our right Course, and to determine which of those forks was the Mesouri River, Some of the Men at our Camp killed 2 fawn Elk near it; those Fawn Skins, we prepar'd to dress, to make moccasins, towards Evening the Wind rose from the North east, and was Cold, Two of our Men that had went hunting from our Camp, returned. They had killed an Elk, and one deer.—and had set 2 Traps to catch beaver.—

1. Lewis's party included Pryor, Drouillard, Shields, Cruzatte, Jean Baptiste Lepage, and Windsor going up the Marias.

2. Clark's party included Gass, Joseph and Reubin Field, Shannon, and York following the Missouri.

Wednesday 5th June 1805. the wind blew high from the N. E. all last night. a cloudy cold windy morning. one beaver caught in a trap last night. I Stayed in Camp dressing Skins for to make myself moccasons &c. one of the men by the name of goodrich has caught a considerable quantity of Small fish. Some of them Skale fish the most part are a [sort?] of a Small-ish sized cat fish.[1] we have caught no large ones this Season as we did last as yet, &c.

Wednesday June 5th The wind blew during last night, from the North east, and we have a cold windy & Cloudy morning; One beaver was caught in the Traps set last night, part of the Men were employed, in dressing Skins to make Moccasins for the party.— One of our party was employ'd fishing; he caught a considerable number of small Cat fish.—

1. Probably channel catfish.

Thursday 6th June 1805. a cold cloudy morning. the wind blew cold from the N. E. Some of the men went from Camp a Short distance and

killed 2 buffalow one fat Elk 2 Deer 1 mule & one common Deers, 2 antilopes &c. a light Sprinkling of rain to day. about 2 oClock P. M. Capt. Clark
& his party returned to Camp. they informed us that the South fork is the
most probable branch to our course which Capt. Clark alowed we would
take. they had been about 40 miles up the South fork. when they got
about 8 miles from our Camp they found a beautiful Spring of water,[1] where
the Small river was not more than 200 yards from the South fork. they
refreshed themselves at the Spring with a drink of good grog.[2] they Saw but
little game on this river. they passed through high plains, where nothing
groes but Short grass & prickley pears.[3] the course of the river as far as they
went about S. W. they Saw a mountain[4] to the South of them covred with
Snow. one of the men by the name of Jo. Fields was attcd by an old hea
bear, which would have killed him if the rest of the party had not been in
hearin to have fired at him which made him turn his course. they killed
3 bear, & eat a part of one of them, & returned by way of the middle branch
which they came down & killed in its bottoms a number of fat Elk Deer &
Saw wolves antelopes & beaver &c. the bottoms of this middle river is like
thee bottoms below the forks, covered with timber. Some cotton trees[5] with
a leaf like the leaf of cherry. they Saw wild tanzey[6] &c— Capt. Lewis &
party did not return this evening.— the party has been employed dressing
Skins &c.

Thursday June 6th We had a Cold Cloudy morning, the Wind still continuing to blow from the North east, Some of our Men went out a hunting a
small distance from the Camp, They killed 2 Buffalo, one fat Elk, 2 deer,
2 Antelope & some <other> small game.— We had a small sprinkling of
Rain this forenoon. About 2 o'Clock P. M. Captain Clark, and the party
that was with him returned, to Camp, the party informed us, that the South
fork, was most probably the Course that we should take, and Captain Clarke
allow'd it would be the case.—

The party that was with Captain Clark, had been about 40 Miles up the
South fork, they had discover'd 8 Miles from Camp a beautiful spring of
water; where the small River which emptied itself into the North fork was not
more than 200 Yards, from the South fork— They mention'd of having
seen but little game on that River; and that they had passed through high

plains, which had short Grass, and prickly pears growing on them.— and that the Course of the River as far as they went, ran about Southwest, they likewise saw a Mountain; lying to the South covered with Snow.— One of the party was attackted by an Old Male Bear, which in all probability would have killed him; had not the rest of the party been near enough to fire at him, which made him turn his course, They had killed 3 Bear, part of one they had eaten,— The party had returned by way of the middle branch (or small River) and came down the same.— They had killed in the bottoms on their return down this small River; a number of fat Elks & deer, and saw Wolves, antelopes Beaver &ca. in the greatest abundance. The bottoms on this small River, are like the bottoms Land below the forks of the two Rivers.— They have fine growths of Timber on them, and <have> the Cotton wood trees in them, having a leaf much like Wild cherry, and plenty of Tanzy.— Captain Lewis and his party did not return this Evening.— The party that remained in Camp employed themselves in dressing Skins, making Moccasins &ca.—

1. The "Grog Spring," as Whitehouse notes, was at the place where the Teton and Missouri rivers approach very closely, in Chouteau County, Montana.

2. Grog is generally taken to be a mixture of rum and water.

3. Probably plains prickly pear, *Opuntia polyacantha* Haw.

4. Probably the Highwood Mountains, in Chouteau County.

5. Probably narrowleaf cottonwood, *Populus angustifolia* James. Only Whitehouse and Ordway compare its leaf to the leaf of a cherry.

6. Perhaps western yarrow, *Achilla millefolium* L. See Ordway's entry for this day and Lewis's entry of June 5, 1806.

Friday 7th June 1805. rained the greater part of last night. a Cloudy wet morning. Some men went out to hunt, and killed 2 Deer, rained moderately all day. Capt. Lewis & his party has not returned yet. we expect the reason is owing to the badness of the weather. nothing further occured this day.

Friday June 7th We had rain the greatest part of last night, and this morning was cloudy and wet weather, Some of our party went out to hunt, They returned in a short time, having killed 2 deer, which they brought with them to our camp— Captain Lewis and his party did not return to us this day; and we supposed they were detained by the badness of the weather, the Men that were in the Camp were all employed in making mockasins & dressing Skins as usual.—

Saturday 8th June 1805. Some cloudy. the wind blew cold from the N. W. Several men went out to hunt. about 9 oC. cleared off pleasant. the Indian goods &c put out to air. we Saw the high mountain to the west of us covered with Snow. the South fork of the Missourie is high & of a yellow coulour to day, & the North fork more white & rile than before, owing as we expect to the rains & Snow melting above, on the mountains. about 3 oClock P. M. Capt. Lewis & party returned to Camp, & Informed us that they had been about 60 miles distant up the north fork, had traveled through high plains the greater part of the way. they found that the N. fork keeps its bigness, pleanty of water, considerable of timber in the bottoms & an amence cite of game. they killed a great deal of Elk Buffalow Deer &c. &c. but Capt. Lewis thinks that the N. fork bears too far North for our course to cross the Mountains, for if we Should take the wrong River, we Should have more mountains to cross & further to go by land to git to the Columbia River, which we have to descend to the west. So the Capt. conclude to take the South fork & proceed, and named the North fork *River Mariah*, but it has the resemblence of the Missourie below the forks in everry respect, & the middle fork they name *Tanzey River* the water &c. of which resembles the Missourie also. the men in Camp generally employed Dressing Skins &c—

towards evening the hunters all returned had killed Sevl. Elk 13 deer and one beaver. the wind blew from the East, a light Shower of rain this evening.

Saturday June 8th This morning we had Cloudy weather, and the Wind blowing from the North west; several of our Men went out to hunt, About 7 oClock A. M. the weather cleared off, and became pleasant, the Indians Goods were all put out to air, We saw on the Weather clearing away, a high mountain; lying to the West of us; which was covered with snow, The South fork of the River Mesouri rose to a great heighth, the Water being of a Yellowish Colour today; and the North fork more White and riffling than it was before, the cause of which, we expect, is owing to the Rain that fell lately, and the snow melting in the Mountains. About 3 o'Clock P. M. Captain Lewis & party returned to Camp, and inform'd us, that they had been about 60 Miles distant, up the North fork of the Mesouri River, & that they had travelled, through high plains, the greater part of the way; they found that the North Fork, kept its width, and plenty of Water, as far as they had been up it.—

The party under Captain Lewis found plenty of timber in the bottoms, the Land extreamly good, and game of all kinds in the greatest abundance, they had killed a great many Buffalo, Elk, deer and other game, Captain Lewis mentioned, that the North fork of the River, bore too far to the Northward, to be our Course to cross the Mountains; and mentioned, that if we should take the wrong river, that we should have more mountains to cross, and a farther distance to travel by land to get to the Columbia River; which we had to descend, it lying to the Westward, Our Officers concluded on proceeding up the South fork of the River, which they deemed as entitled to the Name of the Mesouri River, it being by far the largest; and named the North fork, Maria's River, This River Maria, has the resemblance of the Mesouri below the forks, in every respect. The middle fork they named Tanzey River; from the great quantity of that herb, which grows wild in its bottoms— The Tanzey River, is the small River mention'd, which Captain Clarks party came down, on their return to Camp; after having been to take a view, of the South fork.— The Water, banks, &ca has also the resemblance of the Mesouri River in every respect.— The Hunters returned in the Evening and had killed 7 Elk, 3 deer, & 1 Beaver, which was brought to our Camp, We had a light shower of Rain and the Wind from the Eastward towards Night.—

Sunday 9th June 1805. a clear pleasant morning. 2 men of the hunters went out & killed a verry fat buffalow. took Eight men to bring in the meat. Several men Sent out to the bluffs back in the point, to dig a hole called a Cash to burry Some of the articles which we can Spare best, So that we might have them Safe when we come back &c. the wind rose high from the west. towards evening we had a frolick. the officers gave the party a dram, the fiddle played and they danced late &c we had a light Shower of rain late in the evening.— rope works made.

Saturday [*Sunday*] June 9th   We had a clear pleasant morning, two of our hunters, went out early to hunt; they returned in a short time having killed a very large fat buffalo; and took out of our Camp, eight Men to bring in the Meat of it, Which they did in about one hour.— several of our Men, were sent out to the Bluffs, back in the point, to dig a hole (called a Cashe,) to bury some of the articles which we can spare, and intend leaving behind, in order that they may be safe, when we return, The Wind towards evening rose from the West.   We were employ'd in erecting Rope works, during this day; we had a Shower of rain late this Evening, Our Officers gave each Man of the party a dram of Spirits, and they seem much recruited since we encamped here.—

Monday 10th June 1805.   a beautiful pleasant morning.   the party employed   Some makeing a towing line for the white perogue, others employed digging another hole So that we might bury in different places what we left So that if the Savages Should find one perhaps they would not find the other & we would have Some left Still.   about 10 oClock we halled up the red perogue on an Island, on the North Side of the N. fork which was covered with Small cotton timber.   we halled it among the thicke of trees & ran the bow between two & pined hir on each Side & covered hir over with bushes, & Secured hir as well as possable, branded[1] Several trees with the U S. mark & Capt. M. Lewis & Latd. &c.   The black Smiths[2] fixed up the bellowses & made a main Spring to Capt. [Lewis's] air Gun, as the one belonging to it got broke.   the articles which we Intend to bury all got ready. the loading which came out of the red perogue divided out to the White perogue & Canoes & loaded them.   put a Canister of powder & led accordingly in the ground near the point, between the two Rivers at our Camp. about 4 oClock P. M. we had a light Shower of rain.   the evening pleasant.

Monday June 10th   A Beautiful pleasant morning, our men are all employed in making of ropes, and digging another hole, in Order to deposit what we leave behind in different places, so that in case the Savages should find one of our places of deposit, the other might escape being found.— so that we might have something left, if we should ever return.— About 10 o'Clock A. M. we hawled up one of our pettyaugers on an Island, lying on the North side of the North fork of the River (called Maria's River,) which was cover'd with small Cotton wood Timber.— We placed the pettyauger among the thickest of the trees, and ran her bow between two of them, pinned her on each side, and covered her over with bushes. The officers branded several of the trees with the mark of the United States, Captain Lewis's name, the Latitude of the place &ca— The Blacksmiths fixed their Bellows, to repair the Arms, the rest of the party was busy in burying the Goods, and securing them from Spoiling, which we intend to leave behind;— the loading which came out of the pettyauger which we had hid on the Island, was put on board another Pettyauger & Canoe, We also buried a Cannister of powder & some lead, near a point, between the two Rivers, the place that we are encamped on, The powder was in leaden Cannisters prepared for that purpose.— About 4 o'Clock P. M. we had a light shower of Rain, & in the Evening it cleared up, & we had pleasant Weather.—

1. Lewis's branding iron; see his entry for this day. Only Whitehouse is this explicit about the instrument.

2. Shields, according to Lewis.

Tuesday 11th June 1805. a Clear pleasant morning. about 8 oClock Capt. Lewis, George Drewyer, G. Gibson, Jo. Fields & Silas Goodrich Set out for the South Snowey mountain. we put in the Carsh or hole 1 keg of powder 1 bar led, 1 keg flour 1 keg pork 2 kegs parchcd meal the bellowses & tools augur plains Saw &c Some tin cups a dutch oven, a corn hand mill, packs of beaver, bear Skins horns Buffalow Robes &c. &c. the Blacksmiths compleated repairing the fire arms. the carsh or hole on the high land dug deeper and compleated burrying the heavey articles &c. we got in readiness to ascend the South fork. we have caught more Small fish Since we lay here than we made use of—and one kind of Small flat Scale fish[1] that we never Saw the kind before.—

Tuesday June 11th We had a clear pleasant morning, about 8 o'Clock A. M. Captain Lewis & four Men of our party, set out for the Snowey Mountain, There was put into the holes or Carsh [*erased, illegible*] Yesterday 1 keg of powder, 1 keg barr lead, 1 keg flour, 1 Keg pork, 2 Kegs parched Corn meal, the Blacksmiths bellows & tools, Augers, planes, Saw &ca—. some tin cups, a dutch Oven, a Corn hand Mill, packs of beaver, bear Skins, horns of different kinds, Buffalo robes &ca. &ca—.

The blacksmith, had compleated repairing the fire Arms, and every thing was got in readiness to ascend the South fork or the Mesouri River, which the officers intend doing tomorrow.— We had caught more fish since we lay here encamped, than what we could possibly destroy, among which was a small flat fish having scales, which none of us had before ever seen.—

1. Probably the goldeye, *Hiodon alosoides.*

Wednesday 12th June 1805. a clear pleasant morning. we burryed 3 traps which was forgot yesterday, and Set out about 7 oClock from Camp or point deposit 2508¼ mls from mouth, and proceeded on up the South fork which we Still call the Missourie R. passed a great nomber of Islands [(]5 or 6 at least by noon) before we had got out of cite of the point, which was covered with cotton timber. one of the party caught a beaver on one of them in a trap which he Set last night. passed high black & yellow bluffs on each Side & handsom Smooth plains on each Side. Saw Elk antelopes & Geese &c. found Some penerial[1] the first we Saw on the River. the current verry Rapid. three of the G. D. canoes like to have overset & one in great danger. Several Rattle Snakes has been Seen by the party to day. one man took hold of one with his hand, which was in a bunch of bushes, but luckily he escaped being bit. Our Intrepters wife verry Sick. Capt. Clark killed this evening one Elk & a Deer. Some other of the hunters killed 1 or 2 more. we passed in the course of the day a number of gravvelly Islands & bars. the Shore on each Side is covered with Stone of different Sizes— we Came *18 miles* to day & Camped[2] at a handsom bottom of cottonwood on the N. Side, where the Elk & Deer was killed.

Wednesday June 12th We had a clear pleasant morning, we buried 3 of our Beaver Traps, which we had omitted burying two days past; We set off from our encampment, which we named point deposit, this lies 2,508¼ Miles from the mouth of the Mesouri River; we proceeded on up the South fork, or River Mesouri, and passed by 6 Islands, before we lost sight of the point we had encamped at; These Islands were all covered with Cotton wood timber, One of our party caught a Beaver, as we passed along, in a trap, which he had set last night. We passed some black & Yellow bluffs, which were very high, lying on both sides of the River, & some handsome plains, lying also on both sides of the River, In those plains we saw Elk, and Antelopes, and in the River large flocks of Geese, & found Pennyroyal, the first that we had seen since we enter'd the Mesouri growing along the Shore.—

The current of the River, runs very Strong, and three of our Crafts had like to have overset, and one of them was in great danger of being lost.— Our party saw this day several Rattle Snakes, <this day,> and one of the party narrowly escaped being bit, by a very large one, that lay concealed in a bush, as he passed along with the tow line.— Our interpreters wife got very Sick, and great care was taken of her, knowing, what a great loss she would be, if she died, she being our only Interpreter, for the Snake Indians, who reside in those Mountains lying West of us, and from whom we expect assistance, in prosecuting our Voyage,— Captain Clark who walked along Shore, killed an Elk & one deer; and the <other> hunters, killed 2 more Elk. We passed in the course of this day, a number of Gravelly Islands, & barrs; The Shore on each side of the River being covered with stones, of different sizes,— We came 18 Miles this day, & encamped at a handsome bottom of Cotton Wood trees, lying on the North side of the River, it being the place where the Elk and deer was killed at

1. Ordway also mentions the pennyroyal, but its identity is unknown.

2. In Chouteau County, Montana, in the vicinity of Evans Bend, about five miles downstream from Fort Benton.

Thursday 13th June 1805. a beautiful pleasant morning. we Set out at an eirly hour & proceeded on. passed the Mouth of a Small River[1] on the South Side about 50 yards wide & rapid current & of a muddy coulour. I went over the River to See it. large bottoms of cotton timber for Some distance up. we named it Snowey River, as we expect it comes from the Snowey Mountain, to the South of us. passed verry high bluffs on each Side Some Small bottoms of cotton timber. we Saw abundance of wild or choke cherries & a kind of yallow current,[2] Such as I never Saw before. the Goose berrys are now ripe & abound in the River bottoms— we came 14 miles to day & Camped[3] on the South Side. I was taken verry Sick to day, & a vilont head ack. 2 deer & [*illegible*] buffalow killed to day.

Thursday June 13th We had a Clear & pleasant morning, and set out on our Voyage at sun rise, we proceeded on, and passed the mouth of a small River lying on the South side called Smiths[4] River which was <and> about 50 Yards wide, <which was called Smiths River> the current in this River runs rapid and its water was muddy, I was sent over to this small River by Captain Clark in order to make what discoveries I could, I found large bottoms of land lying along the River, for some distance, and the Land very rich, the growth in those bottoms of Rich land being chiefly cotton wood.— Captain Clark called this River Smiths river, and we expect its source lay in the Mountains; we saw some days past, covered with Snow;— lying to the South west of us. we continued on our way and passed some very high bluffs, lying on both sides of the River, and small bottoms of cotton wood Timber, and found a large quantity of wild Artichokes, Cherries, and Yellow currants, the last of which none of our party had ever seen before, & also Goose berries growing in abundance which were ripe & grew in the River bottoms, The land that we passed through, as we passed along this day; was extreamly Rich, and fertile, The hunters that was out killed one Buffalo this day.— We came 14 Miles this day, and encamped in the Evening on the South side of the River.—

1. Shonkin Creek, Chouteau County, Montana.
2. Probably the buffalo currant, *Ribes ordoratum* Wendl. f., but possibly the golden currant, *R. aureum* Pursh.
3. In Chouteau County, perhaps in the vicinity of Bird Coulee.
4. A clear misreading of Whitehouse's "Snowey River."

Friday 14th June 1805. a fare pleasant morning. 2 men lay out all last night, which walked on Shore one a lame hand the other 2 sick. we proceeded on. passed the place where Capt. Lewis had camped as he went up. had left 2 bear Skins & [*illegible word*] one Deer Skin which they had killed. 2 of the men lay by it last night. at breakfast we came up to the other man which had killed 2 buffalow & a deer. we proceeded on passed verry high bluffs on each Side, & Several Islands of cotton timber. the current verry rapid all day. our Intrepters wife verry Sick & I am verry Sick myself about 4 oC. P. M. we met one man[1] which Capt. Lewis Sent back to meet us. he informed us that he came from the falls to day, & that they were verry bad, &c. about 20 miles from us above, & that Capt. Lewis & the other three men was a going to the head of the falls, in order to examine how far it was before we could take water again. we went 10 miles to day through a verry rapid current, and Camped[2] at a Small bottom on the Lard. Side. we Saw a nomber of dead buffalow floating down the River which we expect was killed in the falls.

Friday June 14th This morning, we had pleasant weather. Two of our Men, <that had> laid out all night; they had walked along shore Yesterday; came to us, the one had a lame hand, and the other was very sick; we proceeded on our Voyage, & passed a place, where Captain Lewis had encamped at, on his way to the falls of this River, he had left there, 2 bear, & One deer, that his party had killed; we found 2 of his party at that place, who were left to take care of it, till we came on

At 9 oClock A. M we halted to break fast, here we found another of Captain Lewis's party, who had killed 2 Buffalo, and one deer, which we had brought to our Crafts, by some of our party, At 11 o'Clock A. M. we proceeded on, and passed very high bluffs lying on each side of the River, and several Islands, cover'd with Cotton wood Timber, We found the current of the River run very rapid all this day, Our Interpreters Wife (an Indian) and one of our party was very sick all this day.— About 4 o'Clock P. M. we met one of Captain Lewis's party which was sent back to us; who inform'd us, that he had come from the falls of this River to day, and that they were very bad to assend & that they lay 30 Miles above us, He likewise mentioned that Captain Lewis and the remainder of his party had gone on to the head of the falls, in order to find out, how far the distance was; before we could undertake, to go by water again.— We came only ten Miles this day; having a very rapid Current setting against us, and encamped in a small bottom, lying on the South side of the River, where we saw a number of dead buffalo <dead> floating down the River, which we expected had been killed in the falls of this River.—

1. Joseph Field, according to Clark.
2. In Chouteau County, Montana, near the mouth of Black Coulee.

Saturday 15th June 1805. a clear pleasant morning. we Set out at the usal hour. proceeded on. passed the rapidest water I ever Seen any crafts taken through, at noon we halted at the Mouth of a creek on the Lard. Side which we named Strawberry Creek,[1] their being a great quantity of Strawberry vines[2] about it. a handsom rapid Stream, the bottoms of it coverd with Small cotton timber. 2 of the hunters went a Short distance up this Stream & killed 2 Deer. choak cherrys, Goose berrys and yellow currents abound on the banks of the Streams in this country. the afternoon verry warm. we proceeded on. passed redish couloured bluffs on each Side of the River which were high rough & in places clifts of dark Rocks. in the evening we Came to a bad rapid which we concluded to not undertake to pass untill morning. So we Camped[3] below on the Stard. Side. the wood Scarse. one man[4] Sent to the falls, for Capt. Lewis. we Came only 12 miles to day by exerting our Selves as much as possable with the towing line

Saturday June 15th   We had a Clear pleasant morning, and set out at the usual hour, and proceeded on our Voyage, and passed through the most rapid running water, that we had met with, since we enter'd the Mesouri River, at Noon we halted at the mouth of a Creek lying on the South side of the River; which we named Strawberry Creek, their being such vast quantities of strawberry Vines along it, This Creek was a handsome one, the Stream running rapid, & and the bottoms along it, cover'd with handsome Cotton timber, Two of our hunters went a short distance up this Creek, and killed 2 Deer,— On the banks of this Southern fork (or Mesouri) their is <an> the greatest plenty of Choak cherries, Goose berries, and Yellow Currants.— In the afternoon of this day, it became very warm, We proceeded on, and passed reddish Coloured Bluffs, lying on each side of the River, which were high, and rough; and in places Clifts of black rock, In the Evening we came to a bad rapid, which we concluded on, not to undertake to pass, untill the morning, We encamped below this rapid on the North side of the River, where we found wood Scarce; Captain Clarke sent one of our Men to the falls of the River this day, to inform Captain Lewis where we were, and our situation. We came only 12 Miles this day, the Men using their utmost exertion in towing our Crafts, which fataigued & tired them exceedingly.—

1. This is the name Ordway and Gass give, but Clark calls it Shields River, after John Shields of the party. It is present Highwood Creek, Chouteau County, Montana.

2. Probably either wild strawberry, *Fragaria virginiana* Duchn. var. *glauca* Wats., or woodland strawberry, *F. vesca* L. var. *americana* Porter.

3. In Cascade County, Montana, a little below and opposite the mouth of Belt Creek, the captains' Portage Creek.

4. Joseph Field again, according to Clark.

Sunday 16th June 1805. we had a Shower of rain & high wind the fore part of last night. a clear morning. all hands went over the Rapids 1st with the canoes about 1 mile & then went back and took up the perogue, and halted to wait the arival of Capt. Lewis, &c. their being a rapid a Short distance above which is impossable to pass with loaded crafts. we caught a considerable quantity of Small flat Scale fish at this place. about 12 oC. Capt. Lewis & the men who accompanied him joined us. Capt. Lewis informed us that he had been 15 miles up the River above the first bad Rapids or Shoot & that the falls continued all that distance in 5 different Shoots, but Some higher than the rest, but the highest about 50 feet perpenticular & verry Rapid water between each Shoot roling waves & white brakers.[1] Capt. Lewis informed us that the Lard. Side would be the best for us to carry our goods and baggage by the falls, also the canoes. So we crossed over to the Lard. Side and unloaded the Canoes & crossed them back to the Stard. Side empty and towed them up the rapid about a mile. then crossed them back to the Lard. Side again, in order that we might git them up a Small River[2] which comes in below the next Shoot to a more convenient place to git them up the bank on to the plains. this little River comes in on Lard. Side close below the next Shoot. opposite to the mouth of this little River on S. S. a beautiful Sulpher or mineral Spring[3] rises out of the Side hills. it is a verry Strong Sulpher water. we git & drink freely of it. in the bottoms is a considerable of wild flax[4] growing all in blossom. Capt. Lewis's party had prepared & dryed buffalow meat and had caught & dryed a large quantity, of fine fish, which we call Salmon troute—[5]

Sunday June 16th   We had in the forepart of last night, Showers of Rain, & high wind, This morning it cleared away, & we had pleasant weather; and we prepared to pass the Rapids which was Effected by all hands that were well passing our Crafts over One at a time.—

We halted above the falls, to waite for the arrival of Captain Lewis & his party.—   and on account of a large rapid which lay a short distance above us; which was thought impossible to pass, with loaded Crafts.—   We caught at this place a considerable quantity of those flatt large scaled fish, mention'd, which was caught, at where the Mesouri forked, and where we had encamp'd called Point deposit, About 12 o'Clock A. M Captain Lewis and his party, came to us; Captain Lewis informed us; that he had been 15 Miles above the first rapids, or Shoot, and that the falls continued all that distance; in five falls or Shoots; and that there was some of them of considerable height, the highest being 87 feet perpendicular, and the water running very rapid, between each fall, with rolling waves & white breakers; Captain Lewis gave it as his opinion, that it would be best to take the Crafts over to the South side of the River, and have them unloaded, and the empty Crafts towed up the Rapid, about a Mile, which Captain Clarke agreed to, and it was accordingly done, altho' with much labour & fataigue to the Men, and they got them, into a small River, which came into this River on the South side, below the next fall or Shoot, it being a convenient place to land   the party then carried all the Crafts loading to them, at this Small River;—   opposite to which we found on the South side, a beautiful Sulphur or Mineral Spring running out of the side of the hills, the water having a strong sulphurous taste, Our party drank a considerable quantity of this water for their healths which had the desired effect, the bottoms lying on this small River<s> had a considerable quantity of beautiful wild flowers, which were all in blossom; Captain Lewis's party that went ahead of us, had prepar'd dinner, for the party (who brought on our Crafts loading;) which consisted of buffalo meat & Salmon trout, the latter of which they had caught a great Quantity, they were by much the largest of any, that we had ever seen, We encamped at this place for the day.—

1. The Great Falls of the Missouri consists of a series of five falls in Cascade County, Montana. For a measure of the various heights, see Clark's survey notes of June 17–19, 1805.

2. Belt Creek, the party's Portage Creek, the boundary between Cascade and Chouteau counties. The party's lower portage camp was just below the mouth of the creek.

3. Sulphur, or Sacagawea, Springs, in Cascade County opposite the mouth of Belt Creek, a few hundred yards from the Missouri.

4. Perhaps blue flax, *Linum perenne* L., or roundleaf harebell, *Campanula rotundifolia* L., which resembles flax.

5. Probably cutthroat trout, *Oncorhynchus clarki* (formerly *Salmo clarkii*), named for Clark.

Monday 17th June 1805. a cloudy morning. Some men employed taking the canoes up the little River about 1¾ miles. 6 men employed makeing Small low waggons to hall the canoes and baggage by the carrying place above the falls. Capt. Clark and five men[1] went to Survey & measure the distance up to the head of the falls, to where we can take water again, & to look out a road for us to go up with the waggons, &c. 2 hunters out to git Elk Skins, to put our Iron boat together above the falls, as we leave our largest craft here. the timber is verry Scarse above the falls. verry high plains the buffalow pleanty. in the evening we got the canoes up the Small River to the falls of it which is about 4 feet perpenticular. we had Some difficulty in gitting them up the rapids to day, as well as a dangerous job one canoe turned upside down in a bad rapid, & was near drowning the 2 men which was in hir. Several others filled with water but we haled them up Safe to the place convenient at the falls to take them up the bank.[2] we caried them out on a livel & turned them up on edge to dry.

Monday June 17th This morning we had cloudy weather, our men were employed, in taking the Crafts up the little River, about 1¾ miles, and some of them were also employ'd making small low truck carriages, to transport our Crafts, and the baggage on by a carrying place, above the falls of the River, Captain Clarke took a small party of our men & went to measure the distance, up to the head of the falls of the River, and to find the best rout for our carriages to go, to that place; where we intend embarking again in our Crafts. Two of our hunters went out hunting in order to procure some Elk skins, to cover the frame of an Iron boat, which we had brought with us, which our Officers intend putting together above the falls.—

Our officers concluded to leave our largest Craft at this place, knowing the difficulty that we should experience in getting them even over the falls, which was on this small River of 8 feet; We found Timber very scarce about those falls, and very high plains, and Buffalo in very great abundance.— In the Evening we got our Crafts up the small River to the falls of it, which was about 8 feet perpendicular, and the Water running very rapid down them,— We experienc'd much difficulty, as well as danger in getting our Crafts up the rapids this day.— One of our craft turned upside down & the 2 Men that were in her narrowly escaped being drownded, several others of them filled with water. With much difficulty & fataigue we hawled those Crafts on our Carriages up to where the falls commenced, and took them up the bank, out to a level piece of Ground, and turned them up on their edges to dry, We encamped here for this night, all our party being much fataigued.—

1. Including Willard, Colter, and perhaps Joseph Field.
2. Apparently they camped on Belt Creek, in Cascade County, Montana, below the falls of the creek.

Tuesday 18th June 1805. a fine pleasant day. in the morning all hands halled out the White perogue, in a thicked of bushes below the bank & covered hir with bushes &c. & Secured hir Safe. 3 men Sent out a Short distance to a knob to dig a carsh or hole to deposite Some of our baggage in, for we mean to leave all we can Spare at this place. Some men at Sorting & repacking the Indian Goods &c. about 12 oC. the 2 hunters came in had killed 10 Deer but no Elk. in the evening we Saw Some buffalow on the opposite Side of the River. Some of the hunters went over and killed 2 of them. the low waggons finished which are all made of wood, & of an ordinarry quality though they may answer the purpose. the wind high from the West.

Tuesday June 18th A fine pleasant day, in the Morning all our Men who were in Camp, were employed hawling up our largest Pettyauger, into a thicket of bushes, which lay below our Camp, where they secured her, after doing of which 3 of our Men were sent a short distance to a knob, in order to dig a Cashe, or hole, to deposit some more of our baggage in, Our Officers intending to leave here, what baggage we can possibly do without, Some others of our party was employed in sorting and repacking the Indian Goods &ca.—

About 12 o'Clock A. M. the hunters that had went out Yesterday, returned to us, they had killed 10 deer, but no Elk, In the Evening we saw some buffalo on the opposite side of the River, some of our hunters went across and killed 2 of them, we this day compleated our Carriages, they were made out of wood of an ordinary quality, though we think they will answer the purpose that they were intended for; The wind rose & blew from the West, we encamped[1] at this place for the day.—

1. At the lower portage camp.

Wednesday 19th June 1805. a clear cool morning. Several men Sent for the meat across the River which was killed last night. the wind verry high from the West. our Intrepters wife Some better. three men[1] Sent over the River to go up to the head of the falls to a river which falls in on that Stard Side, Called medicine River[2] to hunt in order to prepare Elk Skins for the Iron boat. we prepare to move the goods & baggage &c. Saw large gangs of buffalow on the Side hills on the opposite Shore. the wind continues high all day. we are now 2580 odd miles from the mouth of Missourie—

Wednesday June 19th This morning, we had clear & cool weather; some of our party was sent acros the River for the Buffalo kill'd, by some of our party Yesterday. the Wind had blown very hard during the last night, our Interpreters Wife and the others that was sick recover'd fast, three of our party was sent over the River to go up to the head of the falls, to a River which falls into this River, lying on the North side; which we named Medecine River, they were sent to hunt for Elk, in order to get the Skins, to cover the Iron boat.— We were employ'd at Camp in getting every thing in order, to move the Baggage &ca. We saw large Gangs of buffalo on the hills side, on the Opposite shore; the wind continued high, during the whole of this day from the West, We are now 2,585 Miles, from the Mouth of the River Mesouri, We continued at this place this day, The land here is good, being chiefly Priaries, and producing fine Grass in abundance.—

1. Drouillard, Reubin Field, and Shannon, according to Lewis.
2. Sun River, meeting the Missouri at the town of Great Falls, Cascade County, Montana.

Thursday 20th June 1805. Some cloudy & cold. the wind continues high from the west. three or 4 men went across the River to hunt &c. we lay at Camp at the commencement of the carrying place, to wait the arival of Capt. Clark & party. a light Squall of rain about noon. in the afternoon <the> Some of the hunters came in had killed 11 buffalow the most of them verry fat. all hands turned out after the meat, but could not fetch more than half of what was fat. 3 men Stayed all night to butcher the remainder of the buffalow, which lay dead. Saw large gangs come about close to the men which was dressing the meat &c— a little rain.

in the evening Capt. Clark & party returned. they informed us that they traversed the River going up & measured the falls & river found the first to be about 30 feet the highest & middle 87 feet the upper one a 45 feet all of which is perpinticular, a continued rapids between each other.[1] they found it to be 17 miles to the head to where we can take water again. two men was attacted by a verry large White bear one of them A Willard near being caught. Capt. Clark went & relieved them & 3 men with him. but night comming on & the bushes thick it being on an Island they did not kill it. they Saw 1 or 2 other white bear. they Saw also innumerable gangs of buffalow & killed 8 of those animels, & one beaver. they Saved as much of the buffalow meat as possable. <one mile above> 1 mile above the fall of 47 feet 8 Inches is the largest fountain or Spring,[2] as they think is the largest in america known. this water boils up from under the rocks near the river & falls immediately into the river 8 feet & keeps its coulour for ½ a mile which is clear & of a blueish cast. they inform us that their is many Shoots or little falls between the high ones. the large catteract or falls[3] is a large mist quite across the fall, for a long distance from them. Capt. Clark Saw rattle Snakes but Saw verry little timber. they turned back this morning in order to look out the best & Smoothest portage possable to take the canoes & baggage &. up to the medicine River. they informed us that the Country above the falls & up the meddicine River is level with low banks & Smoth water. they Saw a chain of mountains to the west,[4] Some of which particular those to N. W. & S. W. are covered with Snow, & appear to be verry high. Capt. Clark lost a part of his notes which could not be found, as the wind blew high & took them off. they did not look out & marke the road for the baggage &c much more than half way down to Camp it being too late to go round the deep gulleys &c.   Capt. Clark Saw gangs of buffalow attempt to Swim the river abo. the falls.   Some went over.

Thursday June 20th   This morning we had Cloudy weather, and cold; and the wind continued high from the West, four of our Men were sent across the River to hunt, We now lay at Camp, at the commencement of the carrying place, waiting the arrival of Captain Clark & party.—   We had about noon some Squalls of wind, attended with Rain.—   In the afternoon some of our Hunters returned to us; and had killed 11 Buffalo, the most of them, they said were very fat, all our spare hands turned out, in Order to bring the Meat to our Camp.—   they returned, and had brought with them but above one half of it and that was very fat—   Three of the party that went after the meat, staid all night, to butcher the remainder of the buffalo, that the hunters had killed, the party that was sent for the meat mentioned that large Gangs of Buffalo came about close to the Men, who were employ'd dressing the Meat, & that they appeared no ways shy of them.—   We had small Showers of rain this afternoon.—   In the evening Captain Clarke and his party returned to us, they informed us, that they had travers'd this small river, in going up; and had measured the falls—of the Mesouri, of which there was three.—   the first falls being 30 feet high by measurement, the second or middle fall, being the highest 87 feet perpendicular, and the third fall 47 feet 8 Inches also perpendicular, and the Water running exceedingly Rapid, between each of these falls, and found the distance to be 17 Miles to the head fall, where we expect to proceed on again with our Crafts, & take Water.—

The party that was with Captain Clark, mentioned, that two of their Men were attackted by a very large white or brown coloured bear, and that one of them had nearly been caught by that huge animal, & that it certainly had been the case, had not Captain Clark and three of the party releived him, but night coming on, the Bear made his escape among some very thick bushes, and got off from them, this happened on an Island—   They also mentioned of having Seen also two more very large <white> Bear of the same kind, and saw innumerable large Gangs of Buffalo in every direction, as far as their sight extended, they had killed 8 of them, and One beaver, they saved as much of the buffalo meat, as possible, they also mentioned that one Mile above the fall of 47 feet 8 Inches, is the largest fountain or spring, they had ever seen, and that they beleived it, to be the largest, in America that was known; this spring boils up from under the Rocks near the River, and falls immediately into it 8 feet 3 Inches, and keeps it colour for half a Mile in the River, which is Clear & of a blueish colour, and mention'd that there was many Shoots or little falls of water, which lay between the large falls, and at where the Cataracts or large falls lay, that a large mists was quite across them and that it was the same a great distance below each of them.— Captain Clark mention'd that on his route he had seen a number of Rattle Snakes, and but little timber,—

The party under Captain Clark, had left the falls this morning, and had returned back, in order to look out for the best and smoothest Portage, for us to Convey the Crafts and baggage up to the head of the falls on the Mesouri River, they mentioned that the Country above the falls, and up the Medecine River is level, with low banks, & smooth Water.— They saw a chain of mountains lying to the West, and some laying to the North West and South West; <both> all of which chains of mountains appear'd to them to be covered with snow, and lay very high, Captain Clark had lost part of the notes that he had taken which could not be found the Wind blowing hard, had taken them off.— they had not marked the road, above half the way down to our Camp; it being too late to go round the deep Gullys.— The party mentioned of having seen Gangs of buffalo swimming the River above the falls, some of which from the Rapidity of the current, was washed down over them, We remained still at our encampment, preparing every thing necessary in Order to assend to the head of Portage.—

1. See Clark's survey notes of June 17–19, 1805.

2. Giant Springs, now located in a park northeast of the city of Great Falls, Cascade County, Montana.

3. The Great Falls of the Missouri River, in Cascade County, now much reduced by Ryan Dam.

4. Probably the Lewis Range and the main Rockies.

June 21st Friday 1805.   a fine morning the wind from the S. W. off the Mountains & hard.   Capt. Lewis with the men except a fiew take a part of the baggage &c & a canoe up the Hill better than a mile in advance.   Several men employed in Shaveg & graining Skins Elk hides for the Iron boat as it is called. the meat was brought in & the men returned which Stayed out to dress the buffalow last night. they killed 2 or 3 deer and a buffalow calf & a Small Elk. we Saw innumerable numbers & gangs of buffalow & calfs on the high plains on Stard. Side of the Missourie.

Friday June 21st We had a fine morning, the wind blew hard from the South west, off the mountains, Captain Lewis, and greater part of our Men took a part of the baggage, & one of our Craft, up a Hill, better than a mile in advance of where we lay.— part of our Men were employed Shaving & Graining Skins & Elk hides for the covering of the Iron boat.—

This Iron boat,[1] or rather frame was made out of wrought Iron, the keel being 32 feet long and had ribbs, Stauncheons & beams of the same, with holes & screws to fit them. it likewise had screws to fasten the hides or skins that coverd the bottom & sides, and was in shape like a Ships Yawl. The meat of the Buffaloes that was killed Yesterday, & left behind, was brought to our Camp, & the Men returned, who had staid to dress it, They had killed 3 deer, a buffalo calf, and a small Elk, which they also brought into camp, We saw this day innumerable numbers of buffalo in Gangs with their Calves, on the high plains on the North side of the River Mesouri.— We still remained at our encampment

1. Whitehouse gives one of the best descriptions of the iron-frame boat.

Saturday 22nd June 1805. a fair pleasant morning. the wind as usal. the party all raised up eairly. Capt. Lewis and Clark with all the party except 3[1] Set out with a waggon & baggage to take the canoe & loading which was halled on the hill yesterday up to the upper end of the partage,[2] where we Shall form a Camp. Capt. Lewis & 3 or 4 men carried <all> their baggage in order to Stay up their, in order to git the Iron boat in readiness &c. the buffalow around the lower Camp verry thick Some gangs Swam the River Capt. Clarks Servant york killed one which was verry fat. Capt. Clark informed us that he Saw 40 or 50 Swimming the River abv the falls and Some went down over them which he could not See them rise any more. a nomber got to Shore half drowned. in this way great numbers of those animels are lost and accounts for So many as we Saw lying on the Shores below the falls ever Since we came from the Mandans & Gross vauntares but a vast deal pleantier near them [3] the country in general is verry high.   no timber back from the river and but verry little on the river, but bluffs & high clifts the most of the Shores.   we are a little South of the Mandans, but have had no verry hot weather as yet.

Saturday June 22nd   A fair pleasant morning and the wind continued as usual at So West   The party all got up early.   Captains Lewis & Clark with all our party (excepting three) set out with one of our Carriages (or Waggon) & baggage, to take the Craft, and loading which was hawled on the hill Yesterday; up to the upper end of the portage; where they intend to form a Camp, Captain Lewis, and 4 Men carried their own baggage, in Order to stay up there, <in order> to get the Iron boat in readiness &ca—   The buffalo was round the lower Camp in very great abundance.   Some Gangs of them swam the River.—   Captain Clarks Negroe Man shot one of them which was very fat.—

Captain Clark informed us that he saw between 50 & 60 Buffalo swimming the River, above the falls <of the river>; and that some of them, were drove down, by the rapidity current over the falls, and that he did not see them rise again, and that those that reached the Shore, appeared to be half drownded, which accounts for the many Dead Buffalo that we had seen floating along the Shores below the falls, ever since we left the Mandan and Gross Vaunter Villages; but found them floating much pleantier near these falls.—   The country generally here lies very high, and is chiefly Priaries & rich land; having no timber laying back from the Rivers, and but very little Timber on it, bluffs and high Clifts are all along the Shores on both sides of the River— We are at this place a little South of the Mandan Villages, but as yet have experienced no very warm weather.—

1. Ordway, Goodrich, Charbonneau, Sacagawea, and York were left at the lower portage camp to watch the remaining baggage.

2. The upper portage camp, on the Missouri about three-quarters of a mile north of Sand Coulee Creek, Cascade County, Montana, above the city of Great Falls.

3. Whitehouse appears to say that all of the dead buffalo seen on the banks of the Missouri since leaving the Mandan villages had been swept over the Great Falls. If this was his intention,

he should have known better, since the animals undoubtedly drowned in crossing the river in
many places during high water in the spring.

Sunday June 23rd 1805. the wind has Shifted to the East.   Cloudy.   a
light Sprinkling of rain.   in the afternoon one of the hunters[1] came in from
the Medicine River & informed us that one man G. Shannon left them the
first day he left this place, & took with him a Small kittle & Some perched
meal which was for the hunters, and that the other 2[2] had killed 16 buffalow
and a fiew Deer but Saw no Elk.   had dryed considerable of fat buffalow
meat at their Camp on the medicine River.   in the evening Capt. Clark and
party came in from the upper Camp & I with them[3] & informed us that they
had Some difficulty with their truck waggons as they broke Sundry times.
Capt. Clark Surveyed & measured the remainder of the portage, and looked
out the best way for the truck waggons & baggage to Go, and made the distance to the upper camp to where we take water again to be 18 miles a Strait
course.   they put up mile half mile ¼ mile & a half quarty mile Stakes as well
as Several flags as guides for the portage or carrying place &c.   Capt. Lewis
& 3 men[4] Stayed at the upper Camp, to prepare the Iron boat &c &c

Sunday June 23rd   This morning the wind shifted to the Eastward & became Cloudy and we had a light sprinkling of rain—   In the afternoon, one
of the hunters came in from Medecine River, and informed us, that one of
our Men by the name of Shannon had left them, the first day, after they had
left this place; and had taken with him a small kettle & some parched Meal,
which was intended for the hunters, and that the other two hunters had
killed 16 Buffalo, & a few deer, but had seen no Elk, and that they had dried
a considerable Quantity, of fat buffalo meat, at their Camp on Medicine
River.

In the Evening Captain Clark & party (of whom I was one) came in from
the upper camp, we inform'd the party left behind, that we had a great deal
of difficulty, with the truck carriage and that it broke several times—   Captain Clark surveyed, and measured the remainder of the Portage; and had
looked out the best way; for the truck carriages to go,—   and made the distance to the upper Camp to (where we are to take water) 18 Miles, on a strait
course, We put up Mile, half mile, ¼ Mile & half quarter Mile stakes; it being

Priaries all the way, and several flags as guides thro the portage, & carrying places.— Captain Lewis staid at the upper Camp; preparing the Iron boat &ca. this night, We still remain at same place encamped below the falls.—

1. Reubin Field.
2. Field and Drouillard.
3. Clark returned to the lower portage camp and Whitehouse accompanied him.
4. Gass, Joseph Field, and Shields, reports Lewis.

Monday 24th June 1805. a fair morning. we halled out the last canoe, & turned hir up to dry. all the party present Set out eairly with a waggon & baggage &c. for the upper Camp. we had Some difficulty in gitting the loading up on the high plains to where the canoes were left last night, though after a little fatigue we got all the loading which we intended carrying at this load in 2 Canoes & proceeded on to a creek called willow creek[1] 7 miles from the lower Camp & halted to refresh ourselves. made a tongue to one of the truck waggons, & proceeded on the wind blew Steady from the S. East. we hoisted a Sail in, the largest canoe which helped us much as 4 men halling at the chord with a harness. passed through high Smoth delightful plains. Saw a nomber of antelopes & buffalow. towards evening when we were within about 3 miles of the upper Camp. their came up of a Sudden a violent thunder Shower & rained a mazeing hard, for about 15 or 20 minutes, in which time the water Stood on the ground over our mockasons. our water being all gone and all the men thursty drunk harty out of the puddles. at dusk we arived at the upper camp, and unloaded found Some of the baggage wet by it raining in the canoes &c. we found Shannon here. he had been incamped up the medison River. he had killed 3 buffalow 8 Deer & several antelopes but no Elk.

Monday June 24th This morning we had fair weather, We hawled up our last Craft & turned her up to dry; all the party present set off, with a Carriage, having baggage &ca. for the upper Camp. We had some difficulty in getting the loading up, on the high plains where our Crafts was left last night, though after some trouble we got all the loading to where we intended carrying it at this time; in the two Crafts, and proceeded on to a Creek, which we called Willow Creek 7 Miles from the lower Camp, where we halted to refresh ourselves, and made a tongue to one of our Truck Carriages.—

We proceeded on, the wind blowing steady from the South east, We hoisted sail in our largest Craft (or Canoe) which assisted us as much, as 4 Men hawling at a Rope; We passed through, high smooth delightfull plain, where we saw a number of Antelopes & Buffalo in Gangs & flocks.— towards Evening when we were within about 3 Miles of the upper Camp, there came up of a sudden a Violent thunder shower, & it rained amazingly hard; for about 15 or 20 Minutes, in which time the water stood on the ground over our Moccasins— Our Water being all gone, & the Men very thirsty, they drank heartily, out of the puddles of water that lay in the plains— At dusk of the Evening we arrived at the upper Camp and unloaded our Carriage, & found that some of our baggage had got wet, by the rain, (that were in the Crafts.)— We found Shannon, the Man that had left the two hunters, at the upper Camp. He had been encamped up the Medecine River, & had killed 3 Buffalo, 8 Deer & several Antelopes, but had seen no Elk—

1. Now Box Elder Creek, Cascade County, Montana.

Tuesday 25th June 1805. a cloudy morning. we Set out with the 2 truck waggons, and returned back to the lower camp for another load. took up 2 canoes on the high plains. the day proved pleasant and warm the party much fatigued halling the truck waggons & the baggage. Saw large gangs of buffalow and antelopes to day. the evening clear and pleasant we got our loads ready to Start from this for the upper Camp. mended our mockasons &c. below the falls the plains are inferior in point of Soil to those below, more Stones on the Sides of the hills, Grass but a fiew inches high and but a fiew flowers in the plains. Great quantities of choke cherries, goose berrys, red & yellow berrys & red and purple currents on the Edges of the water. we catch great quantities of Trout, and a kind of mullet flat backs,[1] & a Soft fish resembling a Shad, and fiew cat fish &c. Sergt. pryor Sick. the party all of us amused ourselves with dancing untill 10 oC. all in cheerfulness and good humor. we all harnised up our back loads of the baggage to make an eairly Steart in the morning.

Tuesday June 25th   We had a cloudy morning; we set out with the two truck waggons, and returned back to the lower camp, in order to bring on another load, the party hawled up two of our Crafts, to the high plains in our absence, the weather cleared up at about 10 o'Clock A. M; and the day proved warm, and pleasant, the party that had hawl'd the trucks Yesterday, were all very much fataigued yet, We saw large Gangs of Buffalo & Antelopes this day, This evening was pleasant, and we prepared our loading, ready to start for the upper Camp &ca.—   below the falls, the soil on the plains, are inferior to the plains below; and more stoney on the sides of the hills, the Grass on them but a few Inches high, and but few flowers.—   We found in those plains growing Choke cherries, Goose berries, red & Yellow berries, and red & purple Currants growing on the edges of the water, in great quantities, and we Catched in the River near the falls a great Quantity of Salmon trout, [*blank*] and a kind of fish which were soft, and resembling a Shad & a few Cat fish &ca.—   The party all amused themselves, & was very chearfull waiting till the morning, in Order to start off for the loads of baggage &ca.—

1. "Flat backs" are unknown, but could be suckers, of the family Catostomidae. This is much the same as in Ordway which is quite similar to the captains' entries.

June 26th Wednesday 1805.   Some rain last night.   this morning verry cloudy.   the party Set out eairly with our loads to the canoes consisting of pearched meal pork powder lead axes tools Bisquit and portable Soup &c. we proceeded on with the 2 canoes & Some baggage.   verry hot Sun beat down on us as the day proved fair.   we halted at willow creek and made up a fiew dumplings & broiled a little fat buffalow meat & we Saw great numbers of buffalow on the plains in every direction.   the plain appear to be black with them.   Some antelope and Deer.   the wolves pleanty.—   I took sick this evening[1]   I expect by drinking too much water when I was hot.   I got bled &c

Wednesday June 26th   We had some rain last night, and this morning, we had cloudy weather; the party set out early this morning, with their loads to the canoes, it consisted of parched Corn meal, pork, Powder & lead, Axes and Iron tools, Biscuit, Portable soup &ca. the party proceeded on with the 2 Canoes, & the aforementioned Articles, baggage &ca.— The weather cleared up at 9 o'Clock A. M. and the Sun was very hot; We halted at Willow Creek in order to dine, The party that went with this load, mentioned of having seen a Vast number of Buffalo feeding in the plains in every direction, the plains appearing to be fairly black with them. they saw Antelopes, <and> deer, & Wolves in the greatest abundance, As I was one of the party that was sent with the 2 Canoes, that was carried on the truck waggons loaded with Provisions baggage &ca. I had an opportunity of seeing the quantity of Buffalo as related; and I can without exaggeration say, that I saw more Buffalo feeding—at one time, than all the Animals I had ever seen before in my life time put together.— One of the party was taken very Ill, and it was supposed his sickness proceeded from drinking too much Water, when he was warm,

1. The party Whitehouse was with reached the upper portage camp in the evening.

June 27th Thursday 1805. a fair warm morning. I feel Some better but not able to go back to the lower Camp So I remained with Capt. Lewis. Sergt. Ordway and three men went down by the River to See the falls and Spring &c about 4 oClock we had a hard Shower of rain which made the portage so Slipperry we did not expect they would Start from the lower Camp tomorrow with a load of the baggage as usal

Thursday June 27th   This morning we had clear weather, but warm, the Man that was taken Ill Yesterday, had got somewhat recovered, tho' so weak, and was not <to be> able to return to the lower Camp, Captain Lewis and three of the party went down to the River, to view the falls, Springs &ca. About 4 o'Clock P. M. we had a hard shower of rain, which made the Portage so slippey, that we did not expect the party would start from the lower Camp till tomorrow with a load of baggage &ca. for the Upper Camp—

June 28th Friday 1805. a fair morning the wind from the South. I remained with Capt. Lewis assisting with the Iron boat &c.—

Friday June 28th   We had a Clear morning, which continued the whole of this day, the party[1] that was at the upper Camp, were all employed in fitting out the Iron boat &ca.

1. Lewis, Gass, Drouillard, Joseph Field, Frazer, Shields, and Whitehouse.

June 29th Saturday 1805.   a little rain verry eairly this morning.   after clear and pleasant.   in the afternoon their <cam> arose a storm of hard wind and rain and amazeing large hail at our Camp   we measured & weighed Some of them, and Capt. Lewis made a bowl of Ice punch of one of them   they were 7 Inches in Surcumference and weighed 3 ounces.   as luck would have it we were all that Stay at this Camp Safe in a Shelter but we feel concerned about the men on the road.—

Saturday June 29th   This morning very early, we had some rain; which lasted but for a short time, when the weather cleared off, and it became pleasant.—

In the afternoon, there arose a storm of hard wind & Rain; accompanied with amazing large hail at the upper Camp, We caught several of the hail Stones which was measured & weighed by us (I being at the upper Camp), the hail measured 7 Inches in circumference; and weighed 3 Ounces.— Captain Lewis made a small bowl of punch out of one of them, the party that was at the upper Camp, were under a good shelter, but we are all concerned, for the welfare of the party who are on the Road with the baggage from the lower Camp.—

June 30th Sunday 1805.   a fair morning.   I remained Still at the upper Camp assisting with the Iron boat Sowing Skins together &c. &c.   the hunters kill Some buffalow and 3 white bear.   one verry large the fore feet of which measured 9 inches across, & the head to feet 11¼ Inches long and 7 Inches wide.   a bear nearly catching Joseph Fields chased him in to the water   bear about the Camp every night, and Seen on the Islands in the day time.   we look for Capt. Clark & party.

Sunday June 30th   A fair morning & pleasant, the party that were at the upper camp, were all employed, in sewing Skins together for to cover the frame of the boat &ca. some of the hunters kill'd some buffalo, and 3 White or brown Bear, One of which was very large, the fore feet of which, measured 9 Inches across, from the head to the fore feet 11¼ Inches & 7 Inches wide, One of our party had near being catched by one of those huge Animals & he was forced to take to the Water, to make his escape.— The bear are plenty along the upper Camp every night, and we see them in great plenty on the Islands in the day-time. We are at the upper Camp, looking out for the arrival of Captain Clark and his party, with the baggage &ca. fearing that they must have suffered much by the hail.—

July 1st Monday 1805. pleasant and warm. we continued on with the Iron boat as usal. about 3 oClock Capt. Clark and party arived with the last canoe and the most of the baggage. the remainder left only out at the 6 mile Stake. they informed us that the wet weather was what detained them and that they were out in the hail Storm but as luck would have it, the hail was not So big as they were here. Capt. Clark was at the falls at the time had hunted a Shelter in a deep creek with out water when he went in but before the Shower was over the creek rose So fast that he and 3 more[1] who were with him had Scarsely time to git out before the water was ten feet deep. Capt. Clark lost the large Compass a fusiee pouch & horn powder & ball, and Some cloaths &c. the party who were halling Some of them like to have lost their lives, being nearly naked and the most of them without any hats on their heads or anything to cover them and under went as much as any men could and live through it.

Monday July 1st This morning pleasant and warm; the party at the upper Camp were all employ'd in fitting out the Iron boat as usual.— About 3 o'Clock P. M Captain Clarke & his party arrived, with the last of our Craft, and part of the baggage, the remainder being left, at the 6 mile stake, they informed us that they were detained by the wet weather, and that they had been out in the hailstorm, but that the hall was not so large, as that, which fell with us at the upper camp; Captain Clarke was at the falls of the River, at the time the hail fell, and had hunted a shelter for himself, & party from the Rain & hail.— This sheltering place, was in a deep Creek, without any Water in it, at the time it first began raining; & he mentioned that before the shower was over; the Creek rose so fast, that he and those with him, had scarcely time to get out, before the Water was ten feet deep in that Creek— Captain Clarke had lost at that place, a large compass, a fusee, pouch & powder horn, powder, & Ball and some Cloathing &ca   The party that was hawling the Crafts, had nearly all lost their lives, being nearly naked, and the most part of them without hats, <on their heads,> or any thing to cover them, They had no shelter & were Cut and bruised very much by the hail, and under went, as much as Men could possibly endure; to escape with their lives.—

1. Clark was accompanied by York, Charbonneau, and Sacagawea, who had her baby with her. The incident occurred on June 29.

July 2nd Tuesday 1805.   Some rain at day light this morning after which a fair morning.   the men who came in yesterday Set out with the truck wag- gons to go back to the 6 mile Stake for the Boxes and kegs which was left yesterday &c.   we that Stayed at Camp Set at gitting timber &c for the Iron boat.   Musquetoes verry troublesome to day.   about 2 oClock the party arived with the last of the Baggage.   they killed 3 buffalow and one ante- lope.   we put our fire arms in order and about 4 oClock the 2 Captains and the most of the hunters went over on an Island to hunt bear   they killed one and Saved the Skin and greece

Tuesday July 2nd   We had this morning Some rain, which fell at day light, and it then cleared up, and we had clear pleasant weather.   The Men who arrived at the upper Camp yesterday set out with the truck waggons, to go back to the 6 Mile stake, for the boxes & kegs that they had left at that place.—   those of the party that were left behind, were employed getting timber &ca. for the Iron boat &ca.   We found the musketoes very trouble- some at the upper Camp, the whole of this day.—   About 2 o'Clock P M. the party arrived with the last of the baggage, they had killed 3 Buffalo, and one antelope, about 4 oClock P. M. the two Captains and most of our hunt- ers went over on an Island, to hunt bear.   They killed One bear, which they brought into our Camp, and we secured the Oil & Skin of this animal, Some of the party were employed in putting our fire Arms in Order &ca.

July 3rd Wednesday 1805. a clear pleasant morning. Sergt. Gass and 2 men [1] Set out to go down and See the falls & large Spring &c. the men at employed puting the leather on the Iron boat &c. Some burning tar to put on it. We overhalled the Baggage and found Some mice & killed a large curious rat with hair on his tail. we fixed Scaffels to keep the Bags &c from the ground and from the rats. a light Sprinkling of rain in the afternoon. George Drewyer Capt. Lewis' hunter at the upper Camp killed 2 large handsom otter and three beaver. in the evening 2 men went out a Short distance from Camp and killed a fat buffalow. Some men went for meat. Sergt. Gass and the man returned from the falls, had killed Six buffalow and Saved only the brains and tongues. we got the leather on the Iron boat, and took it apart. 8 Seprt. Sections— (2 men burning a tar kill)

Wednesday July 3rd A Clear pleasant morning, A Serjeant and 2 Men set out from Camp to go down to the falls, & large Spring, & to hunt, The Men in Camp were employ'd in putting the leather on the Iron boat, burning tarr to pay the Seams &ca We likewise overhawled the baggage, we found some Mice among it and kill'd a curious kind of a Rat, which was very large, and had hair growing on its Tail, & we fixed Scaffolds to keep the Bags &ca from the ground, and from Rats, We had a light shower of rain in the afternoon. One of our hunters killed at the upper end of our Camp, <killed> 2 large handsome Otters, and 3 Beaver. In the Evening 2 of our Men went out a short distance from Camp, and killed a fat buffalo, and some of our party was sent after the Meat, which they brought to us, The Serjeant and 2 Men that went with him returned towards night; they had killed 6 Buffalo and saved the tongues & Brains only, the latter being wanted to dress Deer leather, with. We fixed the leather on the Iron boat, & then took the boat apart, she had 8 Sections of 4 feet each—

1. Gass says one man, apparently Hugh McNeal. Ordway and Lewis give different counts.

July 4th Thursday 1805. a clear beautiful morning. the most of the men employed putting the Sections of the Iron boat together &c. &c. one of the hunters went on bear Island [1] and killed an Elk and a beaver. we finished putting the Iron boat together and turned hir up to dry. towards evening our officers gave the party the last of the ardent Spirits except a little reserved for Sickness. we all amused ourselved dancing untill 10 oClock in the evening. at which time we had a light Shower of rain, the party all in good Spirits keeping up the 4th of July &c. as Independence.—

Thursday July 4th   This morning we had Clear weather, the most of the party were employed, putting the Sections of the Iron boat together &ca—. One of the hunters went over to bear Island, and killed an Elk, and one Beaver; we finished putting the Iron boat together, and turned her bottom up to dry.—   Towards evening Our officers gave the party the last of the ardent Spirit that we had (excepting a little that they reserved for sickness)— We amused ourselves with frolicking, dancing &ca. untill 9 o'Clock P. M. in honor of the day.   In the Evening we had a slight shower of Rain, but it soon cleared away, & we had fine weather—

1. The White Bear Islands, opposite the upper portage, or White Bear Islands, camp, have virtually disappeared under the Missouri's waters.

July 5th Friday 1805.   a clear pleasant morning.   3[1] men Set out to go down to See the falls &c.   about 9 oClock 12 of the party with Capt. Clark wen[t] in the plains after a gang of buffalow Seen on a hill Some distance off.   the Situation of the plain where the gang of buffalow was Such that we could not git near enofe without being discovered by them.   in attempting it Scared them all off.   then a part of the men went after another gang, the remainder returned to Camp.   towards evening the hunters all came in had killed 3 buffalow 4 miles back in the plains.   brought in Some meat and Skins.   the 3 men returned from the falls.   had killed Several buffalow and might have killed hundreds if they chuse where they were pened in under high clifts of rocks.   they went among them So as might have reached them with the muzzel of their guns, &c.

Friday July 5th   A Clear pleasant morning, Three of our party set out, to go down to see the falls &ca   About 9 o'Clock P. M. 12 of our party went with Captain Clarke <went> out to the Plains after a Gang of Buffalo, which they had seen on a hill some distance off; the situation of the plain where the gang of buffalo was such, that we could not get near them, without being discover'd by those animals; we attempted to advance near them, but they got scared and went off.— part of those Men went after another Gang & the remainder returned to Camp. towards Evening the hunters all returned to Camp.— They had killed 3 Buffalo 4 Miles back in the plains, and brought in some of the Meat & the Skins; the three Men also returned from the falls of the River, they had killed several buffalo, and mentioned that they might have killed hundreds of them, if they chose to do it; they said that the Buffalo were penn'd in, under high clifts of Rocks, & they went among those Buffalo, and were so near, as to touch them with the Muzzel of their Guns.—

1. The number "3" is written over "2."

July 6th Saturday 1805. verry hard Showers of rain and hail through the course of last night. hard Thunder. at day light a hard Shower of rain and large hail one of the men gethered a Small kittle full of the hail which kept the most part of the day— the morning cloudy. 4 men Set out in 2 canoes in order to go down to the head of the falls to kill buffalow for Skins to cover our crafts & meat &c. Some men employed finishing off the Iron boat others dressing Skins &c. the day proved clear. light Showers in the afternoon. the hunters did not return this evening.

Saturday July 6th We had very hard showers of Rain & hail, through the course of last night, and at daylight this morning, we had a hard shower of rain, thunder & hail also; one of our Men gathered a small kettle full of the hail, which he kept most part of the day, without it melting; the morning continued Cloudy, four of our party set out from the Camp in two Canoes, in order to go down to the head of the falls to kill buffalo, for their hides to cover our Crafts, the meat &ca, some of the party were employed in finishing off the Iron boat, dressing Skins &ca— In the afternoon, it cleared up with some light showers of rain, the hunters did not return this Evening.—

July 7th Sunday 1805. a clear pleasant morning. one man caught a beaver last night. 2 hunters Set out across the river this morning to attempt to kill 1 or 2 Elk for their Skins. we finished off the Iron boat and put hir up in an open place to dry. the day warm. I am employed makeing leather cloaths for the party &c. Some Thunder and a light Shower of rain. about 4 oClock the hunters returned had killed Several buffalow, one Elk and Several wolves &c. they brought in Some Skins to cover the crafts with &c. the 2 hunters returned from across the river had killed 4 Deer and one antelope &c.—

Sunday July 7th A Clear pleasant morning, One of our party caught a beaver last night & two of our hunters set out, and went across the River this morning, in Order to kill Elk for their Skins— We finished off the Iron boat, and fix'd her in an open place to dry.— The day proved warm & some of the party was employed in making Cloathes out of dressed leather for the party, We had some thunder, & light showers of Rain. About 4 o'Clock P. M. the hunters returned, they had killed several buffalo, one Elk, and several Wolves, they brought with them some Skins to cover the Crafts with, Meat &ca The two hunters also returned that had went across the River, they had also killed 4 deer, One Antelope &ca.—

July 8th Monday 1805. a clear pleasant morning. one man went across the River a hunting. about 9 oClock A. M. Capt. Clark and all the men that could be Spared from Camp Set out for to go down to the falls a hunting. I remained in Camp makeing leather cloathes &c. the rest of the men at Camp was employed in makeing coal & tallow and Beese wax mixed and payed[1] over the leather on the Iron boat &c. in the afternoon the hunters returned from the falls and plains. had killed Several buffalow, 1 antelope and a yallow fox,[2] also 2 rattle Snakes, &c. Capt. Clark measured the width of the River at the great Spring & middle falls, &c. the hunter returned from over the river and had killed one buck Deer and a buck antelope or goat kind &c. Some Thunder and light Sprinkling of rain, &c.

Monday July 8th A Clear pleasant morning, one of our party went across the River a hunting, About 9 o'Clock A. M. Captain Clarke and all the Men that could be spared from Camp, set out for to go down to the falls a hunting.—

The party of men, left at the Camp, were employed in making leather Cloathing, for the party, burning of coal, & mixing it with tallow to pay the bottom of our Iron boat &ca.   In the afternoon the party that went with Captain Clark to the falls of the River, and those that had went out to hunt in the plains, returned; they had killed several Buffalo, 1 Antelope, & a Red fox, also two very large rattle Snakes.— Captain Clark measured the width of the River at the great Spring & middle falls; which were as follows; at the great Spring 70 Yds wide & at the falls 95 <feet> Yards wide.   In the Evening, the hunter that had went over the River returned, and brought with him, to Camp a large buck deer and a Male Antelope which he had killed, we had this Evening some thunder and light rain—

1. To coat with tar and pitch, but in this case the men used available materials.
2. The swift fox, *Vulpes velox.*

July 9th Tuesday 1805.   a beautiful morning.   the Island near our Camp is covered with black birds.[1]   the musquetoes verry troublesome.   we put the Iron boat in to the water corked Some of the canoes and git in readiness to depart from this place.   in the afternoon we loaded the 6 canoes but did not load the Iron boat for She leaked Some.   Soon after we got the canoes loaded there came up a Storm of wind & Thunder.   the waves dashed over in the canoes So that we had to unload again.   our officers conclude that the Iron boat will not answer our purpose as we cannot git Tar nor pitch to pay the hir over the hides.   the coal Tallow & bease wax would not Stick to the hides, &c.   the time being So far Spent they concluded to burry hir at this place and go about 20 miles up the River and make 2 canoes which would answer much better.   So we Sunk[2] Sd. Iron boat in the River So that Shee may be taken apart the better tomorrow.   about 10 men got ready to go with Capt. Clark to make the canoes, about 20 mls. by water and only about 5 by land from this place.

Tuesday July 9th   A beautiful morning, the Island near our Camp <is> were covered with black birds, we found the Musketoes very troublesome at our Camp during last night; & till after sunrise this morning, We were all employed, in calking of our Crafts; and putting our Iron boat into the waters and getting every thing in readiness to leave this place— In the afternoon we loaded the 6 large Canoes; the Iron boat leaked so much, that we did not put any load into her,— soon after, we had got the Canoes loaded, & a Violent storm of Wind and thunder came on.—

The waves rose to such a height, as to wash over into the Canoes, so that all hands were employed to unload them as quick as possible— Our officers found that the Iron boat would not answer our purpose, we not being able, to get sufficient quantity of tar or pitch, to pay her bottom & sides, and that the Coal, tallow, & grease would not prevent her from leaking, which she did very much; The Season being far advanced for the crossing the rocky mountains, the officers concluded to bury the Iron boat at this place; and to proceed about 20 Miles up the Mesouri, and to make 2 large canoes, to answer our purpose, so they had the Iron boat sunk in the River, that she might be more easily taken apart, which they intend having done tomorrow.— Ten of our party got themselves in readiness to go with Captain Clark, in Order to make the Canoes; they intend going by land the distance being about 5 Miles & 20 Miles by water—

1. Perhaps rusty blackbird, *Euphagus carolinus,* or Brewer's blackbird, *E. cyanocephalus.* The party also apparently called the common grackle, *Quisculus quiscula,* a blackbird.

2. The word "Sunk" is written over "put."

July 10th Wednesday 1805. a clear morning. we took the Iron boat out of the water, and loaded 4 canoes one with baggage & tools for the men at the upper Camp.[1] we Set off eairly with the canoes for the upper Camp Capt. Clark Set out at the Same time with abt. 10 men to go up by land to make the 2 canoes. we proceeded on with the 4 canoes about 8 miles and the wind rose So high that we we[re] obledged to lay by untill toward evening. the wind then abated and we went on untill dark. then camped for the night on N. S. within about 3 miles of the upper Camp. we killed a large rattle Snake. we passed to day 2 or 3 Islands covered with cotton timber and choke cherrys. abundance of cherry yellow currents and box elder timber along the Shores. passed a village of bearking Squerrells & killed one of them on N. S. the musquetoes & nats are troublesome at our Camp this evening. high banks of Sand along the N. Shore.

Wednesday July 10th   A Clear pleasant morning; some of our party were employed, in getting our Iron boat out of the water—   We loaded 4 of our Canoes, one of which had the baggage and tools for the Men, at the upper camp, who intend making the Canoes, We set out early with all the Canoes for the upper Camp.—

Captain Clark set out by land with ten Men to make the Canoes, at the same time, We proceeded on with the 4 Canoes about 8 Miles, when the wind rose to so great a heighth, that obliged us to lay by untill the evening.— the wind then abating, we proceeded on, with them untill dark; and then encamped on the North side of the Mesouri, within about 3 Miles of the upper Camp, We passed on this day 3 Islands, cover'd with Cotton timber, choke cherries & abundance of common wild cherry trees, Yellow Currants, & box Elder growing along the Shores, and passed by where there was a quantity of Priari dogs, whose habitations was as I have before described. One of which animals we killed.—   The Musketoes & Rats[2] were very troublesome at our Camp in the Evening, the Sand banks along the North shore are very high—

1. The "upper camp" was now the one where Clark's party was making canoes. It was in Cascade County, Montana, on the north side of the Missouri, a few miles east of Ulm.

2. The copyist means gnats, as in the first entry.

July 11th 1805 Thursday.   a clear morning, but high wind which obledged us to lay at our Camp untill late in the afternoon except the baggage canoe which went on.   2 of the men went up to the Camp and got Some meat. towards evening the wind abated a little so that we went on arived at the upper Camp about Sunset and unloaded.   the hunters had killed 2 fat buffalow and Several Deer.   I walked a Short distance in the plains to day when we were waiting for the wind to abate, and trod on a verry large rattle Snake.[1] it bit my leggin on my legg I Shot it.   it was 4 feet 2 Inches long, & 5 Inches & a half round.   we took Some fat meat on board and 4 of us Set out with the 8 empty canoes to return to the lower Camp.   we floated apart of the night got about 8 miles   the wind rose So that we halted untill morning— Capt. Clark had got 2 fine trees cut for 2 canoes and got them ready to dig out, &c—

Thursday July 11th A Clear morning, but the wind was high, which obliged us to lay by at Camp, untill the afternoon with our Canoes, excepting the one loaded with baggage & Tools, which proceeded on, two of our party went off to the upper Camp for meat, which they brought to us, towards evening the wind abated, we then went on, & arrived at the upper Camp about sunset,— where we unloaded the Canoes. The hunters had killed 2 fat buffalo, and several deer, One of the party was near being bit by a Rattle snake, which he killed, it measured 4 feet 2 Inches in length & 5½ Inches round.—

A party of 4 Men set out from the Camp, with 3 empty canoes to return to the lower Camp to bring up the baggage &ca left there, they floated down the river a part of the night, & got about 8 Miles, when the wind rose so high, that they were forced to lay by till morning.— Captain Clarks party cut down 2 large trees, and got them in readiness to dig out &ca—to make Canoes.—

1. Rattlesnake incidents had apparently become so common that only Whitehouse reports it. It was a prairie rattlesnake.

July 12th Friday 1805. a clear morning. the wind high from the N. W. we proceeded on down the river. the wind So high that one canoe filled the other 2 took in water, but with difficulty we got to the lower Camp[1] about noon. they while we were gone had killed 2 buffalow. had also put the Irons of the Iron boat in the ground and Some other articles, also. we Scaffelled up the buffalow meat to dry &c. Several men had Set out this morning for the upper Camp, the wind continues verry high all day.

Friday July 12th We had a clear morning, but the wind blew hard from the North West,— The canoes that went off last night to the lower Camp for the baggage &ca proceeded on down the River; the wind continued to blow so hard, that one of those Canoes filled, The other two took in a great deal of water, with a great deal of difficulty they arrived at the lower Camp about noon, the Men left at the lower camp during our absence had killed 2 Buffalo, and buried the Irons of the Iron boat, and several articles that we intend leaving behind us, We scaffolded the Buffalo meat to dry, several of the party that was left at the lower Camp, set out to walk to the upper Camp; The wind continued to blow hard during this day.—

1. Now the White Bear Islands, or upper portage, camp.

July 13th Saturday 1805. clear and calm. we loaded all the canoes eairly and Set out with all our baggage for the upper Camp. Capt. Lewis a Sick french man [1] and the Intrepters wife went across by land. we proceeded on with the canoes abt. 5 miles verry well then the wind rose So high that ob-ledged us to lay too untill towards evening, when the wind abated and we went on about 7 mls. further and Camped. the Musquitoes verry trouble-some untill 9 oClock at night.

Saturday July 13th A clear and pleasant morning, the Men that were at the lower Camp, loaded the 3 Canoes & set out early for our Camp, Captain Lewis, a frenchman that was sick & our Interpreters Indian Wife, went across by land to the upper Camp, The Men with the 3 Canoes proceeded on about 5 Miles very well, The wind then rose so high, that the Men in the Canoes were obliged to halt untill the middle of the afternoon; they then went on about 7 Miles, when they encamped; where they found the Musketoes very troublesome 'till about 9 oClock this night.—

The falls in the Rivor mesouri, being ascertained by different Men belong-ing to our party, as well as our Officers, I beg leave to give my readers a full account of the falls of the same. from its head, Vizt.

to the first great fall is 87 feet Pitch.
to The Second fall lying between 2 falls 19 feet [pitch]
to The Grand Cascade to the upper fall 47 feet 9 Inches
to The upper fall . . . . 26 [feet] 5—

The Total fall above the portage being 362 feet the River descending the whole way and lies in Latitude 47° 8′ 4¾ Seconds North & 2,585 Miles from the mouth of the Mesouri to the [*illegible*] of the great falls.

1. Lepage.

July 14th Sunday 1805. we Set out eairly and proceeded on. the morning clear and calm. passed Several Islands, &c. and arived at the upper Camp about noon. Capt. Clark & men had got the 2 canoes ready to put in the water. we unloaded the canoes put one of the niew canoes in the River about 4 oClock P. M. we had a Small Shower of rain. verry warm the musquetoes troublesome. we put the other niew canoe in the river, and make ready to leave this place. we have considerable of fat buffalow meat dryed. the weeds and grass in this bottom is as high as a mans knees, but the grass on the high land is not more than 3 Inches high.

Sunday July 14th We had a Clear pleasant morning, & the weather Calm, the party that was with the 3 Canoes set off early, and proceeded on for the upper Camp, they passed several Islands lying on both sides of the River, and arrived at the upper Camp about noon, Captain Clark & the Men under him, had got the 2 Canoes ready to put into the Water. The Canoes that arrived from the lower camp was unloaded, and One of the new Canoes, was put into the River. About 4 oClock P. M. we had a small shower of rain, & very warm, the Musketoes were very troublesome, We put the other new Canoe into the water, and all hands were employed in getting every thing in readiness to proceed on our Voyage.—

We have a very considerable quantity of dried buffalo meat at our Camp.—

The weeds & Grass in this bottom is as high, as a mans knees, but on the high land not mor than 3 Inches long, owing to the number of Buffalo that feed on them.—

Chapter Fifty-Eight

Across the Rockies

July 15–October 10, 1805

July 15th Monday 1805. rained the greater part of last night. a clear morning, wind high from the N. W. we loaded the 8 canoes. had Some difficulty to git all the baggage on board. about 10 oClock A. M. we Set out and proceeded on verry well. passed a large Creek or Small River[1] on S. S. passed Several Islands covered with cotton timber willow & Grass fine bottoms on each Side. beaver pleanty. the current verry gentle Since we came above the falls, can Scarsely desern it move as yet. we or Capt. Lewis & Clark & a hunter[2] who walked on Shore to day killed 2 Elk and 2 Deer & one otter. we came about 26 miles by water to day, and Camped[3] on the N. Side.—

Monday July 15th It rained the greater part of last night, and this morning was clear, but the wind blowing hard from the North West, We loaded the 8 large Canoes, and had some difficulty to get all the baggage and Provisions on board,— About 10 oClock A. M. we set out, and proceeded on our Voyage, and passed a large Creek or small River lying on the South side of the River, and several Islands covered with Cotton Trees, Willow and Grass, and fine bottoms lying on both sides of the River, The beaver very plenty, the current of the River running very gentle, since we have come above the falls scarcely descernable in moving and the water very Clear,— Captains Lewis & Clark, and one of the hunters walked on the shore, since we set out this day, they returned to us in the Evening, & had killed 2 Elk,

2 deer and One Otter.— We came only 6 Miles this day & encamped on the North side of the River

1. Smith River, named by the party for Robert Smith, Jefferson's secretary of the navy, meeting the Missouri in Cascade County, Montana.

2. Drouillard.

3. In Cascade County, a few miles southwest of Ulm.

July 16th Tuesday 1805. a clear pleasant morning. Sergt. Ordway went about 4 miles back for an axe which forgot last evening. we proceeded on verry well the current begin to git Swifter. we passed a high round hill a Short distance from the river which at a distance look like a large fortifycation So we named it Fort Mountain,[1] lying on N. S. of the river. we passed a large creek[2] on S. Side 100 yds. wide. passed Several Isld. covered with Timber. also bottoms on each Side covered with cotton Timber, &c. Saw fresh Indian Sign. large Camps back of Several bottoms. the hunters killed 2 buffalow. we Saw verry large gangs in the plains under the rockey mountan which we are now approaching. we Came 20 Miles and Camped[3] at the Entrence of the rockey mountains.—

Tuesday July 16th A Clear pleasant morning, One of our Men went back, about 4 Miles for an Axe that was left last evening, We set out early, and proceeded on, the current of the River being much stronger than Yesterday, We passed a high round hill, which lay a short distance from the River, which at a distance has the resemblance of a large fortification, Our Officers named that place Fort mountain, it lies on the North side of the River.— We passed a large Creek lying on the South side of the River 100 Yards wide at its mouth, and several Islands covered with timber,— and bottoms covered with Cotton wood on both sides of the River, and some fresh signs of Indians, and large Indian Camps lying in the bottoms.— The hunters that were out killed 2 Buffalo, and we saw very large Gangs of them in the Plains, below the Rocky mountains, which we are approaching near to, We came 20 Miles this day, and encamped at the entrance to the Rocky Mountains.—

1. Square Butte, south of Fort Shaw, Cascade County, Montana, but noted by Clark on July 15.

2. Apparently Bird Creek, Cascade County; perhaps the nameless "bayou" noted in Clark's courses for the day.

3. Near Tintinger Slough, Cascade County.

July 17th Wednesday 1805. Capt. Lewis & 2 men Stayed out all night who went up the river yesty. a clear morning. we Set out at Sunrise and proceeded on. about 4 miles came to a hard rapid,[1] ½ a mile where the mountains make close to the river on each Side. Capt. Lewis joined us by the assistance of the towing line and double manning the canoes we took them all up Safe. passed a large Spring[2] which run from under the Mountain on S. S. proceeded on passed verry high Steep rocks & pricipices. these rocky Mountains are broken & verry uneven & appear to be nearly a Solid rock. Some parts of them thinly covered with P. pine and balsom fer[3] timber &c. Some of these knobs we allow to be 700 feet high and a Solid rock. Mountain Sheep on the top of them though they are allmost perpenticular. fine Springs in these mountains, but a desert part of the Country. narrow bottoms on the points. Some willow[4] and high grass with a wide leaf. the current verry rapid, and river Crooked, and only about 100 yards wide. we Came 11 miles this day and Camped[5] on the N. Side in a bottom a little cotton timber on it. the Musquetoes troublesome. we got pleanty of yallow currents[6] this day.—

Wednesday July 17th Captain Lewis, and two of our party that went up the River Yesterday; staid out all last night; We set off at sunrise, and proceeded on about 4 Miles, when we came to a hard Rapid, where the mountains made close into the River on both sides of it. Captain Lewis & the Men with him met us here, we double manned the Canoes, and towing lines, and with much difficulty got them all over safe.— We continued on our way, & passed a large spring which run from under the Mountains on the South side of the River, and some very high Steep rocks & precipeces lying on both sides of the River. The rocky mountains at this place, are very broken and uneven, and appear to be nearly a solid Rock. Some part of them are thinly covered with Pine & balsam for timber.

Some of the knobs on these mountains appear to be from the nearest calculation that we can make <to be> 700 feet high, and it appear'd to be a solid rock, We saw on the very top of those Nobs, Mountain sheep although they appear to be almost perpendicular, In these mountains we saw fine Springs. The Country appears to be a mere desart, and some narrow bottoms are at the points toward the River, Willow and Grass grow in them, The grass grows high and has a broad leaf.— The River at this place runs very Crooked & runs very Rapid, and is only about 100 Yards wide, We came 11 Miles this day & encamped on the North side of the River, in a bottom having, a few Cotton wood Trees growing on it. We found a great plenty of Yellow currants this day, In the Evening the Musketoes was very troublesome.—

1. Half-Breed, or Lone Pine, Rapids, Cascade County, Montana.
2. Perhaps the "small run" noted in passing by Clark.
3. Ponderosa pine and Douglas fir.
4. Any of a number of species of willow, *Salix* sp.
5. In Lewis and Clark County, Montana, a few miles below the mouth of Dearborn River, near where Interstate Highway 15 crosses the Missouri River.
6. See Lewis's entry for a discussion of the area's currants; this one is golden currant.

July 18th Thursday 1805. a clear pleasant morning. we Saw Some Mountain Sheep on a verry high precipice which is nearly Steep from the river up 2 or 3 100 feet. we Set out about Sun rise and proceded on about 3 miles passed the mouth of a River[1] about 100 yd. wide at the mouth   it came in on the N. Side and run Strong. one mile further up   Capt.[2] Clark killed an Elk   Saw a nomber more. we Saw a flock of Mountain Rams on the Side of the Mountain on S. Side with verry large horns. Capt. Clark killd. one   we went near them before they run from us. the mountains appear not So high ahead, but another range Seen a long distance above which appear much higher than any we See in this range and Some we allow to be 700 feet high   the pitch & yellow pine[3] continues Scatering along these mountains &c. Capt. Clark & his Servant york & 2[4] other men Set out to go up one or two days travel by land. we proceded on with the canoes verry well. towards evening we passed a Small River[5] on N. S. about 60 yds wide named [*blank*] River. the mountains continue but not So high as yesterday. we Came 19½ miles and Camped[6] in a narrow bottom on the S. Side. considerable of flax[7] in this bottom half Seded.   we took on board Some deer meat & a Skin which Capt. Clark killed.

Thursday July 18th   This morning clear & pleasant; we saw some Mountain Sheep (Ibex) on a very high Precipice, which is nearly steep from the River, and <nearly> about 300 feet high, We set out about Sun rise, and proceeded on our way, and about 3 Miles from the place we left this morning, we passed the Mouth of a River, about 100 Yards wide at its mouth called Smiths River, it came in on the North side of the Mesouri, its stream run strong for a mile up it, Captain Clark who went ashore here, killed an Elk, and saw a number more of them.— We saw another large flock of Mountain Sheep (Ibex[)] on the Side of a mountain; lying on the South Side of the Mesouri River—

Those animals had larger horns, than any that we had yet seen.— Captain Clark kill'd one of them, We got near to them before they ran from us, The mountains appear not to be so high a head of us, as those we are in at present, We saw another range of Mountains a long distance further above us, Which appear to be much higher, than any that we have seen in this range, (some of which are 700 feet high)   The Pitch & Yellow pine appear to be growing, Scattering along these Mountains   Captain Clark, 3 of the party, & his black Servant, left us, and set out one days travel, up the River by land to make discoveries.— We continued on our Voyage with our Canoes, till towards evening, and passed a small River lying on the North side 60 Yards wide at its mouth which Captain Lewis named Dearbornes River. The Mountains continue, but not so high as they was Yesterday, We came 19½ Miles this day, and encamped in a narrow bottom, lying on the South side of the River; here we found growing considerable quantity's of wild Flax, having seed about half ripe, This flax was in every appearance like the Flax, which is planted & grows in the United States.   We found hanging up at this place the Meat & Skin of a deer, that Captain Clark had killed and left for our party.—

1. Dearborn River, named by the captains for Henry Dearborn, Jefferson's secretary of war, forms the boundary between Cascade and Lewis and Clark counties, Montana, for a short distance above its mouth.

2. The word "Capt." is written over "we."

3. "Pitch" is the familiar ponderosa pine. The most likely species for the "yellow pine" is limber pine, *Pinus flexilis* James.

4. The number "2" is written over "3"; 2 is correct. The men were Joseph Field and John Potts.

5. The captains named it Ordway's Creek, for Sergeant John Ordway of the party; later Prickly Pear Creek, Lewis and Clark County.

6. In Lewis and Clark County, above Holter Dam.

7. Blue flax, *Linum perenne* L. var. *lewisii* (Pursh) Eat. & Wright, named for Lewis.

July 19th Friday 1805. a clear pleasant morning. we Set out as usal, and proceeded on. Capt. Lewis and one hunter walked on Shore Shortly killed a large goat or antelope we took on board the Skin and Some of the meat. the current verry Swift. the mountains verry high & covered with pine & bolsom fir trees many places verry thick. we went on untill about 11 oClock without breakfast expecting to overtake Capt. Lewis as usal. the cause we know knot with Some thing has happened. one of the men killed an otter with his Shocked[1] pole. they are verry pleanty. some beaver also in these narrow bottoms. proceeded on. Shortly found Capt. Lewis. passed the mouth of a Small river[2] on the S. Side. in the afternoon we passed a verry high part of the mountain & Steep up from the River on each Side about 600 feet from the Surface of the water, which we name the gates of the rockey mountains.[3] Several fine Springs come out under these clifs of light couloured rocks. about one oClock their came a Thunder Shower which lasted 1 hour. Saw pine Spruce & ceeder bolsom fer also on the top & vallies of Sd. Mountains. the bottoms on the points verry narrow along the Shores. we Came 19 miles this day through verry rapid water and Camped[4] on the South Side. a light Sprinkling of rain this evening.—

Friday July 19th A Clear pleasant morning, We set out as usual, and proceeded on, Captain Lewis & one of the hunters walked along Shore, & shortly killed a large Antelope. We stopped, and took the Antelope on board of one of the Canoes. We found that the current still run very strong against us, The Mountains appear'd very high as we passed them, and had Pine & Balsam Fir trees growing on them, & in some places they were very thick, We proceeded on 'till about 11 o'Clock, without breaking our fast, expecting to overtake Captain Lewis and the hunter, who were on shore, & as we expected before us, but it not being the case, we are fearful of some accident having befel them— We found the Otter plenty in the River, one of our party killed one of them with the Socket of his setting pole.— We found beaver also tolerably plenty in the narrow bottoms of the River— We proceeded on our way; at 12 o'Clock A. M. [*crossed out, illegible*] we overtook Captain Lewis & the hunter; who came aboard of our Canoes. We passed shortly after the Mouth of a small River lying on the South side of the River which we called Gun brook River— In the afternoon we passed a very high part of the Mountain running up Steep from the River on both sides of it, which appeared to be <200> 600 feet high from the surface of the Water. Our Officers named this place, the Gates of the Rockey Mountains, We found several very fine Springs of water which came out from under the Clifts of these high Rocks, which rocks, are of a lightish colour.— About 1 o'Clock P. M we had a thunder shower, which lasted about One hour.— The Mountains & Valleys here, have Pine, Cedar & Balsam fir, growing on them,—

The bottoms on the points of land that lay along the River shore, is very narrow, The current of the River, run very strong the whole of this day, and the Water very Clear, we encamped in the Evening on the South side of the Mesouri, having 19 Miles this day, shortly after we had encamped we had a light shower of Rain—

1. Meaning "socket," as in the fair copy.
2. Willow Creek, Lewis and Clark County, Montana.
3. The Gates of the Mountains, still as named by Lewis, in Lewis and Clark County.
4. In Lewis and Clark County, a short distance downstream from Upper Holter Lake.

Saturday 20th July 1805. a clear morning. we Set out as usal and proceeded on. at 8 oClock we came to a lower part of the mountains. we found along the Shores a great quantity of currents of all kinds yellow red & black they are now ripe, and we eat pleanty of them the black kind are the most pallatiable.[1] one of the men killed one Elk, and found the Skin of another which Capt. Clark had killed and left a note letting us know that he would only go over the range of these mountains and wait our arival.

the current verry rapid.   passed a Small creek[2] on the South Side.   about
2 oClock P. m. we got through this range of mountains.   Saw an other range
a head.[3]   Saw a smoak in the valley between Some level plains in the valley.
Some timber Scatering along the River.   proceeded on   Saw a great nomber of otter along the Shores.   passed a plain on the N. S. in the valley between 2 mountains.   this valley is uneaven & hilley.   we Came 15 miles to
day and Camped[4] at a Spring on the South Side of the River.   the prickley
pears verry thick &c.

Saturday July 20th   A clear morning, & we set out at the usual hour, and
proceeded on our Voyage, Captain Clark having gone on before us, in order
to make discoveries.   About 8 o'Clock A. M. we came to a part of the Mountains, which was considerable lower than any we had seen since we entered
them.—   We found growing along the shore at that place, a great Quantity
of Currants of different kinds, Yellow, Red, & black, We halted and gathered
a quantity of them, they being Ripe.   We found the most palatable among
them the Black,—   One of our party went out, and killed an Elk, and found
the Skin of another, which Captain Clarke had killed and left, & a Note with
the skin from Captain Clarke, that informed us, that he would go over the
range of [blank] Mountains and waite our arrival.—   The current of the
River run very rapid this day.—   We passed a Creek lying on the South side
of the River.—   About 2 o'Clock P. M. we got through this range of Mountains, and saw another range, lying ahead of us, and a Creek lying in the
Valley, where there was Some level plains.—   We found some scattering
Timber growing along the River.   We proceeded on and saw a great number
of Trees along the Shores on both sides the River.

We passed a plain lying on the North side of the River, which lay in a Valley
between 2 Mountains, this Valley was uneven & hilly.—   We arrived at a fine
Spring lying on the South side of the River where we encamped; having
come 15 Miles this day.—   We found the Prickly pears growing in great
abundance at this place.—

1. All are varieties of golden currant. Whitehouse agrees with Lewis, Ordway, and Gass in
finding the black individuals the best-tasting.
2. Beaver Creek, Lewis and Clark County, Montana.

3. Apparently they passed the Big Belt Mountains on the east and saw the Spokane Hills and the Elkhorn Mountains ahead and to the west.

4. In Lewis and Clark County, on the point of a bend between Soup and Trout creeks.

Sunday 21st July 1805.   a clear morning.   we Set out as usal and proceeded on.   Saw a number of large Swans[1] on the River.   Some of the hunters killed 2 of them.   considerable of pine Spruce and bollsom fir trees along the Shore.   we passed a Small Creek[2] on the S. S. and one[3] on the N. S.   the grass in the valley & on the hills look dry & pearchd. up.   the wind high from the N. W.   in the afternoon we passed through a hill & clifts of rocks on each Side.   the River divides in different channels & Spreads about a mile wide.[4]   the Islands verry pleanty.   Saw beaver Sign on them.   this valley is Smoth in places.   Some timber along the Shores   our hunters on Shore killed a deer.   we Came 15½ miles through verry rapid water.   the men party much fatigued.   Camped[5] on a Smooth plain on the South Side.—

Sunday July 21st   We had a clear morning, and set out early on our Voyage, and proceeded on; we saw a number of large Swans in the River, some of our hunters killed two of them, we saw pine, Spruce, and Balsam fir Trees growing along the Shores on both sides of the River, We passed two Creeks lying on each side of the river, the grass in the Valleys, and on the hills appearing to be dry & parched,—   The wind was high from the Northwest.— In the afternoon we passed <through> a hill, and clifts of rocks lying on each side of the River, We found the River divided here into different channels, & spreading to the width of <a> about a Mile.   We saw a number of small Islands as we passed along, & some signs of beaver on them, We passed a Valley, which was plain & Smooth, and timber growing along the Shores, on both sides of the River.   One of our hunters killed a deer, which he brought to us.   We came 15½ Miles this day, the stream running rapid against us, which fataigued our party much and we encamped on a smooth plain, lying on the South side of the Mesouri River—

1. Trumpeter swan.

2. Apparently Trout Creek, Lewis and Clark County, Montana.

3. Spokane Creek, Lewis and Clark County, which Lewis called Pryor's Creek, after Nathaniel Pryor of the party. This is a confused day in the captains' maps and journals.

4. They passed the Spokane Hills into the valley, in Lewis and Clark and Broadwater counties, now largely inundated by Canyon Ferry Reservoir.

5. In Lewis and Clark County, a few miles east of Helena and about five miles above Canyon Ferry Dam, near the Lewis and Clark–Broadwater county line.

Monday 22nd July 1805. a clear pleasant morning. We Set out as usal and proceeded on   passed verry large Islands covered with grass a fiew trees. a great many currents.   we took a narrow channel behind an Isd. which was about 5 miles through.   we began to think that we had taken an other River, but proved to the contrary.   Some ceeder on Some of these Islands.   passd. 2 large Islds which level and all prarie or plain.   one of the men killed a Deer in a plain on N. S.   about 2 oClock we halted to dine on the N. S. then went on   Capt. Lewis forgot his Thurmometer which he had hung in a Shade.   it Stood today at 80 degrees above o.   I went back and got it then went on after the party.[1]   passed Several Islands covered with cotton & ceeder timber.   the River divides in many Channels.   I took a near cut and at night came out ahead of the party, and went down to the Camp.[2]   Capt. Clark had joined them & his party.   they were all well and had Seen a great deal of Indian Sign along the River and a fire which was burning.   we expect the Snake Indians or a party of them are near this.   perhaps they are alarmed at our firing at the game &c.   we Came 17½ miles this day thro a verry rapid current and a pleasant country.   a pleanty of ripe currents &c. along the Shores.   our Intrepters wife knows the country along the River up to hir nation at the 3 forks.   we are now 166 miles from the falls of the Missourie.—

Monday July 22nd   A clear pleasant morning, we set out Early, and proceeded on, and passed a very large Island, which was covered with grass & had a few trees growing on it, We found growing along the shores of the River, a great quantity of Currants; We took into a narrow Channell, of the River which run behind an Island, which was about 5 Miles through, Our party began to think before we had passed through this Channel, that we had taken the wrong River, For The whole of these 5 Miles, <had> we saw a number of Islands lying a small distance from each other, 2 of which was very large.   They lay very level and were all Priaries.—   We were all well pleased when we passed the last of these Islands, and found that we entered into the

River, which appear'd the same as when we took this Channel, One of our party killed a Deer on the North side of the River, which we took on board our Canoe,— Captain Lewis had forgot his Thermometer which he had hung in a Shade, It stood this day, at 80 degrees above 0.   I was sent back for it, and got it, I then proceeded on after our party, I passed several Islands, which were cover'd with Cotton wood & Cedar timber, the River divided in a number of Channels,— I took a near cut to the River, and at Night got to it, but was ahead of our party, I went down the River to where they were encamped.— Captain Clark, and a party of our Men, had during my absence arrived, and were all well,— They mentioned that they had seen a great deal of Indian sign along the River,— and a fire which from its burning, appeared to have been lately left, our party expect that fire was made by a party of the Snake Indians, who they suppose is near this place, and that they are alarmed at our party firing at Game &ca.   We came 17½ Miles this day <and> through a rapid Current.— We passed this day through a very pleasant Country abounding with Currants &ca.— which grows along the Shores on both sides— Our Interpreters Wife (the Indian woman) informed us, that she knows this Country, along the Shores of the River, up to her nation, (which are the Snake Indians) who she says lives at the 3 forks of this River.— We are now 166 Miles distant from the great falls of the Mesouri River.— These Islands we passed this day we named Whitehouses Islands.

1. Lewis and Ordway say it was Ordway who recovered the thermometer.

2. In Broadwater County, Montana, a few miles upstream from Beaver (the party's White Earth) Creek, on a site now under Canyon Ferry Lake.

Tuesday 23rd July 1805.   Capt. Clark and 3 men[1] Set out in order to go on to the 3 forks, expecting to find the Snake nation, near that place.   Some cloudy.   the Musquetoes verry troublesome.   I cannot keep them out of my face at this time.   the current verry rapid.   we proceeded on.   the river Spreads wide, and full of Islands.   we passed the mouth of a Small River[2] which came in behind an Island on the South Side.   passed livel Smoth large plains, on each Side.   high[3] grass in places & fine Short grass in general.   considerable of good flax now going to Seed.   the thissels[4] also pleanty & high now in blossom.   the timber continues on the Island and along the Shores. the beaver pleanty. the pine timber continues on the Sides of the hills at Some distance from the River. our hunter[5] who Stayed out last night came to us at noon where we delayed to dry the articles wh[ich] is wet in the canoes. he had killed Several Deer, and Saved the most of the meat. we hoisted up our flags and proceeded on the current verry rapid. Came 24 miles this day and Camped[6] on the South Side. the party in general much fatigued. we find pleanty of wild Inions or garlick,[7] in these bottoms & Islands &c. &c.—

Tuesday July 23rd   This morning Cloudy, Captain Clark and three of our party, set out in Order to go to the three forks of the Mesouri River, where they expect to find the Snake Nation of Indians residing, at or near that place.— We set out early, and found the current run very rapid, and the River spreading wide, and full of Islands, we passed the mouth of a small River, which came in behind an Island lying on the South side of the River, & passed level smooth large plains, lying on each side of the River, having fine Grass on it & Flax now going to seed, Thistles high & in bloom, the Timber plenty growing along the Shores, and on the sides of the hills, some distance from the Shores.— Our hunters that had staid out all last night came to us at noon.—

We delayed at the place that the hunters came to us, to dry the articles that was wet in the Canoes, the hunters had killed several deer & had saved most of the meat,— We hoisted our flags on board our Canoes & proceeded on at 2 oClock P. M. the current still running very Rapid, We came 24 Miles this day, and encamped on the South side of the River Mesouri, our Men being very much fataigued, We found here plenty of Wild Onions.—

1. Actually four additional persons, Joseph and Reubin Field, Frazer, and Charbonneau.

2. Whitehouse fails to mention that Lewis named the stream after him. Whitehouse's Creek was later Duck, or Gurnett, Creek, in Broadwater County, Montana.

3. The word "high" is written over "low."

4. Probably elk thistle, *Cirsium foliosum* (Hook.) DC.

5. Drouillard.

6. In Broadwater County, near the south end of Canyon Ferry Lake, a little north of Townsend.

7. Possibly *Allium brevistylum* A. Wats.

Wednesday 24th July 1805. a clear pleasant morning. we Set out as usal and proceeded on. the current verry rapid. we found a goat Skin which Capt. Clarks party had killed and left on Shore. passed a yellow or redish clift of rocks on N. S. Saw considerable of ceeder on the Islands and along the Shores. in the afternoon we passed a large plain on the N. S. the prickley pear abound on it. Saw otter and beaver in great abundance. the willow verry thick on the Islands and along the Shores. the Currents Still abound also the Rabit berrys, which the french call graze the buff.[1] the rapid water continues all day. Some bad rapids which it was with difficulty we passed over them. Came 19½ mls this day and Camped[2] on the large plain N. S. one deer killed this day. a white bear Seen. leant of Elk Sign— we Saw a great many different kinds of Snakes along the R.—

Wednesday July 24th A Clear pleasant morning, we set out as usual, and proceeded on; the current still running very Rapid, and found a Goat skin & the meat which Captain Clark and his party had killed, and left hanging up on the Shore, We passed by a Reddish or Yellow Clift of rocks, lying on the North side of the River, and saw some considerable Quantity of Cedar Trees growing on the Islands & along the Shores.— In the afternoon we passed a large plain lying on the No. Side of the River, which abounded with prickley Pears. We saw some Otter, and <the> Beaver in the greatest abundance.— We also saw some small Islands with Willows growing on them,— along the Shores abound with Currants & Rabbit berries.— The Current run very strong the whole of this day, and we crossed bad Rapids, which we got over with some difficulty, We came 19½ Miles this day and encamped on a large plain, lying on the North side of the River

The hunters killed this day a White or brown bear, and one deer, & saw Elk signs in great abundance, and <we saw> a great many different kinds of Snakes along the River Shores.—

1. It is French, *graisse de boeuf,* "buffalo grease," for the buffaloberry.
2. About seven miles north of Toston, Broadwater County, Montana.

Thursday 25th July 1805. a clear pleasant morning. we Set out as usal and proceeded on. Saw a large white bear on an Island. Saw a number of

otter.   Saw a flock of goats or antelopes one of the hunters killed one of
them.   we Saw a Camp where Capt. Clark had Stayed one night.   discovered mountains a head which appear to have Snow on them, if not Snow it
must be verry white Clay or rocks.   we eat abundance of red & yallow currents.   the timber Island not So pleanty as yesterday.—   large plains on
each Side of the River & looks pleasant and extensive.   in the afternoon we
entered in to Some rough rockey hills[1] which we expect from the Indian
account is the commencement of the Second chain of the rockey mountains, but they do not appear So high as the first nor So Solid a rock.   at the
entrence we found Several bad rockey rapids which we had to pass through
and So Shallow the rocks Show themselves across the River and appear Shallow all the way across.   we double manned and got up Safe.   I cut my foot
with the Stone a towing along the Shore.   Saw excelent Springs which ran
from under the clifts.   we came 16 miles this day and Camped[2] on the N. S.
our hunter killed one goose, which was all that was killed this day—

Thursday July 25th   This morning clear & pleasant, we set out as usual,
and proceeded on our Voyage, and on an Island saw a large White or brown
bear, & in the River numbers of Otters, and a flock of Antelopes on the
Shore one of which our hunters killed.—   We passed by a Camp, where
Captain Clarke had staid all night, We discover'd Mountains lying ahead of
us, which has the appearance of Snow being on them, from their white Colour, we still found abundance of Red & Yellow currants.   We did not find
the Islands or timber so plenty, as it was Yesterday.   We found large extensive
plains lying on both sides of the River, which had a pleasant appearance.   In
the afternoon we <enter'd into> passed some rough rockey hills, which we
expect from the account we have from the Indian Woman that is with us, to
be the commencement of the Second chain of the Rockey Mountains; but
they do not appear, to be so high, as the first chain of Mountains which we
have passed, nor so solid a rock at the entrance of them.—   We found several bad rockey Rapids, which we had to pass through, and <are> the Water
was so shallow that the Rocks appeared above the Water almost across the
River, We double manned our Canoes, and with difficulty got over them, by
hard towing; We saw several excellent springs, which came out from under

the Clifts of Rocks, near the River, We came 16 Miles this day, & encamped on the North side of the River.—

The men were very much fataigued towing the Canoes this day, and some of them had their feet Cut in passing over the Rocks.— Our hunters only killed one Goose, which was all that was killed this day.—

1. Apparently the cliffs Clark labeled "Little Gate of the Mountains," in Broadwater County, Montana, between Toston and Lombard.

2. In Broadwater County, immediately above Toston Dam.

Friday 26 July 1805. a clear morning. we Set out as usal, and proceeded on the current rapid. Saw Several Springs along the Shores. one of the men killed a beaver. the pine and ceeder timber pleanty along the Shores. passed clifts of rocks on each Side but the hills make off lower. we find that we have not entered the 2nd chain of Mountains but can discover verry high white toped mountains[1] Some distance up the River. the River verry wide and full of Islands. the current verry rapid in general. passed over Several verry bad rapids which was difficult to pass. our hunter on Shore killed 4 Deer. the wind blew hard at 2 oClock & a light Sprinkling of rain. we found an Indian bow. took on board a Deer Skin which Capt. Clark had left with a note, that they had Seen no Indians, but had Seen fresh horse tracks. considerable of cotton & ceeder timber on the Islands &c. Came 19 miles this day and Camped[2] on the South Side of the River. found Servis berrys[3] &c.

Friday July 26th We had a clear morning, & set out Early as usual and proceeded on. we found the current of the River to run much stronger, than what we had yet experienc'd, since we entered the Mesouri River; we passed several springs, running from under the Rocks, along the Shores on both sides of the River; and Pine & Cedar Trees plenty; also along the Shores. One of our party killed a beaver as we passed along with the Canoes.— We proceeded on, and passed Clifts of Rocks, lying on each side of the River, but the hills make off lower than they did Yesterday. We now find that we were mistaken, and that we have not as yet, entered into the Second Chain of Mountains, and we discovered very high white topped Mountains, lying some distance up the Mesouri.— The River here is very wide, and full of Islands, and the current runs very rapid in general, We passed several very bad Rapids, which was difficult to pass.— Our hunters that was out since daylight, came to us, they had killed 4 deer, which they brought to us, The wind blew hard from the North west, since 10 o'Clock A. M. and we had a light sprinkling of Rain; We found on the Shore an Indian bow, and took on board our Canoe, a deer Skin which had been left by Captain Clarke, and a Note from him.—

Captain Clark mentioned in this note, that he had seen no Indians as yet, but that he had seen some fresh horse trails.— We passed some small Islands, which had Cotton wood, & Cedar trees growing on them. We came 19 Miles this day, and encamped on the South side of the River in a small bottom

1. Beyond the Three Forks to the south lie the Tobacco Root and Madison mountains.
2. In Gallatin County, Montana, near the landmark of Eagle Rock.
3. Serviceberry, *Amelanchier alnifolia* Nutt.

Saturday 27th July 1805. a clear morning. we Set off at Sun rise and proceeded on. the current as rapid as yesterday. passed clifts of rocks where was villages of little birds [1] under the Shelving rocks &c. the hills not So high as below. the currents of different kinds abound along the Shores. about 9 oClock we Came or arived at the 3 forks of the Missourie which is in a <wide> valley in open view of the high Mountains which has white Spots on it which has the appearance of Snow. Saw large flocks of mountain Sheep or Ibex, and goats or antelopes. the plain on N. Side of the forks has lately been burned over by the natives. we went on passed the South fork, and west fork. went a Short distance up the North fork and Camped on the point which is a Smoth plain.[2] a large Camp of Indians has been encamped here Some time ago. our Intrepters wife was taken prisoner at this place 3 or 4 years ago by the Gross vauntous Indians.[3] their came up Showers of rain which lasted untill evening. Capt. Clark & men returned & Joined us. had found no Indians, but had Seen fresh Sign of horses. Saw one elegant horse in the plains which appeared wild. they had been about 40 miles up the middle or west fork then Struck across the plains to the North fork, and was near the mountains, and informs us that their is considerable of Snow on them. our hunters killed in these bottoms in the forks of the Rivers, 6 Deer 3 otter & a musk rat. Capt. Clark & party had killed Several Deer goats or antelopes and a young bear. this is a verry pleasant handsome place, fine bottoms of timber &c. we expected to have found the Snake nation of Indians about this place, but as they are gone we expect they are gone over the mountains to the River called the Columbian River[4] to fish &c. but perhaps we may find Some this Side of the mountains yet. we Came only 7 miles to day. at this Camp we unloaded all the canoes & conclude to rest & refresh ourselves a day or too &c.— Capt. Clark taken Sick.—

Saturday July 27th A Clear morning, We set off early, and proceeded on; the current was as rapid as it was Yesterday, we passed some Clifts of rocks, where there was a quantity of small bird's nests, built under the shelving rocks. The hills were not so high, as they had been some distance below. We found currants of different kinds in abundance, growing along the shores of the River.— At 9 o'Clock A. M. we arrived at the three forks of the Mesouri River, which lays in a Valley, in open View of the high mountains, which have white spots on them, and has the appearance of being Snow.— We saw on the Hills large flocks of mountain Sheep (or Ibex) and flocks of Antelopes.— The plain lying on the North side of those 3 forks, had been burnt by the natives, We proceeded on, and passed the South and West forks of the Mesouri River; and went a short distance up the North fork, & encamped on the Point, which is a large smooth plain— We found here a large Camp, where the Indians had been encamped sometime past.— Our Indian woman (Interpreter) informed us that she was taken prisoner at this place between 3 & 4 Years ago, by a party of the Gross Vaunter (or big Belley) Indians who had carried her away to their Nation

We had showers of rain that continued till the evening.— Captain Clark and the party that was with him returned; and joined us here.— they informed us, that they had seen no Indians, but that they had come across fresh tracts of horses, and had seen one of the horses, which was elegant, they found this Horse in the plains and he appeared to them to be perfectly wild— They also mentioned that they had been 40 Miles from the best calculation up the Middle or West fork of the River, and then had struck across the plains to the North fork, and had been near the Mountains, and that there was a considerable quantity of snow on them.— Our hunters killed in the forks of these Rivers 6 deer, 3 Otters, and a muskrat, Captain Clarke & his party had killed several deer, Antelope, and a Young bear since they had left us.— The forks that we are present at, is a most delightful situated place, and exceeds any that we have yet seen, it affording a most delightfull prospect, the land extreamly rich & fertile; and the bottoms large and well timbered, and to all appearance must be healthy,— and may be called the Paradice of the Mesouri River. We expected to have found the Snake Nation of Indians here, but they being gone, we now expect that they are gone over the Mountains, to the Columbia River to fish.— The party here are of opinion, that they may find some of those Indians, yet; on this side of the Mountains. We came only 7 Miles this day; to where we are encamp'd We unloaded all the Canoes this day.—

Our officers concluded on the party staying here, for some days; in order to refresh themselves.— Captain Clark was this day taken Ill, which was supposed to be occasioned by fataigue.—

1. Bank swallow, *Riparia riparia.*

2. The Three Forks of the Missouri meet near the Broadwater–Gallatin county line, Montana, about four miles northeast of the town of Three Forks. The first (south) branch they encountered was the Gallatin, then they proceeded on to the junction of the Madison (west branch) and the Jefferson (north branch). Clark's party had reached the forks on July 25. The main party's camp this day was apparently on Barkers Island, between two branches of the Jefferson, northeast of the town of Three Forks, Gallatin County.

3. Sacagawea's capture by Hidatsa (*Gros Ventres*) raiders probably took place near the town of Three Forks. See Lewis's entries for July 28 and 30.

4. Like Ordway, Whitehouse uses the term "Columbia River" broadly. Here it is the Lemhi River, a distant branch of the Columbia.

Sunday 28th July 1805. a foggy morning but clear. Several men went out eairly a hunting. we put out all the baggage to air. Capt Clark verry unwell. we built a bowrey for his comfort. the party in general much fatigued. Several lame, with Sore feet &c. towards evening the hunters all returned. had killed 7 or 8 Deer Some of them fat bucks. one of them who had been a Short distance up the South fork & found it not as large as

the middle or west & North forks, which are near of a Size.   in the evening
we had a fine Shower of rain.   Some Thunder attended it, which cooled the
air much.   the men at Camp has employed themselves this day in dressing
Skins, to make cloathing for themselves.   I am employed makeing the chief
part of the cloathing for the party.   two Elk killed to day also—

Sunday July 28th   We had some fog early this morning, but it cleared
away at Sun rise, & the weather was pleasant, several of our party went out a
hunting, and the remainder was employed in Airing the Baggage &ca.—
Captain Clarke continued still very sick,—   part of our Men were taken off,
from the Baggage &ca. in order to build a bowry, for his accomodation <of
Captain Clark>, which they soon compleated,—   The Men that were hawling the Boats along with the tow lines, for several days past are much fataigued; & some of them lame from Cuts they got in their feet in passing
rockey & stoney parts of the Shores.—   towards the evening the party that
had went out hunting returned.   They had killed 8 Deer, some of which
were very fat.   One of that party mentioned that he had been up the North,
& West (or middle fork of the River Mesouri,) and mentioned that those two
rivers, appeared to him to be nearly one width.   In the evening, we had a
fine shower of rain, accompanied with Thunder, which cooled the Air, &
made it very pleasant, The Men at our Camp, were <Airing> employed in
drying the Baggage &ca <was drying, employed themselves in> & dressing
of Skins to make themselves Cloathing.—   I was employed in making chief
part of the Cloathing for the whole party.—   Our Hunters killed also 2 Elk,
which was brought into our Camp.—

Monday 29th July 1805.   a clear pleasant morning.   Several hunters went
out eairly to hunt.   we conclude to lay at this Camp to day.   Capt. Clark
Some better.   the day verry warm the wind from the East.   the Latitude of
this place is 45° 22m 34s ⁵⁄₁₀th North.   the width of the Rivers at the forks
we alow the North fork to about 60 yards wide, the west fork about the Same,
the South fork about 40 yards wide.   towards evening the hunters came in
had killed 2 fat buck deer, and brought in a curious long leged redish couloured crain.[1]

Monday July 29th   This morning we had very pleasant clear weather, Several of our hunters went out early to hunt, Our officers concluded to lay here this day, Captain Clark had got much better.—   The day proved since 9 o'Clock A. M very warm, the wind blowing from the East.—   Captain Lewis took the Suns altitude, and found the Latitude of this place to be in 45° 2M 34S North—   We measured also the width of the 3 Rivers at the <forks> confluence of them.   We found the North & West forks of the same width of Water 90 Yards wide which is Jefferson & Maddison Rivers and the South fork only 70 Yards wide which they named Galatin River,[2] the North fork having the most rapid Current, all those Rivers having fine Clear water in them.—   towards evening our Hunters returned, and brought in to our Camp 2 large Deer, which were very fat, also a curious long legged reddish Coloured Crane.—

1. Sandhill crane, *Grus canadensis.*

2. The Jefferson was named, of course, in honor of the president, the Madison for James Madison, then secretary of state and later president, and the Gallatin for Albert Gallatin, the secretary of the treasury.

Tuesday 30th July 1805.   a clear pleasant morning.   we loaded the canoes eairly and Set out about 9 oClock and proceeded on.   Capt. Lewis and Several men walked on Shore.   we passed large bottoms of cotton timber.   the River crooked rapid and full of Islands.   the under bushes thick.   the currents abound.   the beaver pleanty.   a nomber of beaver dams behind the Islands &c.   we dined at the upper end of the bottoms close by a clear open prarie or plain.   at this place our Intrepters wife was taken prisoner 4 years ago by a war party of the grossvauntaus.   they took hir as She was attempting to make hir ascape by crossing a Shole place on the River, but was taken in the middle of it.   2 or 3 Indians killed at the Same time on Shore.   the rest of the Snakes made their ascape.   the day warm, and verry pleasant.   one of the hunters killed a deer.   we proceeded on.   the current verry Swift & rapids common.   passed beautiful large plains on L. S. and high land on the S. Side.   we came 13½ miles this day and Camped[1] on the Stard. side. Capt. Lewis did not join us this evening.   these bottoms are low & many beaver dams which causes pond &c.

Tuesday July 30th   A Clear pleasant morning.   we loaded our Canoes early, and proceeded on our Voyage; about 9 o'Clock A. M., Captain Lewis and several of our party walked on shore.—   We proceeded on and passed large bottoms of Cotton timber, the River being Crooked, rapid, & full of Islands, the under wood thick & currants growing along the Shores in abundance.—   Beaver here, <and> were seen by our party plenty, & We saw a number of their dams, laying behind the Islands & other places—   We halted to dine at the upper end of the bottoms, near which lay a Priari or plain, which was Clear & open, & without any bushes on it.—

Our Interpreters Wife the Indian Woman, related to us, that between 3 & 4 Years ago she was taken prisoner at the forks of the three rivers, by a Warr party of the Gros Vaunters or Big belley Indians, and that she had attempted to make her escape, with some others of her nation, but that she was retaken by them in the Middle of the Priari which lies near to us, that 3 of her nation was killed along the Shore, by the same party, that she was taken by but that the greater part, of the party that she was along with (Snake Nation) had made their escape;—   This day was warm but yet pleasant, One of our hunters killed a deer which he brought to us.—   We proceeded on at 2 o'Clock P. M. and found the current running very swift, and a number of rapids, We passed beautiful large plains which lay on the South side of the River & high lands lying on the North side; Towards Evening we encamped on the North side of the River in a fine bottom of Timbered land, and came 13½ Miles this day.—   The Country that we passed through this day, appeared to be rich & fertile, but it lay tumbling on the North side of the River.   Captain Lewis & the party that went with him, did not return to us this Evening— The bottoms along the River this day lies low, and have ponds in them, occasioned by the Beaver Dams, which are very plenty

1. They traveled up the Jefferson and camped in Jefferson County, Montana, just below the mouth of Willow Creek (the party's Philosophy River) and about two miles north of the town of Willow Creek.

Wednesday 31st July 1805.   Capt. Lewis layed out alone all last night.   a fine morning.   we Set off at Sun rise and proceeded on as usal.   the current rapid.   passed the Mouth of a Creek[1] on the Lard. Side, which was damed up by the beaver in Sundry places. the bottoms low on each Side and covered with Small cotton timber & young willow &c. about 8 oClock A. m. we came to Capt. Lewis where he Camped last night. we took breakfast and proceeded on passed a plain on the L. S. the hills begin to make near the River on each Side. passed a verry large Island which is Smoth bottom prarie & but a little timber on it large open plain on L. Side on which grows abundance of flax wild Tanzey thissels &c. the above mentioned handsome Creek runs through this prarie on Smoth bottom without timber. only a little cotton timber on the River we dined about 1 oC. under a delightful Grove of cotton timber on L. Side under the mountain which has large heaps of Snow on it. we now enter the hills on each Side and keeps along under the mountains. Capt. Clark Saw a mountain Sheep with the Spy glass on a round hill towards the mountain. the Game is now gitting Scarser. we are now without fresh meat which is verry uncommon to us. the day verry warm. we proceeded on passed clifts of rocks and high wales along the Shores. Some pine Scatering along the hills. we Came 17¾ miles this day and Camped[2] on a Small Island on the Lard Side. our hunter on Shore wounded a white bear.

Wednesday July 31st About 10 o'Clock last night, the hunters that were out came to our Camp, and had left Captain Lewis, who staid out, all night, We had a fine morning and set out at sunrise; and proceeded on our Voyage; we found the current of the River running strong against us, we passed the Mouth of a large creek which lay on the South side of the River [*erasure*], which was damed up in many places by the Beaver, We passed also by low bottomed land, lying on both sides of the River, which was cover'd with small Cotton wood timber, Willows, &ca—. About 8 o'Clock A. M. we arrived at the place where Captain Lewis was & had encamped last night. We halted at this place and breakfasted. We then proceeded on, and passed a plain lying on the South side of the River. The hills near to this plain begin to make in near the River, on both sides of it. We also passed a very large Island, which lay low, and mostly Priari land, and but little Timber, on it; On the South side of the River opposite to this Island is a large open plain, having a handsome Creek,[3] running through it.— On this plaine we found growing, abundance of Wild flax, Tanzey, thistles & wild flowers, and had grass growing luxuriently on it, There was some timber likewise at this place which grew near the River.   We dined at that place under a delightful grove of cotton timber, which lies a small distance from a Mountain; which had large heaps of Snow lying on it.— We proceeded on about One Mile when we passed hills, lying on both sides of the River, which keeps along under the mountains, Captain Clark saw a Mountain Sheep (or Ibex) with his spy Glass, on a round hill towards the Mountain; We found the Game getting very scarce, & we are now without fresh meat, which was very uncommon with us.   This day proved very warm; We continued on our way, and passed clifts of Rocks, and high Walls of Stone lying along the Shores on both sides of the River.— We saw growing along the hills sides on each side of the River some scattering pine trees.   We encamped in the Evening on a small Island, lying on the South side of the River, having came this day 17¾ Miles. Our hunters that were on Shore wounded a White or Brown bear, but it made its escape.

1. Willow Creek, which they named Philosophy River, joining the Jefferson in Gallatin County, Montana.

2. Near the mouth of Antelope Creek, in either Gallatin or Madison County, a little downstream from the entrance of Lewis and Clark Caverns State Park, and some two miles above where U.S. Highway 287 crosses the Jefferson.

3. Evidently Willow Creek or Antelope Creek.

Thursday 1st day of August 1805.   a clear morning.   we Set out as usal and proceeded on.   Some of the men killed a goose & a beaver   about 8 oClock A. M. we took breakfast under Some handsome ceeder trees on S. Side. Capt. Lewis Sergt. Gass Sharbonoe & Drewyer Set out by land to go on up the River to make discoverys &c expecting to find Indians &c.   we proceeded on.   find currents as usal and choak cherrys along the River.   the current Swift   the hills higher and more pine and ceeder timber on them. we passed high clifts about 500[1] feet high in many places.   considerable of pine on the Sides of the hills   all the hills rough and uneven.   at noon Capt. Clark killed a mountain Sheep, on the side of a Steep redish hills or clifts the remainder of the flock run up the Steep clifts.   the one killed roled down Some distance So we got it and dined eairnestly on it.   it being Capt. Clarks birth day he ordered Some flour gave out to the party.   we Saw Some timber along the Shores resembling ceeder which Some call Juniper,[2] which had a delightfull Shade.   I left my Tommahawk on the Small Island where we lay last night, which makes me verry Sorry that I forgot it as I had used it common to Smoak in.   proceeded on   passed verry high ragid clifts, and a bad rapid at the upper end of a Small Island   the toe rope broke of the Capts. perogue and it was in danger of upsetting.   passed a Spring run or creek[3] on L. Side.   came in to a valley.   passed bottoms of timber and the mouth of a large creek[4] on S. Side, and a Spring also.   we came 13½ miles and Caped opposite the Spring in a fine bottom covered with cotton timber and thick bushes &c.   Saw a white bear.   the hunters killed 5 deer   we took on board 2 Elk which Capt. Lewis had killed and left on Shore for us.   Saw Snow on the Mountains[5] a Short distance to the South of us.

Thursday August 1st   This morning, Clear & pleasant.   We set out as usual, and proceeded on our Voyage, some of our party killed a Goose and a Beaver.   We halted about 8 o'Clock A. M—   where we stopped & took breakfast under some handsome Cedar trees, lying on the South side of the River.—   Captain Lewis, Serjeant Gass & George Drewyer, and Sharbono (<who> the latter of which men had joined us at the Mandan Village,) set out shortly after, to go by land, up Jefferson River, in Order to make discoveries, & to try & find out some Indians.   We proceeded on, and found Currants, & Choke cherries growing along the Shores in great abundance.   the current of the River still running very strong against us; and the hills appearing to us, to be much higher, and more Pine & Cedar growing on them, than those we have passed for several days past, We passed some very high Clifts, of Rocks which were in many places 1,200 feet high &—   on the sides of the hills we saw considerable quantities of Pine & Cedar Trees growing. About noon Captain Clark killed a mountain Sheep or Ibex, out of a flock, which were on the side of Steep reddish hills or Clifts

The remainder of the Flock of mountain sheep or Ibex, ran up the steep Clifts, out of Gunshot, and to such a heighth as is most incredible—   The Mountain sheep that was killed, rolled down the Hill, and we got it.—   We stopped at this place to dine, which was amongst the high Clifts, and it being Captain Clarkes birth day; he ordered some flour to be served out to the party, which with the mountain Sheep made us an excellent meal,—   We proceeded on at 3 o'Clock P. M. and passed by some Trees, growing along the Shore; which resembled in look the Cedar Tree, but it was what is called the Wild Juniper, This Tree afforded a most delightfull shade. we also passed very high rugged Clifts, lying on both sides of the River, and a very bad Rapid, at the upper end of an Island; where the Tow Rope broke of the Canoe, that Captain Clarke was on board & it had nearly upset. We came by a Run or Creek, which lies on the South side of the River, and came in at a Valley, & bottoms of timber'd land, the Mouth of a large Creek, and a large Spring lying also on the South side of the River, We came 13½ Miles this day & encamped opposite this spring, in a bottom covered with Cotton wood Timber, & thick Brush.— We saw a White or brown Bear on the hills some distance from our Camp. The hunters who were on Shore since morning, returned to us, and had killed 5 Deer which we took on board the Canoes & also 2 Elk which Captain Lewis & party had killed and left at this place for us, We also saw Snow on the Mountains, a short distance to the South of our Camp.—

1. Whitehouse may have written "700" initially.
2. Rocky Mountain red cedar, *Juniperus scopulorum* Sarg., and common juniper, *Juniperus communis* L.
3. South Boulder Creek, Madison County, Montana; called "Frasure's Creek" by the party after member Robert Frazer.
4. Boulder River, Jefferson County, named "R. Fields Vally Creek" for Reubin Field.
5. The Tobacco Root Mountains.

Friday 2nd August 1805. a fine pleasant morning. we Set out eairly and proceeded on. the River is now Small crooked Shallow and rapid. passed bottoms of cotton timber &c. Saw abundance of beaver Sign, trees a foot over which had newly been cut down. Saw a pond which was made by the beaver damming up the water as in may places. passed a high bank in which was a village of what is called bank Swallows. high hills a little back from the River on each Side of the River. considerable of pine on them, & covered with Short grass. I have a pain in my Shoulder. we proceeded on passed large beautiful bottom prarie on each Side, & bottoms of timber. Saw a number of old Indian Camps. the beaver houses are verry pleanty & ponds where they resort. the day warm. we proceeded on   passed a nomber of Islands and bottoms.   the River Shallow and rapid.   passed Smoth praries &c.   Saw 2 grey Eagles[1] which had nests on the top of dry trees. Came 14¾ miles this day & Camped[2] on a Smoth plain on L. Side.   Saw a gang of Elk back under the hills.   the country back from the River is broken & Mountainous.

Friday August 2nd   This morning we had fine & pleasant weather, we set out early & proceeded on our Voyage.   We found the River getting very narrow, crooked, shallow & rapid, We passed some rich bottoms of Cotton Timber, where we saw abundance of signs of Beaver, & trees that had been cut down by these animals lately, many of which measur'd a foot over, & a pond which was made by the beaver daming up the Water, We also passed a bank which was very high, and had a vast number of Swallows nests in them. This bank lay a small distance back from the River, on each side of it, & had a considerable quantity of Pine trees growing on them & short grass.—   We proceeded on and passed a large beautiful bottom, and Priaries lying on both sides of the River, and some large bottoms of timbered land.   We saw in those bottoms, a number of Indian Camps which appear'd to have been built some time, & plenty of Houses built by the beaver, & a large pond where those animals resort to, We continued on, & saw a number of small Islands & bottoms, The River getting more shallow; Some level Priaries lying on both sides of the River.—   In the afternoon we saw 2 large Grey Eagles, whose nests we saw on the tops of high Trees which were dead.—   We came 14¾ miles this day, & encamped on a smooth plain lying on the South side of the River, where we saw a Gang of Elk, back of our Camp under some hills.—   The Country this day lying back from the River, is broken, and Mountaneous.—

1. Golden eagle, *Aquila chrysaetos.*
2. Below Big Pipestone Creek, the party's Panther Creek, Madison County, Montana.

Saturday 3rd August 1805.   a clear morning.   we Set out as usal and proceeded on.   Capt. Clark walked on Shore a Short time and killed a Deer. the River verry crooked and filled with Islands.   proceeded on.   Saw 2 deer little a head, one of the hunters went after them and killed a panther on an

Island. it differs Some from those in the States it was 7½ feet long, & of a
redish coulour the turshes long the tallants large but not verry long. passed
verry rapid water So that we had to double man the canoes and drag them
over the Sholes & rapids. passed a large prarie on S. Side. high grass &
bushes along the River. the bottoms has been burned over by the natives I
expect last fall. passed a verry large Spring on L. S. which makes from under the mountains. the beaver has damed up the mouth & built lodges all
through the pond it forms. it falls over the beaver dam in to the River verry
Steep, about 4 feet.— passed over a bad rapid and halted about one to
dine at a bottom of timber on the S. Side. the day pleasant & warm. proceeded on passed Several Springs one large one on L. S. plains and bottoms, Some of which is covred with cotton & birch[1] timber the River Still
getting more rapid and the rapids longer than below. Came 11½ miles this
day and Camped[2] on L. Side Cot. wood.

Saturday August 3rd A Clear morning, & we set out on our Voyage early,
Captain Clark walked on Shore a short time, and killed a Deer.— We
halted our Canoes, and took the Deer on board, and then proceeded on,
We find the River very crooked, and filled with Islands. We continued on,
and saw 2 Deer a small distance a head of us.— One of our hunters went
out after them, this hunter killed a Panther on a small Island, a small distance from us. it differed but very little from those seen in the United
States. It measured 7½ feet long, and was of a reddish colout, its tushes was
very long, the Talons thick but not long, We passed many places in the River,
that the water ran so rapid, that we were forced to double man the Tow ropes
to drag the Canoes over the Shoals & rapids. We passed a large Priari lying
on the South side of the River, high Grass & bushes, growing along the River.
We also passed a very large spring, which lies on the South side of the River,
and comes from under the mountains.— The beaver had dammed up the
Mouth of this large spring, and had built their houses all through the pond
it had formed, it falls over the beaver dam into the River, about 4 feet, We
passed over a bad rapid, and halted about One o'Clock P. M. to dine at a
bottom of timber'd land, on the south side of the River— The day was
warm but pleasant, we proceeded on and passed several springs, one of
which was very large, lying on the south side of the river, & some plains, some

of which was covered with Cotton wood Trees & birch timber.— The River has this day run more rapid, & the Rapids much longer, than any we had yet seen, which fataigued our Men exceedingly.— We came 11½ Miles this day & encamped <in> on the South side of the River, in a place of Wood land.—

1. Perhaps scrub birch, *Betula glandulosa* Michx., which Lewis calls dwarf birch this day.
2. Near Waterloo, with the camp in either Jefferson or Madison County, Montana.

Sunday 4th August 1805. a clear morning. we Set out at Sunrise. a hunter Sent on a head to kill Some fresh meat for us to eat. proceeded on abt. 8 oC. A. m. we Came to Capt. Lewis camp of the 2 ult.[1] he left a note letting us know he left this place yesterday morning, and ment to go on untill this evening, & if they found no fresh Sign of Indian, they would return back a fiew miles & hunt untill we came up. we Saw Several <buffalow &> Elk in a plain on L. Side. proceeded on our hunters killed 2 deer. the rapids bad as usal. we are obledged to use the towing lines where ever the Shore will admit. Some of the Mountains near the River on L. S. has been burned by the natives Some time ago. The timber killed. not So much timber on the River as below. proceeded on killed a goose and a duck. they are pleanty on the River. we Came 15 miles this day and Camped[2] at a bottoms covered with dry timber and wild rose bush which is verry thick on S. Side. the beaver ponds and Sign pleanty &c.

Sunday August 4th This morning we had clear cool weather; we set out at sun rise, having sent one of our hunters to go on, a head of us, in order to procure some fresh meat for our party. we proceeded on, and about 8 o'Clock A. M. we came to where Captain Lewis had encamped the 2nd instant. he left a note, wherein he informed us, that he had left this place Yesterday morning, and that he meant to go on untill this evening, & if he or his party found no fresh sign of Indians, that they would return back a few Miles and hunt, untill we came up. We saw several Elk, in a plain on the South side of the River, We proceeded on, the Rapids being bad as usual, and we are obliged to make use of the Tow Ropes, wherever the Shore will admit, some of the Mountains on the South side of the River has had the Grass burned off from them, & the Timber killed on them.— The timber is not so plenty here, as it is some distance below.   We proceeded on and saw plenty of Ducks & Geese in the River.   Our hunter that went out this morning killed 2 deer, which we took on board.   We encamped in the Evening at a bottom covered with dry timber, and wild rose bushes in great plenty on the South side of the River, where we saw ponds made by the beaver in great abundance.—

1. It should be "inst." rather than "ult."
2. In the vicinity of Silver Star, Madison County, Montana.

Monday 5th August 1805.   a clear cool morning.   we Set out at Sunrise 2 hunters Sent on a head to kill Some meat.   one of them joined us with a deer he had killed before breakfast time.   the wind cold from the South. the Shores and hills rockey & bottom of the River covd. with Small Stones. our other hunter joined us at noon, had killed nothing.   the rapids gits worse that ever.   it is with difficulty we git over them, & verry fatigueing.   at 1 oC. P. M. clouded up.   wind high.   proceeded on   about a mile further up came to a fork[1]   we took the right hand fork which was amazeing rapid. Some of the rapids falls 3 or 4 feet or their abouts in the length of our canoes.   we passed through a channel where the water was rapid and ran through the willows & young cotton wood   the beaver had fell Some of them across the channel and it crooked   it was with much difficulty we got thro.   obledged to forse our way through the bushes and hall by them. Some places out in the water could Scarsely keep our feet for the rapidity of the current.   Saw Several beaver dams verry high.   night came on. Camped[2] on S. Side at a low bottom, which has lately been overflowed.   we expect this little Stream is high from the Snow melting on the mountains. it appears it has lately been higher, but is now falling a little.   was it low their would not be water enofe in it for us to proceed any further by water.   our hunter killed a deer.   Came 8 miles this day.   the party much fatigued and wish to leave the canoes & go by land.

Monday August 5th   A Clear, cool morning, we set out as usual, and sent 2 of our hunters ahead in order to kill some Game for us, One of which joined us before breakfast with a deer he had killed.   The wind blew cold from the South, the Shores & hills rockey & the bottoms of the river, covered with small Stones, The other hunter joined us at Noon, but had not kill'd anything. The rapids of the River, we find here, worse than any that we have yet met with; and it is with great difficulty that we can pass them, and very fataigueing to our party— About 1 o'Clock P. M. the weather clouded up, and the wind got high. We proceeded on about a Mile further up, & came too.— We halted here for a short time, & then proceeded on, and came to where the River forked, We here took the right hand fork, which we found run very rapid, some of the Rapids of the River; here fell 3 feet, and was between 3 & 4 feet in length. We passed through a channel where we found the water run rapid through Willows & Cotton wood trees, The Beaver had cut down some of those trees, which had fell across the Channel, & the River running Crooked, it was with much difficulty we got through them, being obliged to force our Canoes through the bushes, & hawl the Canoes by them. Several of our party were forced to go out into the Water in several places, to hawl along the Canoes, and the rapidity of the Current made it very difficult for them to keep <on> their feet.— We saw several beaver dams, which was very high; Night came on, & we encamped on the South side of the River in a low bottom, which had been lately overflowed. The fork that we are at (or rather small stream of water) is high, which we suppose is occasioned from the Water melting on the Mountains. this River has the appearance of having been considerable higher, than it is at present, and at any common time. we are of oppinion that there would not be water sufficient for our Canoes to proceed any futher.—

We came 8 Miles this day, & encamped; our party are much fataigued, & it is the wish of all of them, that we would proceed on our Voyage by land to the Columbia River— Our hunter joined us at our encampment, and brought with him a Deer, he had killed.—

1. The forks of the Jefferson River. On the right is Big Hole (the party's Wisdom) River and on the left, Beaverhead River, which they continued to call the Jefferson.

2. Clark's party camped a mile or so up the Big Hole River from its mouth, in Madison County, Montana, northeast of the present town of Twin Bridges.

Tuesday 6th August 1805. a clear morning. we Set out as usal, and proceeded on halling the canoes up the rapids. the bottoms low and covered with Small timber. about 8 oClock A. M. we halted for breakfast at a grove of timber. Saw an Indian trale or path. G. Drewyer Came to us and informed us that we had got the wrong fork & that their was 3 forks & Capt. Lewis allowed that the middle fork would be the right course & the best fork for us to go up.[1] Capt. Lewis gone down to the forks. we turned about and went down to the forks with the crafts. in going through a difficult place which we went up thro last evening, one canoe got up Set and everry perticle of the loading got wet. one of the men who was in the bow lost his knapsack and the most of his cloaths &c. I was in the Stern when She Swang & jumped out to prevent hir from turning over but the current took hir round So rapid that caught my leg under hir and lamed me & was near breaking my leg. lost my Shot pouch powder horn full of powder a bunch of thred and Some mockisons &c. the remainder of the loading Saved. we found it difficult to go down over the Sholes. Several canoes ran fast &c. one of the large canoes took in water & was near filling. we got down to the forks found Capt. Lewis & party their. they informed us that they had been about 30 miles up & their was 3 forks and the middle fork was the best for us, to go. we halted here at the forks on L. S.[2] and put out all the articles which got wet to dry. one of the men who went out to hunt this morning has not returned. Several men went out from this place to hunt. we had a Small Shower of rain. the hunters all returned in the evening had killed 3 Deer and one faun Elk. we blew the horn & fired Several guns, expecting the man who went out this morning George Shannon was lost. the Indian goods &c. did not all git dry this evening, &c.—

Tuesday August 6th   A Clear morning, We set out as usual and proceeded on, towing our Canoes up the Rapids, and passed through low bottoms, lying on both sides of this little River; which were covered with Rich growths of Timber, about 8 o'Clock A. M. we halted at a Grove of timbered land for to break fast, where we saw Indian trails or paths, at this place George Drewyer, one of the party that went with Captain Lewis came to us. He informed us that we had taken the wrong fork of the River, and that the River had forked in three places below, and that Captain Lewis allowed that the middle fork, was our right course & the best for the Canoes to ascend,— and that Captain Lewis had gone down the River to where it forked.— We set out at 9 oClock A. M. to return down the River with our Canoes, and in going through that difficult place that we passed Yesterday, one of our Canoes up-set and ev'ry article of her loading got wet, & we were in great danger of losing them.— One of our party who was in the bow of the Canoe, lost his knapsack, and most of his Cloathing.— I happened to be in the Stern of the same Canoe when she swung round and jumped into the water in order to prevent her from turning up, but the current running strong caught my leg, which it had nearly broke.—

I lost in the Canoe, my shot pouch, Powder horn full of powder, the greater part of my cloathing &ca—. the greater part of the load was saved, owing to the Shallowness of the Water.— We found it very difficult in going down the River with our Canoes, and getting them over the Shoals, some of them ran aground, and with much difficulty was got off, and one of our largest Canoes took in Water & was near filling. We got down to the forks about 4 o'Clock P. M. where we found Captain Lewis & the remainder of the party that had went with him.— They informed us that they had been about 30 Miles up above the forks, and confirmed what Drewyer had men-tioned of their being 3 forks,— and that the middle fork was our best way, We halted at the forks on the South side, where we put all the wet articles out to dry, One of our Men that went out a hunting this morning, had not returned to us.— Several of our party went out from this place to hunt, and some time after we had a small Shower of rain, the Hunters that went out from this place returned in the Evening they had killed 3 Deer & 1 Elk fawn, which they brought to our Camp. We blew the horn & fired several Guns, expecting that the Man who went out a hunting this morning was lost & that probably he might hear the report of the Guns and find us out.— The Indian Goods &ca— that was put out to dry, are not perfectly so this evening.—

1. They had missed Lewis's note, which had been carried off by a beaver. The third fork is Ruby River, some distance ahead. They were to stay on the middle fork, the Jefferson, which becomes the Beaverhead above the Ruby.

2. On the Jefferson opposite the mouth of the Big Hole River, Madison County, Montana.

Wednesday 7th August 1805. a clear cool morning. one man out to hunt. we unloaded one of the Small canoes and halled it out in a grove of cotton trees and leave hir here. we put the Indian goods &c. to git throully dry.

Capt. Lewis took an observation & Shot the air gun.   the lost man not returned.   the day warm, the large horse flyes[1] troublesome &c.   about one oClock we packed up all the baggage and Set off & proceeded on up the middle fork.   we find the current not So rapid as the right fork.[2]   the rapids not So bad.   we had Thunder Showers & high wind this afternoon.   passed Smooth plains on each Side &c—   Camped[3] after coming 7 miles on a bottom of wood & bushes L. Side.   our hunter G. Drewyer joined us   had killed a deer.

Wednesday August 7th   A Clear cool morning, We sent one of our party out to hunt & unloaded one of our small Canoes, & hawled it out in a Grove of Cotton trees, as we intend leaving her here.   The Indian Goods &ca— were all put out, in order to get thoroughly dry.—   Captain Lewis took an observation at this place & found it to lay in Latitude 45° 22′ 34S North, he also fired off his air gun several times in order that the Man that went out a hunting from the party that was with Captain Clarke up the North fork Yesterday & who we suppose is lost might hear the report, he having as yet not returned.   This day was very warm & the party was much troubled with large horse flies.—   About 1 o'Clock   P. M. we packed up all the Goods, Cloathing &ca and set off—   We proceeded on up the Middle fork, and found that the current did not run so rapid, as it was in the North fork, nor the Rapids so bad.—   We had Thunder Showers & high Wind in the afternoon, & passed smooth plains lying on both sides of the River, We encamped in the Evening in a bottom of Woodland having a large quantity of bushes, lying on the South side of the River where we were joined by George Drewyer our hunter who had killed a Deer which he brought to our camp.

1. Horse fly, *Tabanus* sp.
2. Jefferson River (middle fork) and Big Hole River (right fork).
3. In Madison County, Montana, just above Twin Bridges.

Thursday 8th August 1805.   a clear cold morning.   4 hunters Sent out eairly to hunt.   we Set out at Sunrise, and proceeded on   passed beautiful Smooth prarie on each Side, but little timber only willows and bushes currents &c.   passed the left hand fork[1] which empties in at 2 places, but is not as large as the middle fork.   Saw a little Snow on the knobs & mountains

at a Short distance back from the [river?]   this large & extensive valley
which looks verry pleasant.   the Soil of these praries is much better than
below, for a long distance.   we proceeded on   passed a fine Spring on L. S.
one of the hunters brought us a deer which he killed.   Saw a nomber of
geese & ducks on the River.   passed delightful prarie on each Side covred
with high grass thissels Small Sun flowers[2] and a number of other kinds of
flowers &c.   at noon R. Fields joined us had been hunting for Shannon but
had not found him.   he had killed a deer & a goat &c.   one of the other
hunters joined us had killed a deer & a goat also—   the day warm & pleasant, in this valley, which is 10 or 12 miles wide & all prarie.   proceeded on
halled the canoes over Several Shole places.   this little River which we call
Jeffersons River is only about 25 yards wide but jenerally eight or 10 feet
deep, and verry crooked.   we passed upwards of 60 points this day in comming [*blank*] miles and Camped[3] in a thicket of bushes on the Lard Side.—
one more deer kill

Thursday August 8th   This morning Clear & cool weather, 4 of our hunters were sent out to hunt, We set out at Sun rise, and proceeded on & passed
beautifull smooth Priaries lying on both sides of the River, which had little
of any kind of timber on them, excepting Willow [*blank*] Hazle[4] & currant
bushes, We passed the left hand fork of the River, which emties itself in to
the middle fork at 2 places.   It was not as large as the Middle fork; We saw
Snow lying on the Nobs & mountains, which lay but at a Short distance from
us, back from the Middle fork lies an extensive Valley which had a beautiful
appearance, & the Soil much better, than what we saw below, for a long distance.   We proceeded on, and passed a fine spring of water lying on the
South side of the River, One of our hunters brought us a deer which he had
killed—   We halted & took it on board & proceeded on and saw a number
of Ducks & Geese in the River, and beautiful Priaries lying on both sides of
it, cover'd with high Grass thistles, Sun & other flowers.   One of our hunters
joined us.   he had been hunting for Shannon, the Man that we had lost, but
had not found him.   He had killed One deer & a Goat, One of our other
hunters joined us also, he had also killed a deer & a Goat, all of which we
took on board.   The day proved warm & pleasant in the Valley which is

between 10 & 12 Miles wide & all Priari. We proceeded on, & hawled our Canoes over several Shoals in this little River, which we call Jefferson River <and> which is about 25 <Miles> Yards wide at this place & generally between eight & ten feet deep, and very crooked, We passed upwards of 60 points this day in coming of 14 Miles, which is the distance we have come. We encamped in a thicket of bushes, laying on the South side of the River. One of our hunters returned to us here & brought in a Deer which he had killed.—

1. Ruby River, their Philanthropy River, which meets the Beaverhead in Madison County, Montana, to form the Jefferson. They continued up the "middle fork," the Beaverhead, which they continued to call the Jefferson.

2. Nuttall sunflower, *Helianthus nuttallii* T. & G.

3. On the Beaverhead, a few miles above the mouth of Ruby River, Madison County.

4. Hazelnut, *Corylus americana* Walt., is not found this far west. It is not clear why the copyist added this or what the plant is.

Friday 9th August 1805. a clear cool morning. Several hunters out on Shore we Set out as usal and proceeded on. the wind high from the S. E. took on board a goat which one of the hunters had killed. we halted abt. 8 oC. for breakfast. George Shannon joined us who had been lost 3 days. he had killed 3 buck Deer, which was fat. he brought in the Skins & a little meat. Capt. Lewis G. Drewyer H. McNeal & John Shields Set out to go on by land a long distance to look out the way for us to go & expect to find the Snake nation of Indians. we proceeded on. took on bord a deer which one of the hunters killed. we Saw no game worth notice except a fiew deer. the River and Smooth prarie the Same as yesterday. <back at the forks our Captains named this Stream Jeffersons River, the N. fork Sensable River,[1] and the South fork>, not known yet. So I expect that ought to be called the head of the Missourie although we are yet on the head branch, which we expect to See the head of it Soon. Some Thunder. the Musquetoes troublesome. the beaver pleanty as usal, &c. Saw Snow on the Mountains Some distance a head. proceeded on passed the old bed of the River where it formerly ran along the high land at South Side of the prarie Some cotton trees along it. the prarie low, Some part of which is soft & boggy which we expect is good turf to burn was dug & dryed.   Thunder Showers passed round or over.   Came 18 miles and Camped[2] on L. S. near a grove of cotton trees & willows.

Friday August 9th   We had a clear cool morning, several of our Hunters left the camp early to go out a hunting & We set out as usual, and proceeded on our Voyage, the wind blowing high from the South east, We stopped with one of our Canoes & took on board a Goat, which one of the hunters, that went out this morning had killed, & left on the bank of the River; we proceeded on till about 8 o'Clock A. M. when we halted to take breakfast.   Here we were joined by George Shannon, one of our party that had been lost, for these 3 days past, he had killed 3 buck Deer, which he said was very fat, he brought with him, some of the Meat and the Skins of them.   Captain Lewis & 3 of our party <here> left us here & set out to go by land a long distance up the River, in order to look out the best way for us to proceed, & to find out the Snake nation of Indians.—   We then proceeded on a small distance, & took on board one of the Canoes, a Deer which one of the hunters had killed & left on the bank of the River also; We saw no Game, excepting a few deer, which were in the bend of the River.   We passed some smooth plains much the same as those we passed Yesterday.   We all expect that we are near the head Waters or source of the Mesouri River, as the River, here is growing much narrower than it was, We had some thunder in the afternoon, and the Musketoes was very toublesome.   The beaver was very plenty to be seen in the River, & along the shores.   We saw Snow on the mountains which lay ahead of us.—   We continued on our way, and passed a place, where we supposed the Bed of the River formerly was, and high land, lying on the South side of the Priaries lying back from the River, with some Cotton wood Trees growing on it, The priaries here lay low on both sides of the River, some part of which is soft & boggy, which we expect would make good turf In the evening we had some Showers of rain accompanied with thunder, We encamped on the South side of the River, near a Grove of Cotton wood trees, & Willows, having come 18 Miles this day.—

1. Perhaps the party's initial name for their Wisdom River, today's Big Hole River.

2. In Madison County, Montana, a little downstream from the Beaverhead County line and the crossing of Montana Highway 41 over the Beaverhead River.

Saturday 10th August 1805. a clear pleasant morning. we Set out as usal. Several hunters out on Shore. we now begin to live on fresh meat & that poor venson & goat meat at this time. as our fatigues hard we find that poor meat alone is not Strong diet, but we are content with what we can git. the high land make near the River on each Side. passed a high clifts of rocks on S. Side.[1] proceeded on the valley gits wider and the hills make further from the River our officers thought proper that the Missourie Should loose its name at the 2nd forks we passed Some time ago where we expected to have found the Snake nation of Indians. So they named the North fork *Jeffersons* River, the west or middle fork *Maddison* River, the South fork *Gallitine* River, on which is a most beautiful Spring abt 2 mls. from its mouth. the Small River that puts in above the forks to Jeffersons River they call phillosify River. So Jeffersons River is the one which we Still keep on. the last 3 forks they call the North fork, Wisdom R. the South Philandrophey and the west or middle fork Still retains its name Jeffersons River it is now gitting Small crooked & Shole in places So that we have to waid and hall the canoes over. about one oClock we halted to dine. had a hard Thunder Shower of large hail and rain thin proceeded on the bottom and river as usal. the hunters killed only one deer this day. Came 13 miles this day and Camped[2] on the Stard. Side.—

Saturday August 10th This morning clear & pleasant, several of our Hunters went out early to hunt, & we set out as usual, We now have nothing to live on, but fresh meat, & that poor Venison & Goats flesh, and our men seem much fataigued; and find that meat only, is too weak a diet, for men undergoing so much fataigue; but they seem all content with what we can get. The high land makes in near to the River on both sides of it, We passed a high clift of Rocks, which lay on the South side of the River, and Valleys, which seem wider, than those which we passed Yesterday, and the hills lies off farther from the River, Our officers were of oppinion (before Captain Lewis left us) that the Mesouri River should lose its name, at the place where the Second fork enter'd this River; which we passed some days past, and where we expected to have found, the Snake Nation of Indians. they named the North fork Jefferson River, The West or middle fork Maddison River, and the South fork Gallatin, River, on which lies a most beautiful spring of Water, about 2 Miles from its mouth; the small River, that puts in above those three forks, to Jefferson River, they named Philosophy river, so that the River that we are now on, is Jefferson River, they also named the last three forks   the North fork they called Wisdom River, & the South fork, Philanthropy River, the middle fork still retaining the name of Jefferson River (and its course runs near West).   The River at this place is narrow, crooked, and very shallow; and in many places, we had to go into the water, and hawl our Canoes along the Shore.—   About 1 o'Clock P. M. we halted to dine, and soon after we had a hard thunder Shower, and large hail.—   At 3 o'Clock P. M. we proceeded on, and passed some bottom land, lying along the River, which were as usual rich Soil.   In the Evening we encamped in a bottom of timber'd land, lying on the River, on the North side having come 13 Miles this day.—   Our hunters returned to us here having killed One deer, which they brought with them [3]

1. If we take "S." to mean starboard, unlike the fair copy which makes it "South," then this can be a reference to Beaverhead Rock. The rock lies in Madison County, Montana, near the Beaverhead County line, along Montana Highway 41, about twelve miles southwest of Twin Bridges and fourteen miles northeast of Dillon. See Lewis's entry of August 8 and Clark's description on August 10.

2. Above Beaverhead Rock, near the Madison–Beaverhead county line.

3. Between this entry and the next in the fair copy is a pointing hand; its purpose is unknown.

Sunday 11th August 1805.   a cool cloudy morning Some rain   we Set out after breakfast and proceeded on   3 men out a hunting.   about 3 miles came to a verry large prarie Island which is 3000 miles from wood River or the mouth of the Missourie.   So we call it 3000 mile Island.[1]   we took up the L. Side of it & had to hall over Several Shole places.   Saw a nomber of geese & ducks.   one of the hunters joined us at noon.   had killed 3 three Deer & 2 otter, Some distance a head.   the day warm.   the large flys troublesome.   we proceeded on   passed Several Sunken ponds and low bottoms which is Soft and boggy   the beaver has cut many channels to their <Shores> houses along the Shores   they are verry numerous in this valley I think they are more pleanty than ever we Saw them before.   towards evening we Came to a fiew Scattering cotton trees along the Shore.   the valley continues to be 8 or 10 miles wide and all low Smooth prarie with timber. we See Mountains a head Some distance which appear high. large Spots of Snow on them. we Came 14 miles this day and Camped[2] on a wet bottom on the Stard Side.— the Mosquetoes troublesome, &c.

Sunday August 11th   A Cool cloudy morning, & some Rain, We set out after having breakfasted, and continued on our Voyage.   Three of our Men went out a hunting, at where we had break fasted; We proceeded on about 3 Miles, & came to a very large Island, being entirely a Priari, which is 3,000 Miles from the mouth of the Mesouri River, we named that place 3,000 Mile Island, We went up the South side of this Island with our Canoes, and had to hawl them over several Shoal places, We saw numbers of Ducks & Geese in the River.   One of our hunters joined us at Noon.   He had killed 3 deer & 2 otters, which had had left some distance a head of us.   The day turned warm & the large flies became very troublesome.   We continued on, and pass'd several sunken ponds, & low bottoms, which were soft and boggy.— The Beaver here had cut a number of channels to their houses, along the <Shores, along the> River shores, and <they are> were very numerous in this Valley, The beaver at this place, are more plenty, than at any place we have been at, since we entered the Mesouri River.   Towards evening, we passed by a few scattering Cotton wood trees, lying along the banks of the River, and Vallies between 9 & 10 Miles wide <and are> which were low smooth priaries, with some timber on them.   We saw Mountains, lying a head of us some short distance; which appear very high, and large spots of snow on them.   We came 14 Miles this day, and encamped in a wet bottom, lying on the North side of the River, where we found the Musketoes, were very troublesome.—

1. The island, in Beaverhead County, Montana, has apparently since disappeared.
2. About halfway between Beaverhead Rock and Dillon, Beaverhead County.

Monday 12th August 1805.   a clear morning 3 hunters out on Shore a hunting.   we proceeded on   the current verry rapid.   passed low Swampy bottoms.   about 2 oClock P. m. a hard Thunder Shower arose rained a Short time.   we then proceeded on the current more rapid   one of the large canoes was near turning over. towards evening the hunters all came in had killed 3 deer and Seen Deer & a goat or antelope. Some timber along the Shore. We came [*blank*] miles and Camped[1] at a Smooth prarie & grove of timber

Monday August 12th We had a clear morning, three of our hunters were still out, a hunting; We proceeded on our way, & found the current of the River running very rapid, we passed some swampy bottoms, lying on both sides of the River. About 2 o'Clock P. M. we had a hard shower of Rain, accompanied with thunder; We continued on, the current of the River running still more rapid; and had nearly overset one of our largest Canoes, towards evening, the hunters came in, and had killed 3 Deer, 1 fawn, & an Antelope, We halted, and took them on board our Canoes; & proceeded on, and passed some Smooth priaries, & Groves of timber lying on both sides of the River; & encamped at a smooth priari, with a Grove of timber on it, We came 14 Miles this day.—

1. There is some question about which side of the Beaverhead this camp was on; see Lewis's entry for this date. It was in Beaverhead County, Montana, a few miles below the mouth of Blacktail Deer Creek, north of Dillon, and a few miles downstream from where Interstate Highway 15 crosses the river.

Tuesday 13th August 1805. cloudy. we Set out as usal & proceeded on. Several hunters out a hunting. passed a handsom Spring run[1] on the L. Side. the hills make a little nearer the River. the valley not So wide & a little higher dry and Smoth. Sun flowers & grass Some places high & other places Short. Some pine timber back on the high hills. we halted & took breakfast near a high clift of rocks on L. Side above which the hills make near the River. proceeded on. the current rapid the plain continues on L. Side and hills on S. Side. Some Scattering cotton trees along the River. we have caught a number of Trout in this Stream. in the afternoon we passed fine Springs & clifts of rocks on S. Side. the current not So rapid in the afternoon Saw a number of large otter along the River. Saw bald eagels[2] ducks &c. took on board a Deer which the hunters killed. Came 15 miles this day and Camped[3] on the Smooth prarie on L. S. Capt. Clark Shot a duck.   considerable of flax in these praries.   Some of the men Save Some of the Seed.   2 hunters did not join us this evening.—

Tuesday August 13th   This morning we had Cloudy weather, We set out Early, and proceeded on our Voyage, We sent several of our hunters out a hunting; We passed a handsome spring run, lying on the South side of the River; The hills make in nearer to the River, as we came along this day, & the Valleys are not so wide, the Valleys laying, higher, and are dryer, than they have been for several days past, & lay level, producing Sun flowers, high Grass &ca—   The Hills which lies a small distance back from the River, having some Pine timber growing on them.—   We halted & took break fast, near a high Clift of Rocks, lying on the South side of the River, <near to which lay a high Clift of rocks,> The current of the River running very rapid, the whole of the way, since we started this morning, and we passed by many very rapid places.   We proceeded on at 9 o'Clock A. M <we> & contined on our way, the current still continuing the same, the Plains lying on the South side of the River, and some scattering Cotton wood trees growing along its banks; we caught a number of fine trout, by gigging them & with the hook & line—   In the afternoon we passed a fine spring, & high Clifts of rocks, which lay on the South side of the River; The current did not run so rapid, as it had done this morning, We saw a number of Bald Eagles & Ducks the latter were in the River; We stopped and took in a deer, which our Hunters had left on the bank of the River, which they had killed.   We came 15 Miles this day, and encamped on a smooth priari, lying on the South side of the River, where Captain Clark shot a Duck, <in this Prairie> we found fine flax growing here.   2 of our hunters did not join us this evening.—

1. Blacktail Deer Creek, which they named McNeal's Creek after Hugh McNeal of the party, reaches the Beaverhead River at Dillon, Beaverhead County, Montana.

2. *Haliaeetus leucocephalus.*

3. A few miles southwest of Dillon, north of where Montana Highway 41 crosses the Beaverhead River and joins Interstate Highway 15.

Wednesday 14th August 1805.   a clear cold morning.   we did not Set out untill we took an eairly breakfast.   the 2 hunters Stayed out last night.   the water in the River is clear and Cold   we are now drawing near the Mountains.   the upper part of the valley pleasant.   passed a Spring run or creek[1] on S. Side a handsome valley Some distance up it.   Some Small timber on its Shores.   about 10 oClock A. m. we came up to the hunters[2] Camp.   they had killed 4 Deer & one antelope.   we proceeded on the current more rapid.   obledged to hale the large canoes over Sholes & rapids.   the Shores & banks of the River Stoney.   halted to dine about one oClock at a dry part of the plain a fine groves of cotten trees &c.   proceeded on took on board a deer and a goat which the hunters had hung on a limb of a tree.   the current continues verry rapid all day.   Capt. Clark killed a buck and one of the men killed a faun deer.   we Came [*blank*] miles and Camped[3] on the L. Side at the foot of the Mountains, on the Smooth plain at the upper end of the valley.

Wednesday August 14th   We had a Clear cold morning, & did not set out on our Voyage, 'till after we had taken an early breakfast; the two hunters did not return to us last night, the River water is here perfectly Clear, and Cool; we are now near the Mountains, The upper part of the Valley is very pleasant. We continued on, and passed a run of water, which came from a spring lying on the South side of the River & where a handsome Valley lay near it, and some scattering timber; lying, along the Shore of the River on both sides of it; About 10 o'Clock A. M. we came to where our 2 hunters, that were out last night were encamped; they had killed 4 deer & one Antelope.— We proceeded on, and found the River running again rapid, which oblig'd us to hawl our Canoes over the Shoals & rapids.   We found the Shores & banks of the River very Stony; About One o'Clock A. M. we halted to dine, at a dry part of the plain, in a Grove of Cotton wood trees.— We took on board our Canoes here, a deer & a Goat which the hunters had killed and hung on the limbs of trees.   Captain Clark and one of our party, had went out hunting this morning; they returned to us, & had killed a Buck Deer & fawn, which was brought to us.   We came 12 Miles this day, and encamped on the South side of the River, at the foot of the Mountains on a smooth plain at the upper end of a Valley.—

1. The party's Track Creek, apparently Rattlesnake Creek, Beaverhead County, Montana.
2. The Field brothers.

3. In Beaverhead County, about ten miles southwest of Dillon and just downstream from Barretts Siding.

Thursday 15th August 1805. a cold clear morning. we Set out as usal and proceeded on   entered the Mountains   verry high clifts of rocks[1] near the River & Steep on each Side.   passed Several Springs on L. Side which run from under the Mountains.   passed Several bad rapids   caught a nomber of fine Trout below the rapids.   the bottoms narrow timber Scarse, the River more Shallow   passed clifts of rocks & high rough mountains on each Side.   passed the Mouth of a creek[2] on the Stard. Side, the warter of a ridish coulour, considerabl rapid and deep.   abt. 7 paces wide.   2 hunters on a head.   we passed where Capt. Lewis had left 3 or 4 Deer Skins the 10 ult. & proceeded on.   the River Shallow   were obledged to hale the large canoes the most part of the time   passed Several cree[k]s   clifts of rocks Steep up from the River about 2 or 3 100 feet in many places.   Some of the knobs are covred with grass & a fine Scattering pitch pines on them.   the River crooked & difficult   Some places Shole & Some deep holes in which we caught a nomber of Trout.   Capt. Clark was near being bit by a rattle Snake which was between his legs as he was Standing on Shore a fishing.   he killed & Shot Several others this afternoon.   Came [*blank*] miles and Camped[3] on L Side at a narrow plain on which was Some old Indian Camps.

Thursday August 15th   A Cold clear morning, We set out as usual, & proceeded on our Voyage, and entered the Mountains, where we found very high Clifts of Rocks lying near the River, and the shores steep on both sides of the River,—   We passed several springs which lay on the South side of the River, and came from under the Mountains, and several rapid places, in the River.   below these rapids some of our party catch'd a quantity of fine Trout.   We passed some narrow bottoms, but found Timber very scarce.— The River this day has been very shallow, We continued on, and passed Clifts of high Rocks, & rough mountains lying on each side of the river; and the mouth of a Creek, lying on the North side of the River; the water of which was of a reddish colour, <and> runs rapid, & is deep; and about 7 paces wide.   We passed where Captain Lewis had left 4 Deer Skins.—   Two of our hunters were sent out ahead of us.—   We found a note, with the deer Skins which Captain Lewis had left, which informed us that he had been at that place the 10th instant.— We proceeded on, & found the River still growing shallower, which obliged our party to hawl the Canoes the greater part of the way, We also passed several Slifts of rocks which went steep up from the River, from 200 to 300 feet perpendicular in many places; some of the knobs, are covered with Grass, & Pitch pine trees. The River got very crooked & difficult to pass, having a number of Shoals & deep holes in it. In those deep holes our party caught a number of fine Trout.— Captain Clarke was near being bit by a Rattle snake this day; it got between his legs, whilst he was standing fishing, he killed it, & a number of the same kind this day, We came 15 Miles this day, & encamped on the So Side of the River in a narrow plain on which was some old Indian Camps.—

1. Rattlesnake Cliffs, so named by the captains, about ten miles southwest of Dillon, Beaverhead County, Montana, near Barretts Siding on Interstate Highway 15.

2. Willard's Creek to the party, after member Alexander Willard; it is Grasshopper Creek, Beaverhead County, Montana.

3. Apparently just below the mouth of Gallagher's Creek, Beaverhead County.

Friday 16th August 1805. a clear but verry cold morning. the Thurmometer Stood at 47°. the water So cold that we delayed untill after breakfast. one hunter out on a head. we proceeded on as usal the current Swift passed a handsom Spring run[1] on L. Side on which is a fiew cotton trees. Capt. Clark our Intrepter & wife walked on Shore and found a great nomber of fine berrys which is called Servis berrys. our Ints. wife gethered a pale full & gave them to the party at noon where we halted at a grove of cotton trees on L. S. our hunter who went out this morning killed a verry large buck. two of our hunters Stayed out last night, & have not returned yet we name this place Servis valley, from the abundance of these berrys along under the hills &c. the 2 hunters joined us here & Informed us that the River forks[2] in about 5 miles a Strait course by land & they think we can go no further than the forks with the crafts. 2 hunters Sent on to the forks to kill meat. we proceeded on over verry Shallow & Swift water passed up a verry bad rockey rapid where we had to waid up to our middle & hale the canoes over the rapid. Saw Several fine Springs & a run above the bad rapid passed high clifts of rocks and high hills on each Side. found pleanty of currents   the water not So bad above the rapid.   Came [*blank*] miles this day and Camped³ on a narrow bottom on L. Side.   no timber   we could Scarsely find any but Small willow to boil our venison

Friday August 16th   We had a Clear, but very cold morning, the Thermometer stood at 47°— from 0, and the water in the River so cold, that we delayed starting 'till after breakfast; One of our hunters was sent on a head, We proceeded on our Voyage at 8 o'Clock A. M. the Current of the River running very strong,—   We passed a handsome spring run, lying on the South side of the River, near to which was a few Cotton wood trees.   Our interpreters Wife (the Indian Woman) went on Shore & found a great number of fine berries, which is call'd service berries.   the Indian Woman gathered a pailfull of those berries, which she brought to our party at noon, where we had halted which was at a Grove of Cotton trees lying on the South side of the River.   Our hunter that went out this morning, killed a very fine buck Deer, which he brought to us.   Two of our Hunters that went out Yesterday had not yet returned.   This place being a Valley, Captain Clark named <this place> it Service Valley, on account of the number of berries, that grew in it called Service berries, Our two hunters that were out came to us, just as we were starting; and informed us that the River forked about 5 Miles ahead, on a strait Course by land, and that it is their opinion, that we can go no further than those forks with our crafts, Captain Clark dispatch'd two of our hunters off, to those forks, to provide some Meat for us, against we arrived there.   We proceeded on at 2 oClock P. M. & found the River running very Rapid & shallow.   We passed up a bad Rapid which was very Rockey; the party had to wade up to their middles in Order to hall the Canoes over it.—

We saw several fine springs, & a run which lay above this bad rapid, and high Clifts of rocks & high hills lying on both sides of the River; We found a great plenty of currants, growing along the Shore, The current of the River did not run so strong, nor the River is not so shallow above the rapids, as it was for some distance below.—   We came 13 Miles this day, and encamped in a narrow bottom, lying on the South side of the River.   We found no timber here, and was obiged to use small dry Willow bushes, for fuel to boil our meat

1. Perhaps Gallagher Creek, Beaverhead County, Montana.

2. The forks of the Beaverhead; see the next day's entry.

3. In Beaverhead County, about four miles below the forks of the Beaverhead and Clark Canyon Dam.

Saturday 17th August 1805. a clear cold morning. we lay last night with 2 blankets or Robes over us & lay cold. Some frost this morning. we took an eairly breakfast and Set out. proceeded on a Short distance. heared a nomber of Indians a Singing on L. Side. directly their came Several of the Snake nation[1] Came to us & told us that Capt. Lewis & party was at the forks. Capt. Clark our Intrepter & wife went with the natives rode their horses to the forks. they kept rideing back & forward to See us comeing up with the canoes. we were obledged to hale the canoes a great part of the way untill we got to Capt. Lewises Camp a little below the forks[2] their was 20 odd of the Snake nation Camped with Capt. Lewis. they appeared harmeless & friendly. Capt. Lewis informed us that he had been over the mountain on the head waters of Columbian River[3] and that this band was Camped on Sd. waters and Creek or Small River on their way across to this place a hunting. the first they Saw was one Spy they had Some distance a head on horse back. Capt. Lewis Swung & held up a blanket as a token of friendship, but as it hapened 2 of the men were a hunting one on each Side of him, which frightned him as he Suposed they wished to take prisoner turned about his horse & rode verry Seedy out of his road & made no halt untill he got to the band, & told his people the news. they met 3[4] Squaws <2> on the Side of the mountain a digging roots 2 of them ran off, the other being old Stood hir ground. Capt. Lewis came or went up to hir & gave hir Some Small presents, and Shewed everry mark of friendship. She then called up the other 2 and they piloted <them> Capt. Lewis & party to the band, which received them with a great deal of fear at first. appared frightened until they lay down their guns and made Some tokens & motions of friendship. the natives then put their arms around their or our peoples necks & appeared glad to See them and used them friendly. they had Some Salmon which they had brought with them from the main river. it is only about 40 miles over the mount to the head waters of the other R. the[y] drank at the head waters or Spring of the Missourie and went only abt. a mile and drank out of the head Spring of the Columbian River which ran west. the natives tell us that their is no timber large enofe for canoes on the head waters &c Capt. Lewis got 2[o] odd of the band to come over with their horses, only 3 women with them. we conclude to leave the canoes at this place and git horses of the natives to take our baggage over the mountains. So we unloaded the canoes and formed a Camp on a Smooth prarie on L. Side. the grass high, but no timber we could git no timber to burn but Small dry willow Sticks about as big as a mans finger &c. a high hill in the point or between the forks of the River. high hills around this valley. the hunters killed 3 deer & 2 goats this day. Capt. Lewis informes us that the game is verry Scarse on the mountain, & that they were without any thing of account to eat for 2 or three days, but the natives tell us that their is pleanty of fish on the columbian River Such as Salmon &c. our officers told the natives that we wanted to git their horses to take our baggage over the Mountain & wanted to buy Some from them also So they Gave them considerable of marchandize divided it among them all. they consented to let us have their horses & assist us over the mo. they tell us that it is only about 8 days travvel a South course to the Spanish country,[5] but these Indians git but little trade amongst them &c—

Saturday August 17th A Clear cold morning; the weather was so cold last night, that our party had to lay under 2 buffalo robes each in order to keep themselves warm, We took an early break fast and set out, we had proceeded on but a short distance when we were alarmed by several voices that were singing— the Voices, came from the South side of the River. We halted our Canoes, when a number of the Snake Nation of Indians came to us; these were the Persons who we had heard singing; They informed us by our Interpreter (the Indian Woman) that Captain Lewis & party was at the Forks of the River waiting for us.— Captain Clark, our french Interpreter & his Indian Wife, went off with these Indians— The Snake Indians that came to us, rode very fine horses, <which> and they let Captain Clark & the Interpreter & wife ride 2 of them to the forks of the River. We proceeded on, the Indians riding their horses back & forward to see us coming on, with our Canoes. We were obliged to hawl our Canoes a great part of the way over shallow places, till we arrived at the place, where Captain Lewis was en-camped, which lay a small distance below the forks of this River. We found between 20 & 30 of the Snake Nation of Indians encamped with him.—

The Indians appeared to be very harmless & inoffensive, Captain Lewis informed us, that he had crossed the Mountains that lay a head of us & had gone on to the head Waters of Columbia River, and that he had found Some of this band of Indians, encamped on the head waters of said River, & a part of them at a Creek or small River, on their way across the Mountains to this place; on a hunting party.— he likewise mentioned, that the first Indian of this party that they had seen, was one of their spies, that was some distance a head of the party on horseback, Captain Lewis swung a blanket as a token of friendship to this Indian, but two of [his, *erased*] Captain Lewis's party who were hunting happen'd to be on each side of <him> that Indian which frightened <the Indian> him, & he supposing that Captain Lewis & party wanted to take him prisoner, he turned about his horse, and rode very speedily out of his Road, & made no halt, untill he got to his band, to who he told the news & of what people he had seen; that afterwards they had met with 3 of their Squaws on the side of the mountain who were digging Roots, 2 of these squaws ran off, & the other being old & feeble stood her ground. Captain Lewis went up to this Squaw, and made her some small presents, and showed her every mark of friendship. This Squaw then called to the other two, who came to her, and those 3 Squaws piloted Captain Lewis & his party to their band; who received them with a great deal of fear at first, & appeared to be much frightened, untill Captain Lewis & his party laid down their guns, & made some motions of friendship, the Indians then hung their Arms (Bows & Arrows) round their own & our Mens necks & appeared very glad to see them, & used them very friendly. These Indians, had some Sal-mon with them which they had brought from the main Columbia River. they mentioned to us that it is only 40 Miles across the mountains to the head waters of Columbia River. The party that was with Captain Lewis men-tioned that they had drank at the head water or Source of the Mesouri River, which was a large spring.— They also inform'd us that about one Mile from that large spring, that they had also drank water out of another spring, which was the head Waters of Columbia River, The Snake Indians informed us by our Interpreter, that there was no timber on the other side of the Mountains, large enough to make Canoes, near to the head of Columbia River— Captain Lewis had persuaded 20 odd Snake Indians of that band to come over with their horses with him.— Our officers concluded to leave our Canoes at this place, & to get horses from those Indians to transport our baggage across the mountains, to Columbia River.— We unloaded our Canoes at that place, & formid a Camp in a smooth Priari, lying on the So— side of the River; where the Grass was very high. We found no timber here, & was forced to make use of small dry willows to cook our Meat with.— In the fork of this River, on a point, lay a high hill, and hills all round where we <are> were encamped at, which is in a Valley. Our hunters killed 3 deer & 2 Goats this day, which they brought to our Camp. Captain Lewis informed us that Game is very scarce to be found on the mountains, & that they were without any thing of any account to eat for 3 days, The indians inform'd us, that there is plenty of fish to be caught in the Columbia River, such as Salmon, &ca. Our Officers informed the Indians that they wanted to get their horses, to carry our baggage over the Mountains, and that they would purchase some of them also, & that they would give them some Merchandise for them, The Indians consented to the officers proposals, The officers gave the Indians some Merchandise for part of their horses, & they agreed to assist us across the mountains. They informed us that it is only 8 days travel, from that place to where the Spaniards have a settlement, which they told us lays a South course from this place but that they have very little trade with them

1. The Lemhi Shoshones, Sacagawea's people. See Lewis's entries of August 11–17 for his meeting with them and his efforts to get them to meet the main party at the forks (see next note).

2. The junction of Horse Prairie Creek and Red Rock River to form Beaverhead River. Here in Beaverhead County, Montana, they formed Camp Fortunate just below the forks on a site now inundated by Clark Canyon Reservoir.

3. Lewis's party had crossed the Continential Divide and met the Shoshones on Lemhi River in Lemhi County, Idaho.

4. The number "3" is written over "2."

5. The "Spanish country" would be New Mexico, but eight days seems an optimistic estimate.

Sunday 18th August 1805. One beaver caught in a trap l. n.[1] a clear morning. Capt. Clark and 11 men got in readiness to Set out with the natives to go over the mountain to the other River, to make canoes &c. Capt. Lewis bought 4 horses of the natives Gave them, Some he gave a uniform coat a knife & a hankerchief. others he gave red leggins a knife a hankch. and a fiew arrow points &c. 2 of the men joined and bought a horse to take their baggage on & gave only one brich cloath one old or poo[r] Shirt & one knife, for a good pack horse. these Indian are verry poor and vallue a little worth a great deal, as they never had Scarsely any kind of a kinife or Tommahawk or any weapons of war or to use. 2 or 3 guns only to be seen among them which we expect they got from Some other nation, who traded with the french or Spanish tradors. gave their horses &c. for them. they are tollarably well dressed with Skins Such as antelope and Mountain rams Skins &c. they have a fiew beeds and ear bobs among them. they gave Capt. Lewis a kind of an ornament which Spread around the Shoulders it was made of wezels[2] tales & Some other ornemental afares. they have little things made of mussell shell which they hang in their ears with their beeds & about 10 oClock A. m. Capt. Clark 11 men and all the natives but 4[,] 2 women & 2 men which Stayed at our Camp, Set out with their horses & considerable baggage to cross the mountain and Send back the horses for us to pack over all the baggage, which we wish to take over we put out the Indian goods &c to air & Sort we had Some Showers of rain this afternoon the one hunter killed one Deer to day—

Sunday August 18th We had a clear morning, Captain Clark and 11 of our men got themselves in readiness to set out with some Indians; to go over the mountains to the Columbia River; in order to make Canoes &ca. Captain Lewis purchased from the Indians that were encamped with us 4 more horses, he gave them for those horses, a Uniform Coat, knives, a handerchief red leggins &ca. two of the Men also purchased one horse from them to carry their baggage, for which they gave them a breech Cloth, an old Shirt & knife. These Indians <are> had the appearance of being very poor, & set a great value, on the most trifling article. they had no knives, or tomahawks among them; or any War like Instruments (excepting 3 Guns which we expect they had got from some other Indians, that had purchased them from French or Spanish traders, for horses,)   These Indians were tolerable well made Men, have very good countenances, but are darker colour'd, than the Mandan Indians, Their dress was made out of the Skins of Antelopes & mountain Rams or Ibex, they had some Beads & ear bobs among them. They gave Captain Lewis an ornament, which, they used to wear round their Shoulders, This consisted of Weasels tails sewed together, and ornamented with Muscle Shells &ca—.   About 10 o'Clock A. M. Captain Clark, 11 of our party & all the Indians excepting 4, (two of which were Men) left our camp, & set out with their horses, & a considerable quantity of our baggage, to go across the Mountain; & intend to send back the Horses for us, to pack & bring over the remainder of them.   We put out the Indian goods to air, & to assort them.—   We had some Rain in the afternoon.—   One of our hunters that was out killed a deer, which he brought to our Camp.—

   1. Meaning last night, as in Ordway's journal.
   2. Long-tailed weasel, *Mustela frenata*. Lewis received such a tippet from Cameahwait, chief of the Lemhi Shoshones; it is shown in vol. 5, p. xii, of this edition.

Monday 19th August 1805.   a cold morning.   we Set our net across this little Stream in hopes to catch Some fish.   Several traps Set for beaver. caught no fish in the net.   Caught one beaver in a trap.   a white frost this morning   a clear pleasant day, all hands employed in dressing Skins & Sorting the Indian goods & packing up the baggage.   Some at makeing pack Saddles &c.   three men out with a horse to hunt.   Some of the men caught a nomber of fine fish, large Trout[1] black Spots all over them.   the hunters returned in the afternoon   had killed 2 Deer.   light Showers of rain.   we packed up the most of the baggage &c.   halled the fish net across the river but caught none any other way but with a hook & line.   Capt. Lewis takes observations here this being the upper fork of Jeffersons River & the extream navigable part of the Missourie close under the dividing ridge of the western Country.

Monday August 19th   This morning we had Cold weather, we set our net across this little stream or river, in order to try & catch some fish, but we had bad luck & catch'd none.   one of our party caught a beaver in a trap during the last night, and several traps were set this morning.   We had white frost this morning, & a clear pleasant day, The Men at our Camp were employed in dressing Skins, sorting Indian Goods, packing up the baggage, and making pack saddles; Three of our party (hunters) went out hunting, and took one of the horses, that belonged to the Indians in Camp with them.   Some of our party caught a number of fine large Salmon trout.   they are the same kind that we have in the United States, only differing from them in having black spots all over them.   The hunters returned in the afternoon, and brought with them 2 deer, which they had killed.   We had a Shower of rain about 3 o'Clock P. M. which lasted but a few minutes.   We hawled our net across the River but again without catching any fish, & find that the only way to catch them is with hook & line.—   Captain Lewis took an Observation this day, this being the upper fork of Jeffersons River, & the extreme navigable part of the Mesouri River and close under the dividing ridge of the Western Country, & found it to lay in 44° 35′ 28¼₀ S   North Latitude & from the Mouth of the Mesouri River 3,096 Miles.—

1.   Cutthroat trout.

Tuesday 20th August 1805.   a clear cold morning.   a white frost.   two men out hunting.   the men at Camp employed dressing Skins &c.   the 2 Indians who Stay at Camp behave well their women mend & make our moccasons.   these Indians behave as well and are as friendly as any Savages we have yet Seen.   our hunters returned had killed nothing.   one beaver caught which ran off with a Steel trap last night.   we found 2 miles down the river.   a nomber of fish caught to day.   Capt. Lewis looked out a place down the river a Short distance for a carsh or hole to put Some baggage in which we can do without untill our return.

Tuesday August 20th   This morning we had a white frost & Clear, Cool weather, Two of our Men were sent out a hunting, and the Men at Camp employed in dressing of Skins, the two Indian men that were in our Camp behave well, & their Women [*crossed out, illegible*] employed themselves in making & mending Moccasins for our men.   they are the most friendly Indians that we have yet met with. Our hunters returned in the afternoon, but had killed nothing. We caught one beaver in a trap, we set last night. he had run off with the trap, & we found it 2 Miles down the river, with the beaver fast in it. The party that went out fishing caught a number of fine fish; which they brought to Camp. Captain Lewis went down the River a short distance to look out a place to have a Cashe, or hole dug to put in some of the baggage which we intend leaving behind us till we return.

Wednesday 21st August 1805. a hard white frost the water which Stood in the Small vessells froze a little. Some deer Skins which was Spread out wet last night are froze Stiff this morning. the Ink freezes in the pen at Sunrise. a clear pleasant morning. one hunter out with a horse a hunting. 4 men Sent to dig a carsh or hole. at 8 oClock A m Some of the party found Ice in Some Standing water ¼ of an Inch thick. Captain Lewis took observations at this place and the Latidude produced is 43D 44m 19s North. in the evening after dark we carried our baggage we conclude to carsh to the place of cashing, So as that the Indians need not discover us, or mistrust that we are going to berry any thing at this place &c &c

Wednesday August 21st We had a hard white frost this morning, the water that stood in small Vessells froze, and some Deer Skins which was spread out wet last night, was froze stiff this morning, & the Ink froze in the pen at Sun rise; The morning was clear & got pleasant, One of the hunters went out hunting on horse back & 4 of our Men were sent down the River to dig a hole or Cashe to deposit some of our baggage in. At 8 oClock A. M. some of the party found Ice in some standing water ¼ of an inch thick, In the evening we carried the baggage that was to be left at the Cashe, or hole that was dug, in order to deposit it there. The evening was dark, & Captain Lewis thought it best to have it done at that time, so that the Indians that were at our Camp, should not mistrust, or discover that we were going to bury anything at this place

Thursday 22nd August 1805. a white frost & cold as usal in the morning. our hunter[1] returned late last night. had killed a faun deer, and informed us that he fell among a party of Indians which were troublesome as they took his gun & rode off   he rode after them and got his gun from out of an Indians hand.   their was Several Squaws which had considerable of their kinds of food and Skins.   they went and left it all   he took it and brought it in with him.   a clear pleasant morning   three men wen to finish in hideing the baggage.   the men at Camp employed dressing their deer Skins & makeing their mockasons &c.   I am employed makeing up their leather Shirts & overalls.[2]   about 11 oClock A. m. one tribe of the Snake nation 50 odd in nomber arived here on horse back some women & children.   they have now come over the dividing ridge to trade their horses &c. with us.   Capt. Lewis counciled with them made 2 of them chiefs, and told them that we had come to open the way and try to make peace among the red people, and that they would be Supplyed with goods and necessaries, if they would catch beaver and otter and Save their Skins which the white people were fond of and would trade with them as Soon as times would admit &c.   Capt. Lewis traded with them & bought 3 horses & 2 mules or half mules, for a little marchandize &c.   we being out of fresh meat & have but little Salt meat we joined and made a fish dragg out of willows   tyed bunches of them together and made it long enofe to reach across the River, and Caught with it 520 different kinds of fine pan fish.   we divided them with the natives.   Gave them a mess of boiled corn which they were fond of.   they appear to be verry kind and friendly.   we trade with them for dressed mountn. rams Skins and otter Skins &c.   our Interpeter & wife came over with them & were all Scarse off for provissions   killed nothing but one or 2 mountain Sheep & rabits &c. they all Camp with us and are peacable, do not attempt to Steel any thing. borrow nothing but what they return.   they appear to live in fear of other nations who are at war with them, but Capt. Lewis tells them that these other nations promise to let them alone and if they do not, their Great father will Send them arms and amunition to defend themselves with, but rather that they would live in peace &c

Thursday August 22nd   This morning we had a white frost & cold weather, Our hunter returned late last night & had a fawn deer with him, which he had killed.   he informed us that he had met with a party of Indians, which took away his <the> Gun from him & rode off, & that he had pursued them, & forced his Gun from one of those Indians. there were several Indian Squaws, with that party of Indians, that he had met, who had a considerable quantity of their kind of food (roots) & some Skins, those squaws ran off whilst he was forcing his Gun from the Indian, & left all, & he took <it> & brought <it> them in which him to our Camp. The morning got pleasant & 3 of our party went and finished hiding the baggage &ca. The Men left in Camp <are> were employed dressing of deer Skins & making moccasins & I am employed in making leather Shirts & overalls— About 11 o'Clock A. M. part of a tribe of the Snake Nation of Indians, fifty odd in number, arrived at our Camp on horse back, they had Women & Children with them, they came across the dividing ridge of Mountain; to trade their-horses with us— Captain Lewis held a Council with them & made two of them Chiefs.— Captain Lewis told those Indians that we had come to open the way & try and make peace among the Red people, & that they would be supplied with goods & necessaries, if they would catch beaver & Otter & save their Skins, which he told them the white people were fond of & would traffic with them as soon as times would admit.— Captain Lewis traded with them & bought 3 horses & 2 Mules for a small Quantity of Merchandise.— We being out of fresh meat, & having but little Salt meat, we joined with the Indians & made a drag out of willows which was done by tying bunches of them together long enough to reach across the River, and we caught with it 520 different kinds of pan fish, We divided them with the Indians, and gave them a mess of boiled Corn, which they <were> appear'd to be fond of & They appeared to be very kind & friendly— We traded with them for mountain Ram (Ibex) skins, which they had dressed & some Otter skins &ca. Our Indian interpreter & his wife came over with those Indians, they were badly off for provisions, they had killed only 2 Mountain Sheep, or Ibex & some Rabits &ca— These Indians all encamped with us, & behave peacable, & do not attempt to steal any thing, & borrow nothing but what they return again.— They appear to be in constant dread of the other Nations Indians, who are constantly at Warr with them. Captain Lewis told them that the other Indian nations promised to let them alone, and if they did not, that their Great father (meaning the President of the United States) would send them Arms & Ammunition to defend themselves with; but that he would rather that they would live peacable with each other, at which they seemed much pleased.—

1. Drouillard; see Lewis's entry of this day for a detailed description of the stealing and recovery of this gun.
2. Heavy trousers worn over regular clothes.

Friday 23rd August 1805. a clear pleasant morning. 2 men Sent out a hunting. Capt. Lewis Commences trading with the natives for more horses, but they do not incline to part with any more horses untill they git over the mountains, but will carry all our baggage over for us. Several of the natives went out with horses to hunt. they rode after the Deer & chased Some in site of our Camp and ran them down So that they killed 4 or 5 of them. this day, we halled all the canoes out in a Small pond on the North Side of the River and Sunk them in the water, So as they may be Safe for us at our return. about 4 oClock P. m. their came another party of the Snake Indians on horseback, about 40 in nomber. they appear the Same as the others did. we expect to Set out tomorrow to cross the mountain 2 hunters Sent on a head to kill Some meat if possable for us by the time we come up with them. our hunter returned in the evening had killed 2 large Deer and three Small Deer[1] and brought them all to Camp on the horse

Friday August 23rd   A Clear pleasant morning, 2 of our Men were sent out a hunting, Captain Lewis commenced trading with the last party of Indians for some of their horses, but they seemed not inclined to part with <any more of their horses> any of them, untill they got over the Mountains, but agreed to carry our baggage, over the Mountains, for us on them <for us>.—

The Indians that came last to our Camp, went out a hunting on horse back, They drove a Gang of deer in sight of our Camp, ran Some them down with their horses & killed 5 of them.   We hawled up our Canoes into a small pond lying on the North side of the River, & sunk them, that they may be safe on our return.   About 4 oClock P. M. another party of the Snake Indians arrived at our Camp on horse back, they <are> were about 40 in number; they appear to be much the same as those who arrived with us Yesterday— We expect to set out tomorrow, in order to cross the mountains. Captain Lewis sent on 2 hunters a head in order to kill some Meat for us if possible, by the time we come up with them. Our hunters returned in the evening, & had killed 2 large deer & 3 Small ones which they brought to our Camp on their horses.—

1. Presumably the large deer are mule deer, while the small ones are western white-tailed deer, *Odocoileus virginianus dacotensis.*

Saturday 24th August 1805. a clear cool morning. we find that the band of the Snake nation who came here yesterday is going down on the Missourie after the buffaloe, and offers Some of their horses for Sale. So we Detain this morning in order to purchase Some of them. we got 3 or 4 more horses and hired 2 and loaded all our horses which was abt. 12 in nomber then the Squaws took the remainder of our baggage and we then Set out about 12 oC. on our way to cross the divideing ridge. proceeded on abt. 3 miles one of the men[1] was taken Sick with the collick, and detained us So that we came only about 6 miles and Camped on the creek.[2] one of the hunters came to us had killed nothing we gave the Indians Some corn, as they had nothing to eat.

Saturday August 24th This morning we had Clear, cold weather, The Snake band of Indians, that came to our Camp Yesterday, informed our Officer, that they intend going down the Mesouri River, to hunt buffalo, and offer some of their horses for sale. Captain Lewis delayed for a while, in Order to try & purchase some of their horses from them. he succeeded in his expectation & purchased 4 <more> horses, & hired from those Indians 2 more, which is intended to be packed with our baggage.— We packed all our horses, being 12 in number, & what baggage remain'd, the Indian Squaws carried for us— We set out about 12 o'Clock A. M. on our way, to cross the dividing ridge of mountains, & proceeded on about 3 Miles. One of our party was here taking very Ill of the Cholic, which detained us some Considerable time, we proceeded on our way, and went only 3 Miles further, and encamped at a Creek, having only came 6 Miles this day. One of our hunters came to us here, he having met with nothing to kill.— We gave the Indians some Corn, to eat, they having no Provisions with them.—

1. Peter Weiser, according to Lewis and Ordway.
2. The party crossed Beaverhead River and followed Horse Prairie Creek upstream along Shoshone Cove, Beaverhead County, Montana.

Sunday 25th August 1805. a clear morning a little frost last night. we loaded up our horses and loaded the Indian horses and proceeded on through the level plain. our hunters killed 3 Deer. passed a nomber of fine Springs and Spring runs. Some willow on the creeks & runs but no timber of any acct. except pitch pine on the hills & tops of the mountains. our hunters killed another Deer. we came about 15 miles this Day and Camped[1] near the creek or run

Sunday August 25th A clear morning with a light frost, we loaded our horses, & those hired from the Indians; and proceeded on through a level plain, Our hunters that we sent a head of us, had killed 3 deer, which they brought to us, We passed a number of fine springs & Spring runs, we saw no timber except some pitch pine trees, which were on the hills, & tops of mountains, and a few Willow Trees which grew on Creeks & Runs. towards evening, our hunters killed another deer, which they brought to us. We came about 15 Miles this day, & encamped near a large Creek or River

1. On Trail Creek, Beaverhead County, Montana, not far from its entrance into Horse Prairie Creek.

Monday 26th August 1805. a clear morning we find it verry cold and frosty every morning. the water froze a little in the Small vessells. we Set out at Sunrise and proceeded on. the mountains make close to the branch on each Side which are partly covd. with pich pine. passed a number of fine large Springs and drank at the head Spring of the Missourie and crossed a high ridge only one mile and drank at the head Spring of Calumbian River running west.[1] the runs all make the Same course Saw a high mountain to the S. W. with Some Spots of Snow on them. Saw Spots of pitch pine and bolsom fer² on the Sides of the Mo. and on the Spring runs, and verry tall. we halted to dine at a Spring within about 8 miles of the Indians Camp which is on the Small River.   one of our Indian women was taken Sick a little back of this and halted a fiew minutes on the road and had hir child and went on without Detaining us.   we then proceeded on after we dined and gave the Indians who were with us a little corn.   passed over Several hills.   when we came near the natives lodges we fired 2 rounds by the requst of the chief then went to their lodges.   they had a large one in the center prepared for us, wher we unloaded and Camped with them.³   their is about 30 lodges here consisting of men women and children, but the nomber of persons would be difficult to find out.   we danced a little this evening.   the natives assembled to See us.   they all appeared verry friendly and peaceable.

Monday August 26th   We had a Clear morning; but very cold & a heavy frost, and the Water froze in a short time in the small Vessells, We proceeded on our way at Sun rise, & found the Mountains running in close to the branch of the River, on both sides of it & <are> were partly covered with pitch pine.   We passed a number of fine large Springs.—   We stopped at a very large Spring & drank out of it.   This spring is the head waters or source of the Mesouri River and lies under a ridge of high mountain's & is 3,124 Miles from the Mouth of the Mesouri River   We crossed this high ridge of mountain's, and proceeded on about One Mile, and came to another large Spring, which <is> we supposed to be the head Waters or Source of the Columbia River, it running a West course, our party also drank water out of this Spring, so that we might all have it in our power to say; that we had drank water from out the head Springs or Source of both those great Rivers.— We passed several runs of water, which all run a West course, and saw very high mountains lying to the South west of us, which had some spots of snow on them & pitch pine & Balsam fir trees growing on the sides of the hills, & on the spring runs.   Those Trees were very tall.—   We halted to dine at a spring within 8 Miles of where the Indian Camp lay, Which is on a small River which was 36 Yards wide & 3,134 from Mo. Mesouri, We proceeded on after dining, having givin the Indians that was with us, some Corn, We crossed several hills, and arrived near, to where the Natives had their lodges.   We fired 2 Rounds with our small Arms, by request of their Chiefs, who were

with us.   We then proceeded on & came to where the Indian lodges lay.—
The Indians had prepared a large lodge for us, which lay in the Center of
their lodges, here we unloaded our baggage, and deposited it.   The Indians
had about 30 lodges here, which was occupied by Indian Men, women &
Children, but their numbers we did not ascertain—   In the Evening our
party had a Dance & the Natives all attended, they seemed pleased with our
mode of dancing, and behaved very peacable & friendly to us.   they were
called the So-so-nee, or Snake Indians.—

1. The sources of Trail Creek, which eventually joins the Missouri, and Horseshoe Bend
Creek, whose waters empty into the Columbia by way of the Lemhi, Salmon, and Snake rivers.

2. Lodgepole pine, *Pinus contorta* Dougl. ex Loud., and grand fir, *Abies grandis* (Dougl.)
Lindl. in this region.

3. The Shoshone camp was probably now located about four miles north of Tendoy,
Lemhi County, Idaho, near where Kenney Creek joins the Lemhi River.

Tuesday 27th August 1805.   a beautiful pleasant morning   we hoisted our
large flag.   Capt. Lewis Gave the head chief[1] a flag also the 2 chief one
they hoisted them on the levil near their lodges.   Capt. Lewis then began to
trade with the natives for horses, after paying off the women who helped us
over the divideing mount.   Mr. Sharbono bought one horse for a red cloak.
the natives brought up Several horses for trade.   2 hunters went out this
morning to hunt with horses.   the natives caught a nomber of fine Trout
which would weigh abt. 8 pound   Some call them Salmon Trout.   others
call them real Salmon, but they are not So red as the large Salmon.   the Indian women are mostly employed gethering a kind of Small black Seed[2] not
So large as buck wheat, which they dry and pound or rub between 2 Stone
and make a Sort of meal of it   they also dry cherries and Servis berryes &
roots &c &c. for food.   they kill but fiew Deer or any wild game except when
they go down on the missourie after the buffalow.   the country in general is
barron broken and mountainious.   an Indian came in with a horse load of
Deer meat, which our hunters killd   our hunters all returned towards evening had killed 4 Deer & 8 or 10 fine Salmon which they had killed with a
wooden gig.   Capt. Lewis has bought 7 or 8 horses this day for a little of
different kinds of Marchandize &c, but they Seem loth to part with any more
without asking more for them.   Some of them play away whatever they git

for their horses, at a game[3] nearly like playing butten only they keep Singing all the while and do all by motions.   more or less play at this game & loose or win more or less they care not   always appear Still peaceable and contented, poor as they be   in the evening they had a war dance.   their women Sang with them they danced verry well, but no So regular as those on the Missourie   they tell us that Some of their horses will dance but I have not Seen them yet.

Tuesday August 27th   We had a pleasant morning.   We hoisted our large flag, and Captain Lewis gave the head Chief a flag, & one other flag each to 2 of their Chiefs, & they had them all hoisted <their flags> in a level near to their lodges.—

Captain Lewis rewarded the Indian Women for bringing our baggage & the Indian Men for the hire of their Horses, packed with our baggage across the mountains, he then began to trade with the Natives for horses, which they had brought to trade with us.   Two of our hunters went out this morning on horse back to hunt by order of Captain Lewis.—   The natives had also sent out some of their Men to fish, & they were very successfull.   They caught a number of fish, which some call Salmon trout, & others Salmon, they weighed in general about 8 pounds, & their flesh were not so red, as the flesh of those caught in the New England States.—   The Indian women <are> were mostly employed in gathering a kind of small black seed, which is not so large as buck wheat, which they dry & pound or grind, between 2 Stones, & make a sort of meal of it.   They also dry Cherries, service berries, & roots, of different kinds which they make use of for food, The Men among them kill but few Deer, or any kind of Game, but when they go down on the Mesouri River after Buffalo—   The Country here is barren, broken, and mountaineous.—   One of the Indians came to our Camp with a horse load of deer meat, which our hunters had killed—   Our hunters all returned towards evening.   they had killed 4 Deer, & 10 fine Trout or Salmon; they had killed those fish with a Wooden Gig, which is the method that the Natives use in fishing—   Captain Lewis purchased 8 horses from the Natives this day for a small quantity of Merchandise.   The natives not wishing to part with any more of them, unless he gave them considerable more, than he paid for those he had purchased of them.   Some of these Natives played away what Goods they had receiv'd at a game nearly like the Game called [*blank*] only with this difference, that they keep singing all the while, and do all by motions; most of the Natives play at this game, and seem very little concerned whether they Win or lose,— they always appearing contented & peacable.— In the Evening they had a warr dance, their women sang & danced with them; they danced very well, but not so regular as those Indians did who live on the Mesouri River.—

1. Cameahwait, Sacagawea's brother.

2. Probably Nuttall sunflower, as mentioned by Gass on August 22 and Lewis on August 26.

3. A variation of the widespread Indian hand game; see Clark's entries of December 9, 1805, and April 18, 1806.

Wednesday 28th August 1805. a clear pleasant morning. we hoisted the large flag. Several men went a hunting and Several a fishing with Iron gigs fixed on poles. about 9 oClock A. m. Capt. Lewis began to trade for horses again and offered nearly double as much as yesterday. Some Spots of Snow continues to lay on the mountain a fiew miles to the South of us. Sergt. Gass joined us about 2 oC. and informed us that Capt. Clark & the rest of the men were about 12 miles down the River[1] waiting for us, but Capt. Lewis Sent down for him to come up as we had So many horses to pack down. Capt. Lewis has bought 5 or 6 more today we have now 25 in all. our hunters killed nothing this day. in the evening 2 Indians arived at this village on horse back from another band which were Some distance to the South near the Spanish country the principal men of the village all assembled to council with them these Savages all like Salt and eat it on meat &c.

Wednesday August 28th This morning we had Clear pleasant weather, & we hoisted our large flag, Several of our men went out a hunting & fishing, the latter fixed Iron Gigs on poles, knowing they would answer better than the wooden ones, that they had, About 9 O'Clock A. M. Captain Lewis began to trade with the Natives again for horses, & offered them nearly double as much Merchandise for them, as what he gave them Yesterday. We saw some spots of snow which continued to lay on the Mountains a few miles to the

South of us.— Serjeant Gass came to our Camp about 2 o'Clock P. M.   he informed us that Captain Clark, & the Men that were with him, were about 12 Miles down the Columbia River, waiting for us.   Captain Lewis sent down for Captain Clark to come up to our Camp.— Captain Lewis purchased from the Native's 6 More horses & we now have 25 horses <in> all to-gether— Our hunters returned, & had killed no game this day.   In the evening 2 more Indians arrived at this Village on horse back.   They be-longed to another band of the Snake Nation of Indians which live some dis-tance to the South of us, and near to where they say Spaniards reside.—

The principal Indians of this Village all assembled, to hold a council with those 2 Indians, which had lately arrived.— These Indians all appear very fond of salt, and eat it with their meat &ca.   This we judged from some Captain Lewis gave them.

1.   At a fish weir on the Lemhi River, about five miles southeast of Salmon, Lemhi County, Idaho.

Thursday 29th August 1805.   a clear pleasant morning.   about 8 oClock A. m. a nomber of Indians arived here from the East Side of the Mountain. they belonged to this nation but had been gone a long time and one of the warries had been Sculped by Some war party in the plain.   a nomber of their relation cryed aloud when they arived in the village.   Capt. Lewis bought 2 more horses.   about 11 oClock A. m. Capt. Clark & party except 2 who Stayed to take care of the baggage arived here.   they informed us the Moun-tains are amazeing high and rough So that it is impossable to follow the River down for the Steep clifts &c. and the River So rapid and full of rocks that it is impossable to go down with crafts, and no game of any kind.   they killed nothing but one Deer, while they were gone.   they lived Several days on Servis berrys and cherries &c.   they passed a lodge of Indians in a Small valley in the mountn. gethering cherries & Servisses.   they Started to run but our men having a guide of their nation with them, he Spoke to them and they were easy.   these Savages had nothing to give our men but Some of their berries.   they got Some Salmon from the natives who Stayed on the River, but Suffered a great deal with hunger.   the Natives tells us that we cannot find the ocean by going a west course for Some of them who are old men has been on that a Season or more to find the ocean but could not find it, and that their was troublesome tribes of Indians[1] to pass. that they had no horses but would rob and Steal all they could and eat them as they had nothing as it were to eat. the country verry mountaineous and no game. these natives do not incline to Sell any more horses without guns in return as they say they must have one or the other for defence, as they could jump on their horses & ride off and carry their children &c. we told them they could not Spare any guns if we Should git no more horses So we put up the goods & make ready to Set out tomorrow on our way round the or between the mountains and Strike Columbian River below if possable. our hunters came in had caught 6 fish and killed one Deer.

Thursday August 29th We had a clear pleasant morning. About 8 o'Clock A. M. a number of Indians arrived at our Camp, who had come from the east side of the mountains, and were part of the Snake Nation of Indians; they had been absent from the Nation a long time, and had one of their warriors killed & scalped by some Warr party of Indians, that they met with in the plains. On the arrival of this party of Indians, the relations of the deceased warrior, that had been killed & scalped set up a terrible Yelling, which was followed by most of the Indians in the Village. Captain Lewis purchased 2 more horses from the Natives for Merchandise this day.— About 11 o'Clock A. M. Captain Clark & all the Men that was with him, (excepting 2 Men that was left with their baggage) arrived at our Camp; they informed us that the mountains which they crossed <are> were amazing high & rough; and that they thought it an impossibility, to go down the Columbia, from the place they were at, from the number of steep Clifts & Rocks, and that the Columbia River, was very rapid & full of rocks, and that it was dangerous for Canoes to descend that River.— They mentioned that Game of all kinds was very scarce, & that they had killed nothing whilst they were gone but One deer,— and that they had lived several days on service berries & Cherries.— They also informed us that they had passed a lodge of Indians which was in a Valley; which lay in between the Mountains.— These Indians they said were a Band of the snake Nation also, they found these Indians before they came to their lodges, gathering cherries & service berries.— On these Indians seeing Captain Clarkes men, they <had>

started to run from them, but our men having a guide of their own nation with them, he spoke to the Indians, and they came to our people and were easy.— These Indians had no kind of food with them but service berries, some of which they gave to our people.— They mentioned that they had met with some of the same tribe of Indians on the Columbia River, from whom they got some Salmon, but that they had suffered very much; on account of hunger.— The Indians at our Camp told us, that we should not find the Western Ocean, by going a West course, and some of the Old Men among them, told us, that they had been that course, a whole Season and could not find it.— They also informed us, that we should if we went that course, <we should> find some troublesome bad tribes of Indians, which we should have to pass, and that they had no horses, but that they would steal all the horses they could, and kill & eat them; that those Indians had nothing to eat & that the country where they resided, was very mountaneous, and that there was no game to be found there, The Indians that we are now among do not incline to sell us any more of their horses, without getting Guns & amunition in return. as they say, they must have either horses or Guns for their defence, As they told us, that on the approach of their enemies, that they could get on their horses & carry off their Wives & Children & make their escapes.—

Our officers told them, that they could not part with any of their Guns, if they should get no more horses.— The whole of our party were employed in packing up the Indian Goods & baggage in order to get ready to start tomorrow, on our way to go round, or between the Mountains, in order to find the Columbia River, a distance below where Captain Clark & his party had been; if possible.— Our hunters came in to our Camp and had caught 6 Salmon & killed One deer, which they brought to our Camp

1. Probably a description of the Tukudika, or Sheepeater, Indians, referred to by Lewis as the Broken Moccasin Indians; see Lewis's entry of August 14, 1805.

Friday 30th August 1805. a clear pleasant morning. we got all our horses up and bought 3 more which makes 30 in all which we now have. we got our loads ready. the guide[1] which we engaged to go with us tells us that we could go a road which would be Smooth & leads to the Southward but we would be 2 days without water and no game on that road.   but he could Show us a hilley rough roud over the mountains to the north of the River which would take us in 15 days to Salt water, or in 10 days to a large fork of the River,[2] where it would be navagable.   So we concluded to go that roud a part of these natives Set out with their horses to go over on the Missourie after the buffalow.   about one oClock P. M. we got ready and Set out with all our horses except 2 loaded with baggage.   our hunter killed three Deer this fornoon.   we proceeded on down this little River bottom   crossed Several Spring runs   passed Several old camps or lodges.   Came about 10 miles and Camped[3] on the bottom near the River.

Friday August 30th   A Clear pleasant morning, and our Men were employed in getting up our horses—   Captain Lewis bought 3 more horses from the Natives, and we now have 30 horses to carry our baggage &ca.— We got all the loads for the horses ready.—   The Indian guide, which our officers had engaged to go with us, from the Indians we are among; informed us, that we could go a Road which would be smooth & which went to the Southward, but that we should be two days, without water, & that there was no game to be met with on that Route,—   but that he would show us a hilly rough road, which went over the mountains, to the North of the Columbia River, which would take us in 15 days to Salt water, or in 10 days to a large fork of the Columbia River; which would be navigable for Canoes.—   Our Officers concluded to take the last mentioned Road—   A party of the Snake Indians that we were with, set out with their Horses to go over on the Mesouri after Buffalo, about 1 o'Clock P. M. we set out, having all our horses (excepting 2) loaded with our baggage &ca.   Our hunters came to us, & brought 3 deer which they had killed with them.   We proceeded on down this little River bottom, & crossed several spring runs, and passed by several old Indian Camps or lodges.—   We came about 10 Miles & encamped in a bottom, which lay near the River—

1. The man they called Old Toby; see Lewis's entry of August 20, 1805.
2. The Snake River, called Lewis's River by the party.
3. Near the Lemhi River, some miles below Baker, Lemhi County, Idaho.

Saturday 31st August 1805.[1] a fine morning. we Set out eairly and proceeded on 2 miles   passed Several Indian lodges where we bought a nomber
of fine Salmon.   the natives have wires [weirs] fixed across the River in
which they catch more or less every night.   a Strange Indian came in Site
of these lodges who they expected to be one of the nation called the flat
heads.[2]   he ran as Soon as he Saw us   Several of these natives followed after
him.   we went on a Short distance further crossed the River and halted for
breakfast.   one man out a hunting.   2 men Sent to Some other Indian
Camps, with Some articles to buy Some more Sammon, but they had moved
their Camps and we got none.   we then proceeded on over rough hills
Some of them high & Steep, deep Gullies and white earth which had been
washed down by rains &c.   went about eight miles and halted to bate our
horses and dine.   4 or five of the natives follow us.   Some pitch pine on the
Mountains which make near the River on each Side.   we proceeded on over
a Smooth plain about 7 miles and passed along [th]e Side of a mountain
near the River,[3] where the Stone lay one [up]on an other and full of holes,
So that it is allmost impossable for horses to pass without breaking their
leggs.   we then passed along the end of this mountain.   Come to a large
creek[4] which falls in on the East Side.   we followed up this creek or Spring
branch.   found pleanty of wild or choke cherries and Servis berrys.   one of
the hunters killed a Deer at the edge of the evening.   we Came [*blank*] Miles
this day and Camped[5] at the Creek where we had Several good Indian lodges
to Sleep in this night.

Saturday August 31st   We had a fine morning, & set out early, and proceeded on about 2 miles, and passed several Indian lodges, and met with
some Snake Indians, from whom we purchased for trifles a number of fine
Salmon, the Natives have Wares fixed across the Columbia River, in which
they catch more or less of them every night—.   A strange Indian came in
sight of the lodges, which we past; which the Snake Indians thought was one
of the Nation of Indians, which they called the flatt head nation:—   he ran
as soon as he saw us; and several of the Snake Indians followed him, We
proceeded on a short distance, and crossed the Columbia River, where we
halted to break fast.   One of our party was sent out this morning a hunting,

and two others of our party was sent to the Indian Camp with some articles to purchase some Salmon,— but the Indians had removed their Camps, & they got none. We proceeded on our way, and crossed over some rough hills, some of them very steep, & passed through some deep Vallies, which had white earth in them, which was occasioned by the Earth being washed down from the Hills of that Collour.—

We went about eight miles & halted to rest our horses & to dine, where some of the Natives followed us. We saw some Pitch pine trees which grew on the Mountains which make near to the River on each side of it. We proceeded on & passed through a smooth plain about 7 Miles & along the side of a mountain; which lay near the River, where the Stones lay very plenty, & the place full of holes, & where we found it almost impossible, for our horses to pass, without breaking their legs. We passed along the Edge of this mountain with great difficulty, & came to a large Creek, which falls in, on the East side of the Columbia River; we proceeded up this Creek, & found plenty of wild or choak cherries and service berries. One of our hunters killed a Deer on the Edge of the Mountain, which we had passed & which he brought to us in the evening; We came 15 Miles this day, & encamped on the Creek, where we found several Indian lodges, which we slept in

1. This is the last entry in this section of Whitehouse's original journal and ends near the top one-third of the page. The remainder of the page is filled with random scribbles, most of them Whitehouse's signature.

2. Also called Salish Indians; see September 4.

3. The Salmon River, which the party considered to be the same as the Lemhi, calling both Lewis's River.

4. Tower Creek, flowing into the Salmon River, Lemhi County, Idaho.

5. A few miles above the mouth of Tower Creek, Lemhi County.

Sunday 1st Sept. 1805.[1] a fine morning we Set out as usal and proceeded on over verry high mountains which was verry bad for our horses to climb up and down them. passed across Several large creeks the water of which is verry cold. considerable of pine & cotton timber on each of those creeks. we find a great pleanty of Servis berrys which are verry Sweet and good at this time. in the afternoon we descended a Mountain nearly as Steep as the roof of a house. went down in to the valley in which runs through a large

Creek.[2]   passed by a plain near the Creek a Short distance.   Camped[3] after coming 23 miles this day & Camped a little before night on account of its raining.   Some of the men giged Several Sammon in the creek.   three men went down to the Mo. of it to purchase Some Sammon from a camp of Indians who Stay at the mo. of the Creek to fish.   they bought about 25 pound with a fiew Small articles.   the hunters killed a Deer and wounded two bear at dark but could not get them.   the wild or choke cherrys abound in this bottom.   we gethered and boiled Some which eat verry well.   a nomber of Indian lodges along the creek.   we had 2 at camp to Sleep in.   Several Small Showers of rain this day & a little Small hail

Sunday September 1st   A fine clear morning, we set out as usual & proceeded on over very high mountains, which were bad for our horses, to climb up & down them; We passed across several large Creeks, the water of which was very Cold, with considerable quantities of Pine & Cotton timber growing on each side of them, & plenty of sweet service berries which was very welcome to us at this time.—   In the afternoon, we assended a mountain nearly as steep as the roof of a house, and went down, into a Valley which had a large Creek running through it,—   and a fine plain a short distance from this Creek, We encamped after having come about 23 Miles this day.— We stopped about 3 hours before night, on account of it raining, some of our party gigged several Salmon in the Creek & three of our men also went down to the Creek in order to purchase some Salmon from a band of Indians, who stay as we were informed at the mouth of the Creek fishing— They bought about 25 lbs. weight for some very trifling articles: the hunters killed a Deer & wounded two bears this evening, but did not get them.— The wild or choke Cherries were very plenty in this bottom, we gather'd some, which we boil'd & they eat very well—   There was number of Indian lodges of the Snake Indians lying along this Creek, & we had 2 of their Camping lodges to sleep in—   during this afternoon we had several small Showers of rain.—

1. Here begins the first entry in the final section of Whitehouse's original journal. In this section the writing is across the page from side to side as in a conventional book, rather than from end to end as in the preceding sections. The first page, which includes this entry and part of the next, is very difficult to read due to fading.

2. North Fork Salmon River, the party's Fish Creek, joining the Salmon in Lemhi County, Idaho.

3. On the North Fork Salmon River, a few miles south of Gibbonsville, Lemhi County, near the mouth of Hull Creek.

Monday 2nd Sept. 1805. a wet cloudy morning. we loaded our horses and Set out about 7 oClock and proced on. the road bad Some places thick bushes and [logs?] to cross. other places rockey. went about a N. E. course up the abo. ment.[1] Creek. Crossed Several large Spring runs. Saw a nomber of large beaver dams & ponds the pine and bolsom fer timber verry pleanty and thick up this Creek Some of the Pine is large enofe for boards [*several words illegible*] we proceeded on through a bad thicket of tall Strait pitch pine bolsom fer & cotton timber we were obledged to cut a road for the horses to go and some places verry Steep and rockey. we followed the creek up, crossed a nomber of fine Spring branches and waided the creek a nomber of times. the mountains on each Side of the Creek is verry Steep and high. the bottoms on the Creek narrow and Swampy a nomber of beaver dams. we Call this place dismal Swamp,[2] and it is a lonesom rough part of the Country. we were obledged to climb Several hills with our horses, where it was So Steep and rockey that Some of the horses which was weak and their feet Sore, that they fell back 3 or 4 fell over backwards and roled to the foot of the hills. we were then obledged to carry the loads up the hills and then load again. one of the horses gave out So that his load was left a little before night. we Came 13 miles this day and Camped[3] in a thicket of pine and bolsom fir timber near the Creek. 2 of the men came up with their horses and loads after dark. this horrid bad going where we came up this creek which we Call dismal Swamp was six miles and we are not out of it yet, but our guide tells us that we will git on a plain tomorrow. Several fessons killed this day, but no other kind of game Seen by our hunters.—

Monday September 2nd A cloudy wet morning, We set out with our horses & proceeded on our Journey, and about 7 o'Clock A. M. we passed some very bad Roads, some being plains with very thick bushes, and low slashes to cross, other places, very rockey, we went a North east course up the

Creek above mention'd.   We recrossed the same Creek near a large spring run,— where we saw a number of high beaver dams.   We saw also Pitch pine & Balsam fir Trees in great abundance, on the Tops of the Mountains, We passed through a bad thicket of tall strait Pitch pine, balsam fir, & Cotton wood Timber <so> which grew so close to each other that we were obliged to cut a road for our horses to pass through.—

Some of those places were very steep & Rockey.—   We continued our course up the side of the Creek already mentioned this day, and crossed a number of fine Spring branches, and waided in the Creek a number of times. The Mountains that lies on both sides of this Creek are very steep & high; the bottoms on this Creek narrow & swampey, And had a vast number of beaver dams, on them   We named this place Dismal swamp, & it was certainly a lonesome rough looking part of the Country.—   We were obliged to Climb several hills with our horses, where the hills was so steep & rockey, <which> some of the horses that was weak & had sore feet fell backward with their loads; and rolled down to the foot of those hills, we were obliged to carry the loads of our horses, on our backs up many of the hills, & then load them again.   One of our horses gave out, so that we were obliged to leave his load.—   We came about 13 Miles this day, & encamped in a thicket of pine trees, and balsam fir timber; near the Creek.—   Two of our Men came up with their horses & loads after it was dark.—   We came about 6 Miles through this bad road, all of which way was very bad travelling, and we are informed by our guide, that we have still further to go, before we get to the plains, which he says will be tomorrow, Our Hunters killed several Pheasants this day, but saw no other kind of Game.—

1. That is, "above mentioned," as in the fair copy. The stream is the North Fork Salmon River.

2. Ordway also uses this term (but not Clark or Gass) for the area around Gibbonsville, Lemhi County, Idaho. The term may refer to the Dismal Swamp of southeast Virginia and northeast North Carolina.

3. Northwest of Gibbonsville, Lemhi County, near U.S. Highway 93. See Clark's entry for this day for a discussion of the exact location.

Tuesday 3rd Sept. 1805.   Cloudy.   we Set out as usal after the load was brought up which was left last night.   we proceeded on up the branch a

Short distance, then took the mountains and w[ent] up and down the mountains all day.   passed and crossed an a bundance of fine Springs and Spring runs.   Some of the mountains was So Steep and rockey that Several of the horses fell back among the rocks and was near killing them   Some places we had to cut the road through thickets of bolsom fer Some of that kind of timber in the vallies of these mountains is verry high about 100 & 60 feet, and verry Strait and handsom.   the most of them are covred with warts full of the bolsom   towards evening we crossed a dividing ridge went some distance on the top of it which was tollarable good and Smoth going.   then passed down a Steep hill in to the head of a cove and branch where we Camped[1] after a dissagreeable days march of only 11 miles with much fatigue and hunger as nothing has been killed this day only 2 or 3 fessents,[2] and have no meat of any kind.   Set in to raining hard at dark So we lay down and Slept, wet hungry and cold.   Saw Snow on the tops of Some of these mountains this day.—

Tuesday September 3rd   We had a cloudy morning, & set out as usual, we brought the load up the hill on our backs, that was left there last night, and then we proceeded on up the Creek a short distance, and then took to the mountains, and went up & down them the whole of this day, and crossed abundance of fine Springs, & spring runs, some of the mountains that we crossed was so steep & Rockey, that several of the horses fell backwards among the rocks & was near being killed.—   We had to cut Roads, through thickets of balsam fir timber, for our horses to pass through.   We found some of that kind of timber in the Vallies which were very high many of them being 160 feet long & very strait & handsome, a number of them full of warts, & full of the balsam.—   towards evening, we crossed a dividing ridge, we went some distance on the top of it, which was tolerable smooth & good travelling, We then passed down a steep hill, at the head of a Cove and branch.—   We encamped at this place after a most diasgreeable days travel of only 11 Miles, being much fataigued & very hungry, our hunters having killed only 3 Pheasants this day,—   and we had no fresh meat with us.   At dark it began to Rain hard, We lay down to sleep being Wet, hungry & Cold, We saw Snow on the Top of these Mountains this day.—

1. The party's route and camp this day are particularly "obscure and enigmatic"; see Clark's entry. Those who have studied the matter disagree whether the camp was in Lemhi County, Idaho, or in Ravalli County, Montana, to say nothing of the exact location. Most likely they crossed the Continental Divide near Lost Trail Pass and entered Montana.

2. Probably some species of grouse; see Lewis's entry of September 20.

Wednesday 4th Sept. 1805. the morning clear but verry cold. our mock-ersons froze hard. the mountains covred with Snow. 2 mountain Sheep Seen by one of the men. we delayed untill about 8 oClock A. m. then Set out and assended a mountain without any thing to eat. the Snow lay on the mout. So that it kep on our mockisons the air verry cold our fingers aked with the cold. we [de]scended the mountain down a rough rockey way and along through a large thicket of bolsom fer timber in which we killed a dozen fessents then descended down in to a large valley[1] on a branch and halted to dine our hunter killed a Deer. Saw fresh Indian Sign. we Eat our deer. our Indian guide and the young Indian who accompanied him Eat the paunch and all the Small guts of the Deer. we then proceeded on down the valley towards evening we arived at a large Encampment of the flat head nation[2] which is a large band of the nation of about 40 lodges. they have between 4 and 500 well looking horses now feeding in this valley or plain in our view. they received us as friends and appeared to be glad to See us. 2 of our men who were a hunting came to their lodges first the natives Spread a white robe over them and put their arms around their necks, as a great token of friendship. then Smoaked with them. when Capt. Lewis and Capt. Clark ari[ved] they Spread white robes over their Shoulders and Smoaked with them. our officers told them that they would Speak with them tomorrow and tell them our business and where we are going &c. the natives are light Complectioned decent looking people the most of them well cloathed with Mo. Sheep and other Skins. they have buffalow Robes leather lodges to live in, but have no meat at this time. but gave us abundance of their dryed fruit Such as Servis berrys cherries different kinds of roots all of which eat verry well. they tell us that we can go in 6 days to where white traders come and that they had Seen bearded men who came a river to the North of us 6 days march but we have 4 mountains to cross before we come on that River. our hunters killed another Deer this evening. Came [*blank*] miles to day and pitched our Camp[3] on the plain near the Creek on the right of the Indians lodges. considerable of large pitch pine in the valley.

Wednesday September 4th   This morning Clear but very cold so that our moccasins froze hard. the Mountains here are covered with snow. One of our party saw two Mountain Sheep or Ibex, We delayed setting out till about 8 oClock A. M. we then set out & ascended a mountain; not having had any thing to eat this day, the snow lay on the Mountain; so that it stuck to our Moccasins, The air was very cold, and made our fingers ache, We descended the Mountain; down a rough rockey way,— through a large thicket of balsam fir timber, in which we killed one dozen Pheasants, We then descended into a large Valley, to a branch of Water; where we halted to dine. our hunters killed a Deer, & told us that he had seen fresh signs of Indians. We eat our deer, & our Indian guide and a young Indian of the Snake Nation that attended him, eat the paunch & small guts of it. We proceeded on down the Valley towards evening, & arrived at a large encampment of the flat head nation of Indians, which were a large band of that nation, They had about 40 lodges, & had between four & five hundred horses feeding in the Valley or plain; which lay in our view. These Indians received us as friends, & appeared to be glad to see us. Two of our Men who were a hunting came to their lodges before we had arrived. The Natives <had> spread a white robe over them, and put their Arms around their necks, as a great token of friendship, then smoaked with them. When Captains Lewis & Clark arrived they spread white Robes over their shoulders and smoaked with them also. Our officers informed them, that they would speak to them tomorrow, and inform them our business & where we were going &ca.—

These Flatt head Nation of Indians are a well made, handsome, light coloured sett of people, the most part of them were well cloathed. Their cloathing were made out of mountain Sheep or Ibex skins & other kinds of Skins; all of which were dressed. Their Lodges were made out of dressed buffalo hides, which they live in. they had no meat among them at this time, They gave us abundance of dried fruit, (Serviceberries & cherries) & different kinds of roots, all of which eat very well. They told us, that they can go in 6 days, to where the white traders come, & that they had seen bearded men, on a River to the North of us, & only 6 days march from this place,— but said we have 4 mountains to cross before we come to them, which lies & is on a River, our Hunters killed one Deer this day, which they brought to our Camp. We came about 10 Miles this day, & pitched our Camp near a Creek on the Plains, on the right of where the Indian lodges stood; and where in a Valley, a small distance from us; grew a considerable quantity of large Pitch pine trees.—

1. Ross, or Ross's, Hole, east of Sula, Ravalli County, Montana.

2. The Flathead, or Salish, Indians; see Clark's entry for this day.

3. In Ross Hole, probably on Camp Creek near its entrance into the East Fork Bitterroot River.

Thursday 5th Sept. 1805. a clear cold morning. the Standing water froze a little last night. we hoisted our large flag this morning. Several men went out a hunting. about 10 oClock our officers held a Council with the flat head nation and told them nearly the Same as they told other nations, only told them that we wanted a fiew horses from them, and we would give them Some marchandize in return. Gave 4 of their principal men meddles made them chiefs gave each of them a Shirt and a nomber of other articles also 2 flags &c. then told them that we could not Stop long with them and that we were ready to purchase their horses, and that we could not talk with them as much as we wish, for all that we Say has to go through 6[1] languages before it gits to them and it is hard to make them understand all what we Say. these Savages has the Strangest language of any we have ever Seen. they appear to us to have an Empeddiment in their Speech or a brogue or bur on their tongue but they are the likelyest and honestst Savages we have ever yet Seen. our officers lay out Some marchandize in different piles to trade with the natives for horses. our officers bought twelve horses and gave a Small quantity of marchandize for each horse. we Swapped 7 horses which were lame &c. Gave Some Small articles to boot. we bought 10 or a Dozen pack Saddles from the natives. our hunters all came to Camp towards evening. one of them had killed 2 young deer and one brarow.

Thursday Septemr 5th This morning was Clear & cold, the water that we had in our small Vessells froze during last night. Our officers had our large flag hoisted at our camp this morning.— several of our Men were sent out a hunting.— About 10 oClock A. M our Officers held a Council with the flat head Indians. they told them that they had come in Order to make peace between all the red people, who were at Warr with each other; & to instruct them in the way of Trade, and that they would open the Path from their Nation to the white people &ca they also informed them that they wanted a few horses from them, for which they would give them some Merchandise in return. They gave 4 of their principal Indians Medals, & gave them Commissions as Chiefs. they also gave each of them a Shirt, a number of small articles & 2 Flags. they informed those Chiefs that we should not stay with them but a short time, & that we were ready to purchase some horses from them, and that they would give them some Merchandise for them, and that they were sorry that they could not have as much talk with them as they wished to have, and that all that they told them, had to be Interpreted through six different languages, before either party understood, what was said, and then hard to make them understand what our officers said to them.— These Indians language is the strangest that any of us ever heard. they all appear to have impediments in their speeches, and pronounce their words with a kind of brogue or burr on their tongues. These Indians were the handsomest & most likely Indians, that we have seen yet.— They behave very kind to our party, and are very honest, not attempting to pilfer the most trifling article from us.—

Our Officers had laid out Merchandise in different piles, in order to trade with the Natives for horses. They purchased twelve horses from the Indians, for Merchandise, & exchanged 7 more horses that were lame with them, & gave them the difference in Goods.— they also purchased some pack saddles from them. Our hunters all came into our Camp towards evening having killed 2 young Deer and a Brarerow which they brought with them.—

1. This number may have been added to a blank space. There were actually five languages: Salish (for the Flatheads), Shoshone, Hidatsa, French, and English.

Friday 6th Sept. 1805. a clear cold morning. we began to pack up our baggage and look up our horses &c. bought a nomber of lash chords and other Small articles from the natives at 10 oClock A. m. the natives all got up their horses and Struck their lodges in order to move over on the head of the Missourie after the buffalow. they make a large Show as they are numerous and have abundance of horses. we take these Savages to be the Welch Indians[1] if their be any Such from the Language. So Capt. Lewis took down the Names of everry thing in their Language, in order that it may be found out whether they are or whether they Sprang or origenated first from the welch or not. about noon we got ready to Set out. we have now 40 good pack horses, and three Colts. we loadd. the horses Several men had to take 2 horses &c. 4 hunters were furnished horses without loads to hunt constant. about 1 oClock P. m. we Set out. the natives Set out at the Same time to go over on the missourie. we proceeded on our journey. crossed a large creek[2] went over a mountain about 7 miles came down on the Same creek and Camped[3] nothing to eat but a little pearched corn. on[e] hunter Stayed out all night. light Sprinklings of rain through the course of the day.

Friday Septemr— 6th A clear cold morning, and we began to pack up our baggage & collect our horses in order to get ready to proceed on our Journey, we purchased a number of Cords & other small articles from the Indians, for some small articles of merchandise. About 10 o'Clock A. M. the Indians collected their horses, & struck their lodges, in order to move over on the head waters of the Mesouri River after Buffalo. they made a large show & were numerous and had abundance of horses. We all suppose these Indians to be the Welch nation of Indians, if there be any such a Nation; & from their language we believe them to be the same. Captain Lewis took down the names of almost every thing in their language in order to find whether they are the same,— or if possible to find out from their language & if there is any thing similiarity between it, & the Antient Welch language, & [*illegible, crossed out*] whether they originated from the Welch.— About noon we got ready to set out on our Journey, & we have 40 good pack horses which our officers had purchased <from> & exchanged with these Indians.

They had also purchased 3 Colts; that in case we should be without provisions, that we might have something for to subsist on.— We loaded our horses, & our hunters were also furnish'd with horses without loads, to hunt on.— About 1 oClock P. M we set out. The natives set out at the same time, to go over on the Mesouri River to hunt buffalo, after taking an affectionate leave of us.— We proceeded on our Journey, and crossed a large Creek, and went over a Mountain about 7 Miles across.— We asscended this Mountain, and came to the same Creek that we crossed this day, & encamped.— We had nothing to eat except a little parched Corn Meal, but our party are all contented. One of our hunters did not return to us this night

1. Whitehouse recalls the myth that some interior Indians may have descended from legendary Welsh travelers. Some persons also applied this myth to the Mandans.

2. East Fork Bitterroot River, in Ravalli County, Montana.

3. In Ravalli County, a few miles northwest of Sula, on the East Fork Bitterroot River, apparently above and opposite Warm Springs Creek.

Saturday 7th Sept. 1805. a cloudy cold morning. we Set out eairly, and proceeded on down the creek.[1] our hunter came up who Stayed out last night. had lost his horse. we proceeded on over a plain. the bottoms narrow and considerable of timber large pine and cotton along the creek high mountains[2] on the Side of the creek which are covred with pitch pine. Some of the highest are covred thick with Snow. one of our hunters killed 2 Deer, which revived us. Some of the hunters killed a goose & a crain[3] Several fessents and a hawk. Several Small Showers of rain in the course of the day. the valley gitting wider the creek larger. the plain Smooth and dry. the Soil verry indifferent. we Came 18 miles this day and Camped[4] on the bank of the Creek. we passed Several creeks and branches[5] which run into the main creek this day. one of our hunters did not join us this evening. a little rain. our course this day is generally N. west.

Saturday September 7th We had a cold, Cloudy morning.— We set out early and proceeded on, we went down the Creek that we had encamped on. The hunter that was out last night returned to us, he had lost his horse, & had killed no game. We proceeded on, and crossed a plain. the bottoms along the Creek are narrow, and had a considerable quantity of Pine & Cotton Wood trees growing on it. On the South side of this Creek, lies high Mountains, which are covered with Pitch Pine. One of our hunters came to us, and had killed 2 deer, Some others of the Hunters also came to us, &

had killed 1 Goose 1 Crane several ferrets[6] & a hawk all of which they brought with them.—

Our party seemed revived at the success that the hunters had met with, however in all the hardship that they had yet undergone they never once complained, trusting to Providence & the Conduct of our Officers in all our difficulties. We had several small showers of Rain in the course of the day. As we pursued our Journey we found the Valleys getting wider & the Creek larger & the plain smooth & dry, but the Soil very indifferent. We came 18 Miles this day, and encamped on the bank of the same Creek, that we had encamped on Yesterday. We passed during this days Journey several Creeks, & branches which run into the creek where we now are.— One of our hunters did not join us this evening, our course during this day has been generally North West.—

1. The party went down the East Fork Bitterroot River to the junction with West Fork Bitterroot River (West Fork Clark's River to the party) and on down the Bitterroot (Clark's) River, Ravalli County, Montana.

2. The Bitterroot Mountains on the Montana–Idaho border.

3. Probably a sandhill crane.

4. Southeast of Grantsdale, Ravalli County, on the east side of the Bitterroot.

5. Including McCoy, Tin Cup, Rock, and Lost Horse creeks, in Ravalli County. See Clark's entry for the day.

6. The copyist's error. He meant "fessents" as in the first entry, for pheasants, otherwise grouse.

Sunday 8th Sept. 1805. cloudy and verry chilley and cold. we Set out eairly and proceeded on down this large creek or Small River. passed over Smooth dry plains. no timber only along the River, which is large pitch pine the bottoms wide. we crossed Several creeks.[1] Saw Snow on the Mountains to our left. high barron hills to our right.[2] about 11 oClock we halted to dine at a branch our hunters all joined us. had killed an Elk & and a Deer, Which they brought with them. the wind from N. W. chilley and cold. the Snow lays thick on the mot. a little to our left. we delayed and let our horses feed about 2 hours, and proceeded on down the valley. had Several Small cold Showers of rain & a little hail. passed over level Smooth plains in this valley. the Mountains are rough on each Side and are covered with pine and the tops of which are covered with Snow. Some places appear to lay thick. one of our hunters found & caught 2 horses and a handsom Colt. we take them along with us though the horses are lame. we expect that to be the reason that the natives left them in these bottoms. we travveled 20 odd miles this day and Camped[3] at the Creek and Smooth bottom where was fine feed for our horses. our hunters all joined us one[4] of them had killed a Deer. crossed Several branches in course of the day.—

Sunday Septemr. 8th   A cold chilly Cloudy morning.   We set out early and proceeded on our Journey.—   We went down this large Creek or small River, we passed over smooth dry plains, but no timber to be seen excepting what grew along the Creek, which were large Pitch Pine trees.—   The bottom land along this large Creek were wide & the Soil very rich.—   We crossed several small Creeks, which made into the large Creek which we left this morning.—   We saw Snow lying on Mountains, which lay to the South of us, & high Barren hills, which lay to the North likewise of us.—   About 11 o'Clock A. M. we halted to dine at a Creek.—   Our hunters all joined us here, they had killed an Elk & one Deer, which they brought to us.   The Wind has been from the N West during this day & the Air chilly & Cold.—

The Snow still continues on the Mountains, a small distance to the South of us.   We delayed about 2 hours to let our horses feed, we then proceeded on down the Valley & had several small showers of rain accompanied with hail.—   We passed over level smooth plains in this Valley, the Mountains on each side of which, are rough, and are cover'd with Pine Trees, the Tops of which are Covered with Snow & the snow appears to lay thick in many places on these Mountains.—   One of our hunters came across 2 Strange horses & a Colt, which he caught.—   We took those horses & Colt along with us, the horses were lame & we expected that the Natives had left them in this Valley, on that account.   We came 25 Miles this day as near as we can guess, and encamped at a Creek, on a smooth bottom of land.   We found here fine food for our horses.   Our hunters joined us in the Evening.   They had killed only one deer which they brought to us.—

1. There are a number of creeks running into the Bitterroot in this day's course, in Ravalli County, Montana; see Clark's entry for the day.

2. On the left are the Bitterroot Mountains and on the right are the Sapphire Mountains.

3. Near Stevensville, Ravalli County.
4. Drouillard.

Monday 9th Sept. 1805. a cloudy cold morning, wind from the N. W. we Set out as usal, and proceeded on down the valley. Smooth pleasant plains, large pitch pine timber along the River. no timber on the plains but they are covred with grass and wild hysop. the Soil poor. crossed Several branches on which is pine timber, also, a little cotton timber &c. the Snow continues on the Mount. each Side of the valley. about 11 oClock we halted at a branch to dine one of the hunters had killed three geese and a wood pecker.[1] Capt. Clark killed 4 fessents or prarie hens. we find wild or choke cherries along the branches. we delayed about 2 hours and a half. then proceeded on down the valley. passed through a large bottom covered with handsom pitch pine timber, from that a pleasant plain the remainder of this day. the afternoon pleasant, but the Snow Still continues on the Mountains as usal. Came about [*blank*] Miles this day and Camped on a plain near a creek[2] which runs in to the River about 2 mls. below. our hunters all but one joined us had killed 3[3] Deer and Several ducks this day, &c. course N. W. and North all day.—

Monday Septemr 9th This morning was cold & the wind blew from the No. West. We set out as usual, & proceeded on our Journey down the Valley, We passed along smooth plains, covered with high Grass & wild hysop, but the soil poor.— There was no timber to be seen here excepting some pitch pine trees, which grew along the large Creek or river side. We proceeded on, and crossed several branches on the sides of which grew Pitch pine & Cotton wood trees.—

The Snow still continued on the Mountains, on both sides of the Valley. About 11 o'Clock A. M we halted at a branch to dine, where one of our hunters had killed three Geese & a wood peckar, which he brought to us. Captain Clark went out here to hunt & killed 4 Pheasants, which he brought to us. we found here wild or choke cherries, growing along this branch— We delayed at this place about 2½ hours and then proceeded on down this Valley & passed through a bottom covered with handsome pitch pine timber, and the remainder of this day we passed through pleasant plains. The Snow continuing as usual on the Mountains on both sides of us. We came about 20 Miles this day, & encamped on a plain, near a Creek which run into the River about 2 Miles below where we were encamped.— Our hunters all but one joined us here. They had killed 3 Deer & a number of ducks this day which they brought to us.— our Course this day has been from North to North West.—

1. Either the red-headed woodpecker, *Melanerpes erythrocephalus*, or the pileated woodpecker, *Dryocopus pileatus.*

2. This was the party's Travelers' Rest Creek, now Lolo Creek. The camp, which they called Travelers' Rest, is in the vicinity of Lolo, Missoula County, Montana, on the south side of the creek, one or two miles above the Bitterroot River.

3. The number "3" is written over "2."

Tuesday 10th Sept. 1805. a clear pleasant morning. not So cold as usal. as our road leads over a mountain to our left, we conclu our Captains conclude to Stay here this day to take observations, and for the hunters to kill meat to last us across the mountain and for our horses to rest &c. Several men and all the best hunters went out a hunting considerable of cotton timber on this creek the choke cherries abound on its bottoms. the natives has lately gethered an amence quantities of them here for food, as they mooved up. considerable of Elder[1] willow and Servis bushes along the Creek &c. theo the day is warm the Snow does not melt on the mt. a Short distance from us. considerable of pitch pine on the mountains, but the Snow makes them look like the middle of winter. the valley and plains are pleasant. towards evening the hunters all came or returned to Camp had killed 4 Deer 2 ducks a faun deer and Several geese. towards evening one of the hunters[2] went up the creek a Short distance came across three Indians[3] a horseback they appeared afraid of him untill he lay down his gun they then came up to him in a friendly manner and took him on behind one of them and rode verry fast down to our Camp. they belong to the nation of flat heads. 2 of our hunters was down the River in cite of the forks to day, and allow it to be about 15 miles down the valley. these three natives tell us that they lay in hearing of our guns all day and was afraid to come to us. they tell us that two of the Snake Indians has Stole 22 of their horses, and these three are in persuit of them. one Stayed to pilot us over the mout. the other 2 proceeded on in order to ride all night after them, intending to git their horses if possable. our guide tells us that these waters runs into Mackinzees River[4] as near as they can give an account, but he is not acquainted that way. So we go the road he knows.

Tuesday Septemr. 10th We had a clear pleasant morning, and the weather moderate, As our Road now lay over a Mountain to our left hand, Our Officers concluded to stay here this day, in Order to take an Observation & attain the latitude of this place & for the hunters to provide us with Meat, sufficient to last us across that mountain; and to rest our horses.— Several of the Men & our best hunters were sent out a hunting.—

We found along this Creek, a considerable quantity of Cotton wood timber, & in the bottoms choke cherries. We found an immense quantities of these berries, which the Natives had lately gathered for food on their way to the Mesouri, Elder, Willow & Service berries bushes grow in plenty along this Creek.— the day continued to grow warm, but the Snow did not melt on the Mountains, which lay a short distance from us. On these mountains are large Pitch pine Trees. The Snow on the Mountains have the appearance of the Middle of winter. The Vallies have a very pleasant appearance.— Towards evening all our hunters returned to our Camp.— They had killed 4 Deer, 1 fawn 2 Ducks & several Geese. The hunters went out again up the Creek a short distance, and came across 3 Indians on horse back, those Indians seemed afraid of our hunters, untill they laid down their Guns, they then came up to them in a friendly manner. these Indians took our hunters up behind them, and rode very fast down to our Camp, We learnt from our Interpreters & Guide, that those Indians belonged to a Nation of Indians called the Flatt head Nation. Some of our hunters that went down the Creek or River, informed us, that they were in sight of the Columbia River this day & allow it to be about 15 Miles down the Valley that we are now in.

The three Indians, that came to our Camp with our hunters informed us; that they had lay in the hearing of the firing of our Guns all this day, and that they were afraid to come to us, not knowing what nation we belonged to. They also informed us, that two of the Snake Nation of Indians had stole 22 of their horses & that they were now in pursuit of them. One of these Indians staid with us to pilot us over the Mountains and the other two started after the theives, intending to ride all the night after them, and to get their horses if possible.— Our guide, informed us, that these Waters, runs into Mackenzie's River, as near as <they> he can guess, or give information, but says that he is not acquainted with that Road or path, Our officers concluded on going the Road that our Interpreter is best acquainted with.—

1. Probably blue elderberry, *Sambucus cerulea* Raf., which Lewis mentioned on February 7, 1806.
2. Colter.
3. Although the party called them Flatheads (Salish), they were probably Nez Perces.
4. See Lewis's account of the connections of rivers in his entry for this day.

Wednesday 11th Sept. 1805. a beautiful pleasant morning. we went out to hunt up our horses, but they were So Scattered that we could not find them all untill 12 oclock, So we dined here. the Latidude at this place is 46° 48m 28s %10 1 North. the Snow on the mountain about 1 mile to the S. W. of us does not melt but verry little. Some of the men who were hunting the horses detained us Untill 4 oClock at which time we Set out 2 and proceeded on up this Creek Course nearly west. the narrow [bo]ttom along this creek is mostly covred with pine timber. passed a tree on which was a nomber of Shapes drawn on it with paint by the natives. a white bear Skin hung on the Same tree. we Suppose this to be a place of worship among them. Came about 7 miles this evening and Camped 3 on a Smooth plain near the Creek, where had lately been a large Encampment of Indians. Saw one house made of Earth. the pine trees pealed as far up as a man could reach. we Suppose that the natives done it to git the enside beark to mix with their dryed fruit to Eat. the Choke cherries are pleanty on &c

Wednesday Septemr—. 11th A Beautiful pleasant morning, and we all turned out to hunt up our horses, but they were so scattered, that we did not find them all untill 12 o'Clock A. M. We dined here and our Officers ascertained the Latitude of this place which they found to lay in 46° 48′ 28%10 S North Latitude and named this place *Travellers Rest.* The Snow on the mountains lying about One Mile to the South West, had melted very little.

Some of the Men that were hunting the horses did not come in till 4 o'Clock P. M. At which time we set out on our Journey again,

We proceeded on up this large Creek nearly a West course, where we found the narrow bottoms along the Creek mostly covered with Pine timber; and passed by a Pine Tree on which a number of figures were painted <on it>, & a White Bearskin hanging on the same tree, the figures were painted by the Natives & the White bear Skin, were placed there also by them. We suppose this place to be a place of Worship among them. We came about 7 Miles this evening, and encamped on a smooth plain, near the Creek that we had left & where there had lately been an encampment (which was large) of Indians. We saw one encampment here made out of Earth & the Pine trees, pealed as high up as a Man could reach, which we suppose the Natives had done in order to get the inside bark, for to mix with their dried fruit to eat; it being the manner in which they prepare it— We found the Wild or Choke Cherries plenty at this place.—

1. The reading may have been added to a blank space.
2. They headed west on the Lolo Trail, along Lolo (Travelers' Rest) Creek.
3. About one half mile east of Woodman Creek, Missoula County, Montana.

Thursday 12th Sept. 1805. a white frost, and clear pleasant morning. the hunters Set out eairly. we loaded up and Set out soon after Sunrise, and proceeded on a Short distance. then took the mountains covred with pitch pine. went up and down a nomber of bad hills and mot. crossed Several runs & about 1 oClock P. m. we descended a bad part of the mot. nearly Steep came down on the creek a gain, and halted to dine.[1] our hunters has killed this day 4 Deer and a fessent. we proceeded on crossed 2 more creeks, and assended a high rough mountain rockey & a verry rough trail to follow. we proced. on along the ridge which was covred with pitch pine timber. night came on and we had to go through the thickets of pine and over logs &c. untill about 10 oClock at in the evening before we could git any water. then descended a Steep part of the mountain down on the Creek <&> which we left at noon, and Camped[2] on the bank of the creek where we had Scarsely room to Sleep. Came 17½ miles this day. Saw high

Mountains to the South of us covred with Snow, which appears to lay their all the year round. Scarsely any feed for our horses.

Thursday Septemr. 12th   This morning Clear weather with white frost & our hunters went out early to hunt; We loaded up our horses, and set out on our Journey, soon after sun rise, & proceeded on a short distance & took up to the Mountains, which were on their Tops cover'd with Pitch pine trees. We then continued ascending & descending Mountains & bad hills & crossed several Runs.—

About 1 oClock P. M. we descended a bad part of the Mountains, which was nearly steep, & came down on the Creek which we had left,— where we halted to dine & where our hunters came to us, & had killed 4 Deer & a Pheasant which they brought to us, We halted for one hour & proceeded on, and crossed 2 Creeks, and ascended a high rough rockey mountain, & followed a very rough trail.   We proceeded on along the ridge of one of these mountains which was covered with Pitch pine timber.   Night came on and we travelled in the dark, through thickets of pine Trees, & passed over logs & bad places untill about 10 o'Clock P. M. before we could get to a place where water was convenient to encamp at, which was at a steep part of the Mountain, which we descended down to a Creek, being the same which we had left at noon.   We encamped on this Creek, where we had scarcely Room to lay down to Sleep, <on> having come about 17½ Miles this day.— We found here, very little food for our horses, and saw Mountains this day which lay to the South of us covered with Snow, which lies on those Mountains during the whole Year.—

1. They traveled up Lolo Creek, passing various branches, and nooned at Grave Creek, where the trail forks, in Missoula County, Montana.
2. About two miles east of Lolo Hot Springs, Missoula County, near U.S. Highway 12.

Friday 13th Sept. 1805.   cloudy.   we got our horses up all but the one Capt. Lewis rode and a colt which our young Indian rode.   we hunted Some time for them but could not find them.   then all but 2 or three loaded the horses and proceeded on   a Short distance passed a warm Spring,[1] which nearly boiled where it Issued out of the rocks   a Short distance below the natives has dammed it up to bathe themselves in, and the water in that place is considerable above blood heat. it runs out in Sundry places and Some places cooler than others. Several of us drank of the water, it has a little sulpur taste and verry clear. these Springs are very beautiful to See, and we think them to be as good to bathe in &c. as any other ever yet found in the United States. a handsom green or Small meadow on the creek near Sd. Springs. a little above we could not git along the Indian trail for the timber which had been blown down in a thicket of pine &c. So we went around a hill came on the trail again and proceeded on untill about 11 oClock and halted to dine and let our horses feed on the main fork of the creek where was Several beaver dams. Capt. Lewis and the men who Stayed back to hunt their horses joined us, but had not found them our hunters gone on a head the mountains rough and rocks which appear above the timber like towers in Some places. the day proved pleasant. we proceeded on assended a high mountain, over took the hunters. they had killed a Deer. 2 of them Sent back after Capt. Lewiss horse. we crossed the dividing ridge found it only about half a mile from the head Spring of the water running East to a branch running west. each heading on an open Swamp, which is level and full of Springs. Came [*blank*] miles this day and Camped[2] on the branch running west where we had good feed for our horses.

Friday Septemr. 13th We had Cloudy weather; We got up all our Horses, but the one that Captain Lewis had rode & a Colt which was rode by the Young Indian, who attended our Interpreter; which we had got from the Snake Nation of Indians

The men all turned out to hunt for this horse & Colt, but returned to us without success. We on the return of our Men loaded our horses with our Goods & baggage excepting 3 which we left for Men, to ride & seek the lost horses, we proceeded on our way a short distance when we came to a Warm spring, where the water was nearly boiling hot, where it issued out of the Rocks. We found a short distance below that place a dam, which the Natives had made in Order to stop the Water, that they might have a bathing place. the water at this Bath was considerable above blood heat, this bath run out at different places, some of which was considerable cooler than others.— Several of our party drank of the Water that was in this Bath, it had strongly the taste of Sulphur, & was very clear. The same kind of Sulphurous springs are to be found near this place, & has a handsome appearance, Our officers were of opinion that those Springs were very healthy to bathe in; Near this spring run lies a very handsome Creek, with a very handsome Meadow lying along it, & this Meadow lay near to the Spring, & a small distance above it— We could not get along the Indian trail, for the timber that had been blown down in a thicket of Pine & other Trees.— We went round this falling timber, and round a hill, and got into the road again. We proceeded on our Journey 'till about 11 o'Clock A. M. when we halted to dine & let our horses feed which was on the Main fork of the Creek,— where we saw several beaver dams, Captain Lewis & the Men that staid behind to hunt the horses joined us, but they had not found them. Our hunters went on ahead to hunt, 'till the evening. The Mountains we found this day were very rough, and Rocks, which appear above the timber like Towers.— The day proved very pleasant, and we proceeded on, & ascended a high mountain; & overtook our hunters who had killed a deer, Captain Lewis sent back 2 of these hunters, to hunt for his Horse & the Colt which was lost— We proceeded on, and crossed the dividing ridge, & found it only about half a mile from the head of a spring where the Water run an east Course, to a branch of Water which run a West course, each heading in an Open Swamp which lies level & abounds with Springs. We came only 18 Miles this day & encamped on the branch which run a West course; where we found good Grass for our Horses.—

1. Lolo Hot Springs, Missoula County, Montana.
2. They crossed the Montana–Idaho state line into Idaho County, Idaho, east of Lolo Pass, and went down Pack Creek (their Glade Creek) to Packer Meadows, camping at the lower end of the meadows.

Saturday 14th Sept. 1805. a cloudy morning. we eat the last of our meat, and Set out as usal. ascended a mountain covrd. with pine. abt. 4 miles we descended it down on the Creek at a fork[1] where it ran very rapid and full of rocks. we then <descend> ascended a verry high mountain, about 4 miles from the forks of the creek to the top of it went Some distance on the top then descended it about 6 miles. Some places verry Steep. came down at another fork of the Creek[2] where it was considr. larger. the Natives

had a place made across in form of our wires[3] in 2 places, and worked in
with willows verry injeanously, for the current verry rapid. we crossed at the
forks and proceeded on down the creek. passed Several late Indian Encampments. our <Intrepter> Guide tells us that the natives catch a great
nomber of Sammon along here. we went down the creek abt. 4 miles and
Camped[4] for the night. Eat a little portable Soup,[5] but the men in jeneral
So hungry that we killed a fine Colt which eat verry well, at this time. we
had Several light Showers of rain and a little hail. Several claps of Thunder.
we came in all [*blank*] miles this day. the 2 hunters joined us with Capt.
Lewis horse which had been lost. Saw high mountan.[6] a little to the South
of us, which are covred with Snow. the most of these mountains are covred
with pine. Saw Some tall Strait Siprass, or white ceeder[7] to day. the Soil
indifferent, and verry broken. the Countrey all mountaineous. our
hunters found a Stray horse on the road. a Small Indian horse came to us
this evening.

Saturday Septemr 14th   A Cloudy Morning, & we did not set out till we
had breakfasted, at which we eat the last of our Meat; we then proceeded on
our Journey, and ascended a Mountain which was cover'd with Pine timber,
and was about 4 Miles from where it began to ascend to the top; we descended this mountain; & came down to a Creek on a fork of it; at this place
the Water run rapid, & it was very full of Rocks.— We ascended then,
another Mountain; which was about 4 Miles from the fork we left to the
top of it.—

We continued on our way on the top of this mountain where we had a
most delightful prospect of the Hills & Vallies which lay below us, & then
descended this Mountain about 6 Miles, which in some places, we found very
steep, and came down on another fork of the Creek, which we last left, which
was considerable larger, the Natives had here made places across this fork of
the Creek, in the form of Weirs to catch fish in, which we found in 2 different
parts of this fork, it was worked in with willows very ingeniously & strong, the
current running very rapid at where these Weirs were set.— We crossed
below this place at where the Creek forked, and proceeded on down the
creek and passed several Indian encampments, which the Natives had lately
left. Our guide informed us, that the Natives catch great Quantities of Sal-

mon at this place, We went down this Creek about 4 Miles & encamped. the Men here eat a little portable Soup, but still are all very hungry.— Our officers concluded on having a fine Colt that we had along with us killed, which was done, & hunger made us all think that it eat delecious, We had towards Evening several small Showers of rain, some hail & several severe Claps of thunder, The hunters that went after Captain Lewis's horse & the Colt, joined us in the Evening; they had found the horse only, We saw in the course of this days travel, several Mountains, which were covered with Snow which lay to the South of us.—

The Tops of most of these Mountains are cover'd with pine, & tall white Cedar Trees. The Soil during this days travell is very indifferent, and the Country broken & very mountaineous. Our Hunters found a stray horse on the Path, & a small Indian horse came to our Camp in the evening.— We came about 18 Miles this day.—

1. Brushy Creek (Gass's Stony Creek) and Crooked Fork, Idaho County, Idaho.

2. Crooked Fork and Colt Killed creeks (formerly White Sand Creek but now restored to Lewis and Clark's name) merge to form the Lochsa River, Idaho County.

3. That is, weirs.

4. On the north bank of the Lochsa, some two miles below the mouth of Colt Killed Creek, near Powell Ranger Station, Idaho County.

5. Lewis purchased this soup in Philadelphia; it may have been kept in the form of dry powder or thick liquid. It was staple army rations of the time.

6. They were traveling through the Bitterroot Mountains.

7. The words, "or white ceeder" appear to have been interlined in another hand, perhaps as a correction to Whitehouse's cypress. It is western redcedar, *Thuja plicata* Donn.

Sunday 15th Sept. 1805. cloudy. we loaded up our horses and Set out at 7 oClock, and proceeded on down the creek a Short distance crossed Several Springs and Swampy places covred with white ceeder and tall handsom Spruce pine,[1] which would be excelent for boards or Shingles. we crossed a creek a Small pond[2] a little below, then assended a high mountain.[3] Some places So Steep and rockey that Several of the horses fell backward and roled down among the rocks 20 or 30 feet but did not kill them. we got on to the ridge of the mot. and followed it riseing over Several high knobs where the wind had blown down the most of the timber. we found a Small Spring before we came to the highest part of the mountain where we halted and drank a little portable Soup, and proceeded on up on the top of the mountain, which is covred with timber Spruce &c and Some Spots of Snow and high clifts of rocks   it is about 10 miles from the foot of this mountain to the top and the most of the way verry Steep.   we marched on top of this mountain untill after dark in hopes to find water, but could not find any, So we Camped[4] on the top ridge of the mountain without finding any water, but found plean[ty] of Snow, which appear to have lain all the year   we melted what we wanted to drink and made or mixd a little portable Soup with Snow water and lay down contented.   had come [*blank*] miles to day.

Sunday Septemr 15th   This morning we had Cold weather, & cloudy, We set out on our Journey about 7 oClock A. M. with all our horses loaded   we proceeded on down the Creek a short distance, and crossed several springs & swampey places, covered with white Cedar, & tall Spruce pine.   We crossed a Creek & a small pond which lay a small distance below it.   We then ascended a high mountain; which in some places was so steep & rockey, that several of our horses fell backward, and rolled down among the Rocks between 20 & 30 feet, but none of them were killed in the fall, We went on, and got on the Ridge of the Mountain.   We followed on the ridge of the Mountain & went over several high knobs on it, where the Wind had blown down the most of the timber on them.   We found a small spring of water, before we came to the highest part of the Mountain; Where we halted & drank some portable soup, We proceeded on, still on the top of the Mountain which was covered with Spruce Trees, & some small Spots of Snow on it, & high clifts of rocks.   This mountain is about ten Miles, from the foot of it, to the top,—   & the most part of the way very steep.—

We proceeded on our way on the top of this mountain, untill after dark, in hopes of finding water, but was not fortunate enough to find any.   We encamped on the top ridge of the Mountain, where we found plenty of Snow, which from appearance had lain there during the whole Year; we melted Snow to drink & make some portable Soup, which was given to all the party & they all retired to rest seemingly content.—   We came about 10 Miles this day.—

1. Engelmann spruce, *Picea engelmannii* Parry.

2. Now known locally as Whitehouse Pond, it is on U.S. Highway 12, a short distance west of Powell Ranger Station, Idaho County, Idaho.

3. They went down the Lochsa River, parallel to U.S. Highway 12, and then north along Wendover Ridge back up to the Lolo Trail on the heights.

4. In Idaho County, on the Lolo Trail, near Forest Road 500.

Monday 16th Sept. 1805. when we awoke this morning to our great Surprise we were covred with Snow which had fallen about 2 Inches the latter part of last night, and continues a verry cold Snow Storm. Capt. Clark Shot at a deer but did not kill it. we mended up our mockasons. Some of the men without Socks raped rags on their feet, and loaded up our horses and Set out without any thing to eat, and proceeded on. could hardly See the old trail for the Snow. kept on the ridge of the mountain Several high knobs to pass over but had more down hill than up. about one oClock finding no water we halted and melted Snow and made a little more Soup, and let our horses graze 1 hour & a half. then proceeded on the Snow is fell So fast that it is now in common 5 or 6 Inches deep. Some places is considerable of old Snow on the moutn. towards evening we descended the mountain down in a lonesome cove¹ on a creek² where we Camped in a thicket of Spruce pine & bolsom fir timber. all being tired & hungry, obledged us to kill another colt and eat the half of it this evening. it has quit Snowing this evening, but continues chilley and cold. Came about 15³ miles to day over a rockey rough road. Some places bare on the top high places of rocks &c.

Monday Septemr 16th We were all surprized when we awoke this morning; to find ourselves covered with Snow, which was 2 Inches deep & had fallen in the latter part of last night & it still continuing to Snow. Captain Clark went out with his Gun & shot a deer on the Mountain but did not get it.— The Snow storm continued and the Men were employed in mending up their Moccasins. some of our party are without Socks, and are forced to wrap Rags round their feet to keep out the cold. We loaded up our Horses, & set out not having anything for to eat, We proceeded on our way, but had great difficulty to follow the Indian trail on account of the Snow that had fell, we still continued on our Journey, along the ridge of the Mountain; and we had several of the Nobs of the Mountain to pass over, but all the way on a descent, about 1 o'Clock P. M we finding no Water we halted, & melted some Snow & made some portable Soup for our party, and turned out our horses to Graze about One hour & a half   The Snow fell so fast that it is now from 5 to 6 inches deep & where old the Snow remained it was considerably deeper, towards evening, we descended the mountain; down into a lonesome looking Cove on to a Creek, where we encamped in a thicket of spruce Pine timber.   The party were all much fataigued & hungry, our officers had a Colt killed and the party eat the half of it this evening.   In the evening it quitted snowing, but the wind was very chilly & Cold, We came about 15 Miles this day & passed over a rough & rockey road, & on the tops of rocks which were quite bare.—

1. Another designation unique to Whitehouse.

2. Near the rock mounds called Indian Post Office (which none of the journalists mentions), perhaps on Moon Creek, Idaho County, Idaho.

3. The words "about 15" appear to have been squeezed into a blank space and perhaps written by another person.

Tuesday 17th Sept. 1805. cloudy and cold.   we went out to hunt our horses, but found them much Scatered.   the mare which owned the colt, which we killed, went back & led 4 more horses back to where we took dinner yesterday.   the most of the other horses found Scatd. on the mountain, but we did not find them all untill 12 oClock at which time we Set out and proceeded on.   the Snow lay heavy on the timber.   passed along a rough road up and down the Mountains   descended down a Steep part of the moutn.   the afternoon clear & warm.   the Snow melted So that the water Stood in the trail over our mockasons in Some places.   verry Slippery bad travvelling for our horses.   we assended verry high mountains verry rockey. Some bald places on the top of the mountn.   high rocks Standing up, & high precepices &c.   these motn. mostly covred with Spruce pine & bolsom fer timber.   crossed Several creeks or Spring runs in the Course of the day Came about [*blank*] miles this day, and Camped[1] at a Small branch on the mountain near a round deep Sinque hole full of water.   we being hungry obledged us to kill the other Sucking colt to eat.   one of the hunters chased a bear in a mountn. but killed nothing. we expect that their is game near a head. we hear wolves howl & Saw Some deer Sign &c.

Tuesday Septemr 17th   We had a cold Cloudy morning, the Men were sent out to hunt our horses, they found them, but they were much scattered, The Mare whose colt we had kill'd Yesterday, went back to where we halted Yesterday, to refresh ourselves, (or eat portable Soup) and took 4 of our horses with her, the other of our horses were found scattered on the Mountain & the whole of them were not found 'till 12 oClock A. M.   We then set out, and proceeded on our Journey, the Snow laying heavy on the trees.   We passed along a rough path, which was up & down the Mountain; & descended a steep part of the same, In the afternoon the weather cleared away, & then it became clear & warm, the Snow melted fast, & the water stood in the trail over our Moccasins, & in some places it was very Slippy, the travelling was very bad for ourselves & horses, We ascended some very high mountains, & very rockey paths & many bare places on the Mountains & high Rocks Standing upright on them.—

These mountains were chiefly covered with Spruce pine, & balsam fir timber.   In the course of this day we crossed several Creek & Spring runs, lying in the hollows of the Mountains.   We came about 16 Miles this day, & encamped at a small branch on a Mountain; near a Round deep Sink hole which was full of water.   The party being all exceeding hungry we were obliged to kill a sucking Colt to subsist on.   One of our hunters went out hunting.   He chased a bear in a Mountain; but did not get a chance to kill it.   The Wolves howled very much in the Night, & we saw some signs of deer, so that we expect that their is game to be had a head of where we are encamped.—

1. Just east of Indian Grave Peak, Idaho County, Idaho.

Wednesday 18th Sept. 1805.   a clear pleasant morning   Capt. Clark and Six hunters[1] Set out at Sunrise to go on a head to try to kill Some game if possable.   we got up all our horses except one which we expect is lost.   one man[2] Sent back Some distance to hunt him.   we Set out about 7 oClock and proceeded on a ridge of the mountains Some distance, then went up and down rough rockey mountains as usal.   but verry little water.   about

3 oClock P. m. we halted on a ridge of the mountn. to let our horses feed a little, and melt a little Snow as we found no water to make a little Port. Soup as we have nothing else to eat. the day moderate the Snow melts a little. the mountains appear a head as fer as we can See. they continue much further than we expected. we proceeded on down a verry Steep part of the mount. then up on the side of another before we found any water, and Campd[3] at dark on the Side of the motn. where we found a Spring by going down a Steep hill where it was dangerous to take our horses to water. we Suped on a little portable Soup and lay down on this Sideling mount. Came 14 miles day

Wednesday Septemr 18th   This morning clear pleasant weather, Captain Clark & Six of our best hunters, set out at sunrise to go on a head; to try & kill some Game if possible, We got up all our horses excepting one, which we expect we have lost, One of the party was sent back to hunt him.   We then set out & proceeded on our Journey, about 7 oClock A. M. we passed on a ridge of mountains, some distance, then ascended & descended rough rockey Mountains as usual, & found but very little Water.   About 3 o'Clock P. M. we halted on a ridge of the Mountains to let our horses feed, and to melt some Snow to make a little portable Soup, having nothing else to eat. The weather moderated, & the snow melted a little.   The Mountains appear a head of us as far as we can see & continue much further than we expected.—

We proceeded on down a very steep part of the Mountain, then ascended the side of another mountain; where we found water.   We encamped on the side of this mountain at dark, & found a spring, which was down a steep hill, which was so dangerous to descend, that we did not take our horses to it for water.   We supped on a little portable Soup, & lay down on a Sideling mountain.   We came about 14 Miles this day.—

1. Including Reubin Field and Shields.
2. Willard.
3. About three miles west of Bald Mountain, Idaho County, Idaho.

Thursday 19th Sept. 1805.   a clear pleasant morning.   we Set out as usal and assended up to the top of Sd. mout. and discovered a plain[1] in a valley about 20 miles from us where we expect is the Columbian River which puts us in good Spirits again. we descended down the mountn. which was verry Steep descent, for about three miles. then assended another as bad as any we have ever been up before. it made the Sweat run off of our horses & ourselves. on the top the ground was froze a little and the ground mostly covred with Snow. the Spruce pine & bolsom timber continues on these motn. as usal. Some places thick bushes. we descd. the mot. down in a narrow valley where we found a run of water and halted to bate our horses and to drink a little portable Soup. one of the men killed a fessent. their is not any kind of game or Sign of any to be Seen in these mout. Scarsely any birds itself. we delayed about 2 hours and proceeded on descended the mountain about 4 miles came to a creek[2] running about East. we followed up the creek. a bad peace of the road, Some places along Side of the mountn. which is high & Steep on each Side of the creek. one of our horses[3] fell backward and roled about 100 feet down where it was nearly Steep and a Solid rock & dashed against the rock in the creek, with a load of Ammunition. but the powder being in canisters did not git damaged nor the horse killed, but hurt. we proceeded on. Came about 17 miles this day and Camped[4] at a run in Sd. mount., our course this day was generally west. the timber continues as usal. we Suped a little portable Soup. the most of the party is weak and feeble Suffering with hunger. our horses feet are gitting Sore and fall away in these mountains, but we are in hopes to git out of them Soon.

Thursday Septemr 19th   A clear pleasant morning, we set out early, & ascended the top of the Mountain on the side of which we lay last night, We discovered from the Top of this mountain; a plain which lay in a Valley, which we suppose to lay about 20 Miles from us, We expect this plain is where the Columbia River is, this revived the drooping spirits of our party.   We descended down this Mountain, which we found dangerous for about 3 Miles, We then ascended another Mountain; which was as bad to ascend as any Mountain we had yet seen, this was very fataigueing to ourselves & horses, the ground was covered with Snow & froze, The Pine & Spruce, balsam Fir timber on the Top of these Mountains, & in some places thick bushes.— We descended this Mountain & came down into a narrow Valley, where we found a run of water. We halted at that place to rest our horses & to eat some portable soup. One of our Men here killed a Pheasant, There was no kind of Game to be seen in these Mountains, & scarcely any Birds. We delayed about 2 hours— & proceeded on, & descended a mountain about four Miles, and arrived at a Creek, whose course run east, we pursued our way up the Creek on a bad piece of Road, some places running along close under the Mountain; which is high & steep on both sides of the Creek, One of our horses fell backwards, & rolled about 100 feet down a steep solid Rock, and dashed against a Rock, in the Creek with his load; which was Ammunition; The Powder, being in leaden Cannisters, was not damaged, nor the horse killed, but much hurt.— We proceeded on, and encamped at a run of Water in the said Mountain; In the evening, our party had a little portable Soup made to subsist on. They all are very weak & feeble & suffer much for want of Provisions, Our horses feet are very much worn, & they have fallen away very much, since we came into the Mountains.

The Men still seem contented; & flatter themselves of soon getting out of the Mountains. Our course during this day, has been chiefly a West course & we came about 17 Miles—

1. The open prairies in Lewis and Idaho counties, Idaho, northwest of Grangeville, including Camas and Nez Perce prairies, observed by Clark on September 18.

2. Hungery Creek, Idaho County; the name was bestowed by Clark on September 18, "as at that place we had nothing to eate."

3. Frazer's horse, fortunately without Frazer.

4. On Hungery Creek, Idaho County.

Friday 20th Sept. 1805. a cold frosty morning. we eat a fiew peas[1] & a little greece which was the verry last kind of eatables of any kind we had except a little portable Soup. we got up our horses except one which detained us untill about 8 oClock before we found him. we then load up our horses and Set out. proceeded on up the creek a Short distance and found a line which Capt. Clark had left with the meat of a horse which they found and killed as they had killed nothing after they left us only three prarie hens or Phesants. we took the horse meat and put it on our horses and proceeded on a Short distance further. then left the creek and went over a mountain S. W. then followed down a ridge, came to a Spring run and halted and dined Sumptiously on our horse meat. one horse Strayed from us which had on him a pear of portmantaus which had in it Some marchandize and Capt. Lewis winter cloaths &c. 2 men Sent back to the creek to hunt him. we proceeded on up and down Several hills and followed a ridge where the timber was fell So thick across the trail that we could hardly git along. our horses got Stung by the yellow wasps.[2] we did not find any water to Camp untill after dark, and then Camped on a ridge[3] found a little water in a deep gulley a Short distance from us. the different kinds of pine continues as usal. considerable of Strait handsome timber on these ridges, which resembles white ceeder but is called Arbervity.[4] no other kind except the pine & bolsom fer, all of which grows verry tall and Strait. the mountains not So high as back but verry broken. Came about 14 miles this day. the plains appear Some distance off yet. it is twice as far as we expected where we first discovred it from a high mountain.—

Friday Septemr 20th This morning was cold, with frost, we did not set out, 'till after we had eat breakfast, which consisted of a few pease & bears Oil, which was the last kind of eatables, that we had with us (excepting a little Portable Soup) we loaded all our horses, but one which had strayed off, which detain'd us untill 8 o'Clock at which time we proceeded on our Journey.— we went up the Creek we had been at last evening a short distance, & found a line from Captain Clark, with the flesh of a horse which the party with him had found & killed. they informed us, that he nor his party had not killed any <thing> kind of game since they left us, excepting 3 Pheasants, We put the horse meat on our Horses, and proceeded a short distance further up the Creek, we then left the Creek, and went over a Mountain a South west course, & went down a ridge, and came to a Spring where we halted, & dined sumptuously on our horse meat.— One of our horses during the time that we were at dinner, strayed away from us; he was loaded with two portmanteaus, which had in them some Merchandise & Captain Lewis's winter Cloathes.— Captain Lewis sent 2 of the Men back to the Creek to look after him, and we continued on our Journey, We ascended & descended several hills, and passed along a ridge of mountains, where the timber had fell so thick across the trail, that it was with great difficulty that we got our horses along, & the Yellow wasps was very troublesome to them, there being a great abundance of them at that place. We did not find any Water to encamp at, 'till after it was dark, and it lay in a gully, a short distance from the Ridge of mountains that we encamped at. We found growing on these Ridges, different kinds of Pine timber, and some tall White Cedar Trees. The Mountains which we crossed this day, are not so high as those Mountains, we crossed some distance back; but are very broken.— We came about 14 Miles this day & the plains appear to lay some considerable distance from us still, & We expect it is double the distance that we supposed it to be, when we first saw them from the high Mountain.—

1. Ordway mentions "Indian peas," which may be the hog peanut brought from the Missouri River in North Dakota.

2. Perhaps the western yellow jacket, *Vespula pensylvanica.*

3. Between Dollar and Sixbit creeks, Idaho County.

4. That is, *arborvitae,* another name for western redcedar.

Saturday 21st Sept. 1805. a clear pleasant morning. we went out eirly to hunt up our horses, but they were much Scatered. we did not find them all untill about 10 oClock at which time we Set out and proceeded on crossed a creek[1] & went on a west course over a hilley rough trail. on Some of the ridges the timber has been killed by fire and fell across the trail So that we had Some difficulty to git a long the trail. in the after part of the day we descended down a hill & came to the forks of a creek[2] where it is large we went down it a Short distance and Camped[3] at a good place for feed near the creek. had Come 11 miles this day. Capt. Lewis killed a wolf. Some of the men killed a duck and three Phesants. we caught Some craw fish[4] in the creek, and eat them.

Saturday Septemr 21st A Clear pleasant morning, some of our party were sent out to collect our horses. they found them after much difficulty, which detained us 'till about 10 o'Clock A. M. at which time we set out, & continued on our Journey. We crossed a Creek, and went on a West course over a hilly rough trail, on a ridge of mountains The timber on this trail, had been killed by fire, and fell across the path so that we had great difficulty to get along it. In the afternoon we descended down a hill, & came to the forks of a creek, where the Creek got to be large.— We went down the Creek a short distance, & encamped at a flatt piece of land which lay along the same Creek, where we found plenty of fine Grass for our horses. Captain Lewis went out to hunt from this place, and took some of our party with him. They killed a Wolf, a duck & 3 Pheasants, & some of the party catched some craw fish in the Creek.— We came about 11 Miles this day.—

1. Either Eldorado Creek or Dollar Creek, Idaho County, Idaho.

2. Lolo Creek, Idaho County, which the captains called Collins Creek after John Collins of the party.

3. On Lolo Creek, Clearwater County, Idaho; the creek at this point serves as the Clearwater–Idaho county line.

4. Some variety of crayfish, *Astacus* sp.

Sunday 22nd Sept. 1805. a clear pleasant morning. a white frost. we were detained Some time a hunting our horses. about nine oClock we found all the horses and Set out ascended a mountain and proceeded on Came on a Smoth level clear place & a run of water. met R. Fields who Capt. Clark Sent back to meet us with Some Sammon and other kinds of food which they had purcd. from Some Indians which they found Encamped about 8 miles from this. we halted and divided out the food and eat it found it verry good. we delayed about one hour & a half then proceeded on. the 2 men who had been back for the lost horse Soon overtook us. they had found the horse & port mauntaus, and took on the horse with the one they took with them untill last night then they lost boath of the horses. they expect that they were Stole by Some of the natives. So they brought the portmantaus &c. on their backs. we proceeded on over a mountain and down in a handsome Smoth valley.[1] ariv at an Indian village[2] in a delightful plain. large pitch pine around it. these Savages was verry glad to See us the men women & children ran meeting us & Seemed rejoiced to See us. we Camped[3] near village at a Small branch. the natives gave us Such food as they had to eat, consisting of roots of different kinds which was Sweet and good also red & black haws[4] &c. the principal roots[5] which they made use off for food are pleanty. this praries are covred with them they are much like potatoes when cooked, and they have a curious way of cooking them. th[e]y have places made in form of a Small coal pit, & they heat Stone in the pit. then put Straw over the Stone, then water to raise a Steem. then they put on large loves of the pounded potatoes, and 8 or 10 bushels of potatoes on at once then cover them with wet Straw and Earth. in that way they Sweet them untill they are cooked, and when they take them out they pound Some of them up fine and make them in loaves and cakes. they dry the cakes and String them on Strings, in Such a way that they would keep a year & handy to carry, any journey. Capt. Clark arived here this evening, and informed us that he had been on a branch of the Columbian River[6] where it was navigable for canoes, and only about 8 & half miles from this place & a good road. the hunters[7] Stayed at the River to hunt. one of them had killed 2 Deer at the River. the natives gave us Some excelent fat Sammon to eat with the root or potatoe bread

Sunday Septemr 22nd This morning clear & pleasant, with a small white frost. We were detained by the party, that went out to hunt our horses till about 9 o'Clock A. M. when we set out again on our Journey. we ascended a mountain, & went on some distance, & came to a smooth level clear place, where there was a clear run of water—. At this run, we were met with by Robert Fields, (one of the party that had went with Captain Clark,) and who Captain Clark had sent back to meet our party; this Man brought with him some Salmon, & other kinds of food, which they had purchased from some Indians, which they had found encamped about 8 Miles from this place.— Captain Clarke had dispatched this Man, shortly after their arrival at this Indian Camp, with what Provisions he could carry on his horse, knowing, what great necessity must have attended us, for want of food, & he was a welcome Messenger.— We halted, & the Provisions were divided out among the party. We delayed about an hour & a half, and then proceeded on our Journey. the two Men that had went back for to hunt for the Horse that had strayed from us the 20th instant; overtook us; they had found the horse that they had went after, on the Mountain, which we had passed, and brought him along with them & also the horse that they had took with them some distance, and mentioned that last night, they had lost both of those horses, & they said that they expected that they were stole by the Natives.— These Men brought the Portmanteus on their backs, to where they overtook us. We proceeded on, and crossed a Mountain; & descended down into a handsome smooth Valley; where we arrived at an Indian Village; situated on a most delightfull plain, where was large Pitch pine Trees growing all around it— The Indians belonging to this Village, appeared very glad to see us; the Men, Women & Children ran out to meet us; & seemed rejoiced at our coming. We encamped near this Village, at a small branch, where the Indians belonging to this Village, brought us such food, as they had, which consisted of Roots of different kinds, which had a sweet taste & was good also Red & black haws & some Salmon. The principal food that those Indians made us of for food, and which grow in great plenty in the Priaries are roots of an oval form these Roots are about the size of the middle Sized Potatoes, & when boiled have both in resemblance & taste of them. The Natives have a curious method of preparing these Roots for food,— which is in the following manner.— They dig holes in the earth much in form of what we dig a coal pit. They then heat a quantity of large stones, which they place in this pit, & cover them with Straw. They then throw water on those Stones, & raise a great Steam, and then place on the Straw large loaves made out of this root which they pounded up as fine as flour to make the loaves with, which they cover with wet Straw & earth, in this way they sweat this Root, untill it is perfectly fit for eating, they then take it out & pound it again, & make it up in loaves & Cakes,— and dry them in the Sun; and string them, they then will keep for a long time; & is used by them on their long Journies.— Captain Clarke arrived here in the Evening; he informed us that he had been on a branch of the Columbia River, and where it was navigable for Canoes, & only about 1½ Miles from this place, & a good Road leading to it. The hunters staid at the River that were with Captain Clark to hunt,— & Captain Clark mentioned that one of them had killed 2 Deer, which he found near to the River.— The Natives gave us at our Camp, some Excellent Salmon, & plenty of those Roots which I have before described, & behaved very friendly to our party.— These Indians <are> were a part of the Polot pello or Flat head Nation.—

1. Weippe Prairie, Clearwater County, Idaho.

2. Nez Perces, whom Clark's party had met on September 20.

3. On Jim Ford Creek, on Weippe Prairie, about three miles southeast of Weippe, Clearwater County.

4. Only Whitehouse noted two varieties of hawthorns. The red is Columbia hawthorn, *Crataegus columbiana* How., the black is black hawthorn, *C. douglassii* Lindl. Lewis noticed the latter on the return trip, April 12, 1806.

5. The most important was camas, *Camassia quamash* (Pursh) Greene.

6. Clark had been to the Clearwater River, the Kooskooskee to the party, at a point about a mile above Orofino, Clearwater County.

7. Including Shields.

Monday 23rd Sept. 1805. a clear pleasant morning. we purchased considerable quantity of Sammon and root or potatoe bread from the natives. these natives are now at war with Some other nation to the west, and the most of the warries, are mostly gone to war, and the women are engaged laying up food for the winter as they tell us that they intend going over to the Missourie in the Spring after the buffaloe &c. Some of the natives have copper kittles, and beeds a fiew knives &c. which they tell us that they got from the traders to the west, which must have Come from the western ocean. they are verry fond of our marchandize. the large blue beeds they are the fondest of but are glad to git anything we have. a Small peace of red cloath, as wide as a mans hand they gave as much for as they would for double the value in any other article. our officers gave the chiefs of this village a flag & one to the chief[1] of the next village about 2 miles further on our road, which they hoisted. these natives live well are verry kind and well dressed in mountain Sheep & deer & Elk Skins well dressed. they have buffaloe robes but are verry choice of them. in the afternoon we got up our horses, all except one which we could not find. we loaded up our horses, left one man who had not found his horse, and went down to the next village about 2 miles and Camped.[2] bought Some more Sammon and Some dressed Elk Skins &c. we had a Shower of rain attended with Thunder this evening. these Savages at this village live the Same as those at the other village. they are numerous and talk loud & confused. they live much comfort in their villages. Several lodges all join. the most of them have leather lodges, and are makeing flag[3] lodges &c.

Monday Septemr 23rd   This morning we had clear pleasant weather. Our officers purchased from the Natives a quantity of Salmon & root or potatoe bread, for which they gave them some small articles of Merchandise.

The Natives informed us, that they were at present engaged in a Warr, with a Nation of Indians who lived to the West of them, and that most of their Warriors were gone out to fight that Nation; The Indian women at this Village, are mostly employed in laying in Provisions for the Winter, and they informed us, that they intend going across the Mountains in the next Spring, over to the Mesouri River; in Order to hunt buffalo. We found among the Natives which are with us, Copper kettles, Beads & a few knives; which they informed us they got from the Traders, living to the Westwards of their Village, and which we suppose came from the Western Ocean. They appeared to be very fond of our Merchandise, & in particular of some large Blue beads, which our officers had. They were likewise fond of Red Cloth. They gave our Officers for a Small piece of that article as broad as ones hand, double the quantity of Salmon & bread, that they would for any article of the same Value, (excepting the large blue beads) however as Merchandise of all sorts are scarce among them, they appeared to be fond of every article that we had of Merchandise among us. Our officers gave the Chiefs of this Village a Flag; they also gave a Flag to a Chief who resided at a Village 2 Miles from this Village on our Road.— They hoisted the flag at the Chiefs lodge, & seemed very much pleased at the present their Chiefs had received.— These Indians live very well. They dress themselves with Mountain sheep, (Ibex) deer & Elk skins, which they dress & make very pliable. They have Buffalo Robes among them, but don't wish to part with any of them.—

These Indians behaved very friendly to us, & gave both our officers & men many small presents.— In the afternoon we hunted up our horses, & found them all but two, & loaded them. We left one of our Men behind, in order to hunt for the horses which was lost. We proceeded on to another Indian Village, which lay on the same Creek, & about 2 Miles distant, and Encamped. Our officers here purchased from the Indians belonging to this Village, Some Salmon & skins of various kinds which were dressed. In the Evening we had a Shower of Rain attended with thunder. The Indians at this Village, live in the same manner as those at the other Village which we left this day, & have Salmon & root bread in great plenty.— The Indians at this Village are far more numerous than those at the first Village that we came to, after crossing the Mountains. They talk very loud, & their language seems confused. This Village is built more compact than the last

Village that we left; several of their lodges join each other, the most of which, are made out of dressed leather. they have also lodges made out of Flags & are preparing to build several others of the same kind.

1. Probably Twisted Hair (Walamottinin); see Clark's entries for September 21.
2. About a mile southwest of Weippe, Clearwater County, Idaho.
3. Probably common cat-tail, *Typha latifolia* L.

Tuesday 24th Sept. 1805. a clear pleasant morning. we went out eairly a hunting our horses, which were Scatered all over the plain. Saw a vast nomber of horses which belong to the natives, the most of which are in good order and good horses in general. Saw a nomber of Squaws digging the wild potatoes in the plains. the Soil verry rich and lays handsom for culti-vation. we loaded up our horses. one man[1] Sent back in the mountains to look for the 2 horses which was lost about 8 oClock we Set out and proceeded on. the day warm. had a fine road mostly plain, Some Scater-ing large pitch pine, but little water. Several of the men Sick, by eating hearty of the Sweet food and Sammon. towards evening we came on the branch or fork of Columbian River,[2] and followed down it Some distance, and went on a Small prarie Island and Camped.[3] a hard rapid at the foot of this Island which the natives tell us is the last bad rapid in this fork of River the hunters joined us with 4 Deer & 2 Sammon which they had killed. Sev-eral of the natives followed after us and Camped with us. high hills each Side of the River thinly covred with pine but not large enofe for canoes, but we expect to find Some near, So that we may leave our horses in the care of a chief and go down by water to the ocean.—

Tuesday Septemr 24th A Clear pleasant Morning, & a number of our party were sent out in order to hunt our horses, which were scattered all over the plain. the party saw vast numbers of horses, which belonged to the Natives, some of which were very elegant, most of these horses were in very good order. They also saw numbers of Indian women, who were employed in digging the bread Root, or wild potatoes in the plain, They found the Soil extreamly Rich, & the Land lay handsomely for Cultivation.—

The party that were sent out to collect our horses returned, they had found them all but one. We loaded them, & sent back one of our party to the Mountains in order to find the 2 horses that was lost. About 8 o'Clock A. M we proceeded on our Journey, the day grew warm & we found the Road extreamly good it being mostly a plain with some large scattering pitch pine Trees, growing on them; & but little water to be found, in them,— Several of our party was taken sick on the Road, which was occasion'd by eating too hearty of the bread & Salmon that we got from the Indians. Towards evening we arrived at <the> another fork of Columbia River, and followed down it some distance, and went on a small Island of Priari land and encamped. At the foot of this Island lay a bad rapid, which the Natives informed us, is the last bad rapid in this fork of Columbia River. The hunters had went a head of us this day, & they all join'd us at this place, they had killed 4 deer & 2 Salmon which they brought to us.— Several of the Natives followed us from the last Village, and came & encamped with us.—

The land on both sides of this fork is hilly, and is thinly covered with Pine Trees, but none of them large enough to make Canoes, but we all expect lower down the fork a short distance that we may find some to answer that purpose. Our Officers concluded to leave our horses in the care of some of the Indian Chiefs, & to ascend the River to the Mouth of the Columbia River, provided we can procure timber to make Canoes of.—

1. Colter, according to Clark.
2. Clearwater River, Clearwater County, Idaho.
3. On China Island, about a mile above Orofino, Clearwater County.

Wednesday 25th Sept. 1805. a fine morning. three men out a hunting. Capt. Clark went with a chief down the River to look for timber which would answer for to make cannoes. the natives have Several Small cannoes in the River one at th[is] place. this River is about Sixty yards wide and gener[ally] deep. Some clifts of rocks along the Shores. the nativ[es] have a fishery fixed in the River little above our Camp, in which they catch large quantity of Sammon. they went withe the canoes and took in Several today. they gig a great many also towards evening Capt. Clark returned had been down about 4 miles at a fork[1] which came in on the East Side. he informs us that their is Some timber at the forks but not verry large & knotty.

So we conclude to move down tomorrow. the natives drive a nomber of their horses from the villages to this place. the man who Stayed at the village for his horse arived here this evening. had got his horse by hireing Indians to git him.

Wednesday Septemr. 25th   A fine morning, Three of our Men went out a hunting. Captain Clark went down the River with an Indian chief to look out for timber fitting to make Canoes of, The Natives had several small Canoes in this fork of the River, & one of them lay at the place where we were encamp'd. The fork of Columbia River which we are at is about 60 Yards wide, and generally very deep, and has some Clifts of rocks along its shores.— The Natives had a fishery fixed on this fork of the River, a small distance above our Camp, in which they catch quantities of Salmon in the fishing season   they went to it with their Canoes, and took out a number of Salmon on this day.— They also procure a number of them which they kill with a Gig,— Towards evening Captain Clark returned, he had been down the fork about 4 Miles, to where <a> another small fork came in to the fork, which we are on, on the East side of it— he mention'd that he had seen some timber at the place where these two forks <made> met but that it was not very large & full of knots. Our officers concluded to move down to that place tomorrow. The Natives drove during this day, a number of their horses to this place. The Man who staid behind to hunt the horse, that was lost, arrived here this Evening; <they> he had the horse with him, which was found by some of the Indians that <they> he had hired at the Village to hunt him

1. North Fork Clearwater River, their Chopunnish River, after the captains' name for the Nez Perces.

Thursday 26th Sept. 1805.   clear and pleasant. we got up our horses and Set out about 8 oClock and proceeded on down the River   crossed a creek[1] which came in on the East Side. then crossed the River at a Shole place, but wide   the water to the horses belleys. proceeded on down the South Side of the River and Camped[2] opposite the fork which came in on the N. Side. we formed our Camp in a narrow plain on the bank of the River.

made a pen of pine bushes around the officers lodge, to put all our baggage in. Some of the natives followed us with droves of horses. Some came down the N. fork whoe had been up Some distance a fishing. had with them a Small raft which they came on with all their baggage Sammon &c. they ran fast on a Shole place about the middle of the River opposite our Camp, and came out to See us. Some Indians came down from our last nights Camp in a canoe with Sammon &c. we went about helving our axes and git in readiness to begin the Canoes. Several of the men Sick with the relax, caused by a Suddin change of diet and water as well as the Climate Changed a little also.

Thursday Septemr 26th We had a clear pleasant morning, the party went out & brought up our horses, and we set out on our Journey about 8 oClock A. M. and proceeded on down the fork of the River, and crossed a Creek, which came into the fork on the East side, and then crossed the fork at a Shoal place which was wide, where the Water was up to our horses Bellies. We proceeded on down the South side of the fork of the River, & encamped opposite to where <a> another fork of the River came in on the North side. We formed our Camp in a narrow plain, on the bank of the Main fork, and made a Pen of Pine bushes round the Officers lodge, to put the baggage in. The Natives still continued to follow us, with droves of horses. Some of the natives also came down the North fork, who had been up some distance a fishing; and had with them a small Canoe with their Baggage, Salmon &ca. they run fast with their craft on a shoal place, in the middle of the River opposite to our encampment. They came to the Shore in Order to see us, some of the Indians also came down with a Canoe from the place where we had encamped last night; they brought with them some Salmon, Root bread &ca. The party employed themselves in making helves for their Axes, and to prepare ev'ry thing necessary for making Canoes. Several of the Men were unwell with <laxes> the dysentry, occasioned by a sudden change of diet, & water, change of Climate &ca.

1. Orofino Creek, Clearwater County, Idaho.

2. At the party's "Canoe Camp," about five miles west of Orofino, Clearwater County, Idaho, on the south bank of the Clearwater River and opposite the mouth of the North Fork Clearwater River. They remained here until October 7.

Friday 27th Sept. 1805. a fair morning. the party divided in five parties and went at falling five pitch pine trees for canoes, all near the Camp. in the afternoon the man who went back to the mountains after the lost horses joined us had found one of the horses, & had killed a large Deer, which he brought to Camp with him.—

Friday Septemr. 27th A fine pleasant morning, Some of our party that were well went out in five parties, in Order to cut down five pitch pine Trees for to make Canoes; which they found near to our Camp, In the afternoon the Man who went back to the Mountains after the horses that we lost, joined us, he had found one of the horses & had killed a large Deer which he brought to our Camp with him

Saturday 28th Sept. 1805. a fair morning. 2 men went out to hunt. all that were able went at work makeing the canoes & oars. the natives visit us. they catch a fiew fresh Sammon which we purchase from them. we fixed Some gigs on poles in order to gig Some ourselves. Several of the party are unwell and all takeing medicine

Saturday Septemr 28th This morning we had clear pleasant weather, 2 of our party set out to hunt, & the remainder that were well, were employed in making the Canoes & Oars. The Natives visited us, & brought some Salmon with them, which we purchased.— We fixed some Gigs on poles, in order to gig some Salmon Ourselves, Several of our Men that were sick took Medicine, in order to recover their healths & <are> were made as Comfortable as possible.—

Sunday 29th Sept. 1805. a fair morning. all hands who were able to work are employed at the Canoes. only two who went out to hunt. about noon the hunters[1] Came to Camp with three Deer, which they had killed. the natives caught a nomber of Sammon which they Sold to us.

Sunday Septemr 29th A pleasant Morning, all our Men that were able to work, were employed at making the Canoes, Two of our hunters were sent

335

out hunting, About noon the hunters returned to our Camp, with 3 Deer which they had killed.   The Natives also brought to us, a number of Salmon, which we purchased of them for some trifling Articles.—

1. Drouillard killed two, Collins or Colter one, reports Clark.

Monday 30th Sept. 1805.   two[1] hunters Stayed out last night.   a fair morning.   the Sick men are gitting Some better.   we continued our work at the canoes as usal.   our constant hunter out to day.   the party in general are So weak and feeble that we git along Slow with the canoes.   our hunters returned towards evening   one of them had killed a Deer & a pheasant.

Monday Septemr 30th   This morning we had pleasant weather, The hunters that went out hunting the 28th instant had not as yet returned, and the Men that were sick belonging to our party are recovering their healths. The party employed at making the Canoes, are so weak & feeble that— they do but little work in the course of the day.—   Towards evening the hunters returned, & brought in with them a Deer, & a Pheasant that they had killed.—

1. The word "two" is written over "one."

Tuesday 1st October 1805.   a fair morning   we continued working at the canoes   built fires on Several of the canoes to burn them out   found that they burned verry well.   the hunters killed nothing this day.

Tuesday October 1st   A fine clear morning, & the party continued working on the Canoes; they made fires on the Canoes to burn them out, & found they burnt very well.   The hunters went out this day, & returned towards evening without having killed any Game.—

Wednesday 2nd October 1805.   a fair morning.   two men[1] Sent up to the villages with Six of our horses and Some marchandize to trade for Sammon and their kind of bread &c.   we continued our work as usal at the canoes. Some hunters out in the hills a hunting.   towards evening the hunters returned   had killed nothing but one prarie wolf, which we eat.   the party are So weak working without any kind of meat, that we concluded to kill a horse and accordingly we did kill a horse which was in tollarable order, and we eat the meat with good Stomacks as iver we did fat beef in the States.— we bought a fiew fresh Sammon & Some root bread from the natives &c.—

Wednesday October 2nd   A pleasant morning, Two of our Men were sent up to the Indian Villages, with six of our horses & some Merchandise to trade with the Indians for Salmon & their root bread.   We continued our work at the Canoes as usual, and some of our hunters were sent out go into the Hills a hunting.   Towards evening those hunters returned & had killed nothing but a Priari wolf, which was eat by our party.—

The party that were at work on the Canoes were so weak for want of meat, that our officers concluded on having a horse killed, which was done & it being in good order, the Men eat the flesh of it with as good a relish as they would have done had it been a Stalled fed beef.—   The Natives came to our camp towards evening, & brought with them some fresh Salmon & Root bread, which we purchased from them.—

1. Frazer and Goodrich, says Clark.

Thursday 3rd Oct. 1805.   a fair morning.   we continued on our work at the Canoes as usal.   Some of them forward &c.

Thursday October 3d   This morning was very pleasant.   The Men employed working on the Canoes went on, with much better spirit than they had done for several days past, being refreshed by the Horse meat that they had eat.—   The Canoes are now in great forwardness, & will be in readiness to receive their loading on board in a few days—   Our Men that had been sick for some time past recovered fast, & we are in hopes that they will be fully recovered by the time we are ready to proceed on down the River—

Friday 4th Oct. 1805.   a fair morning.   two men out a hunting.   we continue at the Canoes   Some of them ready to dress and finish off.   our hunters killed nothing this day.   Some of the men eat a fat dog.—

Friday October 4th   A fair morning, Two of our hunters were sent out a hunting, the party continued working on the Canoes; some of them are ready to be finished off.   Our hunters went out this day & returned without having killed any thing.—   Some of our party killed a fat dog, which they had got from the Indians at the last Village that we passed through.   They roasted & eat it in the Evining—

Saturday 5th Oct. 1805.   a fair cool frosty morning, the two men who had been at the villages trading, returned late last night, with their horses loaded with the root bread and a Small quantity of Sammon, a fiew Elk Skins dressed & otter Skins for caps &c.   we continue on finishing off the canoes.   got up our horses and cropped their fore mane, and branded[1] them with a Sturrup Iron on the near fore Shoulder, So that we may know them again at our return.   a Chief[2] who we Intended leaveing our horses with has engaged to go on with us & leaves the horses in care of his two Sons.   38 in nomber of the horses which we delivered up in their care   towards evening we put two of the canoes which was finished in to the River.   (the distance over the mountn. is estimated to be 160 odd miles from where we left Flatt head River, to this place[)]

Saturday October 5th   This morning was Clear & frosty.—   The two Men who had been at the Villages trading with the Indians returned late last night.   they had their horses loaded with Root bread & a small quantity of Salmon, & a few dressed Elk Skins, also some Otter skins, which we make use of in making Caps &ca.

The Men at work on the Canoes, continued to work on them & finishing them off—   We got up all our horses, and Cropped close off the foretop of each horse, and branded them with a stirrup Iron, on the near fore shoulder, that we may be able to know them on our return.   One of the Indian Chiefs who our officers intend leaving the care of our horses with, intends going on with us, & to leave the horses in the Care of his Two Sons.   We delivered up to this Indian Chief 38 Horses, which he & his Sons took charge of.   Towards evening we put two of the Canoes which our Men had finish'd into the River.   We computed the distance that we came across the Mountains, & estmated it to be 165 Miles from where we left Flatt head River to this place.—

1. Now in the possession of the Oregon Historical Society, Lewis's branding iron bore the inscription "U.S. Capt. M. Lewis."
2. Twisted Hair.

Sunday 6th Oct. 1805. a clear pleasant morning. we continued on with the other canoes, & a carch or hole dug to berry our pack Saddles in. we got poles & oars ready towards evening we got the other Canoes ready to put in the water. Some gig poles prepared &c. a raft Seen floating down the River with Several Indians on it. one of the men killed 2 ducks. berryed the pack Saddles and Some Ammunition &c.—

Sunday October 6th A clear pleasant morning, we continued the party working on the Canoes, and dug a Cashe or hole to bury our pack Saddles in, & made oars & poles for our Canoes. Towards evening, we got the other Canoes ready to put in the Water & prepar'd some Gig poles &ca We saw a raft floating down the River which had several Indians on it. One of our party went out with his Rifle & killed 2 Ducks which he brought to our Camp. We finished digging the Cashe or hole, & deposited our pack saddles & some Ammunition in it.— Our Men that had been sick for some time past, had nearly all got their healths, & are fit to do their duty again We are all in high spirits expecting we shall be able to descend the River tomorrow. This place we named Canoe Camp and lies in Latitude 46° 34′ 56²/₁₀ North Latitude.—

Monday 7th Oct. 1805. a fair morning. we put the other three canoes in to the River and got them in readiness and loaded them. about 3 oClock P. m. we Set out on our way to descend the River.[1] the 2 Indians[2] we came over the mount. with us continues on with us, and a chief & one more Indian[3] who agreed to go down with us has gone by land Some distance down and then Intends comming on board. we proceeded on over a number of bad rapids where the canoes run fast and obledged us to git out in the cold water and hale them off. Some places the water is deep & current gentle

for Some distance, but the Shole rapids are common & rockey.   the River
hills make close to the River on each Side.   Some clifts of rocks, a fiew Scattering pine trees on the hills, but they are mostly barron broken, & covred
over with grass.   Some Small cotton wood along the Shores.   Some of the
rapids which are deep enofe to run clear are So bad that we take water over
the canoes by the waves.   Strike Some large rocks & Slide of without Injury—.   Came 21 miles and Camped[4] on Stard. Side   the officers canoe
leaks So that they changes their Baggag in an other canoe for fear of gitting
the Instruments &c. wet.   the Evening cloudy.   one man taken Sick with
the collick.   we passed Some old Indian Camps this afternoon & a Small
canoe on Shore—

Monday October 7th   This morning we had clear pleasant weather, all
our party that were able were employed in getting the other three new Canoes into the River, which they effected.   they got every thing in readiness
on board of them and got them loaded.   About 3 oClock P. M. we set out
on our way to descend the River, & the 2 Indians of the Snake Nation, that
came to Pilot us across the Mountains, agreed to continue with us.   We also
had a chief & one Indian from the last Town we came through who also
agreed to accompany us.—   These two last Indians, set off down the River
by land to go some distance, & intend to join our party again.   We then
proceeded on our Voyage, and crossed a number of bad rapids, where our
Canoes got fast, & obliged us to get out in the Water (that was cold) and hawl
them off.   we found the Water in some places deep, & the current running
gentle for some distance.   The Rapids were very frequent & Shoal, the bottom of the River rockey, and the hills making close in to the River on both
sides of it.   There is some Clifts of rocks, lying along the Shore & a few
scattering pine trees, growing on some of the hills <but they> which are
mostly broken & covered with grass.   We saw some few cotton wood Trees,
growing on each side of the River along the Shore, We also found, that in
some of the Rapids where we had plenty of water for our Canoes to pass, that
the Waves ran so high that our Canoes took in a great deal of water, & we
struck several Rocks, in passing over them, but the Rapidity of the stream
forced us over them.—

We came about 27 Miles this day, and encamped on the North side of the River.   The Canoe that our Officers went in, leaked so bad, that they were forced to unload it, & put their baggage into another Canoe, for fear of getting their Mathematical Instruments & baggage wet.   We passed this afternoon some old Indian Camps & saw a Canoe lying on the Shore.   The Evening proved cloudy.   One of our party was taken ill, this evening of a Cholic occasioned by being so much in the water.

1. Clearwater River.
2. Old Toby and his son.
3. Twisted Hair and Tetoharsky.
4. On the Clearwater River near Lenore, Nez Perce County, Idaho, opposite Jacks Creek.

Tuesday 8th Oct. 1805.   a fair day.   we dilayed loading &c.   burryed a canister of powder the Northe Side of a broken toped tree.   about 9 oClock we Set out and proceeded on down the River.   Saw Some Indian horses on the Side of the hills   passed over Several bad rapids.   took Some water in the canoes by the waves dashing over the Sides.   the current rapid the most part of the way some places deep.   passed clifts of rocks and bare hills on each Side.   about 12 oClock we Came to Some Indian Camps, on the South Side.   only 4 or 5 lodges of well looking Indians & Squaws.   they had Several Small canoes, and catch considerable quantitys of Sammon.   we purchased Some from them by giving them a fiew green or blue or red beeds, and tin &c.   the day warm.   Some of the men bought 2 dogs from them. they have a great many horses feeding along the Shores and have a nomber of Small canoes.   we proceeded on a Short distance further down came to Some more Indian Camps at the foot of an Isl. & rapids.   we halted a Short time, bought Some more Sammon and Some white roots.   then proceeded on   a Short distance further down 2 chiefs came with us.   as we were descending a rockey rapids at the foot of an Island on which was Some Indian Camps, one of the canoes Struck a rock and wheled round then Struck again and cracked the canoe and was near Spliting hir in too.   <thrung> throwed the Stearsman [1] over board, who with difficulty got to the canoe again, but She soon filled with water, and hang on the rocks in a doleful Situation.

341

Some of the men on board could not Swim, and them that could had no chance for the waves and rocks.   an Indian went in a Small canoe to their assistance.   our little canoe went also and took out Some of the loading, and carried it to Shore.   we unloaded one of the other canoes and went in the rapid and took the loading all out of the canoe which was Stove and got all to Shore below the rapid, and Camped,[2] at dark.   examined found everry thing wet which was in the canoe that was Stove.   Some Small articles lost. a nomber of the natives visit us this evening.   we have come about 18 miles this day before the Sad axident hapened to us

Tuesday October 8th   We had a fair day, We delayed for to load one of our Canoes & burying a Cannister of powder; which we did on the North side of a broken top Tree, About 9 o'Clock A. M. we set out, & proceeded on with our Canoes down the River on our Voyage; we saw a number of the Indians horses feeding on the side of hills, as we passed along, We also passed over several bad rapids, where our Canoes took in Water, occasion'd by the Waves dashing over the sides of them.—

The Current of the River has run rapid the most part of the way this day, & in some places we found the River very deep.   We passed by large Clifts of rocks & naked hills lying on both sides of the River.—   About 12 oClock A. M. we arrived at some Indian Camps, which lay on the South side of the River, in which we saw some well looking Indian Men & Squaws; there was only 5 lodges at this place, and they had several small Canoes, which were tied to the Shore.   These Indians employ themselves in catching of Salmon and catch considerable quantity of them   They were part of the flatt head Nation.—

We stopped with our Canoes some time, & purchased from these Indians some Salmon for which we gave them round Blue & Green beads, & some small pieces of Tin.   some of our party also purchased from those Indians 2 dogs for trifles—   Those Indians had a number of fine horses, which we saw feeding along the Shore.—   The day proved warm.   We proceeded on but a short distance down the River, and came to another Indian camp; This Camp was situated at the lower end of an Island, where lay some rapids.   We halted here for a short time, & purchased some more Salmon and white bread Roots.—

These Indians were also belonging to the flatt head Nation.— We proceeded on and went but a short distance, and took in the Indians that set out this morning by land. we then continued on our Voyage, and as we were descending a rocky rapid at the foot of an Island on which were some Indian camps, One of our Canoes struck a rock, and wheeled round, where she again Struck <a> another rock and Cracked the bottom of it, & was near splitting in two; & threw the Man who was steering her overboard, but he with great difficulty got to her again— This Canoe soon filled with water & hung on the rock in a perilous situation. Some of the Men on board of her, could not swim; & those Men that could, had no chance of saving themselves, the Waves ran so high, and the current was so rapid, that they must have been dashed against Rocks that lay below them a short distance & in all probability must have drownded.— It was very fortunate for those Men, that an Indian who saw their situation from the Island we passed last, came to their assistance with a small Canoe & One of our Canoes went also, & took out some of the loading & landed it safe on the Shore.—

Our officers had one of the other Canoes unloaded and the Men went, and took out the remainder of the loading from on board that Canoes, which had been stove; and got it all on the Shore below the rapid, They experienced much difficulty in unloading the Canoe in the Rapids, the Current being so very Swift & strong. We found the whole of the loading got out of that Canoe, wet & we lost some small Articles of the loading.— Our party were all rejoiced at the fortunate escape that the Men made that were in the Canoe, & think that nothing but the Interference of providence was the occasion. In the Evening a number of the Natives came to Visit us, & behaved with a great deal of friendship to us all, they continued some time with us & took a friendly leave & departed for their Camps. These Indians also belonged to the Flatt-head Nation.— We came about 18 Miles this day before the accident happen'd to the Canoe,— & encamped where we unloaded the Canoes with the baggage.—

1. Perhaps Thompson, who Clark says was "a little hurt."

2. This camp, where they stayed until October 10, is on the north side of the Clearwater, Nez Perce County, Idaho, below the confluence of the Potlatch and Clearwater rivers, a few miles from Spalding.

Wednesday 9th Oct. 1805. a fair morning. we were obledged to delay and prepare or repair the canoe which got Stove last evening, put the loading marchandize &c out to dry. the natives brought us some fresh Sammon. the River hills are high and continue barron on each Side. a fiew Scattering pines along the Shores. but fiew creeks puts in. the natives hang about us, as though they wished to Steal or pilfer Something from us So we had to keep 2 Sentinels to watch the Marchandize &c. we got the canoe repaired and loaded. our officers tryed to purchase a fat horse for us to eat but the Natives did not bring him as they promised. in the evening we purchased a considerable quantity of Sammon, a little bears oil or greese, Some root bread 2 dogs &c. after dark we played the fiddle and danced a little. the natives were pleased to see us. one of their women was taken with the crazey fit by our fire. She Set to Singing Indian and gave all around hir Some roots, and all She offered had to take from hir. one of our men refused to take them from hir. She then was angry and hove them in the fire, and took a Sharp flint from hir husband and cut hir arms in Sundry places So that the blood gushed out. She wiped up the blood and eat it. then tore off Some beeds and peaces of copper &c which hung about hir and gave out to them that were round hir a little to each one. Still kept hir Singing and makeing a hishing noise. She then ran around went to the water Some of her kindred went after hir and brought hir back She then fell in to a fit and continued Stiff and Speechless Some time they pored water on hir face untill She came too. Capt. Clark gave hir Some Small things which pleased hir— <we came>

Wednesday October 9th A pleasant morning, We delayed at the place we encamped at last night, in order to repair the Canoe which got Stove last evening.— We put the loading that was on board that Canoe, which consisted chiefly of Merchandise out to dry. The Natives came to our Camp, and brought us some fresh Salmon, which we purchased from them. The River hills are high at this place, are barren, and a few scattering Pine Trees grow along the Shore, on each side of the River, and but few creeks are to be seen emptying into the River at this place. The Natives appear'd round our Camp the most part of this day, & had every appearance of wishing to pilfer or steal from us, Our officers placed 2 Centinels to watch the Merchandise, & other articles that were laid out to dry, We caulked the Canoe that was stove, & repaired her, the Men then put the load on board of it— Our officers endeavoured to purchase a fat horse from the Indians at our Camp, for the party to eat, but they did not bring the horse after promising to do so. In the evening we purchased from them a considerable quantity of Salmon, a small quantity of Bears Oil, some Root bread & two dogs. After it was dark some of the party began to play on a Violin and the others fell to a dancing, This pleased the Natives very much, & they seemed delighted at our manner of dancing, These Natives continued at our Camp all Night & one of the Women that were among them was taken with a Crazy fit. This Woman began with singing in the Indian language, and then gave all that was round her some roots, & all those who she offer'd them to, had to take them. One of our Men refused taking them from her, at which she grew Angry, and hove them in the fire, and took from her husband who stood near her, a sharp flint stone, and cut her Arms in many places, that the blood gushed out of them, she catched the blood & eat it, She then tore off some beads & pieces of Copper than hung about her neck, & gave all those round her, some of them; she still kept singing, & would at times make a hissing noise. She then ran round the whole of them, & went towards the River. her Relations followed her, & brought her back; when she fell into a fit, & remain'd Stiff & Speechless for some considerable time.— The Natives threw Water on her, & brought her too, & then gave her some small Articles at which she seemed much pleased—

Thursday 10th Oct. 1805. a fair morning. our 2 Indians who came with us from the Snake nation left us yesterday. we Set out eairly and proceeded on down Several bad rapids took in Some water in the canoes. passed Several Indian fishing Camps where we bought Some Sammon from them they have a nomber of Small canoes along the Shore. about 11 oClock we came to a verry bad rockey rapid, where we halted and took one canoe over at a time. one of the canoes ran fast on a rock Stove a hole in hir Side with Some difficulty we got hir to Shore, unloaded and repaired hir Some of the natives caught Some of our oars and poles which was washed away in the rapids. we bought some more Sammon, & a dog or two. about 2 oClock we proceeded on   passed Several more fishing Camps.   passed down Some verry bad rapids which were Shallow.   we had to wade in Several rapids to hale the canoes over.   about 5 oClock P. m. we arived at the forks of the Columbian river.[1]   we proceeded on down it a Short distance and the wind blew So high from the west that we Camped[2] on the Starbord Side.   had come 20 miles this day & mostly a west course   a nomber of fishing camps along the Shores about the forks.   this is a large River afords a large body of water & is about 400 yards wide, and of a greenish coulour.   No timber barron & broken praries on each Side.—

Thursday October 10th   A pleasant morning, the two Indians that accompanied us from the Snake Nation of Indians left us, in order to return home, We set out early & proceeded on down the River & passed over some bad rapids where our Canoes took in Water, We passed several Indian fishing Camps where the Natives were fishing.   We halted at them a short time; & purchased some Salmon from them.—   Those Indians had a number of small Canoes lying along the shore.   About 11 o'Clock A. M. we came to a very bad rockey rapid, where we halted, & took one Canoe over at a time. One of our Canoes run fast on a Rock, & <stove> broke a hole in her side, & it was with much difficulty, we got her to the shore, where we unloaded and repaired her, Some Natives that were below where this accident happened caught the Oars & poles belonging to our Canoes, which we lost in the Rapids as we came along, They brought them to us, & we purchased from them some Salmon & 2 dogs for Provisions.—   About 2 o'Clock P. M. we proceeded on, & passed several more fishing Camps & down some very bad Rapids, which were shallow, We had to waid in the Water at several of those Rapids in Order to hawl our Canoes over them.   At 5 o'Clock P. M. we arrived at another of the forks of Columbia River & proceeded on down it a short distance.   The Wind blowing so hard from the Westward that we were obliged to come too, & We encamped on the North side of the River.   We came 20 Miles this day, & our Course has been nearly West.—   the whole of the way.—

We found along shore near the forks of Columbia River, a number of fishing camps, The River now became large & contained a large body of Water which appears of a Greenish Colour & it is about 400 Yards wide & has no Timber along its shores & the land on both sides of the River is barren & broken Priaries.—

1. Actually the junction of the Clearwater and Snake rivers, on the Washington–Idaho boundary, between Lewiston, Nez Perce County, Idaho, and Clarkston, Asotin County, Washington. The captains first called the Snake the Kimooenem, then called it the Lemhi and Salmon rivers, to which they had given this name.

2. In Whitman County, Washington, opposite Clarkston.

Chapter Fifty-Nine

Winter on the Coast

October 11, 1805–April 2, 1806

<*Wednesday*> Friday *11th Oct. 1805*. a fair morning. we Set out eairly. two[1] more Indians with a Small canoe accompy. us. we proceeded on passed over Some rapid water but the current mostly gentle. about 8 oClock we came to a fishing Camp & party of Indians, where we bought considerable quantity of Sammon, and 8 or 10 fat dogs to eat. Some dryed haws &c. Saw among them Some peace of fish net which they must have come from white people. a tea kittle made of copper Seen also &c. we proceeded on passed a great number of fishing camps where the natives fish in the Spring. the Stone piled up in roes So that in high water the Sammon lay along the Side of the line of rocks while they would gig them. the country is barron a high hills and clifts of rocks on each Side of the River not even a tree to be Seen no place. a fiew willows along the Shores Some places. Some rapids in the River but Some of them roles high waves but a large body of water. we roed 30 miles this day and Camped[2] at a fishing Camp of Indians on the S. Side where we bought 3 or 4 more dogs and Some Sammon &c. one Indian from an other nation came among them f. falls

Friday October 11th This morning clear & pleasant weather. We set out early, and were accompanied with 2 More Indians in a small canoe. We proceeded on down the Columbia River & we passed over some Rapids but found the current mostly run gentle. At 8 o'Clock A. M. we came to a fishing Camp, where there was a party of Indians, where we purchased 10 fat dogs, a Quantity of Salmon & some dried haws, for to eat. We saw among these Indians some pieces of a fishing Seine, which we supposed must have come from some Civilized nation. We also saw among them a Copper Tea-kettle. We continued on our way, & saw a number of fishing Camps, where the Natives come to fish in the Spring of the Year. We also saw Stones piled up in Rows, so that when the River is high the Salmon lies along side the Rocks, at which place the Natives kill them with a Gig.— The Land at this place is a poor Barren, & on each side of the River lies high hills, & Clifts of rocks, and not a tree of any kind is to be seen, & a few willows are only to be seen in places along the Shore. We crossed over some Rapids, where the waves rolled high, and abundance of Water in the River; We came about 30 Miles this day, & encamped at a fishing Camp, laying on the South side of the River, where we found a number of Indians, who are of the Flatt head Nation, We purchased from those Indians 4 dogs & some Salmon for provisions. In the evening an Indian belonging to another Nation of Indians came to the Flatt head Indian Camp.

1. The word "two" is written over "one."

2. On the Snake River, below Almota Creek and Lower Granite Dam, in Whitman County, Washington, in the vicinity of Almota. The camps were those of the Nez Perces and perhaps the Palouses.

<Thursday> Saturday 12th Oct. 1805. a clear pleasant morning. we Set out eairly and proceeded on as usal. the country continues the Same as yesterday Saw a nomber of old fishing Camps along the Shores. the current Swift in Some places, but gentle in general. about 12 oClock we halted to dine on the Lard. Shore. could Scarsely find wood enofe to cook our victules. Capt. Lewis took an Meridian observation. we then proceeded on verry well passed Several more fishing Camps. the wind rose hard from the west our general course west. high clifts of rocks & high prarie on each Side. this River is verry handsom and country pleasant but no timber at all. we Came 35 miles this day and Camped[1] on the Starbord Side at the head of a bad rockey rapid which we expect is difficult to pass. the Indians canoe and our Small pilot canoe went over this evening. we expect that we have got past the numerous flat head nation.[2] only the guides who are with us they tell us that in 2 days more we will come to another nation at a fork which comes in on the St. Side of the Columbian River.—

Saturday October 12th   We had a clear pleasant morning, & we set out early & proceeded on our Voyage down the River.   The Country has the same appearance as it had Yesterday.   we passed a number of old fishing Camps, lying along the Shores on both sides of the River, and found the current of the River run very swift in many places.   About 12 o'Clock A. M. we halted to dine on the South side of the River where we could scarcely find wood enough to Cook our provisions.   Captain Lewis took at this place a Meridian Observation and found this place to lay in Latitude 46° 29′ 21⁷⁄₁₀s. North.   We continued our Voyage at 2 o'Clock P. M. & passed several more fishing Camps, lying on both sides of the River.   The wind rose & blew hard from the West.   We also passed high clifts of Rocks & high Priaries, both lying on each side of the River, & they had a handsome appearance.   The Country has a pleasant appearance this day, but no kind of timber is to be seen.   We came about 35 Miles this day, & encamped on the North side of the River, at the head of a bad Rockey rapid, where we expect to meet with difficulty in passing it.— We got the Indians Canoe & our smallest Canoe over this rapid this evening.   We expect that we have passed the flatt head Nation, which were very numerous.   Our Guides who are Indians inform us, that in 2 days more sailing, that we shall come to another Nation of Indians, who reside near a fork of the River Columbia & that this fork lies on the South side of the said River.—

1. In the vicinity of Riparia, Whitman County, Washington.

2. Whitehouse, like Gass and the captains, uses the term "Flathead" in a very general way, referring to various peoples west of the Continental Divide. The people along the Snake River in this area were Nez Perces and Palouses.

<Friday> Sunday 13th *Oct. 1805.*   a rainy wet morning.   we delayed untill about 10 oClock A. m. then took 2 of the canoes at a time down the rapids.   all the men which could not Swim went by land and carried Some rifles & Instruments &c.   we got Safe below the rapids by 12 oClock.   dined on Sammon and proceeded over Several more rapids   the wind hard a head.   cleard off about 2 oC. P. m.   we Saw Several Old camps where the natives fish in the Spring, but no timber except what they raft down a long distance, and they Scaffel it up verry carefully.   towards evening we came to

a verry rockey place in the River & rapid   the River all confined in a narrow channel only about 15¹ yds. wide for about 2 mile and ran as [s]wift as a mill tale   the canoes ran down this channel Swifter than any horse could run. a great fishery below these rapids.   Saw 2 Indians Swim their horses across the River to the N. S. and follow down the River   they have to ride fast to keep up with us for the current mostly rapid.   the clifts & hills high plains & barrons continues on each Side of the River as usal.   we Came [*blank*] miles this day and Camped² on the Stard Side.   passed a Creek on the Lard. Side this aftr. noon.

Sunday October 13th   This morning we had Rain & delayed setting out till about 10 o'Clock A. M.   We took 2 of our Canoes at a time down the Rapids.   The Men that were among us, that could not swim, went by land, to go below these Rapids.   They carried with them some Rifle Guns & Mathematical Instruments &ca.   We were fortunate in getting all our Canoes safe over these Rapids, by 12 o'Clock A. M. when we halted to dine on Salmon.   We proceeded on our Voyage about 2 o'Clock P. M. & passed several old fishing Camps, where the Natives come to catch Salmon in the spring of the Year.   We crossed several more Rapids which were not difficult to pass.   About 3 o'Clock P. M. the wind rose from the West & the Weather became clear & pleasant.   We saw no Timber this day, excepting what the Natives had rafted down the River a great distance, which they Scaffold up very carefully.   Towards evening we came to a very rockey place lying in the River, which run very rapid.   The River at this place was confined in a narrow channell, & was only about 150 Yards wide for about 2 Miles & ran as swift as Water from a Mill tail.—   Our Canoes descended the River at this place with much more swiftness than a common horse could run the same distance.   We found below these falls a great Indian fishery & saw 2 Indians swim their horses across the Columbia River, to the North side of it.   They followed us down the River & had to ride fast, to come up with us.   The current of the River run mostly very rapid, the Hills & plains high, & some Clifts of rocks.   The land is very Barren on both sides of the River as usual. We came 35 Miles from the best computation we can make this day & encamped on the North side of the River.   Our Course for these several days past has been West.   We passed by a Creek this afternoon lying on the South side of the River which was small.

1. The number "15" is written over another number ending with a zero. The copyist misread this as "150," hardly a "narrow channell."

2. In Franklin County, Washington, opposite or a little below Ayer, Walla Walla County, on the other side of the Snake.

<Saturday> Monday *14th Oct. 1805.*   a clear cold morning the wind high a head & west.   we took an eairly breakfast and Set out and proceeded on. as usal the current mostly rapid about noon we went down a verry bad rockey rapid the worst we have passd in this River.   three of the canoes ran fast on a Solid rock at the head of the rapids two on at a time and was in great dangr. of being lost.   one Struck a rock in the middle of the rapids and luckily escaped being Stove.   as luck would have it we all got Safe down.   a Small Island near the Lard. Side, in the rapids we halted a little below to dine.   two Indians are rideing down the River, and have to ride verry fast to keep up with us.   we proceeded on verry well about 8 miles   then came to a rockey rapid at the head of an Island in which one of the canoes under charge of Sergt. ordway ran fast on a Solid rock and Swung across the rock.   they got out on the rock and attempted to Shove the canoe off the rock, but could not Start hir for Some time.   the waves dashed over hir bow So that when we got hir loose from the rock She filled full of water and considerable of the baggage and bedding washed out.   one of the canoes below unloaded and <came> went to their assistance.   took out Some of the loading.   the canoe then broke away from them and left 4 men Standing on the rock.   the water half leg deep over the Smooth rock & rappid.   a canoe Shortly went and took them off the rock, and got all to Shore except a Small brass kittle & bowl, 2 mens robes & blankets 2 Spoons, one bag of root bread one Shot pouch & powder horn a dressed Elk Skin and Some other Small articles.   we Camped below the rapids on Sd. Island[1] and put out all the wet baggage to dry.   we found Some wood on the Island covered up with Stones where the natives burryed Sammon everry Spring.   wood was So Scarce that we made use of that which was covred So carefully with Stone.   we came [*blank*] miles this day.   the country continues barron.   Some places broken, other places high Smooth plains &c.   Some or one of the men killed 7 or 8 ducks to day

Monday October 14th   A Clear cold morning, the Wind blowing hard from the Westward, We took an early breakfast and proceeded on our Voyage as usual, We found the current to run mostly rapid.   About noon we went down a very bad Rockey rapid, it being the worst rapid that we had passed in this River.   Three of our canoes ran a solid rock & stuck fast. This was at the head of a rapid.   Two of these canoes were fast at the same time, and had nearly been lost.   the other Canoe struck the same rock, & got fast in the middle of the fall, however with great exertion our Men got them afloat again & brought them safe over these falls, & got <brought> them safe down to a small Island lying near the South side of the River, which Island lay still in the rapids.   We continued on a small distance below this Island, where we halted to dine.—   We have since we set out this morning, constantly saw two Indians riding down along the bank of the River, who had to ride fast to keep up with us.—   We left this Island at 1 o'Clock P. M. and proceed on down the River about 8 Miles very well, We then came to a Rockey rapid, which lay at the head of an Island, in passing through this rapid, one of our Canoes, that was in the charge of Serjeant Ordway ran fast on a solid rock, and swung across it.   The Men that was on board this canoe all got out of her into the water on the rock, & attempted to shove her off, but could not for some time start her.   The Water all this while dashed over the bow of this Canoe, & when they got her loose she filled with water & a considerable quantity of baggage & bedding washed out.   One of our Canoes that was a small distance below where this accident happened, unloaded and went to their assistance; and took out some of the loading.— The Canoe that was on the rock then broke away from the Men, & left 4 Men standing on the Rock in the Water half leg deep over the smooth rocks & rapids.   One of our Canoes went in a short time to their assistance & took these Men from off the Rock on board of it.   We saved some part of that Canoes loading & lost a small brass kettle, Buffalo robes, blanketts, Spoons shot pouches & powder horns, dressed Elk Skins, a bag of Root bread &ca. We encamped on an Island lying below the Rapids & put out all the wet baggage to dry.   We found on the Island, some Wood that was covered up with Stones, which the Natives had buried.   The Natives come to this place to fish in the Spring of the Year.   We made use of the Wood that we had found, to dress our Victuals with.   We came about 25 Miles this day,   The land continues to be a Barren & in many places broken & high smooth plains.— In the Evening one of our Men killed 8 Ducks which he got. our Course still continues West.—

1. An island downstream from Burr Canyon, Franklin County, Washington, an area now inundated by Lake Sacajawea.

<*Sunday*> Tuesday *15th Oct. 1805*. a clear cool morning. we delayed here to dry the baggage. Some of the men went out and killed three geese & Several ducks. about 3 oClock P. m. we loaded up the canoes and Set out and proceeded on over Several rapids and Swift water. passed Several Scaffels of wood where it was put up to be Saved for the use of their fishing in the Spring. the country continues as yesterday. we came 17 miles and Camped[1] above a bad rapid on a Sand bar no wood except an Indians Scaffel we had to take Some of the wood for our use this evening.

Tuesday October 15th This morning we had clear & cool weather; We delayed here in order to dry the wet baggage. Some of our Men went out & killed 3 Geese and Several ducks.— About 3 o'Clock P. M. we loaded the Canoes & set out, and proceeded on; & passed several rapids & places where the water run very swift, We also passed Scaffolds of wood, which the Natives had built for the use of this fishery in the Spring season. The Country continued the same as Yesterday. We encamped on a Sand barr above a bad Rapid, we found no Wood, excepting an Indian Scaffold & we took some of it for our use. We came about 17 Miles this day, our Course the same as Yesterday. (West)

1. In Franklin County, Washington, just below Fishhook Rapids.

<*Monday*> Wednesday *16th Oct. 1805*. we Set out as usal and proceeded on over Several bad rapids which was full of rocks. one of the canoes Struck a rock in a rapid and Swung on it they Stayed their untill we unloaded and took a canoe I was on board the canoe which Struck. the Small canoes came to our assistance also. we got the load and canoe Safe to Shore, loaded again and proceeded on over Several more rapids then came to a

verry bad rapid, the worst or had the highest waves of any we have yet passd. we halted above the rapid and carried considerable of the baggage by land about a mile. then took the canoes Safe over, and loaded up and proceeded on down Several more rapids towards evening we arived at the forks of the river[1] which came from a northly direction and is larger than this Columa. R. the country around these forks is level Smooth barron plains not even a tree to be Seen as far as our eyes could extend a fiew willows along the Shores. we found about 2 hundred or upwards[2] Camped on the point between the two Rivers. a verry pleasant place. we Camped[3] near them on the point. the natives Sold us eight dogs and Some fresh Sammon. the whole band came in a body Singing in their form to our fires and Smoaked with us and appeared friendly. they have beeds and brass and coper in Small peaces hanging about them, which they Sign to us that they got them from white people on a River to the north, and Some down about the mouth of this River. we went [*blank*] miles this day. passed Several Islands &c.

Wednesday October 16th   A pleasant morning & we set out early; and proceeded on; we passed over several bad Rapids, which lay quite across the River, which were <was> full of rocks.   One of our Canoes struck on a rock, which was in a rapid, & swung round and remained fast, where she staid, till the Canoe that I was in came to their assistance & a small Canoe belonging to our party.   The Men from the two Canoes got the load out of the Canoe, & got her off the rock & to the shore.   We got the Canoes loaded again & continued on our Voyage.   we passed over several more bad Rapids; and came to a place in the River, where we found a very bad Rapid by far the worst that we had yet seen on this River; & we halted our Canoes above the Rapid.   We carried a considerable quantity of our baggage about a Mile by land below this rapid.—   We got all our canoes safe over this <rapid> difficult place & loaded them and proceeded on down the River; & passed several more Rapids.—   Towards evening we arrived at a large fork that came into this River from a Northerly direction & was much large than the fork which we descended which we supposed to be the Columbia River.—   The country round where the forks of these two Rivers lay <is> was level & <is>

smooth barren plains, with not a Tree to be seen as far as our Eyes could extend. Along the Shores <are> grew a few Willows. We found upwards of 200 Indians, that were encamped on a point of land, that lay between these two Rivers, in a very pleasant situated place. We Encamped near those Indians on the same point of land. These natives came to our encampment & sold us 8 dogs & some fresh Salmon. This whole Band of Indians came in a body, Singing in their manner to our fires, Smoaked with us, & appeared friendly.— These Indians had beads, and small pieces of brass & Copper hanging about them, which they made signs to us, that they got them from White people, who live on a River; lying to the North of this place, & that they also got some of them at the Mouth of this River. We passed several Islands this day & came 26 Miles, the Course with us is the same as Yesterday.—

1. The junction of the Snake and Columbia rivers, in Franklin County, Washington.

2. They were Yakima and Wanapam Indians; the former lived in the immediate vicinity of the Snake–Columbia fork, with the latter nearby. Also nearby were the Walulas (Walla Wallas), Umatillas, and Palouses. All spoke languages of the Shahaptian family.

3. In the point between the rivers, in Franklin County, just southeast of Pasco at the site of Sacajawea State Park.

<*Tuesday*> Thursday *17th Oct. 1805.* a clear pleasant morning. we delay here to day for our officers to take observations &c. the natives Sold us a nomber more dogs and fresh Sammon &c. these Savages have but verry fiew buffalow Robes, but are dressed in deer & Elk Skins. the deer Skins are dressed with the hair on and Sowed together in robes. Some of them have red and blew cloath and a number of articles which came from Some white people. they have Some horses. they Sign to us that their is deer and Elk below this. we Saw an emence Site of fowls on the plain considerable la[r]ger than the prarie or haith hens. Some of the party went out and killed 3 of them. we now call the north fork as it is the largest the Columbian River, and the other which we came down loose it name from Columba. and we call it after the Indian name kimoo-e-nem— the columbia River is more Smooth and the current gentle the Natives have a great number of canoes, and fishing camps along the Shores. Capt. Clark and two men went up the Columb. River in a canoe 3 or 4 miles to the Indians lodges they

Saw a vast quantitys of live Sammon in the River they giged one which was verry larg they Saw a great nomber lay dead on Shores.[1] Some of the men killed Several more haith hens[2] most as large as Turkeys. <our officers gave the chiefs> of these bands <which is not greatly> like <the first> flat <heads we Saw but we Still call them. So we cannot> we cannot find out what nation these are as yet, but our officers gave the principal men meddles a flag and Some other Small articles &c. we bought in all 26 dogs from the natives this day. these Savages are peaceable but verry poor. they have nothing of any account to trade. a number of them have not any thing to cover their nakedness, but the greater part of them have dressed deer & Elk Some rabit Skins &c. to cover themselves. Saw a nomber of horses on the opposite Shore. we have late[ly] Seen a nomber of their grave yards pickeded in &c

Thursday October 17th We had a clear pleasant morning. Our officers delayed this day here, in order to ascertain the latitude of this place &ca. The Natives sold us several more dogs &ca They had very few buffalo robes among them, & were cloathed in deer & Elk skins dressed with the hair on & sewed together, & made into Robes. Some of these Indians had Red & blue Cloth & a number of articles that must have been procured from some Civilized <people> nation. They also had some horses. They made signs to us that there is deer & Elk below this place.— We saw an immense quantity of Fowls in the plains, they were considerable larger than the Priari or heath hen. Some of our party went out with Guns & killed 3 of them.— Our officers were of the opinion that the River which we descended, & which we all took, to be the Columbia River should lose its name at this place and that the North fork being the largest should be called the Columbia River,[3] & the South fork of the River (or rather River) which we had descended, should be named Lewis's River or after the name it bears among the Indians which is Ki-o-me-num River.— The water in Columbia[4] River (or North fork) is much smoother & the current more gentle here than the Ki-o-me-num or Lewis's River. The Columbia River only bearing the name up the North Fork, of these two rivers.— The natives here had a great number of Canoes, & fishing Camps, along the shores, of both these Rivers.— Captain Clark took a party of our Men, and went up the Columbia[5] River in a Canoe, between 3 & 4 Miles, to where these Indians had their lodges. They saw vast quantities of live Salmon in that River. They gigged one of them which was very large, They also saw a great number of Salmon which lay dead on the shores, Some of our Men went out into the plains, & killed <some> several more of the Priari or heath hens, which were nearly as large as a hen Turkey,— & good eating. Our party were all at a loss to know what Nation of Indians the Band which we are among belong to. Our officers gave the principal Men among them Medals, a Flag, & some other presents.— We purchased 26 dogs from these Indians to eat, The Indians that are among us, are handsome, well made & light brown color'd sett of Men, and are very peacable. They have not any thing to Trade amongst them with us, but Salmon, Dogs & a few Elk skins. We saw a number of horses on the opposite shore, and a number of their Grave Yards, which were picketed in. Our Officers took a Meridinal Oservation, & found the Forks of these Two Rivers at their Confluence to lay in Latitude 46° 15′ 13⁷⁄₁₀S North.

1. Either coho salmon, *Oncorhynchus kisutch,* or sockeye salmon, *O. nerka.* They were dying after having laid and fertilized their eggs.
2. Probably sage grouse, *Centrocercus urophasianus.*
3. "Columbia" is written over an erasure that is illegible.
4. Again the word is written over an illegible erasure.
5. Another substitution.

<Wednesday> Friday *18th Oct. 1805.* a clear pleasant morning. we delay untill after 12 oClock today for Capt. Lewis to complete his observations. Capt. Clark measured the width Columbian River and the ki-mooe-nem found the Columbian R. to be 860 yards wide and the ki-moo-e-nem River to be 475 yards wide at the forks. Some of the party killed Several more haith hens about 12 oClock we loaded up the canoes. Capt. Lewis took down Some of three languages of these Savages, as fer as we could make them understand. about 2 oClock P. m. we Set out only two chiefs with us who come with us from the flat heads. we proceeded on down the Colum-bia River, which is now verry wide from a half a mile to three forths wide and verry Smooth & pleasant the country level for about 16 miles down then the hills and clifts made near the River, and Some Rapid places in the River. passd. Several Islands on which was large camps of Indians and Scaffels of

abundance of Sammon. Saw the Sammon thick jumping in the river Some dead in the R. and along the Shore. the Latitude at the forks as taken by Capt. Lewis and Clark is [*blank*] North. we proceeded on over Several rapids places passd. Several large Camps of Indians which have flag lodges and abundance of Sammon, and have a great nomber of horses. we went [*blank*] miles and Saw no timber of any acct. not a tree to be Seen. we Camped[1] on the Lard Side. got a fiew Small willows only to burn. a nomber of the natives came in their canoes to See us. they have a great nomber of Small canoes &c.—

Friday October 18th A clear pleasant morning. Our officers delayed till after 12 o' Clock A. M. to compleat & prove the observation that they had taken Yesterday, and to make farther remarks on those Two Rivers which we are now at. Captain Clark measured the width of both these Rivers. He found the Columbia River (or North fork) to be 860 Yards wide at its Mouth, & the Ki-o-me-num or Lewis's River to be 475 Yards wide at its Mouth also.— Several Men of our party went out in the plains, & killed a number more of Priari or heath hens, which were very large.— Captain Lewis took down in writing, a number of Words spoken by these Indians in their language, & the names of several things, as well as we could make them understand by signs &ca— About 2 o'Clock P. M. we proceeded again on our Voyage; and had Two Chiefs with us, that had come from the flatthead Nation of Indians. We proceeded on down the Columbia River, & found it to be from half to three quarters of a Mile wide, & the water running very smooth. The Country for about 10 Miles level, & then the hills made in near to the River & some Rapid places in it.— We passed several Islands, on which were large Camps of Indians.—

We saw likewise abundance of Scaffolds with Salmon drying on them. The Salmon were very plenty as we came along, & a number of them were jumping in the River as we passed along also, & a number of dead Salmon, lay all along the shores in the River. The Latitude at the forks of the two Rivers we last left taken by Captain Lewis & Captain Clark being fully ascertained is 46° 15′ 13⁷⁄₁₀s North as before mentioned.— We continued on our way, & passed over several bad rapid places. We also passed several large Camps of Indians, who had Lodges built of flags, and they had abundance of Salmon. These Indians had a vast number of Horses. We saw no Timber of any account, & were forced to make use of dry Willows for fuel to cook with, some few of which grew along the Shore, where we encamped. We encamped on the South side of the River where a number natives came shortly after in their Canoes to see us. We came 17 Miles this day, our Course still being West.—

1. Below the mouth of the Walla Walla River, Walla Walla County, Washington, a little above the Washington–Oregon boundary.

Saturday 19th Oct. 1805. a clear cold morning. we took an eirily breakfast. the Natives came to See us in their canoes. brought us Some fish which had been roasted and pounded up fine and made up in balls, which eat verry well. about 7 oC. A m. we Set out and proceeded on down the R. passed high clifts of rocks on each Side passd. over Several rockey rapids. our officers gave one[1] of the Natives we left this morning a meddel. we passed Several Islands on which was Indian fishing Camps. the natives all hid themselves in their flag lodges when they Saw us comming. the Indians are numerous the camps near each other along the Shores the River pleasant only at the rapid which are common we passd. over Several today but no exident hapened. the Country around level plains except Some hills & clifts along the Shores. we discovred a high hill or mountn[2] a long distance down the River which appears to have Snow on it we <came> went 36 miles this day and Campd[3] opposite a large Indian Camp on the South Side. a great number of the natives[4] come over in their canos to see us. when any of these natives die they deposite all their property with them. we Saw one of their grave yards to day, even a canoe was Split in peaces and Set up around the yard Several other art. also.

Saturday October 19th This morning was clear & cold, We took an early breakfast, the Natives still continuing to visit us, bringing with them some Salmon, which they had roasted & pounded fine & made up into Balls, which eat very well; About 7 oClock A. M. We proceeded on down the Columbia River, We passed by Clifts of rocks, lying on each side of the River, & also rockey rapids. We passed by several Islands, on which were Indian fishing

Camps. The Natives all hid themselves (on these Islands on seeing us,) in their Flag lodges. We now begin to find the Indians very numerous, and their Camps lay near each other along the Shores on both sides of the River, We found the day pleasant & the Navigation of the River easy, excepting at the Rapids several of which we passed over this day, without any accident happening.—

The Country as we passed along is level plains, and along some part of the Shores are some hills & Clifts. We discovered a high hill or mountain laying a long distance down the River which appears to have Snow on it.— We came 36 Miles this day, & encamped opposite to a large Indian Camp, which lay on the South side of the River. A number of the Natives came over to see us, & behaved very friendly.— These Indians have a custom among them, that when any of them die, they deposit all their property with them.— We saw one of their grave Yards this day, & even to a canoe, that belonged to the deceased person; was split up into pieces, and set up round the grave Yard

1. Yelleppit, chief of the Walula Indians.
2. Clark saw Mt. Adams, Yakima County, Washington, this day. The previous day he noticed Mt. Hood, Hood River County, Oregon.
3. Perhaps on Blalock Island, between Irrigon and Boardman, Morrow County, Oregon.
4. Probably Umatilla Indians living in the vicinity of Plymouth, Benton County, Washington, but possibly Cayuses.

Sunday 20th Oct. 1805. a clear frosty morning. we Set out eirily. passed a handsom peace of the River the country low Smooth plains on each Side. Saw Some pillicans, and abundance of crows & ravens,[1] as the Shores is lined with dead Sammon. about 12 oClock we came to a large Indian Camp on the point of a large Island. we halted to dine. we bought Several Small articles from the natives and Saw Some articles which came from Some white people Such as copper kittles, red cloth Some arsh paddles &c. we proceeded on passed a great nomber of Indian Camps, where they had abundance of fish hung on Scaffels to dry. passed over Several rapids to day but no exident hapened. the country continues as usal the hunters killed 9 ducks and a goose this day. we Come 46 miles and Camped[2] on the Stard. Side. no wood only a fiew Small Sticks, & green willow &c. we

Saw Some akehorns among the natives which is a Sign of oak being in the country for they boil and eat them. we Saw red cloth which appeared to have come from [white?] people this last Sommer.—

Sunday October 20th A clear frosty morning, We set out early on our Voyage, & passed a handsome piece of the River, where the Country lay low & smooth plains lying on both sides of the River, We saw some Pelicans & a number of Crows & Ravens, which we supposed to be occasiond from the very great quantity of dead Salmon, which the River Shores were lined with.— About 12 o'Clock A. M. we came to where, there was a very large Camp of Indians, laying on the point of an Island. We halted to dine at that place. We purchased from those Indians, several small articles & saw among them some articles which <they> must have been originally purchased from white people. They were Copper kettles, red Cloth, Ash paddles neatly made; knives &ca. We proceeded on, and passed a great number of Indian Camps, which were inhabited in all of which the Natives had abundance of Salmon hung up on scaffolds to dry. We also passed over a number of Rapids but without any accident, happening to us.—

The appearance of the Country is the same as Yesterday. Our hunters killed 9 Ducks, & a goose this day in the River. In the evening we encamped on the North side of the River, where we found no other article to make fire with, but small sticks & green Willows. We saw this day among the Natives, some Acorns, which they roasted & Eat, and some red Cloth, which appeared not to be long Imported from Europe.—

1. Perhaps a subspecies of the common crow, *Corvus brachyrhynchos hesperis*. The raven is *Corvus corax*.

2. Probably in the vicinity of Roosevelt, Klickitat County, Washington.

Monday 21st Oct. 1805.[1] a clear cold morning. we Set out eairly and proceeded on as usal, untill about 8 oClock at which time we halted at an Indian Camp where we bought Some wood and cooked breakfast. bought Some pounded fish from the Natives and Some roots bread which was made up in cakes in form of ginger bread and eat verry well. Saw a number of Rackoon Skins also otter and fisher Skins &c.[2] they gave us any thing we asked for by our giving any Small article we pleased. we proceeded on passed clifts of rocks and River hills on each Side passed over Several verry bad rockey rapids, where the River was nearly filled with high rocks of a dark coulour, and the water divided in narrow deep channels, where we ran through verry fast high waves and whorl pools below. passd. Several Islands and fishing Camps where the natives had a large quantity of pounded fish the best of their Sammon pounded up and put up in Small Stacks along the Shore for winter, & cover them with Straw and pile the Stone around them. the Solid clifts continue on each Side. Saw a little Scattering pine timber on the hills on each Side of the River. Some places the rocks are high and Steep. we went about 32 miles and Camped[3] at Some Indian Camps on the Stard. Side. a handsom Spring run from a clift of rocks near our Camp. we bought Some wood from the Natives to cook with these natives appeer to be mostly covd. in deer and Elk Some rabit & Squerrel Skins. they have Some blew Cloth blankets &. we passed a Small River[4] which came in on the Lard. Side

Monday October 21st A clear cold morning. We set out early, and proceeded on as usual, untill about 8 oClock A. M. when we halted at an Indian Camp, lying on the River side, & bought some wood, with which we cooked breakfast, We also purchased from those Indians some pounded fish, and root bread, made up in the form of ginger bread, which eat very well. We also saw among these Indians, Raccoon, Otter, fisher & a number of other kinds of small Skins, These Indians behaved very kind to us, they gave us any article that we asked for which they had among them, by our giving them any small article ever so trifling we pleased; & seemed very well pleased with us. We proceeded on down the River, & passed Clifts of rocks, & hills, which lay near the river on both sides of it. We also passed over several very bad rockey rapids, where the River was nearly filled with Rocks, which were high & of a dark Colour, & the Water divided into narrow Channels. We ran with our Canoes through those Channels very fast, the Waves at that place run high, & whirl pools lay below the Rocks, which made it extreamly dangerous for us to pass.— We continued on, and passed several Islands & fishing Camps, where the natives had large Quantities of pounded fish. The Natives dry & pound the best of their fish which they put up in small stacks, along the River Shores for winter, & cover them over with Straw and pile Stones up high round them.— The Solid clifts of rocks continue along each side of the River. We saw some scattering pine trees growing on the hills on both sides of the River, & the Rocks are steep & high— We passed a small River which lay on the South side of the River which we called Baptiste River & We came about 32 Miles this day & encamped near some Indian Camps, which were Inhabited by a number of Indians; lying on the North side of the River. We found near to our Camp, a handsome spring of water which ran from under some Clifts of rocks. We purchased from those Indians some wood to Cook with. These Natives were chiefly <covered> Cloathed with deer & Elk skins, which they dress into leather. They had also some Rabbit, & squirrel skins among them.— We also saw with them blue Cloth & blankets, Our Course continues nearly West.—

1. Above the date is the word "this."
2. Raccoon, *Procyon lotor*, river otter, and fisher, *Martes pennanti*.
3. In Klickitat County, Washington, in the vicinity of John Day Dam.
4. John Day River, marking the boundaries of Gilliam and Sherman counties, Oregon. It was named "River La Page" by the party for member Jean Baptiste Lepage. This last sentence appears to be squeezed in between entries.

Tuesday 22nd Oct. 1805. a clear pleasant morning. we Set out Soon after Sunrise and proceeded on passed fishing Camps on the Stard. Side high clifts on each Side of dark couloured rock, and a high rock Island with rough towers of Solid rough rocks on it a verry rough roaring rapid at the Stard. Side which is the main body of the River we went down on the Lard. Side a river[1] puts in on the Lard. Side about 40 yards wide & falls in it. opposite the lower part of the Island high hills & clifts on each Side, but the highest is on the Stard Side. all the natives on this River at the most of their Camps have fish nets which they catch the Sammon in the Spring in great abundance. Saw considerable of Sand along the Shores for Several days past. we proceeded on to the lower end of Sd. Island which is about 4 mile long at the lower end is a great nomber of fishing Camps a Short distance below is the first falls of the Columbian River.[2] we halted little above about noon and bought Some pounded fish and root bread of the natives[3] who are verry thick about these falls. Some of them have [f]lag lodges and Some have cabbins of white ceeder bark   they have an abunduance of dry and pounded [fish?].   bags full of Sammon and heaps of it on the Shores   they have a nomber of Small canoes, and have a nomber of well looking horses. high clifts of rocks near on each Side of the falls.   we found the falls to be about [*blank*] feet of a perpinticular pitch and filled with Solid rocks cut in many channels.   a mist rises contiuually from the falls.   we found that we had to make a portage of about ¾ of a mile on the Stard. Side.   So we went to carrying the baggage by land on our backs.   hired a fiew horse loads by the natives   So we got all the baggage below the falls this evening and Camped[4] close to a high range of clifts of rocks, where the body of the River beat against it and formed a large Eddy.   the natives Sign to us that it is only about Six miles below, to the next or other falls.   we Saw Several Sea otter[5] in and about these falls.   the natives are troublesome about our Camp.   we had went about [*blank*] miles before we came to these falls.   these natives Sign to us that Some white people had been here but were gone four or 5 days journey further down.   the perpinticular clifts at our Camp is [*blank*] feet high.

Tuesday October 22nd   A clear pleasant morning & We set out soon after Sun rise & proceeded on down the River, we passed several fishing Camps of Indians, lying on the North side of the River, and high Clifts of dark colour'd Rock lying on both sides of it.—   We also saw an Island of Rocks, which had towers of solid Rock on it, and a very rough roaring rapid, lying on the North side of the River, on which lies the main Channel & body of it; We proceeded down at this place on the South side of the River & found a small River, which emtied into the Columbia River on the same side.   It appeared to be about 40 Yards wide, & fell into it opposite to the lower part of the Rockey Island.   This River was called the Sho-sho-ne or Clark's River.   We saw high hills & Clifts of rocks, which lay on both sides of the River, the highest of which lies on the North side of it.   We found that the Natives had fishing Seins which we saw during this day, and catch the greatest abundance of fish with them in the Spring of the Year.   The Sand this day, lays in great abundance along the Shores.—   We continued on to the lower end of the Island before mention'd this day, (which we supposed to be at least 4 Miles in length) & found a great number of fishing Camps, a short distance below it,

We came here, to the first falls of Columbia River where we halted, for a short time a small distance above it, about noon. The Natives at this place came to us, and we purchased from them some pounded Salmon, & Root bread, which they had brought with them.— We found the Natives to be very numerous about those falls. They had a number of lodges made out of Flags & Cedar bark, and Cabbins built out of same kind of Cedar wood & covered with Bark; we found also among them, large quantities of dried Salmon, which they had in grass bags of their own manufacture, & we saw a number of small Canoes lying along the Shores of the River. We saw a number of handsome horses feeding in the plains which belonged to the Natives. These falls were perpendicular & we found them by measurement to be about 37 feet 8 Inches feet high, & full of Solid Rocks which by the force of the rapidity of the Waters running, are cut into many Channels. And a constant mist rises at this place occasioned by the great fall of Water. The River at this place <is> was considerable narrower than it was a few Miles above it.—

The Rocks & Clifts lay very high near to the River; on both sides of these falls; & the Water falling in such an immense quantity, makes a roaring that can be heard several miles below it. We found that we should be forced to make a portage of about ¾ of a Mile to get where we could again load our Canoes with safety, to proceed on our Voyage. Our Men were set to carrying on their backs all our Goods baggage &ca. and our officers hired from the Natives a few horses, to carry the most weighty part of it. We got all our baggage safe below these falls, in the Evening and encamped on the North side of the River, close to a high range of Clifts of rocks, where the Main body of the Water ran against them & formed a very large Eddy.— The Natives made signs to us, which we understand to be that about 6 Miles below this falls, that we shall come to another great falls. We saw a number of Sea Otters, in and about these falls. We found the Natives here very troublesome about our camp and we <are> were forced to watch them, for fear of their stealing from us.— These Natives informed us by signs, that some White people had been at this place, but that they had gone 4 or 5 days Journey down the River. The perpendicular hight of the Clifts were we are encamped, is about 250 feet high. We came about 35 Miles this day our course being as usual West.—

1. The Deschutes River, on the boundary of Sherman and Wasco counties, Oregon. The captains first called it Clark's River and later Towanahiooks.
2. Celilo Falls near Wishram, Klickitat County, Washington, and Celilo, Wasco County, Oregon, now inundated by The Dalles Dam.
3. In this area were the party's Eneeshurs, perhaps the later Tenino Indians, and some Wanapams.
4. Below the falls near Wishram, Klickitat County, where they remained until October 24.
5. More likely the harbor seal, *Phoca vitulina richardii,* rather than the sea otter, *Enhydra lutris;* see Clark's entry of October 23.

Wednesday 23rd Oct. 1805. a clear pleasant morning. we took an eairly breakfast in order to undertake gitting the canoes by the falls. about 8 oClock A m. we all went with Capt Clark and took the canoes across the River, then halled them round a perpinticular pitch of 21 feet. we halled all canoes round the high rocks about a quarter of a mile then put them in the water again. this portage has been frequented by the natives halling their canoes round, and it is a great fishery with them in the Spring, and the flees[1] are now verry thick, the ground covd. with them. they troubled us verry much this day. we got the canoes all in the River below the great falls of 22 feet perpinticular then went on board again and ran verry rapid through the whorl pools a little better than a half a mile then came to 2 little falls of about 3 feet each we let the canoes down by ropes one of them got away from us from the Lower Shoot and was taken up by the Indians below. towards evening we got all the canoes Safe down to Camp. the Latitude at this place which is called the grand falls of the Columbia River is 45° 42′ 57′.3. the hight of the falls is in all 37 feet 8 Inches, and has a large Rock Island in them and look Shocking, but are ordinary looking. Some of the Sick men at Camp bought Several fat dogs this day. in the evening one of our chief[s] Signed to us that the Savages had a design to kill us in the night, which put us on our guard. but we were not afraid of them for we think we can drive three times our nomber.—

Wednesday October 23rd   This morning we had Clear pleasant Weather, We took an early breakfast, in order to get the Canoes from where we left them Yesterday; About 8 o'Clock A. M. the greatest part of our Men, set out with Captain Clark and went up to the head of the falls, where we took our

Canoes to the opposite <shore,> side of the River & hawled them out on the Shore.—

The party then hawled the Canoes, round a perpendicular fall of 21 feet, and also round high rocks for about a quarter of a Mile distance and then put them in the Water again. This portage is frequently used by the Natives, in hawling their Canoes round & is a great fishery & used by the Natives as such, in the spring of the Year. we found at this place innumerable Quantities of fleas, the ground being cover'd with them, & they were very troublesome. the place where we put our Canoes last into the Water, lies below a fall of 22 feet perpendicular. The Men embark'd on board the Canoes again, and went with great rapidity through the Rocks in a narrow Channel of the River and crossed a whirl pool, which was better than a half Mile across; & came to where lay 2 little falls of about 3 feet each. They then let the Canoes down through those falls by Ropes. One of our Canoes got away from the Men who was letting her down at the lower Shoot; & was taken up by some of the Natives, just below where we left our baggage &ca. Towards evening we got all our Canoes safe down to our Camp. These falls is called the Grand falls of Columbia River, and lies in Latitude 45° 42' 57³⁄₁₀s North, the heighth of them as before mentioned is altogether 37 feet 8 Inches, and has a large Island of rock, lying in the middle of them, & has a terrifying appearance to pass through. We have some of our Men this day sick at our Camp; owing to fataigue, manner of living, Water &ca. Our party that were left at the Camp purchased several dogs from the Natives. In the Evening one of the Indian Chiefs, that descended the River with us; made signs to us, & let us know, that the Indians who are at our Camp, had formed a design to kill us in the night. We kept up a strong guard all night, but they did not attempt to put their plan into execution.—

1. Fleas belong to the family Pulicidae, but these may in fact be human body lice, *Pediculus humanus*. See Clark's entry of October 26, 1805.

Thursday 24th Oct. 1805. a clear cool morning we loaded up and Set out about 9 oClock and proceeded on down. the current verry rapid. we went through a place wher the river was all confined in a narrow channel of about 20 yds. wide high rocks on each Side the current verry rapid and full of whorl pools we ran down verry fast, passed Several fishing Camps. high barron land on each Side of the River. about 4 oClo P. m. we went down a bad rapid where the River was cut in rockey Isld. &.c. a Short distance below we came to another narro[1] where the River is filled with high rocks. we halted and Camped[2] for the night at a village of Savages[3] or red people, which have their houses in our form only they have them in the ground except the roof which is covred with white ceeder bark Some hewn plank which are verry nice comfortable houses their flag mats &c. we bought from them Some cakes of white root bread and other kinds cramberies[4] &c. we bought a nomber of fat dogs and Some wood for us to cook with. their appears to be Some timber back from the River. their has been white people tradeing among these Savages Saw one half white child among them. Saw also a new copper tea kittle beeds copper and a nomber of other articles which must have come from Some white trader. we had went only 7 miles this day. <this may>

Thursday October 24th We had a cool pleasant morning. We loaded our Canoes & set out about 9 o'Clock A. M. on our Voyage; we found the current of the river running very rapid. We proceeded on, and passed through a part of the River, which was confined in a narrow channel of about 20 Yards wide; having high rocks on each side of it, the Current very rapid, and a great many whirl pools. Our Canoes went with very great rapidity through this place. We got through this dangerous place, without any accident happening to us, & passed by several Indian fishing Camps, & high barren land which lay on both sides of the River.— About 4 o'Clock P. M. we went down a bad rapid, where the River had made channels, in rockey Islands, & dangerous places; and a short distance below that place, we came to a Narrow place in the River, where across the River, was many high Rocks, & several rapid Channels running between them.— We halted above this Narrow, & encamped for the night at a Village Inhabited by Indians. These Indians had their houses built, in the same form that we build our houses in the United States with these exceptions, that they were built in the ground, & the Roofs were made, of white Cedar bark, & neatly put on. They had also some of them covered with hewn plank. They appeared to live comfortable, they had matts to lay on, made out of flaggs & several other household utensials.— We purchased from them some Cakes of white Root bread; Cranberries, a number of fat dogs, Wood to cook with, &ca. We saw some timber here, which grew a distance back from the River.— We conclude that their must have been some white people among these Indians, as they had among them, a new Copper Tea kettle, beads, small pieces of Copper & a number of other articles We saw also a Child among them, which was a mix'd breed, between a White Man & Indian Women. The fairness of its Skin, & rosey colour, convinced us that it must have been the case, and we have no doubt, but that white Men trade among them— We came but 7 Miles this day & our Course was as usual West,—

1. The Short, or Little, Narrows, and the Long Narrows, which they would pass the next day, together constitute The Dalles of the Columbia River, above the town of The Dalles, Wasco County, Oregon. The narrows are now concealed beneath the waters of The Dalles Dam.

2. In Klickitat County, Washington, in the vicinity of Horsethief Lake State Park.

3. Wishram-Wasco Chinookans.

4. Probably American cranberrybush, *Viburnum trilobum* Marsh., restricted to the Columbia gorge in this region.

Friday 25th Oct. 1805. a clear morning. we carrd. Some of our baggage about a mile, which took us below the worst of the rapids, then took one canoe down the rapids and narrows where the whole channel is confined in a narrow channel only about 25 yards wide. one of the canoes nearly fi[lled] running through the rapids waves & whorl pools. we got all the canoes down and loaded them. we have bought a large quantity about 16 common bags of pounded Sammon Some white bread cramberies &c. about 3 oClock we Set out and proceeded on down the narrows which lasted abt. 2 miles verry rapid. 2 ¹ Small Islands of Solid rocks Stood in the channel one of the canoes ran hir bow aggainst the point and glanced off without Injury. the water or River between these narrows and the falls, rises at high water 48 feet perpinticular by its being confined by the different narrows. a little [below] or at the lower end of the narrows we Saw a war party of Indians, with horses. they had deer & bear meat with them the head chief had on a jacket that was made of Some kind of worked Splits which would defend off the arrows. our Capts. gave him a meddle, then he gave our Capts. Some bears oil and a fresh Sammon   our 2 chiefs came to us and told us that their was a nation below that which had a design to kill them and us   So they left us in order to return to their own village again.—   we then proceeded on about eight miles   the hils high   Some pine and oak timbr. to be Seen   the River got Smooth.   we Campd.[2] on a high point of rocks little below the mouth of a creek on the Lard. Side.   timbered country hack from the River each Side.   Saw drumm fish[3] jump in Rivr.

Friday October 25th   This morning clear & pleasant; Our Men that were well (all excepting a Guard left with our Canoes,) set off with the loading to a place, below the worst of the rapids; about one Mile distance, which we carried on our backs, The party that were left with the Canoes, took one of our Canoes down the rapids, and narrows of the River.   The channel of the river lays in a narrow place, not about 25 Yards wide, & with difficulty they got through it.   they then returned, & brought the remainder of the Canoes to us, at the place where we had deposited our loading.   One of the Canoes nearly filled, in passing through the Rapid waves & whirlpools in the Rapids.—   We found an Indian village, laying below these falls, or rapids, <from whom> our officers purchased from the Indians that resided in this Village 16 bags of pounded Salmon; some bread made out of Roots, Cranberries &ca.   The whole of our party having come to us below the rapids; we loaded our Canoes & About 3 o'Clock P. M. & we set out, and proceeded on down through the rapids, which lasted about 2 Miles further & the water running very Rapid, the whole way.—   We found 2 small Islands of solid rock, which lay in the channel of the River in these Rapids.   One of our Canoes run her bow against the point of one of these Islands, & glanced off without receiving any injury.—   The River between the falls & narrows at that place rises at high water 48 feet perpendicular, which is occasion'd by the water being confined by the different narrow places, & particularly at the lower end of them.—   We came too, at the lower end of these falls, and halted for a short time, at which place a Warr party of Indians, came to us. These Indians were all on horse back, & had Deer & bear meat with them. Our officers gave their Chief a medal, & he in return gave them some Bears Oil & a fresh Salmon.—   This Warr party of Indians staid with us but a short time.   The Two Indian Chiefs who descended the River with us, told us by signs, that there was a Nation of Indians, that resided on this River below us, who would certainly kill them; & the whole of our party, and that they must leave us, in order to return to their own Village again. These Indians left us at this place, after taking a friendly leave. Our Officers gave them some presents & they left us much pleased.— The Chief or head Man that had been with us of the Warr party; wore a curious kind of Jacket, This Jacket was made out of a kind of Splits, which were worked in such a manner, as to defend him against the Arrows shot by his Enemies.— We proceeded on, & went about 8 Miles further down the River. The hills the whole of this distance, were high on both sides of the River, and we saw some pine & Oak timber, The River ran smooth all this way, We encamped near a high point of Rocks, a small distance below the mouth of a creek, which lay on the South side of the River; The Country laying a small distance back, from where we are encamped, is cover'd with Timber.— And the Land on both sides of the River, is barren land We saw a Number of fish jumping in the River from where we are encamped which we supposed to be Drum fish.—

1. The number "2" is written over "a."

2. At the party's "Fort Camp" or "Fort Rock Camp," at the mouth of Mill Creek at the town of The Dalles, Wasco County, Oregon, where they stayed until October 28.

3. The fish is not identifiable; see Clark's entry for this day.

Saturday 26th Oct. 1805. a clear pleasant morning. we lay Campd. on the clift or pt. of rocks for Safety. 2 Sentinels to guard us. our officers conclude to delay here for observations and repair the canoes &c. So we unloaded all the canoes Shaved the bottoms Smooth and pay them over and made them in good repair &c. Several men out a hunting. a nomber of the natives visited us. we dryed the articles which got wet in the canoe that filled yesterday. one of the men giged a Sammon Trout[1] in the River. towards evening the hunters returned to Camp had killed 5 five Deer a goose and a gray Squirrel.[2] they Saw a great number of deer in the timbered land. we Saw a great no. of geese and ducks. the Savages came in crafts to our Camp made of Solid wood but are made in form of Sciffs for the convenience of rideing the waves in high winds, or to coast along the Sea Shore. Several of the Indians Stayed with us this night one of them a chief Capt. Lewis compared the languages of these with those which he had taken down all the way this Side of the mountains and find them to be all one nation but differ a little in their languages, caused by the different tribes of them Scatered Such a long distance from each other.[3]   all the way thick along the kimoo-e-nem & Columbia Rivers and to the head of all the Rivers runing in to it.   we think the flat head[4] nation to be ten Thousand Strong in all.   the River began to raise about 4 oClock P. M. and raised Several Inches, the cause of which we think that the tide Swels a little up to this place.

Saturday October 26th   A clear pleasant morning, and we continued at our Encampment near the point of rocks, with 2 Centinals placed to guard us.   Our hunters were sent out in order to hunt for game.   Our officers mean to delay here this day in order to ascertain the Latitude of this place, repair our Canoes &ca.   We unloaded our Canoes, shaved their bottoms clean, payed them over with Pitch.   We also put the loading that had got wet, in the Canoe Yesterday Out in order to dry <them>.   We had a number of the Natives at our Camp, to visit us.   One of our party gigged a large Salmon Trout in the River, which he brought to our Camp.   Towards Evening our hunters returned to the Camp.   They had killed 5 deer, 1 Goose & a grey squirrel.   They informed us, that they had seen a great number of deer, in the timbered land, We saw a great number of Ducks, & Geese in the River this day.—   The Indians came to our Camp this day, on Crafts made out of Cedar Wood.   These Crafts were made in the form of a Skiff, for the convenience of riding the Waves in high winds; or to coast along the Sea shore.—   They were neatly formed & dug out.—   Several of these Indians staid with us all Night, among which was one of their Chiefs.—   Captain Lewis compared the language of these Indians, with the different languages that he had taken down in writing, of all the Indians that we had seen on this side of the Rockey Mountains, & found them to be the same Nation, & to differ but little in their languages, which is occasioned by the different tribes of them, being scattered such a long distance from each other & all the way <thick> numerous along the Kio-me-num & Columbia Rivers & to the heads of all the Rivers that run into them.—

Our Officers as well as the Men, are of oppinion that all the Indians that we met with (since we first met with the flatt head Indians) belong to that Nation; & from the best calculation that we can make suppose them to be

Ten thousand Men strong <in all,> The Columbia River began to rise at about 4 o'Clock P. M. and raised several Inches. The cause of which we suppose to be from the flowing of the tide, which occasions the swell at this place.— The place we are at lies in Latitude 45° 0' North & called the long Narrows of Columbia River.

1. Apparently steelhead trout, *Oncorhynchus mykiss*.

2. Probably the western gray squirrel, *Sciurus griseus*.

3. "This Side of the mountains" is a vague location. However, since they had descended from the Bitterroots and met the Nez Perces, most of the people they had encountered had belonged to the Shahaptian language family, as Lewis had discerned. The Dalles area marked the dividing line between the Shahaptian language (upstream) and the Chinookan language (downstream). The Wishrams lived on the north side of the Columbia, and the closely allied Wascos on the south side; both spoke Chinookan languages.

4. The first "Flatheads" they met were the Salish, of the Salishan language family. From the Nez Perces on down to The Dalles the people were primarily Shahaptian speakers. Now they were among Chinookans. Perhaps they picked up the idea of calling all the people west of the mountains Flatheads from the Mandans and Hidatsas, or maybe from Sacagawea and her fellow Shoshones.

Sunday 27th Oct. 1805. a clear morning. the wind high from the west. 6 of the party went out to hunt, back from the River in the timbered country, Such as white oak and pitch pine. the wind continued high all day in the evening the hunters returned to Camp had killed 4 Deer. we Set the Savages across the River which had been with us all day eating our venison. our officers gave one of the principal men a meddle &c.

Sunday October 27th This morning Clear, but the Wind blew high from the West, which continued so the whole of this day. Six of our party went out, in Order to hunt, back from the River in a timbered Country, the growth of which was white Oak & pitch pine Trees. In the Evening our hunters returned with 4 Deer which they had killed.— We carried the Indians that had been with us all day; across the River, in order that they might go to their Village. Our officers gave the principal Men that was among them Medals & some other small articles.—

Monday 28th Oct. 1805. the wind Seased the later part of last night, and began to rain and rained moderately untill morning, then cleared off we loaded up the canoes and Set out about 9 oClock   the wind raised and blew high from the west.   we proceeded on about 4 miles and halted at an Indian village[1] of about 6 lodges, where we Saw an old Brittish musket and Sword, copper tea kittles &c.   we bought Several 5 fat dogs, Some root bread &c. then proceeded on a Short distance further down   the wind rose So high from the west that caused the waves to roll So that we thought it not Safe to proceed   So we halted under a clift of rocks on the Lard. Side.   had Several Squalls of [wind?] & high all day.   So we Camped[2] for the night.   one of the party killed a Deer this evening, and wounded another near a Small pond a Short distance back from the River.—   a nomber of the natives visited us &c.—

Monday October 28th   The wind ceased blowing the latter part of last night; when it began to rain and continued raining moderately till morning; when we loaded our Canoes, and set out on our Voyage at 9 o'Clock A. M. the wind rose again, & blew from the Westward.   We proceeded on, <and> about 4 Miles, when we halted at an Indian Village of 6 lodges, where we saw an Old British Musquet, a Sword, Copper tea kettles &ca.   We bought of the Natives at this place 5 fatt dogs, some Root bread & several other Articles.—

We continued on our way a short distance further down the River, when the Wind rose so high from the Westward, & the Waves ran also so high, that our officers thought it dangerous to proceed.   We came too with our Canoes under a Clift of rocks, which lay on the South side of the River.   We had several squalls of wind during this day.   We encamped on the So. side of the River.   One of our party killed one Deer, & wounded another; in the Evening, near a small pond; a short distance back from the River, which deer he brought to our Camp.—   We had a number of the Natives to visit us after we had encamped.—

1. The party's Chiluckittequaws (variously spelled), probably Wishram-Wascos.

2. At what Clark called "a verry Bad place," in Wasco County, Oregon, a few miles below The Dalles, in the vicinity of Crates Point, and above Rowena.

Tuesday 29th Oct. 1805.   a cloudy morning.   we Set out eairly and proceeded on about 6 miles and halted for breakfast at Some Indian villages[1] on the Stard. Side, where we bought a nomber more fat dogs   we proceeded on the current gentle   passed a great nomber of Indian villages on the Stard Side which had their houses built like those at the falls.   Saw 2 or 3 Camps on the Lard. Side, which was the first we Saw on that Side of the Calm. R. passed the mo. of two creeks,[2] one on each Side, and a Spring on Lard. Side which ran of a high clift of rocks which looked curious.   the country this day mountaineous high clifts of rocks on each side of the River.   the country mostly timbred Such as pine and oak.   Some cottonwood[3] on Some of the narrow bottoms along the Shores willows also.   we bought Several more dogs at one of the villages.   went 26 miles and Camped[4] at a village on the Stard. Side in a Small or narrow bottom of large cotton trees.   we bought Several bags of pounded Sammon to day.   we Saw Snow on the timbred mountains[5] on the Lard. Side a little back from the River.

Tuesday October 29th   A cloudy cool morning.   We set out early & proceeded on about 6 Miles & halted to breakfast, at some Indian Lodges, lying on the North side of the River; which was Inhabited by a number of Indians. We purchased from those Indians, a number more fat dogs.   We proceeded on our Voyage, & found the current of the River to run very gentle, & passed a great number of Indian Villages, lying on the North side of the River.   The houses in those Villages; were built in the same manner of those that I have already described that lay at the falls of this River.   We passed 3 Indian Camps which were on the South side of the River.   these were the first Indian camps, that we had seen, that lay on that side of the River.   We also passed two Creeks, lying on each side of the River & a spring which lay on the South side of the River, which ran from off a high Clift of Rocks & had a curious appearance.—

The Country this day is very Mountaineous & has high Clifts of Rocks lying on each side of the River.   The Country here abounds with Timber of Pine & Cotton wood.—

The bottoms along the River is small, & has will growing on them.   We purchased of the Natives a number of bags of pounded Salmon.   We saw mountains lying on the South side of the River; a distance back from it; Covered with timber, which had Snow lying on them.   We came about 26 Miles this day, & encamped at an Indian Village, lying on the North side of the

376

River, in a narrow bottom, which was covered with Cotton Wood Trees.—
We found the Natives here very friendly & of the Flatt head nation.

   1. More Chiluckittequaws, living in Klickitat County, Washington.

   2. Klickitat River, Klickitat County, Washington, on the right, and Hood River, Hood River
County, Oregon, on the left. The party named them Cataract River and Labiche River for
François Labiche, respectively.

   3. Probably black cottonwood, *Populus trichocarpa* T. & G.

   4. In Skamania County, Washington, a little below the Little White Salmon River, the captains' Little Lake Creek. The people in this vicinity were White Salmon and Klickitat Indians.

   5. The Cascade Range.

Wednesday 30th Oct. 1805. cloudy. we bought 3 dogs of the Indians, and
Set out about 7 oClock and proceeded on. the river verry Strait and wide.
the Timber thick on each Side. Saw a nomber of beautiful Springs running
out of the clifts on the Lard. Side high hills covred with pine and Spruce.
Some bottoms along the Shores covred with cotton timber, and under brush
&c. the after part of the day rainy and foggey. one of the hunters killed a
Deer. we Saw a great nomber of Swan [1] and geese, turkey buzzards [2] which
had white on their wings &c. Capt. Clark killed a black loon. [3] in the evening we arived at another verry bad rapid or falls, above which the River is
gentle and wide a nomber of Islands and high rocks &c one half mile above
the falls is a village [4] of about 10 well looking cabbins covred with bark, Sunk
in the ground like those at the narrows above, only these are much larger
and verry comfortable, and warm. these Savages were Surprized to See us
they Signed to us that they thought that we had rained down out of the
clouds. a nomber of the party went in the village, and was treated in a
friendly manner gave fish and the best they had to eat &c. we went
15 miles and Camped [5] between the village and falls. continued raining.
high mountains on each Side of the falls &c. we passed the mouth of a
River [6] came in on the S. Side 50 yds wide. [7]

Wednesday October 30th We had a cool Cloudy morning. The Natives
came early to our Camp and our officers purchased from them 3 more fat
dogs. We set out on our Voyage again, down the Columbia River. We
found the River at a short distance from where we started this morning to be

very strait & wide and Trees of different kinds very thick on the Shores, on both sides of the River, and beautiful Springs running from under Clifts of Rocks, along the Shores. We also saw on the South side of the River, a small distance back from it, pine & Spruce Timber; which grew on high hills, and in the bottoms on both shores were Covered with Cotton Wood trees & under brush.— The latter part of this day we had some Rain & it became foggy. One of our hunters that had went out this morning, met us with a deer, which he had killed. We saw a great quantity of Geese & Ducks in the River, & Turkey buzzards which differed in Colour to those we had before seen, having white feathers on their wings. Captain Clark killed along the Shore a black Raccoon. In the Evening we arrived at a very bad Rapid or falls, above which, the River run very gentle & was wide, having a number of Islands & high Rocks in it.— We saw about half a Mile above those falls, an Indian Village.—

This Village contained about 10 well looking Cabbins, (which were covered with bark) sunk in the ground, as those we had seen at the falls, which I have already described & were much more comfortable & larger sized. The Indians belonging to this Village made signs to us as we passed along by their village, that they thought & supposed that we had rained down from the Clouds, and seemed very much surprized at seeing us, they not beleiving that we could possibly descended the River at that season of the Year. A number of our party went to this Indian Village, & the Indians treated them in a very friendly manner, & gave them the best they had to eat. On each side of these falls, lays very high mountains, and about 2 Miles above them, we passed the mouth of a River which lay on the South side of this River, which was about 30 Yards wide & by us called the River La Bache.[8] We came about 15 Miles this day, & encamped between the Indian Village & the falls. The Rain continued the greater part of this night.—

1. Probably Lewis and Clark's whistling swan, now the tundra swan.

2. California condor, *Gymnogyps californianus*.

3. Mentioned this day by Ordway but not Clark. Perhaps the common loon, *Gavia immer*, the Pacific loon, *G. arctica pacifica*, or the red-throated loon, *G. stellata*.

4. Yehuhs, a Chinookan-language people of whom little is known.

5. Just above the Cascades of the Columbia River, on an island in Skamania County, Washington, nearly opposite Cascade Locks, Hood River County, Oregon.

6. The captains named it Cruzatte's River, after Pierre Cruzatte of the party; it is now Wind River, Skamania County.

7. Beginning with "high mountains," these last several sentences are crowded in between entries.

8. They had passed Hood (Labiche) River the previous day.

Thursday 31st Oct. 1805. Some cloudy. we got in readiness to carry our baggage past the portage, which we expict will be about two miles. about 9 oClock cleared off pleasant. as the road was Slippery we concluded to take Some of the canoes down to day. So we took down two canoes 1 at a time over high rocks on rollers, by main Strength and by being in the water which ran between Sd. Stone & large rocks. we had to hall them in that way past 2 of the worst rapids then took them a half a mile below, where we intend loading which will make the portage in all only about one mile, but a verry bad one. in the evening 2 Indian canoes came to our Camp 5 Indians in them which were going down the River tradeing with fish &c.

Thursday October 31st This morning was cool & Cloudy. Our party were employed in getting every thing fixed in order to carry the baggage &ca. below the Portage, which we expect will be about 2 Miles. About 9 o'Clock A. M. the weather cleared off, and became pleasant. The Road being slippey, Our officers concluded to have only part of our Canoes hawled down this day. We proceeded on with 2 of our Canoes on Rollers at a time; over high Rocks, by main strenghth hawling them all the way, which was about ½ Miles & passed two of the worst Rapids, & went about half a mile further below them, at which place we intend loading the Canoes again, making the whole of the Portage to be only about 1 Mile— and all this way bad Road. In the Evening 2 indian Canoes came to our Camp. They had 5 Indians in them, & were going down the River in Order to trade away fish &ca. which their Canoes were loaded with

Friday 1st Nov. 1805. a clear morning. the wind high from the N. E. and cold. So we carryed all our baggage past the portage the Indians carried their Baggage and canoes past the portage. we drew out one of the canoes to repair it. then went at tak[ing] down the other two large canoes, and th[e] Small one. towards evening we got all Saf[e] below the big rapids and

Camped.[1]   three canoes arived at the head of the rapids a nomber of men and women on board of them.   they are loaded with pounded fish and dry Sammon for trade.   they Sign to that they are going down to the white traders to trade their fish for blue Beeds

Friday Novemr. 1st   A Clear morning, the Wind high from the No. East & cold.   We set off and carried all our baggage below the Portage.   The Indians that were at our Camp last night, also carried their Canoes & loading below the portage.   We hawled out the remainder of our Canoes, one of which we repaired, and towards evening we got them all down below the big Rapids, and Encamped.   During the time we were at the head of the Rapid, three Canoes also arrived there.   These Canoes had on board of them, pounded Salmon for to Trade; & the Indian Men & women that was on board of them, made signs to us, that they were going down the River, in order to trade away their pounded fish for Blue beads &ca. with the Indians who resided on the Sea Coast.—

1. In Skamania County, Washington, above Bonneville Dam and near the communities of Fort Rains and North Bonneville.

Saturday 2nd Nov. 1805.   a clear morning.   we carried a part of the baggage below the other last rapids one mile further and ran over one canoe down the rapid at a time.   about 10 oClock A. m. we got all below the last rapids we have any acct. of from the Savages, then loaded the canoes agn. and about 12 oC Set out and proceeded on over Several more rapids at the foot of large Islands.   Saw 2 old ancient villages below the big rapids which was evacuated, the bark taken off of one of them and put in a pond to Soak. the frames verry large.   the mountains verry high on the Lard. Side and on the S. Side a little back from the River.   proceed. on abt. 4 miles then the Riv. got Smooth the current verry gentle &c   the River wide and Strait the remdr. of the day   we passed a creek[1] on L. Side &c.   great number of Spring runs, and Springs flowing from the high clifts and mountains and fell off down 100 feet or more.[2]   high clifts on each Side.   the Indians over took us with their canoes, which they carryed past the big rapids   Saw 2 Indians dressed in red Scarlet and one in blue cloth which appeared new.

they had a Musket which was made all of brass and copper, a powder flask &c. towards evening the River got more wide could Scarsely perceive any current at all. the mont. and clifts cont. all day. went 21 miles and Camped[3] under a Shelving clift & a green on the Lard. Side. Saw this day abundance of geese and killed 16 of them. Saw Some Swan and brants[4] ducks &c. passd. one village this after noon on the S. Side. passd. Some narrow bottoms high towers of rocks &c. the country is timbred but mostly Spruce and Pine. Some oak &c—

Saturday Novemr. 2nd A Clear morning but cool. Our party were all engaged in carrying a part of our baggage &ca below these rapids, to a place below the last part of them. On our party returning; they carried the whole of our Canoes down the last Rapid one at a time. About 10 o'Clock A. M. we got them all safe below it. This Rapid is the last, that we have any account of, that lays on the Columbia river, from the Indians. We loaded our Canoes & about 12 o'Clock A. M. We proceeded on down the Columbia River, & passed over several small rapids which lay at the foot of an Island. We saw lying below the big Rapid this day, 2 old ancient looking Indian Villages, which were without any Inhabitants. The bark had been taken off one of those huts in this Village & put into a pond to Soak.— The frames of these huts were very large.— We saw large high Mountains which lay on both sides of the River, a small distance back from it.—

We proceeded on about 4 Miles when the River that had been running rapid this day & rough, became quite smooth & gentle. The River at this place is wide & strait, & remained so during the whole of this day. We passed a creek which lay on the So. side of the River, & a great number of springs & Spring runs flowing from the Clifts & mountains which lay high & fell from off these Clifts & Mountains upwards of 100 feet into the River. The high Clifts & rocks lies on both sides of the River. The Indians that we had left at the <east> first fall (or rapid) overtook us with their Canoes, which they had carried below the big rapid. We saw on board those Indians Canoes 2 of the Indian Men, who were dressed in Scarlet & one of them dressed in blue Cloth all of which appeared to be new. Those Indians had a Musket which the Stock was made of Brass & Copper & a Powder flask.— Towards evening the River got rather wide, & we could scarcely perceive any current running in the River. The Clifts and mountains continued back a small distance from the River all this day. We passed in the afternoon an Indian Village which lay on the South side of the River. We also passed some high towers of Rocks & Narrow bottoms of land which lay along the River on both sides of it. The Country this day is Timbered land, the growth Spruce, Pine & some Oaks; & the soil very poor. We saw this day in the River, Geese, Swans, Brants & ducks.— Some of our party shot 16 Geese, which we got. We came 21 Miles this day, & encamped under a shelving rock lying on the South side of the River, Our course Continuing West.—

1. Perhaps Tanner Creek, Multnomah County, Oregon.

2. Probably Multnomah and other falls in Multnomah County.

3. In the vicinity of Latourell, within Rooster Rock State Park, Multnomah County, Oregon.

4. *Branta bernicla.*

Sunday 3rd Nov. 1805. a foggy morning. we delayd. untill abt. 9 oClock. Several men went out a Short distance to hunt. we Shot Several geese flying over our Camp this morning. one canoe belonging to the Savages and Several Indians camped with us last night. a handsom Spring run came in near our Camp. the fog So thick this morning that we cannot See more than one hundred yards distance. agreeable to all calculations it cannot be more than two hundred miles from this to the ocean. one of the men[1] killd. a large buck Deer we then Set out abt. 9 oC. and proceeded on the fog continued So thick that we could Scarsely See the Shores or Islands passed Several Isld. abt. noon we halted to dine at the mo. of a River[2] which came in on the Lard. Side, the mouth of which was filled with quick Sand So that we could run a pole 6 or 8 feet in it, and it emptyd. in at Several places thro a verry large Sand bar which lay at the mo we then proceeded on passd. the mo. of a Small River[3] on Stard. the after part of the day clear and pleas[ant] we Saw a high round mountain on the Lard Side which we expect is the Same we Saw abo. the great falls and the Same that Lieut. Hood gave an account off.[4] (it is nearly covd. with Snow) we proceeded on the River verry wide better than a mile in general. a nomber of large Islands &c. towards evening we met Several Indians in a canoe who were going up the River. they Signed to us that in two Sleeps we Should See [the Ocean vessels and?] white people &c. &c. the Country lower and not So mountanous the River more handsome the current verry gentle. Some bottoms covered with cotton and pine &c. passd. a nomber of large Islands. went about 13 miles and Camped[5] on a verry large & long Island which was mostly prarie and handsome. a large lake on it. we have Seen a great many Sea otter in the River ever Since we came to the Big falls. the geese and Swan ducks and brants &c. we killed Several Swan geese and brants &c. this day. a nomber of the Savages Camped with us. at Sunset we got a Small canoe from them and carried it out to the pond or lake and killed a nomber of large Swan and geese.

Sunday Novemr. 3d   A foggy morning & we delayed setting out till about 9 oClock A. M.   Several of our men went out a short distance for to hunt.— The party that remained at Camp, shot this morning several Geese as they were flying over our Camp. One of the Canoes that we saw at the large rapid stopped at the place we encamped, & the Indians that were in her, & several others of the same Nation that came by land staid with us all night. The fog got so thick that we could not see 100 Yards distance from the Camp. We find agreeable to the best calculation we can make that we are not more than 200 Miles from the Ocean. One of the party that went out hunting this morning returned to the Camp and brought with him a large buck Deer which he had killed. The remainder of the hunters also returned, & had killed a number of Geese & Ducks. We then set out on our Voyage, the fog continuing so thick, that we could scarcely see the Shores or Islands as we passed along   We saw about 12 o'Clock A. M. several Islands & halted to dine at the Mouth of a River, which came into the Columbia River on the South side. The mouths or entrance of this River is filled with a quick sand, which we run a pole 8 feet down, & had no solid bottom and it emptied itself by several Mouths

At 2 o'Clock P. M. we passed also the Mouth of a small river, lying on the North side of the Columbia River. The weather now got clear & pleasant. We continued on, and saw a high round Mountain, lying on the South side of the River, which we supposed to be the same Mountain, that we saw above the great falls of this River, and believe it to be the same Mountain; that Lieutenant Hood gave an account of when on a Voyage round the World with Captain Cook, This Mountain appeared nearly covered with Snow. We proceeded on, the River being nearly One Mile & a quarter wide in general, & a number of large Islands in it, laying on both sides of it.—

Towards evening we met with several Indians, who were in a Canoe, & who were going up the River. The Indians made signs to us, that in 2 Sleeps, (meaning 2 days,) that we should come to a place, where we should see two Vessells, white people &ca. The country during this day, appears to lay lower than it had been for some time past, & but few mountains to be seen. The River had a handsomer appearance & the Current of it very gentle. We passed by some bottom land, lying along the River, which were cover'd with Cotton wood & Pine Trees, and a number of Islands. We encamped on a very large long Island by us called Swan Island, which was chiefly a Priari, and had a large lake in it, having gone about 13 Miles this day. We saw in the River ever since we came through the great falls, a great many Sea Otters, Geese, Swans, brants, ducks & other water fowl.— Our party killed several Geese Swans & Ducks <of them> this day. A number of Indians came to the Island that we were encamped on, in Canoes, & encamped with us. Some of our party borrowed a small Canoe from those Indians, & carried it out to the lake, where they killed a further quantity of Swans & Geese.—

1. Collins, according to Clark.

2. Sandy River, Multnomah County, Oregon; Quicksand River to the party.

3. Washougal River, joining the Columbia River near Washougal, Clark County, Washington.

4. Mt. Hood, Hood River County, Oregon, was named for British Admiral Sir Samuel Hood by Lieutenant William Broughton of George Vancouver's seaborne exploring expedition in 1792. They passed his farthest point up the river this day.

5. Either Government or McGuire islands, opposite and above Portland, Multnomah County.

Monday 4th Nov. 1805. Some cloudy. the tide [swell?] about two feet perpinticular last night and on the rise this morning. one of the men went out on the Island and killed a Deer & goose. about 7 oClock we Set out and proced. on abt. 8 mils. passd. Several large Islands[1] covd. with cotton timber & praries the River wider. we Came to a verry large village[2] on L. Side the Savages verry nomerous in it, about 35 Cabbens. it is but a new village.

they have a vast quantity of pounded Sammon in their cabbins. they have 50 canoes at their handsome village or landing they have cloths of different kinds among them. the timber Such as cotton and pine is thick in these bottoms the River is now handsome— we bought 2 dogs and Some excelent roots[3] which we found nearly as good as potatoes. we then proceed. on a Short distance and halted to dine on the Stard Side. 2 canoe loads of Savages followed us from the village. they Stole Capt. Clarks pipe Tomahawk which we could not find. [*page torn*] all the way on [*page torn*] timbered bottoms on each Side covd. with cotton and oak timber. a little back from the River the hills is covred with pine and Spruce from which the Savages git the bark to cover their villages. passd. Several more verry large villages on each Side. the Savages are verry numerous. the country appears to be good, the Soil rich and game tollr. pleanty. we Saw the Indians bring in Several deer to day which they had killed with their bows and arrows. towards evening we met a large canoe loaded with Indians one of them could curse Some words in Inglish. they had a Sturgeon on board. they canoe had images worked on the bow & Stern. they had five muskets on board. we discovered a high round mountain Some dis[tance] back from the River on Stard. Side which is called mount Rainy.[4] we are not yet out of Site of Mount Hood which is covd. with Snow. Saw a great many Sea otter in the River we went 28 miles to day and Camped[5] after dark on the Starbord Side. the Swan and geese are verry pleanty on the River brants al[so]

Monday Novemr. 4th This morning was cold & foggy. We are now tide way, the tide fell during last night 2 feet perpendicular, and is on the rise this morning. One of our party went out early this morning on the Island & killed one deer & a goose which was brought to our Camp. About 7 O'Clock A. M. we set off & proceeded on about 8 Miles, and passed several Islands, which were large & covered with Cotton wood Trees & Priaries. The River still getting wider, & we then came to where lay a very large Village of Indians, which lay on the South side of the River. This Village had about 35 Cabbins which appeared to have been lately built.—

The Indians at this Village was very numerous, & had a vast quantity of pounded Salmon in their Cabbins, & had about 50 Canoes laying at a landing at this Village. This village was by far the handsomest of the kind that we had yet seen. It was situated on a rising piece of ground, & lay along the River. The bottom land near this place is cover'd with Cotton wood & pine timber, the Soil tolerably good, & the River had a pleasant appearance, being wide & the current of the tide running very gentle.— These Indians had Cloths of different kinds among them, which they made signs to us that they had got from white people at the Ocean. Our Officers purchased from these Indians, 2 fat dogs, & some excellent roots, which we found to eat nearly as good as potatoes. We continued on our way a short distance, & halted to dine on the North side of the River, The Indians in the Village that we last left, sent 2 Canoes loaded with Indians after us, and they came to the place that we halted at. They proved to be a thievish set of Savages; for after being treated well by us, they stole Captain Clarks pipe Tomahawk; & not withstanding the stricktest search that we could make, we could not find it.— We proceeded on our Voyage, and passed a number of Islands, lying on the South side of the River, & some handsome bottom land which lay along the River, <which was> covered with Cotton wood and Oak timber. We saw lying a small distance back from the River, several hills, which were covered with Pine & Spruce Trees, which were very large, The Indians get the bark from these Trees to cover the roofs of their houses with. We passed this day, several more large Indian Villages, which lay on each side of the River. The Indians appear'd to be very numerous, The Country pleasant, the Soil rich & Game tolerably plenty.—

We saw the Indians bringing into their Villages several deer, which they had killed with their Bows & arrows. Towards evening, we were met by a number of Indians, who were in a Canoe (which was very large) One of these Indians, could curse in English which he did. They had a large Sturgeon on board this Canoe. This Canoe had Images carved on its head & stern, and the Indians had five Muskets with them. We discovered a mountain, which lay on the North side of the River, some distance back from it. It appeared to be round, and is called Mount Rainey. We are not yet out of sight of Mount Hood, which from this place appears to be covered with Snow. We saw this day a considerable number of Sea Otters in the River. In the Evening we encamped, on the North side of the River, where we saw, Swan, Geese, Brants & ducks in the greatest abundance in the River. We came about 28 Miles this day, our Course being nearly West.

1. The party's Diamond and Image Canoe islands; the first is apparently later Government and McGuire islands, the second Hayden and Tomahawk islands. Later in the day they passed Sauvie Island, the party's Wapato Island.

2. The people Clark calls Shahalas; they were Watlalas, speakers of an Upper Chinookan language. The village, now long destroyed, was within the limits of modern Portland, Multnomah County, Oregon.

3. Wapato, *Sagittaria latifolia* Willd.

4. Not Mt. Rainier but Mt. St. Helens, Skamania County, Washington.

5. Probably near Salmon Creek, Clark County, Washington.

Tuesday 5th Nov. 1805. began to rain abt. one oClock last night and rained untill morn. the morning cloudy. we Set out eirly and proceeded on verry well the River verry Strait. passd. Islands as usal[1] abt. 10 miles [*page torn*] the largest village we have [*page torn*] the S. Side. the cabbens [*page torn*] they had a great no[mber] [*page torn*] Some of them got in their [canoes and] came out in the River to See us. they wanted to trade us Elk Skins for muskets. we proceeded on 20 miles Since we Started this morng. and halted about 1 oC. to dine on an Isl.[2] Several men went out a Short time to hunt, and killed one Swan and Several brants. we then proceeded on. passed one or 2 more villages had Several Small Showers of rain the Isld. continues all the way covd. with cotton timber. the bottoms cont. as usal. we went 31 miles to day and Camped[3] on the Lard. Side where the pine hills make close to the River and Some clifts of rocks on L. Shore. the River about a mile wide this evening rainy.—

Tuesday Novemr. 5th It began to rain about one o'Clock last night, and continued till day light & This morning was Cloudy. We set out early on our Voyage, & found the River run very strait, & grew wider. We passed a number of large Islands for the distance of 10 Miles, and then went by the largest Indian Village that we had yet seen on this River; This village lay on the South side of the River. The Cabbins in this Village all joined, and the Indians belonging to this Village, had a great number of Canoes. Some of the Indians from this Village, came out with their Canoes in the River to us; & wanted to Trade us Elk skins, for Muskets, or Guns of any kind, but our Officers refused, we having not more Rifles than what we wanted. We proceeded on, and halted about 1 o'Clock to dine on an Island, where several of our Men went out & killed a swan & several Brants.—

We continued on our Voyage at 2 o'Clock P. M, & passed 2 More Indian Villages, lying on the South side of the River. The Islands still continued as we passed down the River all the way, we went this day; & we had frequently small showers of rain. The Islands I have last mentioned, were covered with Cotton wood, & other timber. The bottom land along the shore, continue the same as those I last mentioned. We came about 31 Miles this day, & encamped on the North side of the River, where hills covered with pine Trees made close into the River, & some Clifts of Rocks. This evening continued Rainey. the River was about 1 Mile wide at this place.

1. Including Bachelor Island, their Green Bryor Island, near the mouth of Lewis River, the boundary between Clark and Cowlitz counties, Washington.

2. The captains called it El-lal-lar or Deer Island; it is still Deer Island, Columbia County, Oregon. The Indians of this day are the Cathlapotles.

3. Perhaps near Prescott, Columbia County.

Wednesday 6th Nov. 1805.[1] Several Showers of rain in the course of last night. the guard had to attend to the canoes to keep them loose as the tide Ebbs & flows abt. 3 feet pertular. a cloudy wet morning. we Set out eairly and proceeded on. Shortly passed a Small village on Lard. Side. Some Indians came out in the River to us with their canoes. we bought Some fresh fish from them, and bought Some fine roots from a canoe which was going down the R. with a load trading at noon we halted to dine at a large bottom which was covd. with cotton timber on the S. Side. Several hunters went out abt. one hour and the underbrush So thick that they could not [go] any distance back. we proceeded on. passed high clifts on L. S. abt. 100 feet from the S[urface] of the water. the hills on each Side are [covered with] different kinds of pine

Wednesday Novemr. 6th   We had several showers of rain during last night; Our officers placed a guard on our Canoes during the night, to attend them, the tide rising & falling 3 feet perpendicular. This morning was cloudy & wet. We set off early, & proceeded on our Voyage. We passed a small Indian Village, which lay on the South side of the River. Some Indians came to us in Canoes; from whom we purchased some fresh fish of different kinds, And also purchased, some Roots from <some> Indians who over took us in Canoes; & were going down the River with loads of this root &ca to trade.   About noon, we halted to dine, at a large bottom, which was covered with Cotton wood Trees, lying on the South side of the River.   several of our hunters went out for about an hour, & found the underbrush growing so thick; that they could not go any distance.— We continued on, & passed high Clifts of rocks lying on the South side of the River, which were about 100 feet high, from the surface of the Water, & hills on both sides of the River, covered with different kind of Pine & White Cedar, & a wood called Abervity, Red wood[2] &ca.—

We proceeded on & passed large bottoms having Cotton wood Trees & white Oak[3] timber growing in them, & two old Indian Villages which were evacuated & had been left sometime past.   We also passed several springs. Towards evening we had the Wind blowing hard from the Westward & the Waves ran very high.   We came 27 Miles this day & encamped[4] on the North side of the River, under a Clift of Rocks.—

1. This is the last entry in the original version of Whitehouse's journal (see Introduction to this volume). There are edges of perhaps three or four pages remaining and some writing is visible but not legible. There is no way of determining to what date this notebook continued.

2. White cedar, *arborvitae*, and red wood are all names for one species, western redcedar.

3. Oregon white, or Garry, oak, *Quercus garryana* Dougl. ex. Hook.

4. In southwestern Wahkiakum County, Washington (see Clark's entry for this day).

Thursday Novemr. 7th[1]   A cool foggy morning.   We set out early, & proceeded on 'till about 10 o'Clock A. M. when we arrived at an Indian Village,[2] consisting of 4 cabbins which were inhabited by the Natives.   We halted at this place a short timber; & purchased from the Indians, some fish, roots, & a number of dogs.   We continued on our Voyage, and passed a number of Islands, which lay low.   These Islands were Marshy & were covered with Grass, & had Water laying in different parts of them.   Towards evening, we passed another Indian Village, which lay on the North side of the River, where we stopped a short time, & purchased from the Natives some fresh fish, Roots &ca.   The Indians who lived in this small village, where from their appearance a dirty, indolent sett of beings.   They had among them Elk meat & Venison; pounded fish, roots &ca.   The Indians both at this, & the other Indian village that we passed this day, made signs to us that there were vessells lying at the Mouth of this River. Some of them signed to us that the Vessells were gone away from it. We saw among these Savages, long planks or puncheons; which they used to cover their Cabbins with. The Men among these Indians go entirely naked, & the Women have pettycoats made out of a sort of grass & platted,[3] which they wear; the other part of their body, being entirely naked. We continued on, & saw some high rough hills, which was covered with pine Trees, high clifts of rocks & some Springs of water.—

We went about 35 Miles this day, & encamped at a Springs run, which lay on the South side[4] of the River, opposite to which lay in the River a high round Rock, which had very much the resemlance of a Tower; Our hunters killed this day several Geese & Swans, which they brought to our Camp.—

1. This entry begins the material that comes exclusively from Whitehouse's fair copy. It continues through April 2, 1806, the end of his known journal writing.

2. A Wahkiakum Indian village in Wahkiakum County, Washington.

3. This same garment also attracted the attention of the captains and prompted Lewis's detailed description of January 19, 1806, apparently copied by Clark under the present date, November 7, presumably because this was where they first noticed this style.

4. Gass also places this camp on the south side, which is misleading. The camp was in fact on the north side, opposite Pillar Rock, in Wahkiakum County, between Brookfield and Dahlia.

Friday Novemr. 8th   This morning we had cool cloudy weather. We set out on our Voyage early. Shortly after the wind rose & blew from the So East very hard, & the River got so rough, that we were tossed very much in our Canoes. We continued on our Voyage, & went round a point of the River, & entered into a Bay,[1] or wide place about 7 Miles wide, which continued as far as our Eyes could descern; & we expect that the River continues its width to the Mouth of it. We halted about noon, at some old Indian Cabbins lying on the South side of the River in order to dine. We saw vast quantities of Geese & Swans in the bend of this River, or bay. Our Hunters killed some Ducks, which they brought to us. We continued on our Voyage, & found the Waves running so high, that we were obliged to land about 3 o'Clock P. M, which we did on the South shore, & took up our encampment for the Night.[2]   Our party had to watch our Canoes constantly, in order to prevent them filling, the waves still continuing to run very high.   We found the River water at this place brackish.   We came 24 Miles this day.—

1. Grays Bay, in Pacific and Wahkiakum counties, Washington. The party called it Shallow Bay.

2. They camped here until November 10, either near the Pacific–Wahkiakum county line, or farther west near Frankfurt, Pacific County, and Grays Point.

Saturday Novemr 9th   It rained the greater part of last night, & the Wind blew very hard from the So. East, which caused the Waves to run so very high, that all hands were employed before day light this morning, in unloading the Canoes to keep them from sinking.   The morning we had wet weather & rainey, & it rained the most part of this day.—   The wind continued high, which caused the tide to rise, much higher than at common tides.   this obliged us to remove our Camp & the baggage &ca to a place some small distance from the River, some of our Men went out and killed several ducks. it ceased raining in the evening.—

Sunday Novemr. 10th   We had rain the greater part of last night & a wet rainey morning, but the Waves did not run so high as they did Yesterday. We loaded our Canoes & set out.   We proceeded on, and passed high hills with pine trees growing on them, some high Clifts of rocks & several fine Springs of fresh water.   We saw in the River a number of Porpoises,[1] & Sea Otters, Sea Gulls[2] & Ducks in the greatest abundance.   We continued on our way, it raining hard on us, 'till about noon; when it ceased.   The Waves then ran so high that we had to turn back and went up the River about 2 Miles, before we could find a harbour to unload the Canoes.   We at last found a convenient place, at which we unloaded our Canoes.   We halted at that place, where we staid till towards evening, when we loaded our Canoes again, and proceedd on up the River in hopes to find a safer harbour, than the one that we had left.   We went a small distance from the place we left, & came to a large Spring run; lying on the South side, in a bend of the River, where we stopped & Encamped.[3]   we again unloaded the Canoes, & had scarcely room to lay down, the hills making in so close to the River.   We went about 7 Miles this day, our course being nearly West.—

1. Perhaps the harbor, or common, porpoise, *Phocoena phocoena*.

2. *Larus* sp.

3. They remained here until November 15, on the eastern side of Point Ellice, Pacific County, Washington, east of the Astoria Bridge near Melgar.

Monday Novemr 11th   It rained hard the greater part of last night, which made it very disagreeable to us all.   The greater part of our Men had nothing to shelter them from the rain, & were obliged to lay down in it, & their Cloathes were wet through.   This morning continued wet & rainey, the wind was high, & the swell in the river ran very high, & We did not attempt to move from this place.—

About 4 o'Clock P. M. 4 Indians came down the river in a Canoe, & halted at where we were encamp'd.   They had a quantity of fresh Salmon trout, & some Roots &ca   We purchased from them some of the Salmon trout. They informed us by signs that they were going down to the Mouth of the River, to trade with white people; & mention'd in english the name of a particular white Man who they called Mr. Haley,[1] & made signs to us that they traded with him.   These Indians staid but a short time with us, & then set out.   they crossed to the other side of the River with their Canoes, through high waves & breakers, which we all consider'd too dangerous to attempt. Some of our party Shot & gigged 16 Salmon trout in a Creek, a short distance above our Camp.—

1. Perhaps Samuel Hill of Boston, captain of the brig *Lydia*, who traded with Indians of the lower Columbia (see Clark's entry for November 6).

Tuesday Novemr 12th   We had a hard storm the greater part of last night, & hard thunder, lightning, & hail this morning.   We saw a high mountain[1] which lay on the opposite to where we are encamped covered with snow. The Rain continued hard during the most part of this day.   We were employed in putting Stones in our Canoes to ballast them.   Towards evening we moved our Canoes & Camp a short distance up the River; to the mouth of a creek; where our men gigged several more fine Salmon Trout.

1. Perhaps Mt. Hood, some distance to the southeast in Hood River County, Oregon.

Wednesday Novemr. 13th   The storm continued & hard rain during last night, and this morning rainey disagreeable weather.   Our Buffalo robes are getting rotten, and the most part of our baggage were wet.   We have a very disagreeable time of it, the most part of our Men having slept in the rain, ever since this storm began, & are continually wet.   In the afternoon three[1] of our party set out in our smallest Canoe, in order to go down to the Mouth of the Columbia River to make discoveries

1. Colter, Willard, and Shannon, according to Clark. The canoe, which Gass praises on this date for its seaworthiness, was one they had obtained from the local Indians.

Thursday Novemr. 13th[1]   The storm continued hard during the whole of last night, and this morning we have rainey disagreeable weather.   The waves continued to run very high and we continued at our encampment waiting for moderate weather.   We have nothing to subsist on but fresh fish, & pounded Salmon; which is by no means nourishing.   One of the Men[2] that had went down the River Yesterday [*crossed out, illegible*] returned by land.   He informed us that he had been at an Indian Village near the mouth of the River, but had not seen any white people.   Captain Lewis & 4 of our party[3] set out in order to go down to that Indian Village by land.   The waves continued high & the Storm continued during the whole of this day.—

1. Misdated and clearly the activities of November 14.
2. Colter, reports Clark.
3. Drouillard, Joseph and Reubin Field, and Frazer, says Clark.

Friday Novemr 15th   We had a considerable quantity of rain during last night, & this morning we had wet rainey weather.   About 10 o'Clock A. M. the weather cleared off, & in the afternoon it became tolerable calm weather.   We loaded our Canoes and went with the ebb tide down the River about 4 Miles, and passed a large Indian Village, which was evacuated & some springs, or small Creeks, which lay below Clifts of rocks on both sides of the River.   The Country appeared to lay lower than it had been.   We encamped at a sand beach, at the head, or upper part of a large bay.[1]   One of the Men[2] that had went down the River in the Canoe, joined us here.   He informed us, that the Indians had stole several of their Guns last night; but they scared the Indians so much; that they gave them up to them this morning. He mentioned that Captain Lewis had gone on, to another Bay. We found plank to make up our Encampments with.—

1. They had rounded Point Ellice and entered Baker Bay, Pacific County, Washington, which the captains called Haley's Bay, after a sea captain–trader who used the bay as an anchorage, and whom the Indians had described as their favorite trader (see Clark's entries for November 6, 1805, and January 1, 1806). The camp was southeast of Chinook Point, on the east side of Baker Bay, and west of McGowan. The main party remained here until November 25, with perhaps a short move on November 16 (see Clark's entry for November 16, 1805).

2. Shannon, accompanied by five Indians; Willard had joined Lewis's party.

Saturday Novemr 16th A clear cool morning. several Indians staid near our Camp last night. several of our party went out a hunting; We put out our baggage to dry.—

The hunters all returned but one, to our Camp. they had killed 4 deer, & a number of Ducks, Geese & brants. A Number of Indians staid with us all day. We are now in plain view of the *Pacific Ocean*. the waves rolling, & the surf roaring very loud. on the opposite shore to us we discovered, the Tops of trees which we supposed to be on an Island laying a very great distance in the Ocean.[1] We are now of opinion that we cannot go any further with our Canoes,[2] & think that we are at an end of our Voyage to the Pacific Ocean, and as soon as discoveries necessary are made, that we shall return a short distance up the River & provide our Selves with Winter Quarters, & We suppose that we shall find a considerable Quantity of Game low down on the River.

1. Depending on what Whitehouse considered the opposite shore, and perhaps on the visibility at the time, this could refer to Sand Island, in the mouth of the Columbia, or Point Adams on the other side of the river in Clatsop County, Oregon.

2. In both his entries for this day Clark seems to say explicitly that the main party moved two miles on this day. Whitehouse, like Ordway and Gass, gives no indication of such a move.

Sunday Novemr 17th This morning we had clear pleasant weather. several of our hunters went out to hunt, and took with them, some of the party to help bring in the Game that they might kill to our Camp. In the afternoon the hunters all returned to Camp. They had killed 2 Deer, and a number of Brants & Ducks, which they, & the Men that went with them brought to us. In the Evening Captain Lewis, & the Men that was out with him also returned. They informed us, that they had been about 30 Miles down on the Sea Coast, & that they had seen no white people or Vessells.[1] They learnt from the Indians along the Coast that some white people & Vessells had been lately there but that they were all gone. Captain Clark concluded to go down with a party tomorrow to the Ocean in order to make his obsersvations of the Coast &ca.

1. Lewis has left no known account of this reconnaissance, but his party clearly reached the Pacific Coast near Cape Disappointment and went up the coast some miles in Pacific County, Washington.

Monday Novemr 18th   We had a cloudy morning.   Captain Clark, 2 Serjeants & eight of our Men[1] set out in Order to go down to Cape disappointment, (the Name of the Cape) in Order to get a satisfactory View of the Ocean &ca.

The Indians came to our Camp, from whom we purchased some dry Salmon.   Towards evening our hunters returned to our Camp; they had killed One Deer, 2 brants & a squirrel & also a large fish called Flounder,[2] which they brought with <us> them to our Camp.—   Our officers named this Cape Cape disappointment[3] on account of not finding Vessells there.—

1. According to Clark, the sergeants were Ordway and Pryor, and the men were Charbonneau, Joseph and Reubin Field, Shannon, Colter, Weiser, Labiche, and York. The captain's second entry for the day adds Bratton.

2. Probably starry flounder, *Platichthys stellatus*.

3. Actually named as such by Captain John Meares in 1788 when he missed the Columbia and concluded that a river did not exist here.

Tuesday Novemr. 19th   A cloudy morning.   Our hunters went out & killed 3 Deer this day, which they brought to our Camp.   A number of Indians came to visit us at our Camp.   They wore Robes made out of the Skins of swans, Squirrel skins, & some made out of beaver skins also—   Some of these Indians Wore hats which they make out of white Cedar & bear Grass.[1]

They sold one of these Hatts to one of our party for an old Razor blade. These Indians are a handsome well looking set of People,[2] and were far the lightest colour'd Natives that we had seen since we have been on our Voyage. Some of these Inc.ians about 15 in number encamped near us, and staid during this night.—

1. Beargrass, *Xerophyllum tenax* (Pursh) Nutt.

2. A very different impression of the appearance of the local people from that of Lewis; see the captain's entry for March 19, 1806. They were Chinooks, of the Chinookan language family.

Wednesday Novemr 20th   A clear pleasant morning.   Captain Lewis gave one of the Indians who had encamped near us a Medal.   One of our hunters[1] went out & killed two deer & several Brants.   About 4 o'Clock P. M Captain Clark & party returned to our encampment.— they mentioned of having been about 10 Miles North of Cape disappointment, along the Sea Coast; & that they found the Country <after> six miles travel from our Camp mountaineous; and than a flatt low country, mostly covered with Spruce pine timber, some ponds, & low Priaries, as far as they could see. they had killed One Deer, & 40 fowl of different kinds, such as ducks, Brants, &ca.   They had seen the Natives on the Sea shore, who they mention'd were a dirty lazy sett of people.   They also had seen among them a Sturgeon[2] which was about 8 feet long & had killed a very large uncommon Sized bird.—[3]

This bird had the resemblance of a Buzzard, it measured 9 feet from the point of one of its wings to the point of the other wing, the body was 3 feet 10 Inches in length, & the head & neck 67 Inches long & was white under its wings.

1. Labiche, reports Clark.

2. Perhaps an exaggerated description of the green sturgeon, *Acipenser medirostris*.

3. Their first specimen of the California condor, taken by Reubin Field.

Thursday Novemr 23d[1]   A Cloudy morning, and a light sprinkling of rain fell.   The Indians all left our Camp.   Two of our hunters left the Camp to go out ahunting.   The Swell in the River ran so high that it detain'd us, at our Camp from going up the River again, to look out for Winter Quarters, which our officers intended as soon as the Weather would permit, and the Season of the Year advancing made it absolutely necessary that it should be the case.— The Season of the Year, is generally cold at this place, but at the present time it was very pleasant. We are now convinced that the wide part of the River, or bay we entered into a few days past; is a bay only, and is called *Haleys bay* the Latitude is as follows of the point above the said Bay, & Bay; both these lying in the same Latitude which is 46° 19′ 7S North. The Indians here, set a high value on the Sea Otter skins. Our officers were very anxious to purchase <an> a Robe made out of the Skins of two of these animals. They offered the Indians a great price in Cloths & trinkets for it; but they refused their offer, & would take nothing but beads for them. They at last offered to let them have it for 5 New blankets, which our Officers would not give them. They at last purchas'd it from them for a Belt which had a number of beads on it, which our officers procured from the Indian woman our Interpreter, which we got at the Mandan Nation, as Interpreter to the Snake nation; who is still with us. I mention this in Order to show the high value that they set on these Skins, which were very beautiful.—

I also mention this circumstance, in order, to show the very high value, they also set on Beads. The Sea Otter is plenty, between this and the great falls of the Columbia River; but are very difficult to be got. They are rarely to be caught in traps, & when shot they sink immediately, which makes the procuring of them so difficult. The evening was rainey & a number of Indians both Male & female came to our Camp this evening.—

1. Again a misdate, this time for November 21.

Friday Novemr 22nd A hard Storm arose in the course of last night accompanied with Rain, & it continued raining very hard & the Wind high from the So West, This caused the Tide of flood to rise much higher, than it commonly did at this place. The Swell ran also to an amazing heighth. One of our Canoes floated off a small distance & the sides of it was considerably split; before we could hawl it out of the Water. We had also to move some of our Camps, the water being all round them & a rising. It continued raining hard all day.—

Saturday Novemr 23d   We had a hard wind blowing the greater part of last night, & it rained powerfully.   This morning it moderated, both with regard to Wind & Rain.   Several of our party went out to hunt, & remained but a short time; when they returned bringing 3 deer in with them, which they had killed.   The evening was pleasant, & one of our Hunters went out & killed 21 fowls of different kinds.   We had during this day a number of Indians at our Camp, they came across the bay to our Camp on a Visit.—

Sunday Novemr 24th   A White frost this morning, & the weather clear & pleasant.   Several of our hunters went out a hunting, & we put out our baggage &ca. to dry—   The River Columbia at this place is 3 Miles from the Sea & 660 Yards wide.   Our Officers went out and took down Notes on several remarkable points &ca. which they could not before have done, on account of the badness of the weather.   We had during this day a number of the Indians that came across the river Yesterday, at our Camp.   These Indians were part of 2 Nations, who resided along the Sea Coast.   They are called the Clattsops & Chi-n-ups[1] Nations.—   These Natives were well made & handsome featured generally, & very light coloured.   They behaved themselves very well & friendly—   In the Evening our Officers had the whole party assembled in order to consult which place would be the best, for us to take up our Winter Quarters at.[2]   The greater part of our Men were of opinion; that it would be best, to cross the River, & if we should find game plenty, that it would be of an advantage to us, for to stay near the Sea shore, on account of <procuring> making Salt, which we are nearly out of at this time, & the want of it in preserving our Provisions for the Winter, would be an object well worth our attention.—

1. Clatsop and Chinook Indians (see Clark's entries of November 15 and 21).
2. See Clark's entry for this day for a record of the vote.

Monday Novemr. 25th   We had a clear pleasant morning.   Our Officers had concluded on crossing the River, & endeavor to find out a suitable place, for our Winter Quarters.   Our officers purchased from the Natives 2 more Sea Otter Skins.   We loaded our Canoes, and set off in order to go up the River, & to cross over the River where it was narrower.—   We proceeded on up the River about 9 Miles, where we attempted to cross it, but the Waves ran so high that we found it impracticable. We kept on about 4 Miles farther & encamped.[1] The place we encamped at, was in the Wide part of the River which is called Shallow bay, from the Shoalness of the Water here.— This place lay on the No side of the Columbia River.—

1. They went around Grays Bay and camped near Pillar Rock, Wahkiakum County, Washington.

Tuesday Novemr. 26th   A cloudy wet morning, & we set out early.   we proceeded about 1 Mile up the River & then crossed it.   In doing of which we passed through several Islands.   We proceeded on down the South side of the River, & came to an Inhabited Village of Indians.[1]   We halted at this place for a short time; where the Indians gave us plenty to eat consisting of Roots not unlike potatoes & behaved friendly to us.—   They also gave us a few of these Roots or wild potatoes to take with us.   We continued on still down the River; the day being wet, cold and very disagreeable.   We encamped[2] in a thicket on the South shore.   Several Indians came to us in a Canoe, with Roots to sell.   We saw along the shore, a number of Islands that lay very low & marshy.   The Geese, swan & Ducks are in the greatest plenty at this place, & our Hunters killed a number of them.   We purchased the Roots the Indians had brought with them in the Canoe, and they left us well pleased.—

1. The people were Cathlamets, speaking Kathlamet, a Chinookan language, and their village was at Knappa, Clatsop County, Oregon.
2. In Clatsop County, near Svenson.

Wednesday Novemr. 27th   A rainey wet morning & cold.   We set out early and coasted along shore round a large Bay.   we then turned a Sharp Cape,[1] & went about one Mile; where the Swell ran so high, that it became dangerous for us to proceed on.   We halted at an old fishing camp,[2] where we unloaded our Canoes & hawled them up on the Shore.—   The Rain continued hard all this day.—

1. The captains called it Point William, probably after Clark; it is now Tongue Point, Clatsop County, Oregon.

2. On the west side of the neck of Tongue Point, Clatsop County, just east of Astoria. Most of the party would remain here under Clark until December 7.

Thursday Novemr 28th   We had a very heavy Storm during the whole of last night, & the wind blowing hard from the Westward this morning.   Several Men of our party turned out to hunt.   It rained the greater part of this day.   The hunters returned, not having killed any kind of game.   They mentioned that they had found the Country very broken, & so thicketty that it was impossible to hunt in it.   The Wind rose from the North West & became a perfect storm

Friday Novemr 29th   It rained very hard all last night, & continued showery this morning.   Captain Lewis & five of our Men,[1] set out in our small Canoe, in order to go down towards the Mouth of the River, to look out for a place to Winter at.   The weather continued showery, & some hail fell during this day.—   Some of our party are unwell owing to our having nothing to live on but pounded Salmon.—   & being continually wet.—

1. Drouillard, Reubin Field, Shannon, Colter, and Labiche, reports Lewis.

Saturday Novemr 30th   We had several hard showers of rain, & some hail fell during last night, and this morning after day light it cleared off.   We put a Canoe into the River in order to try & kill some Geese & Ducks, which we saw plenty of, in a bay a small distance above where we are encamped.   We put out our baggage &ca to dry, as they appear'd to be in danger of spoiling by the wetness of the weather.   Our Hunters went out but did not kill any thing but 3 Ducks.   They mentioned of having seen several Elk, but that they were so shy, that they could not get within Rifle Shot of them.—

Sunday Decmr. 1st   A dark cloudy morning.   We had in the course of this day a little rain, & are all anxiously waiting for the arrival of Captain Lewis.   Several of our party are still unwell, & we have nothing still to subsist on but pounded Salmon.   Our hunters went out & saw several Elk but got none of them

Monday decemr. 2nd   A cloudy wet morning.   Several of our Men[1] went out hunting.   They returned towards evening.   One of the hunters[2] had killed an elk & had come to Camp to get help for to bring it in to us.   Six Men were sent off with a Canoe after the Meat, the road being so bad by land, that it was impossible to bring it that way.   This party & two of our hunters staid out all night

1. Joseph Field, Pryor, and Gibson; York and two others went in a canoe looking for "fish and fowl."
2. Joseph Field.

Tuesday Decemr 3rd   This morning cloudy.   At 10 o'Clock A. M. the Men returned with the Canoe, & Elk meat, which was a very welcome sight to us all.   A Canoe loaded with Indians came to our Camp, but soon left us & went down the River.   In the Evening the 2 hunters[1] that had staid out 2 days returned to our Camp   they had killed 6 Elk about 5 Miles from this place & had seen a number more of them.—

1. Pryor and Gibson.

Wednesday Decemr 4th   A rainey wet morning.   Serjeant Pryor & six men of our party set off, to go out to where the Elk meat was left, to take care of it & to bring it to the River, against we should move our Camp down.   The day continued Rainey, the Wind blew hard & the weather was stormy.   We have not as yet heard from Captain Lewis.—

Thursday Decemr. 5th   We had hard rain & stormy weather; which was very disagreeable.   About 12 o'Clock A. M. Captain Lewis & 3 Men who were part of those that went with him returned to Camp with the Canoe. They informed us, that they had found a tolerable good place,[1] to build our Winter quarters at.   The place they said lay up a small river,[2] about 4 Miles on the South side; & about 15 Miles from this place.   They had killed seven Elk; and had left 2 of the Men to take care of the meat hides & had also killed 5 deer.   They brought some of the Meat with them.   It continued raining the whole of this day.—

1. The site of Fort Clatsop; see Whitehouse's entry of December 7.
2. The party's Netul River, now Lewis and Clark River, Clatsop County, Oregon.

Friday Decemr 6th   A rainey disagreeable morning, & the Wind continued high; We <are> were obliged still to lay at where we were encamped. About 1 o'Clock P. M. it blew a storm, and the tide rose about 2 feet perpendicular higher, than it had been, since we are at this place, & over flowed some of our Camps, which obliged us to move them to higher ground, than they were first at; the Storm still continued, & the Rain extinguish'd our fires, & made it exceedingly disagreeable to us.   Towards evening the Weather cleared up, & it became a little more pleasant,

Saturday Decemr 7th   This morning clear & cold, We put our Canoes into the River & loaded them.   We set off to go to the place appointed for our Winter Quarters & proceeded down along the Coast.   We passed a number of fine Springs or Spring runs, which came in along the Shore.   The Country was covered with pine Trees & under brush.—

The wind rose, & the wind caused the Waves to rise also.   We saw our 6 Men, who had been for the Elk meat, on the Shore.   The Waves ran so high, that we could not land where they were, and had to turn a point of land, to make a harbour; the 6 Men joined us at this place.   They had with them 4 Elk hides, but had none of the Meat.   They mentioned to us, that the distance was so great, & the weather so bad, that it was out of their power to bring it.   We cooked the greater part of a Young Deer, which the hunters had killed, & left near this place.—   We set off, the Waves running very high.—   Captain Clarks negroe Man servant, not having come up, with the Men whom he had went out with, he waited with his Canoe for him.   We proceeded on to a deep bay[1] about 8 Miles, & went up <the> a River,[2] which was about 100 yards wide.   We then unloaded our Canoes & carried all our baggage, about 200 yards to piece a rising ground in a thicket of tall pine Trees;[3] where we intend building Cabbins, & stay if Game is to be had through the Winter season.—[4]

1. Youngs Bay, Clatsop County, Oregon, which the party called Meriwether's Bay, in honor of Lewis.

2. Lewis and Clark River, Clatsop County.

3. Perhaps Sitka spruce, *Picea sitchensis* (Bong.) Carr.

4. Fort Clatsop on the Lewis and Clark River, Clatsop County, southwest of Astoria. There the party remained until March 23, 1806.

Sunday Decemr 8th   We had a hard white frost & cold, & windy morning. Our officers sent off 12 of our party[1] early, in order to bring the Meat which was left by the 6 Men to camp.   They embark'd in two Canoes for that purpose.   One of our Canoes was carried off by the tide, during last night. Captain Clark & another party of our Men[2] went across by land to the Ocean, in order to blaze a road, & to look out a convenient place for to make Salt.   Towards evening the party that went with the Canoes returned with them, loaded with Elk & deer meat.   The latter part of the day was cold & cloudy, & in the Evening we had a little Rain & high Wind from the North East—

1. Gass says he was in charge.

2. Including Drouillard and Shannon, according to Clark's entry of December 9.

Monday Decemr 9th   We had rain the greater part of last night, & it continued raining this morning.   Captain Clark & the men that went with him to the Ocean, did not return.   Captain Lewis sent a Serjeant[1] & eight men after the remainder of the Meat, which was left by the party Yesterday.   They embarked in two Canoes.   In the Evening they returned & brought the meat and the Canoe which had been floated off by the rising of the tide with them.   Three of our party took our small Canoe and went after an Ax, which was left behind, at the place we last encamped at.   They returned before night, & had found the Ax.   Four Indians came in a Canoe with them & staid with us all night.

1. Ordway, according to Ordway.

Tuesday Decemr. 10th   Captain Clark and the party that went with him to the Ocean did not return this morning and the Indians that staid with us during the last night, left us this morning.   The party that was at Camp all turned out & were employed in cutting of Pickets & carrying them to the

place where our Officers intend erecting a fort. It rain'd the most part of
this day. Towards evening Captain Clark & three of the Men that went with
him returned from the Ocean.— They informed us that they had blazed a
Road, through the Woods, from the Ocean; which they supposed to be about
7 Miles. They found 3 Indian huts,[1] which lay on the Edge of the Ocean,
which was Inhabited. The Indians who resided in these huts, informed
Captain Clark & his party, that there was a considerable number of Indians;
who resided further up along the Coast. The party that were with Captain
Clark had killed one Elk, and saw two Gangs of the same kind of animals.
The Indians at those huts, gave our Men plenty of pounded fish & Roots to
eat, & behaved very friendly. The land between this & the Ocean is cover'd
with Pine Trees, & on the Coast, low flatt land considerable Priaries & some
swamps, in which grows Cranberries, [*illegible*] berries &ca.—

Our officers concluded on to build our huts of logs, & to picket them in
from the Corners

1. A Clatsop Indian village at the site of present Seaside, Clatsop County, Oregon, at the
mouth of the Necanicum River.

Wednesday Decemr 11th A wet morning & the party continued on cutting logs, Pickets &ca. We raised one line of our huts this day. It continued
raining the greater part of this day— One of our party by the name of
Gibson was taken very ill occasioned by being constantly wet.—

Thursday decemr. 12th It was cloudy the whole of this day. In the af-
ternoon 10 Indians[1] came to our encampment in Canoes; some of these
Indians lived on the Sea Coast & the remainder lived up the Columbia
River.— These Indians brought with them some Roots to trade with us.

1. Including Coboway, a Clatsop leader, according to Clark.

Friday decemr. 13th We had rain & Cloudy weather, during the whole
of this day. We raised another line of our Huts. they had 2 Rooms in each
hut, & were 16 feet in the clear. We finished raising the huts, & began the
foundation of another line of them in the same Manner, of those we had
raised. the three lines composed 3 Squares, & the other square we intend

picketting in, & to have 2 Gates at the two Corners. We had several more Indians at our Camp this day. they came in Canoes to see us, & to trade. Captain Lewis purchased several kinds of Skins from these Indians, some of which were unknown to us & a curiosity <to us>.—[1] Our two hunters that had been out hunting for some days, returned to our Camp; they informed us that they had killed 17 Elk, Geese, Ducks &ca.—

1. Skins of the Oregon bobcat, *Lynx rufus fasciatus,* and the mountain beaver, *Aplodontia rufa.* See Ordway's entry for this day.

Saturday Decemr 14th   This day we had moderate Rain.   We continued on getting our Huts raised.—   Two of our party were employed in splitting plank to cover them.   We finished raising the line of huts, & began to cover one of them, which Our officers intend for a Meat house &ca.—

Sunday Decemr 15th   We had cloudy weather.   Captain Clark with most of our Men set out with 3 Canoes, to go up the Little River about 3 Miles, after the 17 Elks &ca. which the 2 hunters who returned to Camp Yesterday had killed, & left there.   We proceeded on, & came near to the place with the Canoes & halted.   The party had carried each 2 loads of Meat to the Canoes and went out for a third.   The woods at that place and under brush lay so thick, that the Men got scatter'd & some of them were lost.— Serjeant Ordway, three of the Men[1] & myself were among those that had lost themselves.   We were obliged to stay out during the Night.   It rained all that night & the wind blew very cold & being without fire, we suffered considerably both from the Rain & wind.   Four of the party also got lost, but they came to the place where the party was with much difficulty after dark.—

1. Colter, Collins, and McNeal, according to Clark.

Monday Decemr 16th   The party that I was with found our way this morning to where the Canoes lay.   We took on board them the Meat that was brought by the whole of this party, and returned down to the fort with our Canoes.   It rained very hard during this day.[1]   We unloaded the Canoes, & deposited the Meat in the house prepared in the fort, for that purpose.   We finished covering the Meat house.   Some of our party was left behind in the

Woods, to bring in the remainder of the meat, left by the party that went with Captain Clark.   We had hard Rain & some hail in the afternoon also.

1. Clark called it "one of the worst days that ever was!"

Tuesday Decemr. 17th   We had during last night some Snow & hail, & it continued the same this morning.   We were all employed in building Chimneys in our huts, & splitting out planks to cover our huts with.   We cut up the Meat, & hung it up in the Meat house, in Order to save it.   A little snow remained on the pine trees the whole of this day.   The Man that was sick (George Gibson) got much better.—

Wednesday Decemr. 18th   This day was cloudy with some Rain, some of our party were sent across the River or bay with Canoes, to bring plank. They returned towards evening with the Canoes loaded with plank, which they had got at an Old Indian fishery.   The day grew very cold, & some hail fell.   We continued finishing our huts &ca.

Thursday Decemr 19th   It rained hard all last night, & continued the same this morning.   Serjeant Ordway was very sick, but the Men in general continue in good health, notwithstanding the bad weather & hardships that they undergo.—   We continued to work on our huts, but have not a sufficiency of plank to cover them.   We had during this day a number of Indians in our camp.   they came in Canoes to see us.—

Friday Decemr 20th   A Cloudy wet morning, & continued so the whole of this day.   We continued on building our huts, notwithstanding the badness of the weather.—

Saturday Decemr 21st   A cloudy wet day as usual, but rather warm.   We are still employed in finishing our huts & picketting in the fort &ca

Sunday 22nd Monday 23 Tuesday 24th December   We had during these 3 days Cloudy & wet weather, the Air Warm & the Wind blowing from the Southwest; we continued in finishing our Huts, picketting in the fort &ca.— & nothing extraordinary happened.—

Wednesday Decemr. 25th We had hard rain & Cloudy weather as usual. We all moved into our new Garrison or Fort, which our Officers named after a nation of Indians who resided near us, called the Clatsop Nation; Fort Clatsop.— We found our huts comfortable, excepting smoking a little.—

We saluted our officers, by each of our party firing off his gun at day break in honor to the day (Christmass[)] Our Officers in return, presented to each of the party that used Tobacco a part of what Tobacco they had remaining; and to those who did not make use of it, they gave a handerchief or some other article, in remembrance of Christmass. We had no ardent spirit of any kind among us; but are mostly in good health, A blessing, which we esteem more, than all the luxuries this life can afford, and the party are all thankful to the Supreme Being, for his goodness towards us.— hoping he will preserve us in the same, & enable us to return to the United States again in safety. We have at present nothing to eat but lean Elk meat & that without Salt, but the whole of our party are content with this fare.—

Thursday Decemr. 26h We had Stormy weather the whole of this day. We found that our huts smoaked occasion'd by the hard wind; & find that we cannot live in them without building Chimneys.— It rain'd most part of this day.—

Friday Decmr. 27th It continued raining hard during the whole of this day. We were all employed in building Chimneys in our huts, which we compleated, & found our huts comfortable & without smoak. In the Evening some Indians[1] came to our Fort, they informed us by signs, that a large Fish was drove by the Wind & waves on the shore near to where their lodges were, & we all suppose from the description they gave of it, that it must be a Whale.—

1. Coboway and others, says Clark.

Saturday decemr. 28th This morning it rained & the wind was so high, that it prevented us from going to see the Whale. Five of our Men[1] went out & took kettles with them in Order to go over to the Sea coast to build a Camp & make Salt.   Three of our hunters were sent across the River to hunt.   In the Evening two hunters that were out returned with One deer which they had killed.—[2]

1. Clark names Joseph Field, Bratton, Gibson, Willard, and Weiser as going to the saltmaking camp at Seaside, Clatsop County, Oregon.
2. Clark gives the names of the day's hunters as Drouillard, Shannon, Labiche, Reubin Field, and Collins.

Sunday Decemr 29th   This day was fine clear pleasant weather, the first fair day we had for a long time past.   Several Indians who belong'd to the Chinook Nation;[1] came to our fort.   These Indians brought with them Roots which they called Wappetoes & dryed Salmon in their Canoes to trade with us.   Our Officers purchased the whole of these articles from them, for which they gave them some articles of Merchandise.   This supply of fish & Roots came in good time as our Meat was nearly spoiled.   The most part of our Men were employed in putting up the Pickets &ca.—

1. Clark says they were Wahkiakum Indians.

. Monday Decemr 30th   We had several showers of Rain during last night, and this morning was fair; and the Sun shone a little which was very uncommon to us.—   Our Men finished putting up the Pickets & Gates of the Fort.   About 2 o'Clock P. M. three of our hunters[1] came in to the fort, who informed us that they had killed 4 Elk but a Short distance from the Fort.   Seven Men set out immediately with them from the Fort; and took a Canoe & brought in the meat.   This supply of Meat came very seasonably, as what meat we have in hand, is nearly spoiled   Our Officers placed a Centinel in the Fort.—

1. Clark names Drouillard as one of them.

Tuesday December 31st   A Cloudy morning.   Several more of the Natives[1] came in their Canoes to our Fort; they brought with them Wapeto Roots to trade with us.   We purchased several bags of these Roots from them.— The party of Indians that came to our fort two days ago, left us.— Our Men built 2 Centry Boxes & dug two Sinks[2] &ca.—

1. Clark identified them as Wahkiakums and Skillutes. The latter were probably Watlalas, an Upper Chinookan–language people living near the Cascades of the Columbia.
2. Latrines.

Wednesday January 1st At day break, the Men at the fort fired several Guns, as a salute to our Commanding officers; & in honor of the day. The Morning was pleasant. Two of our party were sent out to hunt. Several Indians[1] came to the fort on a visit. They were entirely naked, excepting a breech Cloth which they wore & Skins thrown over their Shoulders. This is the manner which the Natives in general go cloathed. The Winters here are not very Cold, & the ground has not as yet been cover'd with Snow this Winter. In the afternoon the hunters returned to the Fort, they had killed 2 large Buck Elks <bucks>

1. Clatsop Indians, say Lewis and Clark.

Thursday Janry 2d It rained the greater part of last night, and continued to rain hard this morning. fourteen of our Men went out from the Fort, & brought in the Elk meat, which our hunters had killed Yesterday. We had hard Showers of rain during this whole day. Our Commanding Officers Issued an Order,[1] for the Regulating of our Fort. We are expecting 2 Men of our party to arrive at the fort from the Ocean, where we are making Salt with some of that article, as we are entirely without

1. See the Orderly Book entry with Lewis and Clark's materials for this day.

Friday Janry 3rd We had hard thunder, hail & Rain the greater part of last night, & light showers of rain this morning; Two of our Men left the fort to go out hunting. Serjeant Gass went over to the Ocean in order to go to the Camp where some of our party <are> were making Salt. About 10 o'Clock A. M. a number of Indians[1] came to our Fort on a visit; they belonged to the Clatsop nation. In the Evening three of our hunters[2] returned to the Fort, & had killed 1 Deer, 1 Swan, 2 Geese 4 Ducks & a Raven. The Raven they had eaten on New Years day, & the remainder of the Game they brought in with them, but mentioned they had seen no Elk. One of our hunters caught an Otter during last night.

1. Including Coboway and six other Clatsops, report Lewis and Clark.
2. Reubin Field, Collins, and Potts, but Potts was not included in Clark's list of December 28.

Saturday Janry 4th   We had small showers of rain & some hail this morning.   a number of Indians belonging to the Clatsop Nation that came to the fort Yesterday staid near the Fort last night.   They sold our party some sweet Roots fish, 1 dog &ca.   Towards evening they all left us.   The Rain continued the greater part of this day.—

Sunday Janry 5th   A Wet rainey morning.   In the afternoon one of our hunters[1] returned to the fort & had only killed a brant & 2 Ducks which he brought with him.   Two of our party[2] also returned from where some of our party were making Salt near the Ocean.   these Men brought with them about 2 Gallons of excellent Salt, which was made there & mention'd that the party there could make plenty of it.   they had killed 3 elk & 2 Deer. They told us that the Indians had brought a vast Quantity of the Whale, which they Informed us of, to their Indian Village; and that the Natives eat the Oil made from the whales flesh, & that they had eat of it & that it was very good.—   These Men brought part of the Whale with them, which they got from the Indians

1. Colter, say the captains.
2. Willard and Weiser, whose return ended some concern about their absence from the saltmaking camp since December 28.

Monday Janry 6th   Captain Clark & 12 of our Men[1] set out this morning with 2 Canoes in order to go & get some of the whale, which lay on the Sea Coast.—   About 7 o'Clock the Weather cleared off, & became warm & pleasant which continued during the whole of this day.—

1. Clark's party apparently included Pryor, Cruzatte or Weiser (probably the former), Frazer, Colter, Werner, Lepage, Reubin Field, Potts, McNeal, Labiche, Windsor, Shields, Charbonneau, Sacagawea, and Jean Baptiste Charbonneau. See Clark's entries for January 6.

Tuesday Janry 7th   We had a clear pleasant night, & it still continues so this morning; which is rare to be met with at this place at this Season of the Year.   One of our hunters[1] went out about 3 Miles from the Fort, to where he had set 2 traps.   He found in them One Otter & a Beaver, he brought in with him the flesh of the Beaver & the Skin of the Otter.   this Otter skin was very black & handsome.—

1. Drouillard.

Wednesday Janry 8th   A fine warm morning.   two of our Men[1] went out from the Fort to hunt.   The Crows & Ravens are very plenty about this place, & Geese, Brants, Cranes & Ducks are plenty in the Marshes a short distance from the Fort.

1. Drouillard and Collins, says Lewis.

Thursday Janry 9th   It rained the greater part of last night, & the two hunters that went out Yesterday did not return.   the Weather cleared off this morning & became warm & pleasant.   the Men in the fort were employed mending their Clothes, airing the baggage, making moccasins dressing Skins &ca.—

Friday Janry 10th   A Clear pleasant day, about noon, the two hunters that had went out two days past from the fort hunting returned.   they killed one Elk & wounded two more of them.   Towards evening 12 Indians[1] of the Clatsop Nation came to the fort.   They brought Wapatoes & other Roots to trade with us.   We purchased from them some of these Roots & 2 of their dogs.   In the evening late Captain Clark & some of the party returned to the Fort.   they informed us that they had been about 25 Miles along the Sea Coast, nearly a South course to see the Whale,[2] expecting to get some of the Meat of it, and that they had to pass over rough rockey mountains,[3] to get to the place where the whale lay, & that the Indians had showed them, to where a whale lay; which had been a long time Dead, which was on a very large Rock. It was about 105 feet long & every way proportionable. the head was shaped they said like the bow of a Vessell nearly. The party got some of the Jaw bones &ca. They mentioned, that there was several small Indian Villages along the Coast that they had been, & that they belong'd to different tribes of Indians,[4] which lived on the Whales that was thrown ashore by the Waves, in tempestuous Weather. These Indians had a great Quantity of the flesh of Whales, which they had got, from some other place, than the one, that they had been at. they also mentioned, that the Bones of whales lay along the shore in great abundance. they also informed us, that one Night whilst they were gone, that they lay near a Creek, & that one of their party had went to an Indian Village, without letting the party know it, & that while he was eating some fish, which <the> an Indian had given him, that an another Indian made signs to him to follow him, that he went along with him, not thinking that any harm was in the way. This Indian had a design to kill the Man belonging to that party, for his blanket. Some other Indians belonging to a different Nation, from the one that our man had went with, called over the Creek to our party of Men. The party finding that one of their party by the name of McNeal was missing, dreaded the consequence & several of the party went to his assistance. The Indian that had carred off this Man of the party, on hearing the noise made by the other Indians fled; leaving our Man McNeal by himself.[5] This Creek was named by Captain Clarke McNeals folly,[6] & the Montain he named *Clarks View*. The party purchased some of the meat of the whale & Oil from the Natives, & brought some of it to the fort. Captain Clark had left some of the party at the Salt Camp.—

1. Including Shar-har-war-cap, a chief, and eleven others of the Cathlamet tribe.

2. Probably a blue whale, *Balaenoptera musculus*, at Cannon Beach, Clatsop County, Oregon. See Clark's entries of January 6–10, 1806.

3. The rugged headland they called Clark's Point of View, now Tillamook Head, on the coast of Clatsop County.

4. The people living in the vicinity of the whale site were Tillamooks, Kilamox to the party, belonging to the coastal branch of the Salishan language family.

5. Clark reports this incident in his entries of January 8 and 9.

6. Clark does not mention this name for the river he called Ecola Creek after the Chinookan word for whale, but Ordway uses it. The creek's name, formerly Elk, has been restored to Clark's designation; it is in Clatsop County.

Saturday Janry 11th We had a number of Indians encamped near the fort last night, And this morning, we had pleasant weather. Our small Canoe had went adrift during last night. Our officers sent several of our Men up the River, in Order to bring the Elk meat, which the hunters had killed Yesterday to the fort. Several of our Men were sent down the river, to look after the small Canoe, but did not find it. We returned in the Evening with the Elk Meat— The Indians left the fort, in order to return to their Villages. We had Rain towards night.—

Sunday Janry 12th A Clear pleasant Morning. Two Men[1] went out hunting from the fort, & 3 other Men were sent to take another Search for our small Canoe. they returned without being able to find it. Several of our Men[2] returned from the Salt Camp on the Ocean, to the Fort,—
In the Evening the two hunters returned to the fort, they had killed 7 Elk within about 2 Miles of the fort,

1. One was Drouillard, according to the captains.
2. Including Gass, Shannon, Frazer, and Gibson.

Monday Janry 13th It rained during the whole of last night and continues Raining this morning. Captain Lewis & all our party (excepting the guard) set out in Order to bring in the Elk meat. They brought the 7 Elk in at 2 loads, & Six of the Men set at cutting up and Scaffolding the meat to day &ca.—

Tuesday Janry 14th A fine pleasant morning. One of our Canoes got loose from the landing last night, but we found her this morning up a Creek, where the Tide water had taken her. Six of our Men are employed in Jerking Meat the remainder dressing Skins &ca.

Wednesday 15th Thursday 16 January It rained hard, & we had stormey Weather during these two days

Friday Janry 17th   It continued stormey all last night, and this morning Wet & rainey.   Three of our Men went out a hunting.   A number of Indians[1] came to the Fort.   About noon one of the hunters returned to Camp with a Deer, which he had killed

    1. Clatsops, including Coboway.

Saturday Janry 18th   It rained hard all last night, & still continued the same this morning, Two Indians came to the fort & staid a short time.   it continued Raining during the whole of this day.

Sunday Janry 19th   This morning we had moderate showers of rain, 4 Men[1] of our party went out from the fort a hunting.   the Men in the fort were employed in dressing Elk skins, Several of the natives visited us, & sold our Men several Hatts, which were made out of splits.   They were very handsome & curiously worked

    1. According to Lewis, the hunters were Collins, Willard, Labiche, and Shannon. "Collins" may be an error for Colter; see Lewis's entry.

Monday Janry 20   Wet & rainey weather during the whole of this day. nothing material occured worth mentioning

Tuesday Janry 21st   A Cold cloudy day with Rain.   In the afternoon 2 of our Men[1] came in from hunting.   they had killed 2 Elk.—

    1. Shannon and Labiche, according to Lewis and Ordway.

Wednesday Janry 22nd   A hard storm of Wind & Rain   14 of our party & myself went with a Canoe after the Elk meat, & had a very disagreeable time of it.   Three of our hunters[1] staid out hunting all this day.—

    1. Reubin Field, Shannon, and Labiche.

Thursday Janry 23d   We had during last night thunder & some hail Showers.   two of our Men[1] were sent down to the Camp for Salt.   It rained & we had high wind during this day.—

    1. Thomas P. Howard and Werner, say Lewis and Clark.

Friday Janry 24th   Last night we had a light snow, which hardly made the ground white, & some showers of rain & hail fell during this day.   In the afternoon 2 of our hunters[1] that were out returned to the Fort, they had killed 4 Elk, & brought in with them 2 Deer which 2 other of our other hunters had killed, These 2 Deer where brought in an Indian Canoe by them & 3 Indians to whom this Canoe belonged.   They brought also the Meat of the Elks in this Canoe, and had given these Indians 2 Elk skins & a considerable of the Meat to them, for packing & bringing in their Canoe, the whole of the Meat left, the Skins &ca.

1. Drouillard and Lepage, according to the captains.

Saturday Janry 25th   We had snow during last night & it continued snowing lightly this morning.   The ground had froze a little.   One of the hunters[1] returned to the Fort, who had killed one of the 2 Deer which was brought in the Canoe Yesterday.—

1. Or two men, one of whom was Collins.

Sunday Janry 26th   during last night we had considerable Snow & it continued Snowing this morning.   the weather was cold & freezing & the Snow lay on the ground during this day 5 Inches deep on a level   It continued Snowing 'till the Evening.   The Men in the fort were all employed <at the Fort> in dressing leather, making Moccasins &ca.—

Monday Janry 27th   It froze hard during last night, & this morning was clear & cold.   One of our hunters[1] was sent out, to hunt in order to supply the Men with Meat at the Camp where they are making Salt & 2 of our party <was sent> who went out in Order to go to that place on the 23d instant, had not as yet returned.—   About noon one of our hunters[2] that had been out hunting returned to the fort.   he informed us that he had killed 5 Elk & that another of the hunters had killed 3 Elk, & that another of the party had also killed two Elk but that these last were killed at a long distance from the Fort.

1. Collins again.
2. Shannon, according to Lewis, Clark, and Ordway.

Tuesday Janry 28th   A Clear cold morning, & freezing weather.   I was sent with 13 Men [1] of our party in Order to go after the Meat of the Elk killed Yesterday.   We set out from the fort early, and arrived where they had left those Elk.   The hunters that had killed these Elk were with me.   We could find only three of them, the Snow having covered them.   We returned with the Meat of these 3 Elks in the Evening to the fort.   The 2 Men [2] that had went, to where the Men were making Salt, & had been gone for several days, returned also to the fort & brought some Salt with them.   I got during this day my feet severely frost bit.—

1.   Apparently Ordway was also along.
2.   Howard and Werner, who left on January 23.

Wednesday Janry 29th   It froze very hard during last night, & this morning was clear cold weather, Some of the Men in the fort were employed cutting wood for our fires, and others in making Cloathes for our party.   The two Men who came from the Salt Camp last evening killed a large handsome Otter, & brought in the Skin with them

Thursday Janry 30th   This day Cold & Cloudy, & some Snow fell, in the fore part of this day.   In the Evening we had clear cold weather,

Friday January 31st   A Clear cold morning with frost.   Serjeant Gass & six of our party set out from the fort in a Canoe, in order to go up the River to hunt, They soon returned, & informed us that the River was froze across a short distance up it, & that they could not proceed.—   In the afternoon One of the hunters [1] came in from the Salt Camp, & informed us, that they had killed 2 Elk up the River some distance which were the first they had killed a long time.

1.   Joseph Field, who had been hunting with Gibson and Willard, according to the captains.

Saturday Febry 1st   A clear cold morning.   Serjeant Gass & five of our Men left the fort to go on a hunting party, four Men also left the fort with the hunter,[1] in order to help him to carry the meat of the 2 Elk he had killed to the Salt Camp.—

1. Joseph Field, write the captains.

Sunday Febry 2nd   We had a clear morning, & the day was moderate.   In the evening it was cloudy & a little Snow fell.—

Monday Febry 3rd   We had a little frost, & the weather has moderated since Yesterday.   About noon two of our hunters[1] came to the fort from hunting.   they informed us that they had killed 7 Elk & caught 1 Large beaver.   Six of our Men[2] set out with a Canoe to go after the Elk meat, but soon returned the wind being too high for them to proceed, down to the Bay.   In the evening they attempted it again, but the tide was so low that they could not get near the Shore, for the sholes & sand Barrs.   five men came in from the Salt camp, with 2 bushels of Salt & the flesh of part a whale which we found tolerably good eating.—   The natives call the whale meat E-Co-ley.—[3]

1. Drouillard and Lepage, according to Lewis and Clark.
2. Led by Pryor, report Lewis and Clark.
3. The Lower Chinookan term for whale, *ikuli.*

Tuesday Febry 4th   A Clear plesant morning.   about Noon six of our men[1] set out again from the fort with a Canoe to go for the Elk meat.   We had a very high tide this day.   The party at the Fort were employed in making & mending their Cloathes mockasins &ca.

1. Again led by Pryor, write Lewis and Clark.

Wendesday Febry 5th   We had a beautiful pleasant cool morning. About noon one of the hunters[1] called to us from the opposite side of the River.   Three men[2] were ordered to go over to him.   They proceeded to the place where he was in a Canoe, & found our small Canoe (which had been lost for some time past,) up on a Marsh, in a Creek, where the Water had drove her. The man who hallowed to us, had killed Six Elk, & mentioned that he had heard the other two hunters fire, but could not say what they had killed, but he expected they had killed also some Elk

1. Reubin Field, say the captains.
2. Led by Gass, according to Lewis and Clark.

Thursday Febry 6th   This morning we had pleasant weather, Our Officers sent Ten Men[1] of our party from the fort, in order to bring in the Meat of the Elks which the hunters had killed.   they found them about 2½ Miles from the fort, & the way very bad.   they cut up 5 of the Elk this evening, & packed some of it together; two of these Elk were in very good order.   They formed a camp close to where the meat lay.— Nothing material happened at the Fort.   the Men that remained there were employed in dressing Skins &c.—

1. Including Ordway, Gass, Reubin Field, and Weiser; see Lewis for February 6 and 7.

Friday Febry 7th   The weather continued pleasant.   the Men that went after the Elk meat, carried it on their backs to a marsh near to the River, where they could come with a Canoe.   they then encamped at that place. Two Men[1] were sent from that place with a Canoe & part of the Meat to the fort.   Nothing worth mentioning happened at the fort this day.   The Men there were employ'd as Yesterday.   A short time after dark we had a hard Rain—

1. Ordway and Weiser, report various journalists.

Saturday Febry 8th   It rained very hard the greater part of last night; the Men that went after the meat had a very disagreeable time of it.   they remained waiting for the return of the Canoe.   the Canoe arrived, & they put the meat on board & returned to the Fort.   The party[1] that had been down to the Sea Coast after meat returned & brought 2 Elk with them.   they then went up the River to where our other hunters were.   They returned again in the Evening & brought with them in the Canoe 4 more elk, which the

2 hunters that were up the River had killed.　We had several small Showers of rain & hail in the Evening.

1. Pryor, Shannon, Labiche, and others, write the captains.

Sunday Febry 9th　We had small showers of rain during this day, six of our party were employed in Jerking the Elk meat, and two were sent out to hunt, the remainder of our party, were employ'd at the fort, making Cloathing, moccasins & dressing Elk Skins.—

Monday Febry 10th　We had some Snow fell during last night and this morning the weather was clear & pleasant.　In the evening, two of our Men [1] came in to the fort from the Camp, where our people were making salt, they informed us, that one of the Men there, was very sick, and another of the Men there, was unwell, they told us also that they had killed 6 Elk, but did not save much of the Meat.　The two hunters who went out Yesterday, returned to the fort, but had kill'd no kind of Game.—

1. The captains say that Willard came from the saltworks, with an injured knee, and reported that Gibson and Bratton were seriously ill.

Tuesday Febry 11th　We had a fine clear day.　Serjeant Pryor & four Men, were sent with a Canoe to go round to the Salt Camp in order to bring the Men that were sick there,[1] to the Fort; and two more of our men [2] were sent to the Salt works to supply the place of the Men that were sick.　Three of our hunters [3] left the fort to go a hunting.　the latter part of the day was rainey.—　The remainder of our party at the fort, were employ'd dressing Skins, making Cloathes &ca.—

1. Pryor's party went to the saltworks to bring Gibson back, and Bratton if necessary.
2. Colter and Weiser, say the captains.
3. Gass, Reubin Field, and Thompson, according to Lewis and Clark.

Wednesday Febry 12th　This day was rainey & wet, An Indian came to our fort & staid during last night; this Indian sold one of our Men a Sea otter skin.　He left us this morning well pleased with the Sale he had made.—

Thursday Febry 13th   It rained the greater part of last night, and this morning was Cloudy.   the Men at the fort were employed making of Moccasins & mending their Cloathing &ca.

Friday Febry 14th   This morning was warm, & we had showers of rain during the whole of this day.—   The Men at the fort were employed in repairing the Carpenters Tools, making Moccasins & dressing Elk & Deer Skins.—

Saturday Febry 15th   A clear morning.   In the Evening the party returned from the Salt works.   they brought with them the 2 Sick Men, One[1] of which they were forced to bring in a blanket, to & from the boat; the other Man[2] came with one of the party by land.   the Man who was brought in a blankett was very sick.   These Men were taken good care of, & supplied with every necessary that we had in the fort.   Two of our Men[3] were sent out from the fort a hunting this day.—

1. Gibson, say Lewis, Clark, and Ordway.
2. Bratton, according to the captains and Ordway.
3. Drouillard and Whitehouse, report the captains.

Sunday Febry 16th   We had har[d] rain during last night.   Three Men[1] were sent out hunting in order to try & kill some fowl or Elk for the sick Men.   We are employed at the fort, in making Cloathing &ca.

1. Shannon, Labiche, and Frazer, write the captains.

Monday Febry 17th   during last night some Snow fell.   this Morning the weather Clear.   the three hunters that went out Yesterday returned this forenoon, and brought with them, an Elk which they found dead in the River & which they supposed some of our hunters had killed.   In the afternoon Serjeant Gass & 2 of our hunters[1] returned to the fort; they had killed 8 Elk & had Jerked the meat of 2 of them.   One of our Men[2] came from the Salt works.   He came to get some help from us, to help move in the kettles &

Salt from the Salt works.   One of our hunters killed a very large Grey Eagle.[3]
Two of our hunters[4] also came to the fort   they had killed One Elk.—

1. Reubin Field and Thompson; see the entry for February 11.
2. Joseph Field, report the captains.
3. Lewis says Shannon brought a golden eagle to him.
4. Drouillard and Whitehouse, report Lewis, Clark, and Ordway.

Tuesday Febry. 18th[1]   This morning clear & pleasant weather, Six of our
Men[2] went from the fort with 2 Canoes to go round on the Sea coast to the
Salt works.   Ten Men[3] of our party was sent at some time, in order to bring
in the Elk meat, which was left by our hunters Yesterday.   The party that
were going to the Salt Camp on arriving at the bay, found the wind blowing
so hard, that they had to return to the fort.—

We had several squalls of wind attended with rain in the course of this
day.—   About noon several Indians belonging to the Clatsop Nation came
in Canoes to the Fort.   They brought with them some Roots to trade with
us,—, which we purchased of them.   Towards evening these Indians left
the Fort & embarked in their Canoes in order to return to their Village.—
Two of our hunters[4] also returned to the Fort, but had killed no Game of
any kind.   The Men remaining at the fort were employed as usual in dressing Skins &ca.—

1. At this point a page has been cut from the notebook, but apparently no text is missing.
2. Led by Ordway. Whitehouse says he was with Ordway the next day when he tried again,
but it is not clear that he was along this day, also.
3. Led by Gass, as he relates.
4. Collins and Windsor, report the captains, who say that, in fact, they brought in
one deer.

Wednesday Febry. 19th   We had a hard Storm of Rain & high Wind, blowing from the So. West; this morning I left the fort with 6 of our party[1] in
order to go to the Salt works, <in order> to bring the Kettles, Salt & Mens
baggage to the Fort.   We proceeded on about half way, when the Storm was
so high in the Priari, & on the Sea Coast, that we could not proceed without
suffering by the Sand blowing in our faces—   and the Rain that fell froze &

cut our faces likewise   We Crossed a Creek, which took us middle deep, which benumbed & Chilled the party very much.   We came to an Old deserted Indian hut, in which we made a fire.   we staid at this place all night in expectation of the weather being better by morning.—

1. Led by Ordway; see previous entry.

Thursday Febry 20th   The wind still continued very high, blowing from the South West.—   the party that had gone to the Salt works continued on their way.   the Wind fell a little.   they had to wade through another Creek, & came to where some Indians were living,[1] from whom that party brought some E-co-ley or whale meat & Oil.—   The party left at the Fort were employed in dressing Skins &ca.

1. Clatsop Indians living at present Seaside, Clatsop County, Oregon, where the saltmaking camp was located.

Friday Febry 21st   A Cloudy morning.   The party who were at the Salt works, set out early with all the Salt that was made at that place, the Kettles baggage &ca.[1]   they proceeded on their way to the fort.   They had come about half way, when it set in to raining very hard, and the wind blew so hard, that they could not cross the Creek in a Canoe.   this party had to wade this Creek.   It continued raining very hard which occasioned that party to hurry on & they walked very fast till they arrived at the fort, which was at half an hour past 12 o'Clock A. M.   One of our Serjeants by the name of Ordaway, was taken very unwell.   The party that was sent after the Elk meat, arrived with it at the fort the 19th Instant.—

1. Closing the saltmaking camp at Seaside, Clatsop County, Oregon.

Saturday Febry 22nd   We had a pleasant morning but cool, the Men that were Sick in the Fort, were all getting better.   Several Indians of the Clatsop Nation came to the fort in Canoes.   They brought with them Split & Straw or Grass hatts for sale.   they make those kind of hatts by platting them very ingeniously & they <are> were truly handsome.—   Towards Evening they left the fort, and one of our Hunters (George Drewyer) accompanied them. Some of our Men in the fort were employed in making Cloathing &ca.

Sunday Febry 23d   A pleasant Morning.   Six of our party are unwell, but not dangerously ill.   Three of those sick men has the Influezy;[1] nothing further occurred of consequence this day at the Fort.—

1. Ordway was one, and Lewis considered him the most ill.

Monday Febry. 24th   This morning we had Cloudy weather.   in the afternoon George Drewyer who went with the Clatsop Indians two days past returned to the fort; he was accompanied by a number of the Natives.[1] They all came in Canoes & brought some Straw & Split hatts, fresh fish &ca for sale.   These Indians catch Sturgeon & other fish in great abundance Our officers purchased of these Indians a Sea Otter skin & several of their hatts.   These Indians staid at the fort during this night.   they were a part of the Clatsop Nation & behaved themselves very well.—   Our 2 hunters[2] returned to the fort & had killed One Elk.—

1. Coboway was among them.
2. The captains write that Shannon and Labiche had been unsuccessful in the hunt.

Tuesday Febry 25th   This morning a hard Storm of wind arose accompanied with Rain.   The Indians all left the fort, in order to return to their Village.   The Storm continued during the whole of this day.—   The Men that is sick in the fort are still on the recovery.—

Wednesday Febry 26th   A pleasant morning & Clear weather, four of our Men went out from the fort to hunt, & 2 of our Men went in a Canoe in order to go to the Clatsop & Cathlamah<t> Village in order to purchase some fish from the Natives.[1]   We found the fish that we had purchased from them 2 days past, to be well tasted & fat, especially the small fish, which had the resemblance of a herring but much better tasted

1. The captains say that Drouillard, Cruzatte, and Weiser were sent either to catch sturgeon and "anchovey" (eulachon, or candlefish, *Thaleichthys pacificus*), or purchase them from the natives.

Thursday Febry 27th   We had a rainey wet morning.   One of our party left the fort to go hunting.   In the afternoon one of our hunters returned & had killed an Elk.   All our sick Men at the fort excepting One[1] is still on the recovery.   We have no fresh meat in the fort which is hard for the Men that are sick.—

1. Willard.

Friday Febry 28th   It rained the greater part of last night & this day proved wet & Rainey.   Seven of our Men,[1] set out Early from the fort with a Canoe, after the Elk meat, & brought it in to the Fort.   In the Evening, 3 of our hunters[2] returned.   they had killed 5 Elk.   Two of our Men[3] staid out all night, in Order to hunt.   The Men at the fort were employed in Cleaning their Arms &ca.—

1. Apparently with Pryor in charge.
2. Shields, Joseph Field, and Shannon, according to Lewis and Clark.
3. Reubin Field and Collins, the captains indicate.

March 1st Saturday   A pleasant morning, Twelve Men[1] left the fort to go after the Elk meat.   About noon the two hunters that were out returned to the fort, & had not killed any kind of game.   The afternoon proved Showery & wet.   In the evening, the party that went after the Elk meat returned, & brought the meat with them.   Four of our Men went out hunting.   they went up a River called by the Natives Ir-rum-mack-hill,[2] & the River that our Fort lay near, is called by the Natives Ne-tul.[3]   These hunters staid out all night—

1. Led by Gass, as he says himself.
2. Youngs River, in Clatsop County, Oregon, which the captains called Kilhow-a-nah-kle River. This party discovered Youngs River Falls. The term is Chinookan, *gitawanaxt.*
3. Lewis and Clark River, also in Clatsop County; the Chinookan word is *nitul.*

Sunday March 2d   This morning rainey & Wet, In the evening, three of our men[1] returned who had been trading at the Clatsop Village.   they brought with them a considerable quantity of those small kind of fish,[2] which

424

we purchased from the Natives some days past; These fish were a size smaller than the herring.— they likewise brought several Sturgeon[3] Wapetoes Roots &ca. which they had purchased from the Natives. The natives gave them some fish without any recompence being made to them. These Indians catch great quantities of different kinds of fish in a Creek lying a small distance above their Village.

1. Drouillard, Cruzatte, and Weiser, who had left on February 26.
2. Eulachon.
3. Either the white sturgeon, *Acipenser transmontanus*, or green sturgeon. See Clark entries for November 19, 1805, and Lewis for February 25, 1806.

Monday March 3d We had hard rain all last night, & this morning it still continued the same, & lasted during the whole of this day. The greater part of the Men in the fort were employed in dressing Skins, making Moccosins &ca.

Tuesday March 4th It rained hard all last night, & continued the same during the whole of this day. Nothing material happened at the fort worth mentioning.—

Tuesday March 4th[1] It rained very hard all last night & continued so during this day, & nothing material happened during this day.—

1. In slightly different wording, Whitehouse's copyist repeated an entry.

Wednesday March 5th A pleasant morning. a number of the Natives[1] came in Canoes to the fort. they brought with them, some Sturgeon & some small fish to trade with us. Our officers purchased the whole of them. The Men at the fort were all employed in dressing Skins &ca.

1. Clatsops, according to the captains.

Thursday March 6th We had a pleasant morning. Our hunters returned last night, but had not killed any Game.— Six Men[1] were sent out a hunting from the fort this morning. they were in different directions.

Serjeant Pryor & 2 Men set out with a small Canoe, in order to go up the Columbia River to the Cath-le-mah Village & fishery;— in Order to purchase some fresh fish, Wapatoe Roots &ca. Our old friend the Clatsop chief[2] visited us this day. We hawled up our Canoes in order to repair them &ca

1. Including Drouillard, Collins, and Labiche, according to the captains' entries of March 7.
2. Coboway.

Friday March 7th A Rainey wet morning. Serjeant Gass & one of our Men were employed in repairing our Canoes. towards evening our Two hunters[1] returned & had killed One Elk.—

1. Drouillard and Labiche, say Lewis and Clark.

Saturday March 8th We had showers of hail during last night; and we have Showers of Rain & hail this morning. four of our hunters[1] came to the fort from hunting. They had killed 2 Elk & One deer, & had lost the Canoe which they took with them. Six of our party[2] set off with a Canoe after the Elk meat. Two of our hunters[3] went out a hunting. In the Evening the Men returned with the Canoe loaded with Elk meat &ca.

1. Collins, Shields, Reubin Field, and Frazer.
2. Including Labiche, say the captains.
3. Drouillard and Joseph Field, write Lewis, Clark, and Ordway.

Sunday March 9th This morning we had Snow & hail; 11 of our Men[1] set out from the fort on foot & brought in with them the Meat of 2 Elk. Several of the Natives came to the fort. They brought with them Some Small fish, Bees Wax &ca to trade with us. Our hunters[2] returned to the fort & had not killed any kind of Game.—

1. Led by Ordway, as he says.
2. Drouillard and Joseph Field, report Lewis and Clark.

Monday March 10th   We had Showers of rain, with Snow and hail.   several of our Men[1] went out a hunting.   the wind blew hard this day.   Our party are engaged at the fort in repairing the Canoes & dressing of Skins &ca.

1. According to the captains, two parties hunted along the Lewis and Clark River, and another, consisting of Drouillard, Reubin Field, and Frazer, went beyond Youngs River. See the captains' entries for March 10 and 11.

Monday March 11th   We had during last night some Snow & this morning we have fair Weather.   Serjeant Pryor & the two Men that went out with him returned with the Canoe to the fort.   They had wish them some Sturgeon & a considerable quantity of small fish.   they also brought some Wapa-to or bread Root &ca.   Three of our Men[1] went out hunting.   four of our Men[2] went also, to look for the lost Canoe.   these four Men returned but had not found it.—

1. Drouillard, Joseph Field, and Frazer, according to the captains, went across Youngs Bay to hunt east of Youngs River.
2. Led by Gass, according to the captains.

Wednesday March 12th   A fair morning.   One of our party went out in Order to hunt, And several of our Men[1] went in search of the lost Canoe. they all returned without success.   Two of our party were employed in making of Oars,—   and pitching our Canoes.

1. Led by Ordway, according to Ordway.

Thursday March 13th   A Clear cold morning, I was ordered to go up to the Cath-le-mah Village, in Order to purchase fish &ca.   I took two Men & a canoe with me, & proceeded on but a short distance; when the wind blew so hard that I was forced to return with them to the fort.   The three hunters[1] that were out returned to the fort.   They had killed 2 Elk & 2 Deer, Two others of our party went out hunting.   Some of our Men[2] went out & brought into the Fort the meat of One Elk, Our Officers sent one of our party[3] to the Clatsop Village, in order to purchase a Canoe from the Natives.

In the Evening one of our hunters returned that went out this morning; he had killed 2 Elk & wounded 2 more of them, which he mention'd was by a Short distance from the fort, across the River.—

1. Drouillard, Joseph Field, and Frazer.
2. Led by Ordway, as Ordway relates.
3. Drouillard.

Friday March 14th   This morning was Cloudy.   Seven of our party[1] went in 2 Canoes across the River, in order to bring the Elk meat to the fort, And four of our Men went out to hunt, The party that went for the Elk meat soon returned with it to the fort.   In the afternoon, the Man[2] that went to the Clatsop Village Yesterday; returned; with several Clatsop Indians to the fort. these Indians brought a Canoe with them to trade with us.—

1. Led by Gass, as he says.
2. Drouillard.

Saturday March 15th   A pleasant morning, the Indians remained at the fort during the last night.   they seem not inclined to part with their Canoe this morning, Our Officers sent Six Men[1] in a Canoe in order to go up the River to the Cath-le-mah Village, in order to purchase a Canoe if possible. Our hunters that went out Yesterday returned to the fort.   they had killed 4 Elk.[2]   a number of the Men went from the fort and brought in the Meat of the 4 Elk to the fort.   In the afternoon a number of the Chinnock Nation of Indians—[3]   came to the fort.   The Cath-le-mah Village[4] is situated on the So Side of the Columbia River 45 Miles above fort Clatsop   it contained 105 Lodges & about 1500 Inhabitants & are a band of the Flatt head nation.

1. Including Drouillard.
2. The party consisted of Collins, Joseph Field, Shannon, and Labiche; the last killed all four elk, according to the captains.
3. From the captains' account these included the Chinook chief Delashelwilt, "the old baud his wife," and six women whom the captains urged their men to stay away from. A Clatsop named Catel and his family also came to visit.
4. These last two sentences seem out of place. It may be the Cathlamet village near Knappa, Clatsop County, Oregon, which was considerably smaller than Whitehouse's esti-

mate. See Clark's entries of November 11 and 26, 1805. They are not Flatheads (Salish), here apparently used as a generic designation. Drouillard and a party of five men left this day to try to obtain a canoe from the Cathlamets.

Sunday March 16th[1]   A Rainey wet morning.   The party that went to the Cath-le-mah Village traded with the Natives.   The Men at the fort were employed in dressing Skins, making blanket Coats &ca.   nothing further extraordinary happen'd this day—

1. Portions of the entries for this day and for March 19 and 20 appear to be in another hand.

Monday March 17th   A Cloudy day, and showery; The Men who went to the Cath-le-Mah village, purchased from the Natives Some Roots a few small fish, the small fish not unlike a herring getting scarce among the Natives, Those Men returned in the Evening, & brought the Canoe that they had bought[1] & the other Canoe with them.   Nothing material happened at the fort this day.—

1. Drouillard had purchased the canoe with Lewis's uniform coat and some tobacco.

Tuesday March 18th   We had showers of rain, some hail & thunder this morning.   the hands were employ'd in repairing our small Canoe, & getting everything in readiness in order to ascend the River on our way homewards.—   Our officers sent 4 Men over the River, to a Priari which lay near the Ocean in order to get a small Canoe which belonged to the Clatsop Indians.   They returned in the Evening with the Canoe.[1]   They had put 2 Men of the party on shore who also returned having killed an Elk[2] on their way to the Fort.

1. In plainer language, they stole the canoe. See Ordway for this day, and the captains' entries for March 17.
2. Joseph Field killed the elk.

Wednesday March 19th   We had a fair morning.   some of the Men were sent from the Fort & brought in the Elk meat.   In the afternoon we had showery disagreeable weather,

Thursday March 20th   A Rainey wet day.   We are now waiting for fair weather in Order to make a Start to the United States.   the party has killed 155 Elk[1] & 20 Deer since we came to this place.   The party has now among them 338 pair of good moccosins.   The most of them are strong & made out of Elk skins

1. Ordway counts "150 odd" and Gass, 131.

Friday March 21st   It rained hard all last night & contined the same this morning.   The Natives came to the Fort & brought some dried fish, which the Indians called All-Can,[1] we purchased some of these fish from them. We are all employed in getting things still in readiness in Order to return.—

1. The captains wrote it "ol-then," a Chinookan term, ú-ƚxan, for dried eulachon; see Lewis's entry of March 25.

Saturday March 22nd   It continued raining.   Three of our hunters[1] set out in a small Canoe to go on up the Columbia River, in order to hunt untill we come up to them.   Six of our men were also sent out, in order to hunt. About noon a number of the Clatsop Nation of Indians[2] came to the fort. They brought some Straw & Cane hatts & dry'd fish to trade with us.   We purchased some of those articles from them.   In the Evening all our hunters that went out by land this day returned (excepting one of them).[3]   We are all getting in readiness to start which we expect if the weather permits will be tomorrow—

1. Drouillard and the Field brothers, as the captains note.
2. Including Coboway.
3. Colter.

Sunday March 23d   It rained very hard, during the whole of last night. One of our hunters did not return to the fort during that time; This morning it still continued raining, & the Weather appeared very uncertain.   Our Officers were undetermined, whether they would set out, on our homeward bound Voyage; or not.   About 9 o'Clock A. M., the hunter[1] that had staid out during last night, returned to the Fort; he had killed one Elk, which he mention'd, he had left about 3 Miles from the Fort, towards Point Adams. About 12 o'Clock A. M. it ceased raining; & the weather became Clear & pleasant, & we loaded our Canoes, & got every thing in readiness to ascend the Columbia River.   We have been at Fort Clatsop from the 7th day of December last past; and our party had lived as well, <as they> as could be expected, & can say that they never were, without 3 Meals each day, of some kind of food, either Elk meat, Roots, fish &ca. notwithstanding the repeated rainey Weather; which fell (with a few days intermission) ever since, we passed the long Narrows of Columbia River; which was the 2nd of November last past.—   Fort Clatsop is situated on the South side of Columbia River, and about 1½ Miles up a small River (which empties itself into the Columbia River) called by the Natives Ne-tul, and lay a small distance back, from the West bank of said River.   The fort was built in the form of an oblong Square, & the front of it facing the River, was picketed in, & had a Gate on the North & one on the South side of it.   The distance from the head waters of the So fork of the Columbia River; (<or> Kiomenum or Lewis's River), to fort Clatsop is 994 Miles, (this being the fork which we descended) & from the Mouth of the River de Bois 4134 Miles, the place from whence we took our departure, <& in> Latitude 46° 19′ 11¹⁄₁₀s North, The River Columbia at its mouth also, lay: in Latitude 46° 19′ 11¹⁄₁₀S North, & Longitude 124° 57′ 0¹⁄₁₀S West from Greenwich; & is 21 Miles wide from Cape disappointment on the No side, to Point Adams on So. side of the River; which is where the Columbia River enters into the Western or pacific Ocean.   the Tide rises & falls, about 8 feet at the small River, <on> near which was built Fort Clatsop. We have been 60 Miles from Cape disappointment (Where the Chinnock Indian village lays) which is on the No. side of the River & or its entrance into the Ocean to the No. North West.   The two points, Cape disappointment, & point Adams; lay nearly opposite to each other, & about 10 Miles below fort Clatsop   The distance that we have went to the Mouth of Columbia River; from the River du Bois, from whence we took our departure is 4,144 Miles, fort Adams being the extreme So point, & lay near to where our party made Salt.—   We found that Bands of the flatt head Nation of Indians; are far more numerous that we expected; they extending from the head waters of the Ki-o-me-num River, to the Mouth of the Columbia River; & to the head of all the Rivers, which runs into the No. fork of Columbia River; & to the head of the same.   This information we received from numbers of Indians belonging to the different bands of that Nation.— They are called flatt heads from the custom they have among them, of binding flatt pieces of wood, on the foreheads, & back parts of the heads of their Children, when born, which occasions their foreheads & back part of their heads to be flatt.— End of first Volume.[2]

Sunday March 23d[3]   At 1 o'Clock P. M. we embarked, on board our Canoes from Fort Clatsop, on our homeward bound Voyage.   We proceeded on up the South side of the Columbia River, when we were met by a party of the Chinnock tribe of Indians,[4] who belong to the Flatt head nation.   These Indians were in Canoes, & were on their way to Fort Clatsop in Order to trade with us; they had with them a Canoe & a Sea Otter Skin, which they Intended trading with us.   We halted a short time, & Captain Lewis purchased the Sea Otter skin from them.   We then continued on our Voyage, and went round a point of land called by our officers Merryweather point[5] (the Sirname of Captain Lewis) when the wind rose & blew hard from the South West, & the waves ran very high.   We proceeded on, & passed another point of land called point William[6] by our officers the Sirname of Captain Clark.   We halted a short distance above this last point, at a Camp where the two hunters[7] that were sent on ahead of us were.   These two hunters had killed 2 Elk, which they informed us lay 1½ Miles from this place.   We encamped[8] at that place having come 16 Miles this day.—

1. Colter.

2. In this notebook there are several remaining pages, so the note could refer to the end of a volume in the original journal. It could be also that the copyist sees a new beginning with the party's departure from Fort Clatsop this day.

3. Here begins another portion of the fair copy of Whitehouse's journal. It is introduced by the following words: "Volume 2nd Journal of a Voyage from Fort Clatsop, on the River Netul, one of the Rivers that empties itself into the Columbia River, across the Continent of North America, to Saint Louis in the Territory of Louisiana; under the direction of Captains Merryweather Lewis, & William Clark, & patronized by the Government of the United States by Joseph Whitehouse."

4. Including Delashelwilt and "the old baud and hir Six girls," as Ordway puts it.

5. Astoria, Clatsop County, Oregon.

6. Tongue Point, Clatsop County.

7. Actually three, Drouillard and the Field brothers.

8. Just below the mouth of John Day River, the captains' Kekemarque Creek, Clatsop County.

Monday March 24th   This morning early, Our officers sent 15 of our party[1] out, in order to bring in the Meat of the 2 Elk, which our hunters had killed; that party returned & brought it in with them, about 8 O'Clock A. M. At half past 9 o clock A. M. we embarked & proceeded on to an Indian Village of the Cath-le-mah Tribe,[2] which lay on the South side of the River.   this village consisted of about 9 Lodges & about 100 Inhabitants.—   We delayed at this village about 2 Hours, and proceeded on, & passed through a number of Islands called the Seal Islands,[3] which lay on the So side of the River, and came to where stood an old Indian Village which is on the So. side of the River, opposite to the lower War-ki-a Cum Village.   We continued on about One Mile & encamped[4] on the So. side of the River, Towards evening two of the Natives came to our Camp.   These natives could speak some words of english & mentioned the Names of some of the Traders, Sailors &ca. who had been trading among them.   We saw a large burying place of the Natives a short distance below where we were encamped.   The method that the Natives take to deposit their Dead is, by placing them in a Canoe.   The body of the deceased is rolled up in Skins of some kind of Animal.   The Canoe is raised on forks & poles some distance up from the ground, & all the property that the deceased died possessed of is put into the Canoe, with the body of the deceased Indian.

1. Led by Ordway, as he notes.

2. A Cathlamet village on Cathlamet Bay, in the vicinity of Knappa, Clatsop County, Oregon.

3. Karlson and Marsh islands in the Columbia River.

4. Northeast of Brownsmead, Clatsop County, on Aldrich Point opposite the downstream end of Tenasillahe Island.

Tuesday March 25th   This morning early a Canoe with some of the Natives of the Clatsop Tribe came to where our Canoes lay, their Canoe was loaded with fish & Wapatoes roots.   the wind & tide being against us, We had to delay at our encampment, until 1 o'clock P. M. at which time we proceeded on our voyage, and met two Canoes with Indians, who were descending the River. We continued on, & crossed over to an Island, on which we found a fishing Camp[1] of the Cath-le-mah Indians, These Indians had a great number of Sturgeon laying tied at the Edge of the water, which were fastened to Stakes drove into the ground. One of our party purchased a Sea otter Skin from these Natives. the price he gave for it was a dressed Elk skin, & an old silk handkerchief. We proceeded on. the remainder of the day proved Stormy. we continued on till after dark, & came to another Indian fishing Camp,[2] laying on the South side of the River; where we encamped[3] for the night

1. On Puget Island, Wahkiakum County, Washington.
2. Cathlamets.
3. In Columbia County, Oregon, below one of the mouths of the Clatskanie River, opposite Cape Horn on the Washington shore; see the captains' entries for the day.

Wednesday March 26th The wind & tide rose very high during last night. the water raised so much that it obliged several of our party to move their Camps. Our Officers gave one of the Indians, who belonged to the fishing Camp near us, A. Medal, & the Indian in return, gave them a large Sturgeon. At 8 o'Clock A. M. we proceeded on ascending the Columbia River, & halted at an Island called by our Officers Fannys Island[1] to dine. We continued on our way at 2 o'Clock P. M. and towards evening we halted at an Island & encamped[2] for the night in a Thicket of Woods on the same.

1. Supposedly named for Clark's sister, Frances; later Crims Island, Columbia County, Oregon.
2. On one of the small islands, including Walker and Dibblee islands, below Longview, Cowlitz County, Washington, in Columbia County, Oregon.

Thursday March 27th This morning early it commenced raining, which continued during the whole of this day. At 7 o'clock A. M. we proceeded on, & crossed over to an Island, which lay on the North side of the River, where we halted. We found on this Island, an Indian Village of the Chilutes Tribe[1] it contained 7 Houses.— These Indians treated us in a friendly manner. At 10 o'Clock A. M. we left this Island and continued on & passed several Indian fishing Camps. A number of Indians followed us with small Canoes. Our Officers purchased from these Indians a large Sturgeon. We continued on & passed the Mouth of a River called by the Natives Calamus,[2] & encamped[3] on the South side of the River a small distance above the said River. Our officers sent 6 of our hunters in Canoes to go on a head, to an Island called Deer Island,[4] in order to hunt, untill we came up with them— These hunters left us this afternoon. We have still hard rain this evening. We encamped on the South side of the River, where we found plenty of Oak & Ash wood to make our fires with.—

1. A Skillute village, say the captains' entries for March 25 and 27, 1806. The captains say it contained only two houses; the copyist may have misread the numeral in the original. They also place it on the starboard side, near present Rainier, Columbia County, Oregon, which is hard to reconcile with Whitehouse's island on the "North side."

2. The Kalama River in Cowlitz County, Washington.

3. In the vicinity of Goble, Columbia County, opposite and a little above the Kalama River, Cowlitz County, Washington.

4. Still Deer Island, in Columbia County.

Friday March 28th It continued raining the greater part of last night. We set out early this morning & proceeded on our way to Deer Island at which place we arrived & halted at the Camp of our hunters.[1] About 11 o'Clock A. M. the hunters joined us. They had killed 7 deer. We hawled up our small Canoes on the Island, and repaired them. The remainder of this day was Squally & the wind high. Several of our Men were sent out in order to bring the Vension to where our Canoes lay, & a number of our hunters went out a hunting. Our officers concluded to stay on this Island 'till tomorrow, & we fixed our Encampment for the night. We found innumerable quantities of Snakes[2] on this Island of different kinds. One of our hunters killed a wild Cat,[3] & the others of our hunters killed several Eagles &ca.

1. Near the upper end of Deer Island, Columbia County, Oregon.

2. Lewis described the Pacific red-sided garter snake, *Thamnophis sirtalis concinnus,* a new subspecies, on this day.

3. Oregon bobcat.

Saturday March 29th   We set out early this morning & proceeded on, the Columbia River being very high & the current running very swift.   in the afternoon we passed the Mouth of a River,[1] which was large & the Water in it very high, and makes into the Columbia River with a greadt deal of rapidity; This River lies a small distance below a large Indian Village of the Kalute Tribe[2] <Nation> & called the Kalute River & at which place we halted & purchased from the Natives 10 fat dogs.   Captain Clarke also purchased from these Indians a Sea Otter Skin robe, for which he gave, a small piece of blue Cloth, & part of an old flag.   he also purchased from them some dried fish, Wapatoes &ca   These Indians, are a much decenter looking sett of Natives, than those who reside on, or near the Sea Coast.   The women among them wore a soft leather Breech Cloth, which they drawed tight about their breech, & is tied with a belt, & comes up forward in the manner that a breech Cloth does, & those on the Coast & near it, wore a short pettycoat, made out of Straw.   The remainder of their bodies being exposed to the Weather.—   Our Officers made a Chief, of one of those Indians, and gave him a medal; which he gave to his wife.   These Kalute tribe of Indians, are a part of the flatt head Nation.   Towards evening we proceeded on our Voyage, & went a short distance & encamped[3] at a handsome green where their had formerly been an old Indian Village; laying on the So side of the River.   We saw on the River this day, Swan & Geese in great plenty & the Indians that we were among kill plenty of deer, if we are allowed to judge from the quantities of Vension & Skins which we saw among them.[4]

1. Lewis River, the boundary between Clark and Cowlitz counties, Washington.
2. Nahpooitle, a village of the Cathlapotles, an Upper Chinookan–language people, in Clark County, just above the mouth of Lewis River and behind Bachelor Island.
3. Behind Bachelor Island, Clark County.
4. The last portion of this sentence, from "if we are" on, is crowded between entries.

Sunday March 30th   We set out early this morning, & proceeded on. The River still continuing rising, and is so high, that the tide has no Effect, as high up the River as where we now are.   A number of the Indians accompanied us in their small Canoes.   We saw a considerable quantity of drift wood floating down the River.   We passed two large Indian Villages which

were on a large island. This island was very long and is called Waptoe island,[1] it is about 25 Miles long, & is partly Wood land & the remainder Priari
land, & is very rich Soil. A number of the Indians who resided on this Island,[2] came out in their Canoes to see us. We saw this day Mount Rainey[3]
& Mount hood; they appeared white & was covered with Snow.— At sunset
we encamp'd[4] at a handsome place on the North side of the River, where
the land was Priaries & Groves of White Oak & cotton timber, & the Country
laying much lower than the Country below

   1. Sauvie Island, Multnomah County, Oregon.
   2. Various Upper Chinookan–language people lived on and around Sauvie Island, including the Katlaminimins.
   3. As in Whitehouse's entry for November 4, 1805, this is probably not Mt. Rainier, but
Mt. St. Helens, Skamania County, Washington.
   4. At Vancouver, Clark County, Washington.

Monday March 31st A clear pleasant morning, We set out early and proceeded on, & passed a Village[1] which lay on the So. side of the River. This
Village when we descended the River was large, but the greater part of the
houses were removed & lay scattering along the Shore, for the convenience
of the Inhabitants fishing. One of our hunters[2] killed a deer, & mention'd
that he had seen a number of them, Elk &ca Several of the natives followed
us from the last Indian Village, in small Canoes. In the Evening we passed
the Mouth of a river lying on the North side of the River & encamped[3] a
short distance above it, on a handsome high Priari laying on the North Side
of the River & Opposite to Quick sand River.[4]

   1. The captains called the people Shahalas; they were probably Watlalas. The village was
within Portland, Multnomah County, Oregon, probably on the site of the airport.
   2. Probably Drouillard; see Lewis's entry for the day.
   3. In Clark County, Washington, above the entrance of Washougal River (the party's Seal
River), near Washougal, where the party remained until April 6.
   4. Sandy River, in Multnomah County.

Tuesday April 1st This morning our Officers sent Serjeant Pryor & 2 of
our party in a Canoe in order to go 5 or Six Miles up <Quick Sand or>
Quicksand or Sandy River, (the River we passed last Evening) & Several of

our Men[1] were sent out a hunting. A number of the Natives visited us in their Canoes, as they were passing down the River. these Canoes were loaded with fish Roots &ca— I went up Quick Sand River about 4 Miles. The backwater from the Columbia River went only a quarter of a mile up that River, & then it is a continual rapid as far as I went, & full of Islands, and Sands barrs. Serjeant Pryor killed on his route 1 Deer which he & his party brought to our Camp. Our hunters also returned, & had killed 4 Elk 2 Deer & an Otter. On my route up Quicksand River I saw a Creek[2] which lay on the East side of that River which was about 50 yards wide. The Quick Sand River is 350 Yards wide & only 50 Yards of Water the remainder being entirely a Quick Sand.— I found this river part of the way up it, 6 feet deep, & the remainder as far up it as I went, only 6 inches deep of water & 4 inches quick sand. we saw a high mountain laying a great distance off to the Southward of us, which appeared to be covered with snow. Our Officers named this Mountain Jefferson Mountain.[3] We had a number of Indians encamped near us for the Night. they came in 2 Canoes

1. Gibson was one.
2. Probably either Smith Creek or Big Creek, Multnomah County, Oregon.
3. The captains named Mt. Jefferson, Linn County, Oregon, on March 30.

Wednesday April 2nd[1]   We sent some of our party out last evening to bring in the Meat of the Elk & deer; that our hunters had killed, and they staid out all night. Our officers agreed to stay at this place, untill our hunters[2] kill 9 or 10 Elk & Jerk the meat to take with us, The best of our hunters[3] crossed over to the South side of the River Columbia to hunt; on their arrival there, they went out in different directions, in hopes of succeeding.— The natives that were still with us, informed our Officers, that there was a large River,[4] which emptied itself into the Columbia River, on the South side, below Sandy River,— Captain Clark took me & Six more of our party,[5] and one Indian as a guide, in Order to go down the Columbia River to take a view of that River, We proceeded on in a Canoe down the South side of the River, about 10 Miles.— & passed an Indian Village[6] of 21 houses lying on the same side of the River. This Village lay behind an Island, called Swans

Island,[7] & altho we had been on this Island, on our way in descending the River, none of our party had ever seen <it> this Village before.   We proceeded on 9 Miles further down the River, & halted at a Village of Indians. These Indians belonged to a band called the Wyahoots,[8] which are a part of the flatt had Nation.— We found in this Village, a few old Indians of that tribe; who gave us a few dried Salmon to eat, which were not very good.   We proceeded on, on to the Mouth of this great River, which the Indians had given our Officers an account of.— The Mouth of this River came in behind an Island[9] lying on the So. side of Columbia River; We arrived at the mouth of this river, about Sunset, & went up it, about 7 Miles, when we encamped at an old Indian lodge.   The party <under Captain Clark,> resolved upon sleeping in this lodge, but on our entering it, we found the fleas in such great plenty, that we were forced to quit it.   The great River is called by the natives the Mult-no-mack River; it is 500 yards wide at its mouth; & continues that width, as high up, as where we ascended it to.   The Indian guide that was with us, told us that it heads Near the head Waters of the California, & that there is a large Nation of Indians who reside some distance up that River <&> who live on a So. fork of this River & that Nation is called the Clark-a-mus Nation[10] <& also another Nation> and that 30 Towns belong to them.   Our guide also informed us, that there is another nation of Indians who reside a further distance up that River, by the name of the Callap-no-wah nation;[11] who he said were also very numerous; & that they reside up this River, where it is quite small.— The guide also mentioned that it is 20 days travel to the falls of this River,[12] which falls is 40 feet <fall> perpendicular into that River & that the Tide water runs up to it,—   & that the Natives have a very large Salmon fishery at that place.   Our guide also mentioned that he had seen one of the Indians of the Clark-a-mus Nation, & that this Indian was <almost> white, & that he mentioned they had fire Arms among them.   From the above information received from our guide, I am of opinion, that if any Welch[13] nation of Indians are in existence, it must be <the> those Indians, & not the flatt head Nation, as before mentioned; this I believe, from their Colour, numbers of Towns, & fire arms among them, which I flatter myself will be confirmed, whenever the River Mult-no-mack is fully explored.—

1. Whitehouse's final entry in the fair copy and the end of his known journal writing.

2. One party included Drouillard and the Field brothers.

3. Gass led this party, which included Windsor and Collins. They remained in the area until April 4, then returned to the main party camp.

4. The Willamette River joins the Columbia at Portland, Multnomah County, Oregon.

5. Including Thompson, Potts, Cruzatte, Weiser, Howard, and York.

6. Probably the archaeological site in Blue Lake Park, in northeast Portland. See Clark's entry for this day.

7. Actually behind the party's Diamond Island, now Government Island. Whitehouse's "Swans Island" may be the party's White Goose Island, now McGuire Island.

8. Apparently a branch of Watlala Chinookans. Whitehouse again uses the term Flathead very generally and not correctly in a tribal sense. See Clark's entry for this day.

9. The party's Image Canoe Island, now Hayden and Tomahawk islands.

10. Clackamas Indians.

11. Perhaps Kalapuya Indians.

12. Willamette Falls, Oregon City, Clackamas County, Oregon.

13. Whitehouse revives the myth of Welsh Indians one last time.

Sources Cited

Betts, Robert B. "'The writingest explorers of their time': New Estimates of the Number of Words in the Published Journals of the Lewis and Clark Expedition." *We Proceeded On* 7 (August 1981): 4–9.

Clarke, Charles G. *The Men of the Lewis and Clark Expedition: A Biographical Roster of the Fifty-one Members and a Composite Diary of Their Activities from All Known Sources.* Glendale, Calif.: Arthur H. Clark, 1970.

Cutright, Paul Russell. *A History of the Lewis and Clark Journals.* Norman: University of Oklahoma Press, 1976.

Jackson, Donald, ed. *Letters of the Lewis and Clark Expedition with Related Documents, 1783–1854.* 2d ed. 2 vols. Urbana: University of Illinois Press, 1978.

Moulton, Gary E., ed. *Atlas of the Lewis and Clark Expedition.* Lincoln: University of Nebraska Press, 1983.

Wheeler, Olin D. *The Trail of Lewis and Clark, 1804–1806.* 2 vols. New York: G. P. Putnam's Sons, 1904.

Index

Index